T0325361

Sino-Asia Agricultural Trade and Development Cooperation

www.royalcollins.com

Kevin Chen and Rui Mao

Sino-Asia Agricultural Trade and Development Cooperation

Progress, Challenges, and Outlook

Books Beyond Boundaries

ROYAL COLLINS

Sino-Asia Agricultural Trade and Development Cooperation:
Progress, Challenges, and Outlook

Kevin Chen and Rui Mao

First published in 2023 by Royal Collins Publishing Group Inc.
Groupe Publication Royal Collins Inc.
BKM Royalcollins Publishers Private Limited

Headquarters: 550-555 boul. René-Lévesque O Montréal (Québec) H2Z1B1 Canada
India office: 805 Hemkunt House, 8th Floor, Rajendra Place, New Delhi 110008

ISBN: 978-1-4878-1176-1

To find out more about our publications, please visit www.royalcollins.com.

Contents

AGRICULTURAL TRADE AMID THE COVID-19 PANDEMIC   253

List of Figures

List of Tables

Acknowledgment

This book consists of 12 selected articles focusing on the topics of agricultural trade and cooperation in the Sino-Asia region. These include a general overview of the countries' efforts for agricultural development, both domestically and through trade with their partners and competitors. With this book, we take a particular lens from the development of the Global South countries in Asia on their agricultural trade and cooperation. We have reviewed the regional agricultural trade and development in Southeast Asia, South Asia, and Central Asia regions. As the outbreak of the COVID-19 epidemic in recent years has created great shocks to the agricultural sector, we also reviewed fluctuations in the agricultural sector since the outbreak in December 2019. Due to the closeness and importance of the Asian countries for Chinese agriculture development, one of the main focuses of this book is the Sino-Asia partnership in agricultural trade. The goal of this publication is to foster a stronger trade relationship between China and the developing Asian countries by enhancing a better understanding of the current agricultural trade conditions. It is our hope that this book will foster a stronger trade relationship between China and the rest of Asia, especially through an emphasis on a tripartite relationship among production, consumption, and trade based on a global trading system.

We would like to acknowledge the financial support from Central Asia Regional Cooperation Institute, East and Central Asia Office of International Food Policy Research Institute, One CGIAR Research Initiative "Fragility to Resilience in Central and West Asia and North Africa (CWANA)," ASEAN-CGIAR Regional Program of Innovate for Food, Zhejiang University-IFPRI Center for International Development Studies, National Natural Science Foundation of China (72273123, 71873119), Major Program of National Fund of Philosophy and Social Science of China (23ZDA035, 22ZDA029, 21&ZD092) and Major Program from Ministry of Education Key Research Institute of Humanities and Social Sciences (22JJD790078). We deeply appreciate the authors who contributed their time and knowledge to the completion of this book, including Shaoyin Sun, Mengyao Li, Mengying Xing, Kamiljon Akramov, Allen Park, Jarilkasin Ilyasov, Sarvarbek Eltazarov, Huaqi Zhang, Yanwen Tan, and Ziyi Jia. We thank the Academy of Social Sciences and China Academy for Rural Development at Zhejiang University for funding this book and Royal Collins for providing the publication services for this project. We also thank the editorial teams from China Renmin University Press who helped with the publication process.

Dr. Kevin Chen

Qiushi Chair Professor and International Dean, China Academy for Rural Development
and School of Public Affairs, Zhejiang University
Director, ZJU-IFPRI Center for International Development Studies, Zhejiang University
Senior Research Fellow, International Food Policy Research Institute

Dr. Rui Mao

Professor and Deputy Dean, China Academy for Rural Development
and School of Public Affairs, Zhejiang University
Deputy Director, ZJU-IFPRI Center for International Development Studies, Zhejiang University
Non-Resident Fellow, International Food Policy Research Institute

Abbreviations and Acronyms

ACPC	Agriculture Credit Policy Council
ADB	Asian Development Bank
AFSIS	ASEAN Food Security Information System
AIIB	Asian Infrastructure Investment Bank
AISA	Afghanistan Investment Support Agency
APEC	Asia-Pacific Economic Cooperation
APP	Agriculture Production and Productivity
APTERR	ASEAN Plus Three Emergency Rice Reserve
ASEAN	Association of Southeast Asian Nations
BEA	Bureau of Economic Analysis
BRCA	Balassa Revealed Comparative Advantage
BRF	Belt and Road Forum
BRI	Belt and Road Initiative
CAFTA	China-ASEAN Free Trade Agreement
CAREC	Central Asia Regional Economic Cooperation
CCPIT	China Council for the Promotion of International Trade
CEPII	Center d'Etudes Prospectives et d'Informations Internationales
CICA	Conference on Interaction and Confidence Building Members in Asia
CIDCA	China International Development Cooperation Administration
CIF	Cost, Insurance and Freight
CIIE	China-International Import Expo
CPEC	China-Pakistan Economic Corridor
CPTPP	Comprehensive and Progressive agreement for Trans-Pacific Partnership
EU	European Union
EEU	Eurasian Economic Union
EHP	Early Harvest Program
EOC	Emergency Operations Center
FAO	Food and Agricultural Organization
FTZ	Free Trade Zone
FTA	Free Trade Agreements

FDI	Foreign Direct Investment
FDA	Food and Drug Administration
GACC	General Administration of Customs of China
GCC	Gulf Cooperation Council
GDP	Growth Domestic Product
GHG	Greenhouse Gas
GIS	Geographic Information Systems
HHI	Herfindahl-Hirschman Index
HRS	Household Responsibility System
H1N1	Influenza A
IATF-EID	Inter-Agency Task Force on Emerging Infectious Diseases
ICWC	Interstate Commission for Water Coordination
ICSD	Interstate Commission on Sustainable Development
IFPRI	International Food Policy Research Institute
IFAD	International Fund for Agricultural Development
IFAS	International Fund for Saving the Aral Sea
IHR	International Health Regulations
IPCC	Intergovernmental Panel on Climate Change
ISF	Irrigation Service Fee
KPEC	Khyber Pass Economic Corridor
LMNSE	Law on the Management of the Nation in a State of Emergency
MDG	Millennium Development Goal
MEWR	Ministry of Energy and Water Resources
MOA	Ministry of Agricultural and Rural Affairs
MoCI	Afghanistan Ministry of Commerce and Industries
MOFCOM	Ministry of Commerce
MOU	Memorandum of Understanding
NADF	National Agricultural Development Framework
NEPA	National Environmental Policy Act
NRCA	Normalized Revealed Comparative Advantage
ODA	Official Development Assistance
ODF	Official Development Finance
OIE	Office International des Epizooties
OECD	Organization for Economic Cooperation and Development
OFDI	Outward Foreign Direct Investment
PHEIC	Public Health Emergencies of International Concern
PRC	People's Republic of China
RASFF	Rapid Alert System for Food and Feed

RCA	Revealed Comparative Advantage
RCEP	Regional Comprehensive Economic Partnership
SAR	Special Administrative Region
SARS	Severe Acute Respiratory Syndrome
SCO	Shanghai Cooperation Organization
SITC	Standard International Trade Classification
SME	Small and Medium Enterprises
SPFS	Special Program for Food Security
SPS	Sanitary and Phytosanitary Standards
TBT	Technical Barriers to Trade
TFP	Total Factor Productivity
UAE	United Arab Emirates
UNEP	United Nations Environment Program
UNDP	United Nations Development Program
UNODC	United Nations Office on Drugs and Crime
USAID	United States Agency for International Development
USDA	United States Department of Agriculture
VDB	Vietnam Development Bank
WCA	Water Consumer Associations
WFP	World Food Program
WHO	World Health Organization
WRI	World Resources Institute
WTO	World Trade Organization
WUA	Water User's Associations

CHAPTER 1

Evolution of China's Deepened International Agricultural Cooperation

Kevin Chen, Shaoyin Sun, and Rui Mao

I. Introduction

The People's Republic of China (PRC) has achieved substantial agricultural and rural development since its foundation, following the introduction of the Reform and Opening-Up policy that stemmed from the rural areas in 1978. In the 1980s and 90s, the country established market-based agricultural production and sales systems, effectively increasing agricultural outputs and reducing the rural surplus labor and poverty incidence. With its accession to the World Trade Organization (WTO) in 2002, the development of China's agricultural sector has further accelerated as it is increasingly integrated with the world market. In fact, China has made strong commitments to reduce tariffs on agricultural products. In the ten years afterward, China has fulfilled its promise with tariffs on agricultural products reduced to 15% and has become one country with the lowest tariff level for agricultural products in the world (Cheng, 2012). In addition, with the combined effect of the international market prices and domestic resource costs, the effect of China's agricultural trade policy restrictions has also been significantly reduced ten years after China's accession (Wu & Zhu, 2014).

With increased integration into the world market, China's agricultural trade has experienced a continuous deficit since 2004, with ups and downs over time. From 2004 to 2008, the deficit grew at an annual rate of 40.7% and exceeded US$10 billion for the first time in 2008. Affected by the global financial crisis and the international food crisis, China's trade deficit in agricultural products declined in 2009 but expanded rapidly again, reaching US$48.94 billion in 2012. The deficit decreased again until

2016 and expanded in 2017, breaking through US$50 billion for the first time (Zhu et al., 2018). Though there is a constant shift and changing statistics of China's agricultural trade pattern, China has stayed as an agricultural product trader with a significant trade deficit since its accession to WTO. Due to an increased dependency on the international agricultural market, it is important for China to keep a consistent involvement in the international market with its agriculture opening-up.

While new opportunities are provided, the deepened integration could also raise many new challenges. Domestic food security could be at risk as the country's agricultural development is more dependent on the international market. For instance, as a major agricultural importer, China's agricultural system would be more fragile to trade barriers and import refusals during periods of global crises, such as the COVID-19 pandemic. Developing Asian countries are important trade partners with China, especially due to their geographical conveniences. In this introductory chapter, we aim to provide a thorough review of the current situations and challenges for agricultural cooperation in the region. Through the identification of specific areas of improvements for future agricultural cooperation between Sino-Asia, we aim to foster a stronger trade relationship between China and developing Asian countries. We have divided the chapter into five sections. First, we provide a general overview of China's gradual agricultural opening-up. We will then review the impacts of China's accession to WTO, particularly on the Asian continent. Then, we will provide country-specific reviews on agricultural development in selected Asian countries. As the outbreak of the COVID-19 epidemic in recent years created great shocks to the agricultural sector, the fourth section discusses the fluctuations and influences on the agricultural sector caused by the outbreak since December 2019. With a brief review of the potential challenges to the agricultural sector in the last section, we conclude with an outlook for agricultural cooperation opportunities in the future, particularly among the Sino-Asia countries in the post-pandemic era.

II. China's Rural Reforms and Agriculture Opening-Up

China has made and reformed various agricultural and rural development policies since the founding of the country in 1949. Before the Reform and Opening-Up policy in 1978, China was developing as a socialist society. At this stage, agricultural development was promoted to increase grain yield and farmers' income. Introducing the reform policy has served as an essential turning point in the agricultural and rural development process, with the opening of a new era led by a "socialist market economy." It has promoted a household responsibility system (HRS) in which the households are held responsible for the profits and losses of their production yield.

This has created a de-collectivization of the agricultural system with privatization through a market economy. In particular, the farmers have self-justified with increased production of labor-intensive agricultural products due to the huge population in China. Driven by decades of urbanization and import competition pressures, China has prioritized addressing the "San Nong" (i.e., agricultural, rural, and farmer) issues with the publication of five consecutive *No. 1 Central Document* between 1982 and 1986. At this stage, the de-collectivization of the agricultural system has increased agricultural output significantly, which also opened a door for China to become an exporter of food with predominantly labor-intensive products, such as vegetables and fruits, due to its large population.

Since 2004, as the country moving toward a more progressed stage of agriculture, the Central Committee of the Communist Party of China has promulgated the *No. 1 Central Document* annually, all focusing on the "San Nong" issues. Since then, several radical domestic policy reforms were implemented, including the abolishing of agriculture tax, repurposing of agricultural subsidies, and alleviating poverty with precise targeting. At this stage, foreign investment in agriculture has also begun to take shape. Several new ideas for rural and agricultural development were also introduced, including the promotion of the new socialist countryside, the establishment of strategies for modern agricultural development, the introduction of a new "Giving More, Taking Less, and Loosening Control" policy, and the promotion of rural revitalization. In alignment with the domestic policies, agricultural trade, and the international cooperation have become increasingly significant for China in adjusting the consequent surplus and shortage in agricultural products and ensuring sufficient supply according to its comparative advantages. Specifically, it would help with alleviating domestic resource misallocation: as China exports labor-intensive products, it has also become an important importer of land-intensive commodities like soybeans and cotton. Today, China is emphasizing its stand as a "socialist market economy" with a Chinese characteristic, especially with the promotion of a more open rural operational mechanism. Moreover, this strategy has further developed, especially with its entry into WTO.

III. China's Agricultural Trade and Cooperation Within Asia

With the rapid growth in the scale of agricultural product trade, China is taking an increasingly important role in the world agricultural trade market. On December 11, 2001, China officially became the 143rd member of WTO. Since then, international agricultural trade has taken an important stand in China, especially through its adjusting of resource allocation for economic optimization within and outside of the country. Several high level commitments to the agriculture opening-up have been made, such as lowering its trade barriers (Ye, 2020). At this stage, international agricultural trade took an important stand in the Chinese agricultural system, especially through its adjusting of resource allocation for economic optimization. For instance, the share of its global agricultural product trade continued to increase, with a growth from 3.6% in 2001 to 10.1% in 2019 (International Food Policy Research Institute, 2021). Specifically, in the first decade after the accession, most Chinese imports were driven by land-intensive bulk commodities such as soybeans and cotton; at around 2012, however, import of consumer-oriented products such as meat, dairy, and horticultural products kept growing while meat imports are growing more rapidly in recent years (Statista, 2022).

However, although remarkable progress was made in China, some developing Asian countries still face low agricultural productivity and inefficiencies in the agricultural value chain. Li, Mao, and Chen (Chapter 2) discussed in detail the various policies and initiatives China has introduced to strengthen its regional agriculture cooperation with the surrounding Southeast Asia, Central Asia, and South Asia regions. It has reviewed several ambitious policies introduced by China, including The Belt and Road Initiative (BRI), the "Going Global" strategy, and the South–South Cooperation. It argues that enhanced cooperation with China could promote their national economies to become more connected regionally, build stronger institutions and closer intraregional supply chains through investment and trade, and reduce the risk of food security. It further concludes that China is a significant investor, trading partner, and donor to these developing countries upon the several regional cooperation strategies introduced.

Since China acceded to WTO, its international agricultural trade and cooperation have become further intertwined with the international market. Specifically, trade with Asian countries constitutes a major part of Chinese agricultural trade activity due to its regional proximity. Revolving China's agricultural development with the developing countries in the same region, Xing, Mao, and Chen (Chapter 3) reviewed China's agricultural trade and cooperation with Southeast Asia, Central Asia, and South Asia. They have examined the trade scale, commodity structure, and market structure of China's agriculture trade with the region after its accession into WTO. In their review, Southeast Asian countries have dominated Chinese agricultural imports with predominantly unprocessed products, such as palm oil and rubber; meanwhile, most of the Chinese exports are consumer-ready products, with more than 60% of the products exported to the East Asian countries and the developing Southeast Asia countries. Though, due to a lack of proper facilities, trade with South and Central Asia has kept low, China is no doubt an important import and export country to other

Asia countries, and China's accession to WTO is serving an increasingly important role in Asia. They have further suggested that developing countries could foster their economic development through deepened agricultural trade ties with China under regional cooperation frameworks, such as Regional Comprehensive Economic Partnership (RCEP) and BRI.

IV. Agricultural Development in Developing Asia

Agriculture development varies on a country-specific basis due to their different historical, cultural, and socioeconomic conditions. Together, Kamiljon Akramov, Kevin Chen, Allen Park, Jarilkasin Ilyasov, and Sarvarbek Eltazarov reviewed nine country-by-country cases for agricultural development from the Central and South Asia region (Chapters 4–8), including China, Kazakhstan, the Kyrgyz Republic, Tajikistan, Turkmenistan, Uzbekistan, Mongolia, Afghanistan, and Pakistan. Among these countries, China plays an important role in promoting regional integration as a world-leading developing country. In Chapter 4, the authors reviewed land reform and agricultural development policies, as well as its land use, crop, and livestock production patterns and value chain development. Though given certain natural resource constraints (discussed in detail in Chapter 4), the country's introduction of BRI as one of its greatest development policies has the potential to foster regional collaboration in the Eurasia continent. With the country's legacy from its ancient Silk Road in bringing domestic products to the west for trade, the BRI extends this legacy for the economic development in the Eurasia continent today. Particularly, the introduction of modern trade routes provides various opportunities for the development of fundamental infrastructures within the region (Rippa, 2018), particularly through various forms of aids and investments (Hofman & Ho, 2012). BRI could provide an opportunity for regional economic development through utilizing the comparative advantages in each country for agricultural production.

The countries of Kazakhstan, the Kyrgyz Republic, Tajikistan, Turkmenistan, and Uzbekistan, are the main economic entities in Central Asia, according to the World Bank. They share a common political history as former Soviet Union States. Since the dissolution of the Soviet Union, these countries have undergone a series of reforms in their agricultural sector. Particularly, former agricultural policies have collapsed, and they have to shift their focus to agricultural production, primarily focusing on domestic food sufficiency and security (Chapter 5). In addition, as a cohort of inland countries, they have to collaborate in water resource management for agricultural development due to the unique geographical conditions. Chapter 6 provided a detailed review of the water use and management policies in Central Asia. Specifically, water use conflicts between the downstream (Kazakhstan, Turkmenistan, and Uzbekistan) and upstream (Kyrgyz Republic and Tajikistan) countries is an urgent problem to solve. They proposed several regional collaborations as needed for future agricultural cooperation and development. However, as a fundamental step, the construction of infrastructure for regional connectivity is a basic requirement.

For decades, the economic and agricultural development in Mongolia depend heavily on its trade with the Soviet Union. The dissolution of the Soviet States had a huge impact on the agricultural sector in Mongolia. Chapter 7 provides a review of the agricultural development in Mongolia, with a focus on animal husbandry as the country's major agricultural production sector. It argues for improved science and technological development as poor natural conditions could result in variations of livestock production. The country's involvement in the Central Asia Regional Economic Cooperation (CAREC) program could also provide an opportunity for the country's further integration into the international agricultural market. As for the two South Asian countries of Afghanistan and Pakistan, the development of their agricultural sector depends heavily on the involvement of smallholder farmers (Chapter 8). Particularly, grain production constitutes a major trade sector in Pakistan; however, agricultural production is more fragmented in Afghanistan due to its political tensions. Today, Pakistan and India compose two major trade partners for Afghanistan, while there were little interactions with the Central Asia region because of historical reasons. Along with Mongolia, the five Central Asia countries, and China, they are all members of the CAREC program. They could all work together to enhance regional connectivity from this program.

Aside from the Central and South Asia region, Southeast Asia is also an important agricultural trade entity in Asia. Zhang and Chen (Chapter 9) have written a specific case on Myanmar's agricultural trade with its major competitors. By examining Myanmar's agricultural export performance with varies of its trading partners, mostly from Asia, they suggest that the country should diversify its export portfolio, strengthen export promotion and development, and attract foreign direct investment to enhance its agricultural value chain. Moreover, Myanmar is a country that highly depends on its agriculture sector; hence, with its excellent purchasing power, China could serve as one of Myanmar's major export partners. China has fostered economic growth within the Asian continent through trade and cooperation with its neighboring countries; besides increasing the agricultural demand of the country, there is also space for China to make policy improvements to support the Myanmar government in its trade promotion.

V. Agriculture Trade Amid the COVID-19 Pandemic

In recent years, agricultural development has faced many challenges across the globe. Since the beginning of the COVID-19 pandemic in January 2020, China's total export value has plunged dramatically. WTO predicted that it would hit a new low for global trade since the global financial crisis in 2008, including international agricultural trade. Chen and Mao (Chapter 10) explored the influence of the erection of tightened border controls on international agricultural trade. They argue that tight border control could further shatter the global food system. Apart from the restrictions, it also noted that if the COVID cases are still endured globally, the imposition of trade barriers against affected regions might be kept even when infections are controlled. The restrictions could further restrict exports of vital food products like grain. Based on the global crisis, they advised that to prevent trade barriers that may demolish the global food system, coordination to reduce barriers on border control should be made to create a formal WHO-WTO coordination scheme in reviewing and assessing trade measures. Capacity building of quality enhancement by agricultural exporters from the least developed countries should also be made.

Focusing mainly on the COVID-19 pandemic in China, Tan, Li, and Chen (Chapter 11) explored the impact of the pandemic on agricultural cooperation between China and the Association of Southeast Asian Nations (ASEAN) countries. They found stricter trade restrictions from the ASEAN countries after the pandemic, leading to insufficient supply and slow-selling speed of some agricultural products. The effort to ensure an adequate supply of agricultural products during the pandemic has become a significant problem for the ASEAN countries. Policies to increase the adequate supply of agricultural products, stabilize the price of agricultural products, restrict the export of essential agricultural products, and enhance agricultural financial support have been implemented in the ASEAN countries. However, such policies have also created a short-term interruption of the agricultural product supply chain that influences investment, trade, and regional food security. It has also impacted the ASEAN's economic development. The authors suggest that, in order to reduce the negative impact on food security after the pandemic, trade consultations should be strengthened to stabilize the regional agricultural product supply chain, cooperation should be deepened in the China-ASEAN region to prevent and control the epidemic, and establish an early warning mechanism for agricultural cooperation risks through scientific study.

Further, viewing the pandemic from a global perspective, Mao, Jia, and Chen (Chapter 12) explored the responses of the U.S. Food and Drug Administration (FDA), import refusals, and subsequent trade impacts on agricultural exports from developing countries. Through empirical economic analysis, they examined the impacts on agricultural exports that the US imported from developing countries during four pandemics: severe acute respiratory syndrome (SARS), influenza A (H1N1), Ebola, and COVID-19. Their study shows increased import refusals and amplified trade-impeding impacts on agricultural exports during pandemic outbreaks of both SARS (2002–2003) and COVID-19 when China was the epicenter. It also noted that refusals are focused primarily on foodstuffs, and subjective evaluations made a larger share of decisions. The authors suggest that China, as the world's largest agricultural importer, should play a greater role in establishing coordinated schemes between WHO and WTO to monitor unilateral trade-restrictive measures imposed during the pandemic. There should be a call for an international effort to design unilateral import regulations by sovereign states to meet WTO's principles of non-discrimination using an evidence-based approach.

VI. Challenges and Outlooks

Today, a series of challenges are creating various levels of difficulties and poverty across the global community, including political tension and climate change. The resulting shocks within the agricultural sector could cause enormous negative consequences. For instance, prevention and control policies for agricultural trade introduced after the COVID outbreak have led to shortages of fundamental agricultural production factors. The lack of labor in production is affecting the food supply with various forms of delay. Traffic disruptions and food purchase panics would lead to relevant blockade policies, disrupting the food supply chain, affecting trade and supply, and increasing food prices. Moreover, since the Russian-Ukrainian conflict at the beginning of 2022, the agricultural sector and its international trade system experienced a period of extreme difficulty through the disruption of agricultural production and supply. There was a sharp drop in Ukrainian wheat production and exports, as most of Ukraine's high-yielding farmland is in the eastern region where the war has been most intense. Though policies have been relaxed, strict restrictions on their agricultural exports were still temporarily imposed for a short period. Various drought events were happening around the globe in the summer of 2022, resulting in various production uncertainties through the increased droughts, further affecting domestic and international food security. These increasing challenges make us desperate for improved international agricultural development and trade for the future of cooperation.

At the 20th National Congress of the Communist Party of China, President Xi Jinping emphasized the importance of food security in alignment with the goal to advance rural revitalization, claiming to "ensure that China's food supply remains firmly in its own hands" (Xi, 2022). We believe it is only when a country is self-sustained through its own production it can then offer a helping hand to other countries. In July 2022, a new initiative on international food security cooperation for China was proposed, summoning the G20 countries to take responsibility for building a cooperative partnership for agricultural commodities (Wang, 2022). The foundation of this new initiative lays underneath a tripartite framework of "production-consumption-trade," which was proposed as an enhancement to the biliteral development framework of "production-consumption" domestically (International Food Policy Research Institute, 2021). With China's commitment to be self-sustained in food, an enhanced integration into the global agricultural trade market is made possible in the foreseeable future.

We believe that a tripartite relationship could serve as a holistic approach to international agricultural cooperation and development, especially with a good overall arrangement to ensure the stability of the supply chain. In particular, the comparative advantages of each country for agricultural productions should be identified first to formulate trade relationships with other countries for a more efficient resource allocation. And it is fundamental to plan import and export trading strategies along with adequate domestic support from the country's agricultural department. For China, fostering a stronger connection to agriculture development with its nearby developing Asian countries serves to create a deeper agricultural integration in the region. The introduction of Chinese policies, such as the South–South Cooperation and the BRI, has served well in connecting its agricultural sector within the region. In addition, the development of the transportation system could also improve regional connections to foster agricultural trade, build stable import and supply channels for important agricultural products, accelerate the cultivation of new advantages in the international competitiveness of agricultural exports, and help with the development of a regional agricultural system in general.

However, even if a small disruption occurred in the agricultural trade system could impose serious challenges, such as the trade barriers imposed during the pandemic. As a result, a higher level of institutional opening-up could be beneficial in coping with such challenges. China's creation of a high level, institutionalized opening-up pattern has distinct characteristics: its basic requirement is to build a new domestic and international dual-cycle development pattern, with the promotion of free trade as a strategic goal. With its continuous commitment toward the construction of a high-level socialist market economic system, resource allocation plays a decisive role besides the government. Specifically, attentions are paid to the service industry market, the market-oriented factor reforms, the people-oriented scientific and technological innovation incentive mechanism, and the legitimate rights and interests of entrepreneurs. In sum, a market-oriented, legalized, and internationalized trading environment could be promoted through effective market supervision, while adapting to digital economic development, a service industry market supervision system in line with international advanced standards are important elements to concern.

China's entry into WTO has expanded its global footprint through international cooperation and deepened its integration with the global agricultural economy in its effort to build international agricultural partnerships, expand agricultural relations with developing countries, and use multilateral and regional cooperation platforms. The pandemic has offered the agriculture sector lessons, innovations, and opportunities. Through actions, the world could work together to limit the frequency and severity of shocks, improve communities' ability to anticipate shocks, and build capacity to achieve a more resilient, inclusive, efficient, sustainable, and healthy international agriculture system. Through the increased promotion of social protection policies, we could protect vulnerable populations in times of economic, health, or environmental crises. By constructing infrastructure in developing Asia, we could also build more convenient access to the global market, increasing the expansion induced by a more inclusive and strengthened agriculture trading system. Together, through the advancement of sciences and technologies, the global community should come together to work for a better world yet to come.

References

Ahearne, A., Fernando, J, G., Loungani, P., & Schindler, J. W. (2006). *Flying geese or sitting ducks: China's impact on the trade futunes of other Asian economies* (Working Paper No. 887). Board of Governors of the Federal Reserve System. https://www.federalreserve.gov/econres/ifdp/flying-geese-or-sitting-ducks-china39s-impact-on-the-trading-fortunes-of-other-asian-economies.htm

Cheng, G. (2012). Ten years after the accession into WTO: Miracles and enlightenment of the Chinese agriculture sector. *Journal of Huazhong Agricultural University* (Social Sciences Edition), *3*, 1–8.

Chirathivat, S. (2002). ASEAN-China free trade area: Background, implications, and future development. *Journal of Asia Economics, 13*(5), 671–686.

Fukase, E., & Winters, L. A. (2003). Possible dynamic effects of AFTA for the new member countries. *World Economy, 26*(6), 853–871.

He, M., Huang, Z., & Zhang, N. (2016). An empirical research on agricultural trade between China and "The Belt and Road" countries: Competitiveness and complementarity. *Modern Economy, 7*, 1671–1686.

Hofman, I., & Ho, P. (2012). China's "developmental outsourcing": A critical examination of Chinese global "land grabs" discourse. *The Journal of Peasant Studies, 39*(1), 1–48.

Holst D. R., & Weiss, J. (2004). ASEAN and China: Export rivals or partners in regional growth? *World Economy, 27*(8), 1255–1274.

Huang, J., Otsuka, K., & Rozelle, S. (2008). Agriculture in China's development past disappointments, recent successes, and future challenges. *China's Great Economic Transformation*, 467–505.

Huang, J., Rozelle, S., & Chang, M. (2004). Tracking distortions in agriculture: China and its accession to the World Trade Organization. *The World Bank Economic Review, 18*(1), 59–84.

International Food Policy Research Institute. (2021). *2021 global food policy report: Transforming food systems after COVID-19*. https://doi.org/10.2499/9780896293991

Lei, Z. (2013). Chinese agricultural development policies and characteristics since the Reform and Opening Up in China. *Asian Culture and History, 5*(2), 110–114.

Lu, L. (2006). The analysis on the similarity of China and ASEAN's agricultural products. *World Agricultural Economy, 1*, 36–40.

Putterman, L. (1992). Dualism and reform in China. *Economic Development and Cultural Change, 40*(3), 467–493.

Putterman, L. (1993). *Continuity and change in China's rural development: Collective and reform eras in perspective*. Oxford University Press.

Qiang, W., Liu, Q., Cheng, S., Kastner, T., & Xie, G. (2013). Agricultural trade and virtual land use: The case of China's crop trade. *Land Use Policy, 33*, 141–150.

Rippa, A. (2018). Centralizing peripheries: The belt and road initiative and its role in the development of the Chinese borderlands. *Journal of Business Anthropology, 7*(1), 1–21.

Rong, J., & Yang, C. (2006). Empirical study on competitiveness and complementarity of China and ASEAN's agricultural products. *International Trade Problems, 8*, 45–50.

Tongzon, J. (2005). ASEAN-China free trade area: A bane or boon for ASEAN countries? *World Economy, 28*(2), 91–210.

Wang, Y. (2022). *Wang Yi proposes China's initiative on international food security cooperation*. Ministry of Foreign Affairs of the People's Republic of China. https://www.mfa.gov.cn/wjbzhd/202207/t20220708_10717772.shtml

Wu, G., & Zhu, J. (2014). A Study on agricultural trade policy adjustment and comparative advantage changes in China—ten years since WTO accession. *Journal of Northwest A&F University* (Social Sciences Edition), *14*(1), 47–55.

Xi, J. (2022, October 16). *Hold high the great banner of socialism with Chinese characteristics and strive in unity to build a modern socialist country in all respects—report to the 20th National Congress of the Communist Party of China*. http://www.gov.cn/gongbao/content/2022/content_5722378.htm

Ye, X. (2020). The development trend and strategic adjustment of Chinese agriculture since WTO accession. *Reform, 315*(5), 5–24.

Zhou, L., & Leung, D. (2015, January 28). *China's overseas investments, explained in 10 graphics.* World Resources Institute. https://www.wri.org/insights/chinas-overseas-investments-explained-10-graphics

Zhu, J., Li T., & Lin D. (2018). Chinese agricultural trade during the opening progress: Development process, challenges, and policies. *Issues in Agricultural Economy, 468*(12), 19–32.

REGIONAL OVERVIEW FOR SINO-ASIA AGRICULTURAL TRADE AND COOPERATION

CHAPTER 2

China's Agricultural Cooperation in Southeast, Central, and South Asia

Mengyao Li, Rui Mao, and Kevin Chen

I. Introduction

Agricultural cooperation is an important manifestation of economic globalization in the agricultural field. It refers to the integration of the global value chain and the international division of labor, as well as the participation in global economic cycles to optimize the allocation of production factors, including capital, technology, labor, resources, and information (Zhang et al., 2019). China has historically striven for domestic food production self-sufficiency. In the 1990s, views that China's growing food consumption would pose a threat to international grain markets emerged. In response, as well as the realization that a longer-term vision for national food security was important, China's central government issued a White Paper, *The Grain Issues in China*, in 1996, which set a 95% self-sufficiency target for grains, including rice, wheat, and corn (China Power, 2017). Food security, defined as national food (grain) self-sufficiency in the Chinese context, has been a high priority ever since. The Communist Party's *No. 1 Central Document* have dealt exclusively with questions of agriculture and rural development, showing both the historical and continued centrality of these issues on state legitimacy and socio-political stability in what is still a highly agrarian society.

China's domestic production has, for the most part, increased to meet the country's growing demand. In China's previous Five-Year Plan, which runs from 2016 to 2020, two remarkable objectives are set in the agricultural sector: achieve self-sufficiency in cereal grains and absolute food security. As for the self-sufficiency target, supply and demand in the most populous country are roughly in balance for grains such as rice, corn, and wheat, which provide the bulk of calories in most people's diets. However, decades of economic growth have generated a new set of demographic and dietary demands. While China's population growth is leveling off, continued urbanization and economic growth have resulted in a dietary transition that includes diets with a higher concentration of dairy, meat, and vegetables. This transition is already resulting in increased demand for major crops, including corn, soybeans, and wheat as livestock feed. China's ongoing economic development has sparked the largest urban migration in the world's history, with about 875 million people expected to permanently reside in cities by 2020 (UN, 2019). While urbanization is strongly correlated with economic growth and better standards of living, it could also result in food and nutrition insecurity. The twin challenges of maintaining economic growth while feeding its growing urban population with a countryside that features only 0.19 acres of arable land per capita have come at a high cost.

In order to meet the growing demand, yields on Chinese farms have increased steadily since the 1960s, as increasing mechanization and the promotion of best practices have spread through the farming community. Along with China's quick industrialization, modern production in both primary and secondary industries has resulted in severe environmental damage in China. It is estimated that one-six of China's land has been affected by soil contamination due to toxic runoff (Wong, 2013). Water scarcity is also a concern, as the government reported that nearly 60% of China's underground water is polluted and unfit for drinking without treatment. Pressures brought by tremendous environmental degradation, encroaching on urbanization, and the negative impacts of a changing climate will constrain domestic food production (Fu, 2016).

The shift from a grain-oriented diet to the increasing appetite for resource-intensive foods, such as livestock and dairy products, and China's domestic agricultural problems, including the shortage of arable land and serious environmental degradation, have further exacerbated China's increasing food pressures. Instead of promoting self-reliance at all costs, the Chinese government has realized that it has no choice but to look overseas for alternative food sources to offset its domestic agricultural limitations. Therefore, since the mid-1990s, addressing food security concerns through agricultural cooperation can be seen as part of China's "Going Global" strategy, a foreign policy framework designed to direct Chinese firms and their investment to foreign markets.

The Asian continent supplies 60% of the world's food from approximately 23% of the world's agricultural land. Given the right conditions, countries in Southeast Asia, South Asia, and Central Asia could benefit from the influx of Chinese agricultural cooperation in a number of ways (Luo et al., 2011). As a guarantor of food available to its citizens and a source of employment directly and through agriculture-related value-adding activities, the agriculture sector has played and continues to play an important role in Asia. Although Asia has made remarkable progress in improving food security, some developing Asian countries still face low agricultural productivity and inefficiencies in the agricultural value chain. The agriculture sector in Asia also faces uncertainty due to climate change. For example, in the Mekong Delta, a major rice planting area, floods exceeding the normal depth of between 0.5 m and 4 m are becoming more frequent, increasing the risk of food insecurity (Asian Development Bank, 2017). China's impact on global agricultural markets is increasing with its booming economy and changing consumption patterns. The BRI is also expected to boost China's outward investments in agribusiness and baseline infrastructure spending to facilitate greater agricultural trade. Capital investment from China also has the potential to contribute to agricultural modernization and poverty eradication in developing Asia. Hence, regional cooperation and integration with China could promote national economies to become more connected regionally, build stronger institutions and closer intraregional supply chains through investment and trade, and reduce the risk to food security.

II. An Expanding Global Footprint: China's Overseas Agricultural Cooperation Strategies

1. Early Stages

China has been engaging in overseas agriculture projects since the late 1950s, both through its aid program and through direct investment (mostly since the 1990s). In the early days, national and provincial state-owned agribusiness companies supported agriculture development in African and Southeast Asia countries by providing technical support. The evolution of agricultural aid and investment in Africa provides useful insights into China's changing approach to overseas agriculture. In the 1960s, financed by its foreign aid program, China established a number of large state-owned farms in Africa, including in Tanzania, Mali, Madagascar, and Sierra Leone. These projects included, among others, irrigated rice, dairy farms, poultry, and sugarcane. Although China continued to finance large farms up to the mid-1980s, in the 1970s, the focus moved toward "demonstration" farms. By 1985, China supported 35 agricultural aid projects across the world, including 25 in Africa. In the late 1980s, the approach of the past two decades had limited success. Projects were not sustainable without ongoing support from China, and many failed due to the lack of funds and limited management and technical capacity in the recipient country. Chinese aid projects were hindered because China had limited funds and a lack of experience operating in societies with market economies, and projects struggled to integrate into local markets and supply chains. Chinese technicians also had little knowledge of African languages, culture, and local economies.

Since China's economic reforms in the early 1980s, the operation of foreign agricultural projects has become more commercialized, with a focus on "mutually beneficial" agriculture projects. During the 1990s, small and medium-sized investors began to invest in overseas agriculture, such as planting crops in neighboring countries. The Chinese government also developed policies toward supporting Chinese agribusiness companies to implement and maintain Chinese aid projects.

2. "Going Global" Strategy

With only 7% of the world's arable land, much of which has been damaged by the country's efforts to boost domestic production, the Chinese government initiated efforts seeking agricultural cooperation. China's general "Going Out" or "Going Global" strategy began in the 1990s and was most linked to food security concerns initially.

The first phase of the Chinese "Going Global" strategy was from the 1990s to the early 2000s. During the 1990s, a food security White Paper issued by the State Council advocated a 95% self-sufficiency rate for the main food crops. However, food self-sufficiency is different from food security. According to FAO (1999), food self-sufficiency refers to the extent to which the country can satisfy its food needs from domestic production, while food security focuses more on whether households have sufficient income to maintain an adequate diet. For China, the gap between its domestic production and its effective demand remains the key challenge for agricultural policy. On December 2001, China became a member of WTO, and made substantial commitments to freer trade in agriculture in its accession agreement (Chen & Duncan, 2008). After joining WTO, China reduced agricultural import tariffs to 15.2%, only one-fourth of the world's average tariff, and agricultural product export subsidies were canceled (Ministry of Agriculture and Rural Affairs of the People's Republic of China, 2019). With the substantial increase in market openness, agricultural trade has developed rapidly. In 2004, China became a net food importer (Figure 2.1), showing its dependence on the world market is largely irreversible. In 2018, China's agricultural trade reached US$217.88 billion (with a 12.8% annual growth rate over 2001), including US$137.1 billion in imports and US$79.71 billion in exports. China has become the world's second-largest agricultural trader; the largest importer of cereals, cotton, soybeans, pork, and lamb; and the largest exporter of vegetables and aquatic products (Ministry of Agriculture and Rural Affairs of the People's Republic of China, 2019).

Figure 2.1

China Agricultural Trade Balance, 2001–2018

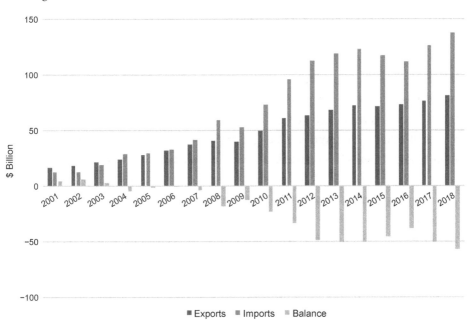

Source. China Customs.

The second phase of the Chinese "Going Global" strategy was from 2006 to 2012. Since the end of 2005, the Ministry of Commerce has unveiled a series of policies to encourage economic and trade cooperation zones in foreign countries. In China's 11th Five-Year Plan, a national food security plan was outlined, advocating for "Going Global" by utilizing China's abundant labor resources to develop foreign land, water, and energy resources and to narrow the gap between domestic production and effective demand. In 2006, Ministries of Commerce, Ministry of Finance, and Ministry of Agriculture jointly issued *Opinions on Accelerating Agricultural "Going Global."* The Ministry of Agriculture's Five-Year Plan for agricultural development outlined a broad "Going Global" strategy. However, the sharp rise in international food prices in 2007 indicated that it might harm Chinese domestic food price stability if China relied greatly on direct cereal imports from foreign grain traders. Therefore, in 2007, prominent Chinese Communist Party policy document, *No. 1 Central Document*, on rural policy, advocated outward agricultural investment to establish a stable grain production and market for the first time. During this period, overseas investment by Chinese enterprises has increased exponentially and has eclipsed China's aid budget. After the 2008 global financial crisis, in the face of the economic recession and downturn in international market demand, a large number of Chinese enterprises directly invested overseas by some encouraging policies, such as the Opinion on the Agreement for the Promotion of the Construction of Overseas Economic and Trade Cooperation Zones (State Council, 2008).

The third phase of the Chinese "Going Global" strategy starts with a revised food strategy issued in late 2012 and is highlighted by the One Belt One Road Initiative in 2013. The revised national food security strategy advocated for a proactive approach to boosting domestic production through technology and greater efficiency, narrowed commodities targeted for self-sufficiency to rice and wheat, and allowed for "moderate" imports of other commodities (Cheng, 2013; COFCO, 2015; Han, 2012; Ye, 2014). Supportive statements from officials, training programs, and subsidies for agricultural "Going Global" increased after the new food security strategy was released. In 2013, a new food security strategy was developed at China's Central Economic Work Conference, which for the first time recognized that imports would be part of China's basic food security strategy and called for "utilizing international markets and overseas resources in a way that ensure a dominant role for Chinese companies in the supply chain."

China's "One Belt One Road" initiative, also known as the "BRI," was launched by Chinese President Xi Jinping in 2013, and became a major driver of "Going Global" in agriculture and other industries by combing infrastructure investment, cooperation in science and technology, and trade to create new economic corridors across Asia, Europe, and Africa (Ernst & Young, 2015). The 2015 and 2016 *No. 1 Central Document* called for enhancing cooperation with trading partners to facilitate customs clearance, inspection, and quarantine for agricultural products.

The inter-ministerial joint mechanism for agricultural cooperation was first established in 2015 and has operated for six consecutive years. With the Ministry of Agriculture and Rural Affairs as the chief convener, 21 ministerial-level departments, which include all parties involved in agriculture, established this institutional mechanism to lay a strong organizational guarantee for foreign agricultural coopera-tion. In April 2016, the General Office of the State Council issued *Several Opinions on Promoting Foreign Agricultural Cooperation*. In May 2017, the *Vision and Action on Jointly Promoting Agricultural Cooperation on the Belt and Road* was compiled and released to the public, together by the Ministry of Agriculture, National Development and Reform Commission, Ministry of Commerce, and Ministry of Foreign Affairs. In 2017, guidance on outbound investment was issued by China's State Council that repeated the emphasis on BRI and identified agriculture as one of six priority sectors for which investment is encouraged.

From 2014 to 2020, as shown in Table 2.1, the Chinese central government pre-sented in its guidance documents that China should fully use international agricul-

Table 2.1

Strategies for Agricultural Foreign Investment in China Policy Documents

Year	Strategic statements related to foreign investment in agriculture
2014	Accelerate the agricultural foreign investment strategy. Foster large, internationally competitive grain and oils enterprises.
2015	Promote foreign science and technology demonstration parks. Implement policies to support facilities, equipment, and inputs needed for foreign agricultural production.
2016	Strengthen agricultural investment with countries along the "One Belt One Road" path and bordering countries and regions. Foster international grain traders and agricultural conglomerates.
2017	Support multinational agricultural businesses that are developing foreign production bases, processing, storage, and logistics focused on "One Belt One Road" objectives. Foster large internationally competitive conglomerates.
2018	Actively support agricultural foreign investment. Foster large, internationally competitive grain-trading and agricultural business conglomerates.
2019	Enhance agricultural cooperation with countries along The Belt and Road. Proactively expand imports of agricultural products in short supply at home. Diversify importing channels. Foster the development of multinational agricultural corporations.
2020	Make good use of both international and domestic markets and resources to supplement domestic market demand, optimize domestic agricultural structures, and alleviate pressure on resources and environment. Strengthen agricultural cooperation with countries along The Belt and Road.

Note. Drawn from *No. 1 Central Document* issued by China's Central Communist Party Committee that summarize rural policy priorities for the year.

tural resources and markets, establish stable cooperative relations with major grain producer countries, cultivate internationally competitive agribusiness enterprises, and encourage firms to set up business overseas, especially in countries along the "One Belt, One Road" path (Ministry of Agriculture and Rural Affairs of the People's Republic of China, 2014–2019). The target industry not only included crop farming, but also extended to animal breeding, agri-food processing, and manufacturing. Although China's overseas agriculture investments have received a considerable amount of attention in the global media, agriculture receives only a small portion of China's recorded outbound investment. According to official statistics from China's Ministry of Commerce (MOFCOM), mainland China's outward foreign direct investment (OFDI) flows reached a record high of US$145.67 billion in 2015. By the end of 2018, China's agricultural foreign investment exceeded US$18.98 billion, with more than

850 agricultural enterprises established overseas in 96 countries and regions around the world (Ministry of Agriculture and Rural Affairs of the People's Republic of China, 2019).

To better support the agricultural "Going Global" strategy, the Chinese government also launched a series of policies. First, the government provides financial support through direct funding, interest subsidy, equity investment, as well as a regional development fund and aid loan program provided by the China Exim Bank and China Development Bank. Second, it provided tax support for enterprises investing abroad for specific agricultural projects. Third, it provided information on investment risks and the current situation of international markets. The Ministry of Commerce established the "Going Global" Public Service Platform to provide a series of "Guidelines on Foreign Investment Abroad." Fourth, the government promoted agricultural cooperation with foreign governments by signing bilateral or multilateral agreements to settle trade disputes and labor restrictions (Ministry of Agriculture and Rural Affairs of the People's Republic of China, 2019).

In practice, China's agricultural cooperation has been concentrated in neighboring areas that are geographically accessible and with abundant endowments of resources. According to the Ministry of Agriculture and Rural Affairs of the People's Republic of China (2019), Asian countries accounted for 36% of China's overseas investment in agriculture in 2017, the highest among all the six continents (Figure 2.2). Approximately 65% of Chinese agricultural exports by value in 2018 were delivered to Asian countries (Figure 2.3), whereas a smaller percentage of China's total imported agricultural goods arrived from Asia (19%) (Figure 2.4).

A mixture of politics and economics factors has caused China's overseas agricultural strategy to evolve. China has been constrained by resources after several decades of economic growth and therefore has relied on boosting domestic production but also increasingly on international markets to make up the gap between supply and demand. There is an important link between China's desire to play a vital role in global governance and its food security. The food security strategy of China has shifted toward overseas investments, moving from "greenfield investment" or land grabbing to supporting whole supply chains. China also hopes to help promote the development of the agricultural sector and the welfare of the people in other developing countries by providing funds and using agricultural technology to stimulate its agricultural production potential (Amanor & Chichava, 2016). Therefore, China's agricultural investment is not only motivated by its quest for food security, but also its interest in supporting economic development in other developing countries.

Figure 2.2

Regional Distribution of China's Agricultural Overseas Investment

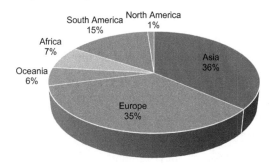

Source. Ministry of Agriculture and Rural Affairs of the People's Republic of China (2019).
Note. The distribution is measured by value.

Figure 2.3

Regional Distribution of 2018 China's Agricultural Exports

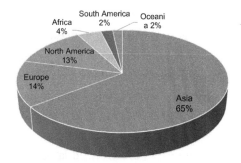

Source. Ministry of Agriculture and Rural Affairs of the People's Republic of China (2019).
Note. The distribution is measured by value.

Figure 2.4

Regional Distribution of 2018 China's Agricultural Imports

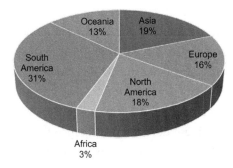

Source. Ministry of Agriculture and Rural Affairs of the People's Republic of China (2019).
Note. The distribution is measured by value.

3. China's Agriculture Aid and South–South Cooperation

As China now attaches greater importance to an innovation-driven sustainable development model and more political willingness to play leadership in global sustainable development, it has gradually developed into an emerging major donor with much more influence (Reinsch, 2019). The OECD defines development aid programs in two types. The first is Official Development Assistance (ODA), which consists of technical aid, official grants, or loans, and has concessional terms with a grant element of at least 25%. The second is Official Development Finance (ODF), which consists of "non-concessional development lending by multilateral financial institutions" and "other officials flow for development purposes which have too low a grant element to qualify as ODA" (Charels et al., 2013). However, the terminology of foreign aid used by the Chinese government lacks a clear definition, only stating the mutual benefit through economic and technical cooperation between developing countries (State Council of China, 2011).

Official Chinese documents explicitly distinguish three forms: grants, interest-free loans, and concessional loans. The loans and investments that comprise most of China's aid programs have lower grant elements than the percentage ODA requires and hence would more appropriately be considered as ODF.

According to the aid data released by Chinese official papers, China's foreign aid expenditures increased steadily from 2003 to 2015, then dropped sharply to US$2.3 billion in 2016, and have since rebounded to a new high of US$3.3 billion in 2018 (Figure 2.5). Many African countries have received large shares of Chinese aid over the past two decades. Elsewhere, countries in Southeast Asia, Central Asia, and Latin America account for a much larger number of infrastructure megaprojects than Africa. Estimates of the overall scope of Chinese-funded infrastructure financing through the BRI range from US$1 trillion to US$8 trillion (OECD, 2018).

The State Council of China released two White Papers on Foreign Aid in 2011 and 2014, respectively, the only two official documents that disclosed China's foreign assistance. Chinese government differentiates its aid as mutually beneficial, and through its aid program, to develop a strong foundation for economic and trade cooperation with other countries (State Council of China, 2011). Table 2.2 shows that China's aid to Africa accounts for 57.9% of its total amount, followed by Asia (24.9%). By analyzing AidData's Chinese Official Finance to Africa Dataset 2000–2013 (Version 1.2), Dreher et al. (2018) found that Chinese development finance to Africa is driven by foreign policy considerations and influenced by economic factors, such as natural resources, financial risks, and institutional quality. As for Asia, China provided US$14.9 billion in ODA-like flows from 2000 to 2014. South Asia is the largest recipient region (39.8%),

Figure 2.5

Chinese Global Foreign Aid Expenditure, 2003–2018

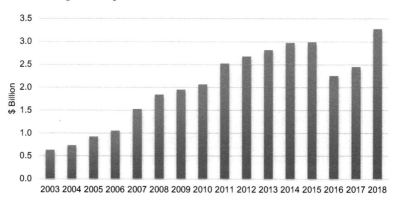

Source. MOF (2020).

Table 2.2

Regional Distribution of Aid by China, 2000–2014 (%)

	China (%)
Sub-Saharan Africa	57.9
Middle East and North Africa	0.8
Latin America	12.5
Central and Eastern Europe	3.5
Asia	24.9
South Asia	9.9
Southeast Asia	7.5
Central Asia	4.4
East Asia and Pacific, non-Southeast Asia	3.1
Total	**100**

Source. AidData (2017).

followed by Southeast Asia (30.1%) and Central Asia (17.8%). The econometric analysis by Oh (2019) shows that Chinese aid to Asia is mainly associated with commercial interests, not particularly with foreign policy interests.

Supported by aid programs, China sent experts and technicians to provide training on growing crops, raising animals, processing products, and Chinese agricultural technologies. China has also built farms and "demonstration centers," constructed irrigation infrastructure, and supplied machinery, tools, and processing equipment. Besides establishing bilateral programs, China is now also engaging with established donor platforms by joining trilateral cooperation projects with other multi and bilateral development institutions. For instance, in order to support low-income food-deficit countries in their effort to improve their national food security through rapid increases in food production, FAO initiated the Special Program for Food Security (SPFS) in 1994. Following the food crisis of 2008, food security issues, especially in low-income and food-deficit countries, became the focus of international attention. To support the mutual exchange of development solutions—knowledge, experiences and good practices, technology, and resources—among countries in the global south, the FAO and China established the South–South Cooperation Program in 2009 as part of the SPFS. Experts from China shared their knowledge and technologies with local farmers in Asia and Africa to raise agricultural productivity and sustainability in areas such as cereal production, animal husbandry, horticulture, fisheries and aquaculture, and water and soil management and conservation. Additionally, in 2014, the Chinese government announced a contribution of US$50 million to FAO to expand its partnership modalities and thematic areas (such as values chains in aquaculture) (FAO, 2018a).

As China's foreign aid has increased, the Chinese government has sought to improve the efficiency and management of aid distribution and improve coordination among various ministries involved with aid disbursement. For a long time, the administrative office of China's foreign aid was the Department of Foreign Aid within the MOFCOM. In March 2018, China formally established its first independent foreign aid agency, the China International Development Cooperation Administration (CIDCA). CIDCA aims to elevate the political importance of foreign aid and to better align the country's aid agenda with its overall foreign policy. Before CIDCA, China's aid structure consisted of three government agencies: the Ministry of Commerce, the Ministry of Foreign Affairs, and the Ministry of Finance. The Department of Foreign Aid in the Ministry of Commerce was tasked with managing China's foreign aid portfolio. The Ministry of Foreign Affairs coordinated aid policy formation and annual planning with the Ministry of Commerce and sought to ensure that the aid agenda aligned with broader foreign policy goals. Meanwhile, the Ministry of Finance coordinated the aid budget with the Ministry of Commerce and was responsible for China's financial contributions to multilateral development agencies and banks. However, poor coordination among relevant government bodies, minimal information sharing, and the lack of oversight and accountability sometimes produced poor implementation or led to negative environmental and social outcomes that damaged the Chinese government's reputation. The emergence of CIDCA replaced the Ministry of Commerce as the lead coordinating body of Chinese foreign aid and outlined a number of new policies that could help improve China's aid system in 2018 (Rudyak, 2019). The establishment of CIDCA addresses a long debate in China about its foreign aid reform and the creation of an independent aid agency that is geared more toward the strategic design and interagency coordination of China's foreign aid administration (Sun, 2019).

III. China's Agricultural Cooperation in Southeast Asia: Mechanism, Policies, and Practices

Agriculture is vital to most ASEAN economies and an essential driver for growth and poverty alleviation. Some ASEAN member countries have chosen to focus their development policies on more "export-oriented" agriculture (for example, palm oil and rubber in Indonesia and Malaysia, high-value beverages like cacao and coffee in Vietnam), while others have recognized the importance of both export and food security needs (for example, Thailand and Vietnam). The agricultural sector in the Southeast Asia region has experienced modernization in the last few decades, resulting in steady agricultural growth since the 1980s, though progress has slowed down since the early 2010s (IFPRI, 2019). The region has become a net agro-food exporter, with around US$139 billion in exports in 2014, compared with US$90 billion worth of agro-food imports (World Bank, 2017). In 2016, this region accounted for about 7.7% and 15% of the agricultural production in the world and Asia, respectively, in gross production values (FAO, 2018b). It is home to two of the world's largest rice exporters (Thailand and Vietnam) and the top three exporting countries for pineapples, bananas, mango, sugar crops, coffee, cashew nuts, and cassava (Teng & McConville, 2016). With growing agro-food exports and imports, the region's producers and consumers are both more exposed to international markets and more reliant on these as a source of income and food.

On one hand, China's fast-growing purchasing power and huge market size are important for agricultural exporting countries in this region. On the other, China's agricultural exports to ASEAN in vegetables and fruits, processed food, and fish (mainly labor-intensive products) will assist the food security of ASEAN counties and their transition to different farming activities or to help farmers move to non-agriculture sectors. At the first China-ASEAN Agricultural Cooperation Forum held in Guangxi Province, the vice minister of the Ministry of Agriculture at that time, Mr. Qu Dongyu stated, "Agriculture has become a priority area of cooperation between China and ASEAN and will be further deepened and promoted." At the country-level, the nature of investment and the patterns of food trade vary widely among ASEAN countries but have been largely driven by profit and geopolitics. China's agricultural investment has expanded rapidly in neighboring countries, such as Laos and Myanmar, but has proceeded at a much slower pace in more distant countries, such as the Philippines where the political situation has been tenuous at times. In addition, China has invested much less in grain production than in profitable crops such as palm oil, which can be turned into biofuel.

1. Growing China-ASEAN Agricultural Trade

The ASEAN-China Free Trade Agreement was signed in 2002 to draw the country and region closer together and to support an important phase of Chinese investment in and trade with ASEAN (MFA, 2018). In 2005, China became ASEAN's third-largest export market, after the US and Japan. In November 2018, the two sides upgraded the protocol of their free trade agreement to build the largest free trade zone (FTZ) among developing countries. The FTZ aims to further elevate the trade partnership between China and ASEAN members and send a clear signal of safeguarding multilateralism and free trade, Chinese Premier Li Keqiang said in Singapore while meeting with ASEAN nations' leaders in November last year. In the China-ASEAN Strategic Partnership Vision 2030 adopted last year, the two sides agreed to realize a goal of US$1 trillion in two-way trade and US$150 billion in investment by 2020.

The total trade volume (imports plus exports) of agricultural products between China and ASEAN continued to rise from US$16 billion in 2010 to US$36 billion in 2018. China exported around US$17.56 billion in agricultural products to ASEAN countries, mainly concentrated on vegetables, fruits, and aquatic products. China imported around US$18.48 billion in agricultural products from ASEAN, mainly concentrated in vegetable oils, fruits, agricultural products, and grains, making the region the second-largest exporter to China in agriculture, only after Brazil.

The planting of durians has picked up steam across Malaysia in recent years owing to increasing demand from China, the world's largest market for this thorny and pungent "king of fruits," according to news on Xinhua Net (2019a). Durian exports to China are expected to contribute around US$120 million to Malaysia's total export value annually. Besides durian, other agricultural products, such as palm oil, are expected to grow dramatically (Xinhua Net, 2019a). In 2017 and 2018, China bought more than two million tons of tropical fruits, becoming the largest foreign market of the Philippines. China has also become the largest Cambodian rice importer and imports a variety of other agricultural products such as cassava, maize, and banana.

2. Agricultural Investment and Industrial Parks

According to the Report on China's Agricultural Foreign Investment Cooperation published by the Ministry of Agriculture and Rural Affairs (Figure 2.6), in 2017, China's agricultural investment flows to ASEAN countries amounted to US$620 million, accounting for 30.3% of total flows abroad. At the end of 2017, there were 333 Chinese agricultural enterprises investing in ASEAN countries, accounting for 39.1% of the total agricultural enterprises that invested overseas. These agricultural companies hired 21,694 local staff.

Figure 2.6
Chinese Agricultural Investment in ASEAN, 2013–2017

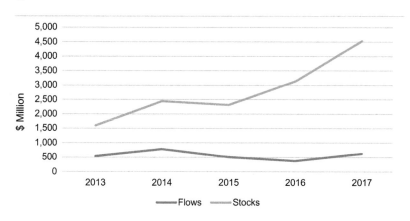

Source. 2013–2017 Statistical Bulletin of China's Outward Foreign Direct Investment

Most ASEAN countries have an agriculture-based economy that is complimentary with China's, making the extension of production technologies natural. In addition to proximity, there are four criteria that Chinese companies generally use for choosing locations for agricultural investment:

- abundance of land, water, and other natural resources needed for agricultural production and food processing;
- presence of production, processing, and logistics assets targeted by Chinese companies in "whole industry chain" strategies;
- countries targeted for technical assistance in agriculture, especially for "South–South" cooperation between China and less-developed countries;
- countries where agricultural ventures may be tied to diplomatic overtures or initiatives like One Belt One Road (Ye, 2014).

Chinese companies began to build industrial parks in Southeast Asia in 2005. Guangxi Province built a modern agricultural industrial park with Brunei in 2014 and Hunan Province has worked together with Laos to build parks principally focusing on the rubber industry, and has also built industrial parks with Thailand. Agricultural industrial zones, such as the China-Indonesia Julong Agricultural Industry Cooperation Zone with five parks on the Kalimantan Island, were promoted to a state-level overseas economic and cooperation zone in August 2016 (Xinhua, 2016).

The Agreement on Comprehensive Economic Cooperation between ASEAN and China was signed in 2002 and came into effect in 2005. Two important components related to food and agriculture are included in this agreement. In 2004, leaders of China and ASEAN agreed to strengthen cooperation in the field of food inspection and quarantine to support the establishment of the ASEAN-China Free Trade Zone. As in 2007, China and ASEAN issued the Nanning Joint Statement on strengthening China-ASEAN food safety cooperation, promoting food trade and protecting consumers' rights. On August 15, 2009, the Agreement on Investment of the Framework Agreement on Comprehensive Economic Cooperation between China and the Association of Southeast Asian Nations was signed in Bangkok, Thailand.

Under the BRI, China views ASEAN as part of the land bridge connecting China to Southeast Asia, South Asia, the Indian Ocean, and the China-Indochina Peninsula Corridor Sea route (Jusoh, 2018). The Asian Infrastructure Investment Bank (AIIB) established by China, with all the ASEAN countries as its founding member states, formally opened its doors for capacity and product cooperation, the establishment of various industrial parks, and the construction of railways between China and Thailand, and China and Laos (Westad, 2012).

3. Bilateral and Multilateral Mechanisms

China works with other countries in the region multilaterally through the Food and Agriculture Organization of the United Nations, the Asia-Pacific Economic Cooperation (APEC), China-ASEAN Agricultural Cooperation Mechanism "10 + 1," ASEAN and China-Japan-Korea Agricultural Cooperation Mechanism "10 + 3," and the Greater Mekong Sub-region Economic Cooperation Mechanism. China also led the creation of dialogue platforms, such as the Lan-Mei Cooperation Mechanism, the ASEAN-China-Japan-Korea Food Security Cooperation Strategy Roundtable, and the China-ASEAN Agricultural Cooperation Forum, and actively participated in the ASEAN-China-Japan-Korea Rice Emergency Reserve (APTERR) and ASEAN Food Security Information System (AFSIS).

China and ASEAN countries are also working toward a RCEP agreement, which is expected to boost trade and economic integration among all ten countries in ASEAN and five of its major trading partners—China, Japan, South Korea, Australia, and New Zealand. A study from the Brookings Institution suggests that RCEP has the potential to grow global real incomes by US$285 billion annually if put into place before 2030, which in absolute acquires is twice that of the Comprehensive and Progressive Agreement for Trans-Pacific Partnership (CPTPP) (CSIS, 2019). Together, the 15 countries make up close to one-third of the world population and global GDP, which is larger than other regional trading blocs such as the European Union (EU), according to a Reuters report. RCEP is primarily beneficial for goods trade because it will progressively reduce tariffs on many products. In addition, the deal will allow businesses to sell the same goods within the bloc but do away with the need to fill out separate paperwork for each export destination (Tostevin, 2019).

China has also signed a number of bilateral agricultural cooperation memoranda with most ASEAN countries and has established bilateral agricultural cooperation committees or working groups, such as the China-Philippines Agricultural Coopera-tion Joint Committee, which meet regularly.

4. Dialogue Platform Through Expo, Cooperation Forums, and Assistance

In November 2018, China held the first China-International Import Expo (CIIE) in Shanghai, attracting more than 3,600 companies from 172 countries, regions, and international organizations to showcase their achievements and seek more chances of international cooperation. The import fair, which will be held on an annual basis in the years to come, will serve as evidence of China's support for globalization and willingness to share growth opportunities with the world. China has also been holding an annual China-ASEAN Expo in Nanning, the capital of southwest China's Guangxi Zhuang Autonomous Region, since 2004.

China also provides agricultural assistance in various forms, such as training, financial aids, demonstration centers, and technical assistance, which target new ways to plant and grow crops more efficiently and with greener methods in pest and disease prevention and control. In 2007, China's Ministry of Agriculture and ASEAN signed a five-year MOU on agricultural cooperation, including a commitment from China to provide training on hybrid rice, cultivation methods, fertilizer use, water management, and training for specialists from ASEAN as well as sending experts from China to provide short-term services. China and Cambodia signed an agreement on establishing an agriculture promotion center in 2014, expecting to train 4,000 technical personnel and professional farmers, and with agricultural technologies extended over 10,000 hectares by 2018 (Zhang, 2019). In 2015, a Chinese-invested agricultural park was commenced between a Chinese City, Zhangzhou, at Fujian Province, and Cambodia, with the aim to facilitate investment from Zhangzhou and enhance agricultural techniques and reduce poverty. This is a case that illustrates the link between Chinese agricultural aid and investment is closely connected.

In 2014, China and Myanmar announced a joint statement on deepening bilateral cooperation, including providing agricultural concessional loans and constructing an agricultural demonstration center in Myanmar (Xinhua, 2014). Although there is no publicly accessible list that complies with Chinese aid projects in the Southeast Asia region, there are some media reports of China donating equipment and machinery, including tractors, vehicles, plows, pumps, and other agricultural equipment, to countries such as Cambodia and Myanmar (China Embassy, 2011).

IV. China's Agricultural Cooperation in Central Asia: Mechanism, Policies, and Practices

Agriculture is important to the economies of each of the five Central Asian countries (Kazakhstan, the Kyrgyz Republic, Tajikistan, Turkmenistan, and Uzbekistan). Central Asia's land resources have the potential for agricultural development, but the cropping industry, mainly consisting of grains, cotton, fruits and vegetables, and oil crops, suffers from low productivity. Except for Kazakhstan, which is a large food producing and exporting country, the remaining four countries are not food self-sufficient.

In June 2004, the former Chairman of the People's Republic of China Hu Jintao visited Uzbekistan. Hu said in a speech at the Uzbek Parliament that China was delighted with the progress made by the Central Asian countries in economic development and hoped for stability and sustained development in the region. Along with the international community, China was willing to renew its efforts to preserve stability and promote development in Central Asia, said Hu. Meanwhile, Hu recalled that China and Central Asian nations fostered close ties through the "Silk Road" by learning from each other as early as the second century BC. The traditional friendship opened a new chapter in the past decade when the two sides further developed a neighborly friendship based on equality and mutual benefit, and expanded cooperation in various fields, said Hu.

In June 2019, President Xi visited Kyrgyzstan and Tajikistan. While in Kyrgyzstan, President Xi attended the 19th meeting of the Council of Heads of State of the Shanghai Cooperation Organization (SCO), as well as strengthened bilateral relations with Kyrgyzstan in meetings with President Jeenbekov. In Tajikistan, President Xi attended the Conference on Interaction and Confidence Building Members in Asia (CICA), as well as met with President Rahmon to build on Sino-Tajik relations. In attending these summits, Beijing will not only strengthen bilateral ties with Kyrgyzstan and Tajikistan but affirm its global role through the multilateral SCO and CICA.

Agricultural cooperation between China and countries in Central Asia is mainly conducted under the framework of bilateral cooperation agreements, such as *China-Kazakhstan Cooperation Agreement on the Control of Locusts and Other Crop Diseases and Pests (2002)*, *China-Kazakhstan Cooperation Agreement on Animal and Plant Quarantine (2004)*, and *Memorandum of Understanding on Agricultural Cooperation between China and Kazakhstan (2009)*. China and Kyrgyzstan have conducted animal quarantine and other cooperation under the framework of the *Memorandum of Understanding on Agricultural Cooperation between China and Kyrgyzstan (2006)*and the *Cooperation Agreement on Animal Quarantine and Animal Health (2007)*. Under the framework of the *Memorandum of Understanding on Agricultural Cooperation between China and Ukraine (2009)*, the strategic importance of stronger cooperation in agriculture between two countries in safeguarding food security was emphasized. In 2011, the Memorandum of Understanding on the Establishment of Ukrainian-Chinese Agricultural Technology Park was signed, and the First Meeting of the Agriculture Subcommittee of the China-Ukraine Intergovernmental Commission on Cooperation was held in China.

With the development of regional infrastructure construction and economic and trade exchanges, China and Central Asian countries learned from each other's strengths and agricultural cooperation has continued to expand. Agriculture in cooperation has shifted from pure planting and breeding to include intensive processing of agricultural products, comprehensive development of agricultural resources, agricultural investment, and other developments (FECC, 2017).

1. Agricultural Trade

China is becoming an increasingly important trade partner with Central Asia, but at present, China's agricultural trade volume with Central Asia is relatively small. China's agricultural imports from Central Asia mainly concentrated in Kazakhstan and Uzbekistan during 1998–2017, which accounted for 74.19% and 16.67% of China total agricultural imports from the region, respectively. The main products of China's imports from Central Asia are cotton, wheat, and plants during 2010–2017. China's main export products to Central Asia are medicinal materials, fruits, animal products, grain products, sugar, cotton and linen, nuts, and vegetables, mainly to Kazakhstan and Kyrgyzstan. Central Asia has the potential to become an agricultural hub to supply the Chinese market in the coming decades as demand in China grows, particularly for fruits and vegetables (Grant, 2019). At present, the trade balance is negative: Central Asia imports more from China than it exports to China.

China and the five Central Asian countries have separately signed agreements on economic and trade cooperation, protecting investment, banking cooperation, and other areas of cooperation. China and the Central Asian nations have also organized joint, bilateral committees for economic, trade, and scientific and technical cooperation. On several occasions, the government of China has also provided the Central Asian countries with loans on favorable terms as well as gratis economic assistance. In addition, there are also numerous joint ventures involving China in Central Asia.

2. BRI and Economic Corridors

Located between China and Western markets, the Central Asia region has been key to the BRI vision since Xi Jinping unveiled it in Kazakhstan in 2013. Two of the proposed belts will cross Central Asian territory (Asian Development Bank, 2019). The northern belt will cross from Kazakhstan and the Russian Federation to Europe, while the central belt will pass through several Central Asian countries to the Middle East. In support of this initiative, major rail infrastructure has already been completed to boost trade capacities between China, Kazakhstan, and the Kyrgyz Republic (Rastogi & Arvis, 2014). Moreover, the PRC and Kazakhstan have created a special economic zone on their common border at Khorgos. The BRI has also established three economic corridors that involve the construction of transport infrastructure to enhance market connectivity:

- PRC-Mongolia-Russian Federation economic corridor;
- PRC-Pakistan economic corridor;
- PRC-Central Asia-West Asia economic corridor.

Agro-industrial parks are expected to be established along the corridors to serve as a base for processing, logistics, and research activities. Additionally, financial platforms such as the Silk Road Fund and the Asian Infrastructure Investment Bank will inject financial resources into infrastructure development and support the construction of agricultural export production bases. Longhai Railway and the Lanxin Railway will be used to complete the integration with the Central Asian Railway Trunk Line and promote the export of agricultural products to the five Central Asian countries (Yu, 2017).

3. Multilateral Mechanism: Shanghai Cooperation Organization

While continuing to recognize Russia's role as a privileged power in Central Asia, China has sought to carefully cultivate relationships with Central Asian republics and deepen its engagement in the region. This attempt was first justified through the framework of the SCO, a regional security organization founded in 2001. In addition to Russia and China, Kazakhstan, Uzbekistan, Tajikistan, and Kyrgyzstan are the funding member states. The organization expanded its membership to eight countries when India and Pakistan joined as full members on June 9, 2017.

Through this multilateral platform, China advocates for a new form of multilateralism that promotes cooperation based on the principle of sovereign non-interference. The SCO was initially designed to foster security cooperation but later found great success in promoting China's economic and trade relations with Central Asia states. In 2015, Chinese Premier Li Keqiang proposed that the SCO establish platforms for cooperation in six areas: security, production capacity, connectivity, financial mechanisms, regional trade, and social affairs. BRI, today the primary driver of the China-Central Asia relationship, is in many ways an extension of the pre-existing SCO framework. Economic cooperation is a key area of cooperation for the SCO and serves as the material foundations and guarantee for the SCO's smooth development. In 2017, the total agricultural investment flowed from China to SCO countries were US$210 million, accounting for 10.3% of total Chinese agricultural investment overseas, with grain crop outputs of 818,000 tons (Ministry of Agriculture and Rural Affairs of the People's Republic of China, 2019).

4. China's Aid to Central Asia

Although there are no detailed official accounts or records available of China's assistance to Central Asia, the numerous reports in the media, often of multi-billion-dollar projects, reveal that Chinese involvement in the region has grown exponentially in recent years. China's assistance to the region slowly started expanding in the first half of the 2000s, taking the form of investments in and financing of infrastructure projects, and then rapidly increased in recent years. In just a few years, China has grown to become the single largest donor in the region. Its assistance today goes primarily to the construction and upgrading of transport infrastructure (roads, tunnels, bridges, and railways, especially in Kyrgyzstan and Tajikistan) and extraction infrastructure. The focus on infrastructure is set to further increase with the Silk Road Economic Belt now well underway (Peyrouse et al., 2012). Apart from facilitating domestic trade, the new transport infrastructure increases trade with China, bringing more Chinese products to Central Asian markets.

China's overwhelming presence in the region also has generated a considerable number of controversies. Most concerns regard the lack of sustainability of China's assistance (Bossuyt, 2016). Chinese assistance has been criticized for lacking capacity building and therefore does not help Central Asian economies to become autonomous actors in their own development. On the contrary, it aggravates their economic dependency on China's assistance and products. As local industries are unable to compete with imported Chinese products, China's aid may lead to further trade dependency of Central Asia on China.

However, there is no assurance that Central Asia will become an agricultural hub for China. Though investment figures suggest progress, the awe-inspiring size of a mega-project, like the BRI projects, does not guarantee a natural path to success. The lack of transparency, corruption issues, and potential environmental costs pose great risks to the benefit and sustainability of BRI projects in energy, mining, agriculture, and communications (World Bank, 2019). Meanwhile, agricultural cooperation between China and Central Asia also faces certain obstacles. First, the decline of soil quality in Central Asia and water conflicts destabilize the region and creates hurdles for agricultural development (Zhang, 2019). Massive extraction of irrigation water for agriculture leads to ecological deterioration and declining crop production (Hamidov et al., 2016). Second, the similarity of agricultural production conditions and products between Xinjiang Uygur Autonomous Region and Central Asian countries inevitably will generate competition. This region, which borders Kazakhstan, Tajikistan, and Kyrgyzstan, generates the bulk of China's high-quality cotton, fruits and nuts.

V. China's Agricultural Cooperation in South Asia: Mechanism, Policies, and Practices

South Asia is a key node on the "Belt and Road" with outstanding geographical advantages and strategic significance for China. Most of the countries in South Asia are traditional agricultural economies. In May 2017, the Ministry of Agriculture, the Ministry of Commerce, the Ministry of Foreign Affairs, and the National Development and Reform Commission of China jointly issued the *Vision and Actions for Promoting Agricultural Cooperation in The Belt and Road Initiative* to deepen agricultural cooperation with countries along The Belt and Road. Advancing the development of agricultural product trade provides a top-level design and action plan. It proposes deepening agricultural trade and investment cooperation in China-Pakistan Economic

Corridor (CPEC), Bangladesh-China-India-Myanmar Economic Corridor, and other economic corridors to establish a "new type of agricultural international cooperation relationship."

1. BRI and Economic Corridor

During the visit of Pakistani Prime Minister in Beijing, Chinese Prime Minister Li Keqiang said China would "continue to promote the development of the China-Pakistan Economic Corridor, strengthen cooperation in infrastructure, economy, trade, finance, and industrial capacity, take strong measures to facilitate a more balanced development of bilateral trade and expand the export of competitive Pakistani products to China" (Xinhua, 2019b). While the first phase of the China-Pakistan Economic Corridor focused on power generation and infrastructure development, the second phase will turn to agriculture, industrialization, and the development of the social sector. In October 2019, the "Pakistan-China Agricultural Cooperation Forum" that aimed to strengthen the exchanges and cooperation between the two countries in the agricultural field, was held in Islamabad. The governments of both countries called for technical exchange and cooperation in fields, such as intensified agro-industrial development, water and irrigation investment, land remediation, disease control, livestock, and poultry breeding, animal and plant epidemic prevention and control, and mechanization demonstration (Consortium for Development Policy Research, 2018).

One example of successful cooperation in research is wheat-breeding technology that was transferred from the People's Republic of China to Pakistan, which may have contributed to a 50% increase in hybrid wheat yields in Northern Pakistan in 2018 (Zhang, 2018). The second occurred when China sent a team of locust experts to Pakistan to assist with an outbreak of desert locusts in Pakistan in early 2020. China provided pesticides and machines that are much needed in Pakistan. In March 2020, the two countries signed a MOU on Strengthening Cooperation in Prevention and Control of Plant Diseases and Pests. Moreover, the topics of disease control and the quality of pesticides are important issues in this corridor. During the Second Belt and Road Forum, the Ministry of Agriculture and Rural Affairs of the People's Republic of China, the Ministry of Food Security and Research of Pakistan, and counterpart ministries of Bangladesh, Cambodia, Myanmar, Nepal, the Philippines, Thailand, Sri Lanka, and Vietnam released a joint Statement of Intent for Cooperation on Promoting Specification-Setting for Pesticide Quality under the BRI (Ministry of Foreign Affairs of the People's Republic of China, 2019).

2. Agricultural Trade

South Asian countries account for a small percentage of China's total agricultural trade. Most countries in the region import from China but flows in the opposite direction are considerably more modest (World Bank, 2016). In 2001, South Asian countries accounted for 1.5% of China's total agricultural trade. In 2012, the share of South Asian countries in China's total agricultural trade rose to a peak (3.4%). During 2012–2017, the share of South Asian countries in China's total trade in agricultural products fell continuously to 1.5% in 2017, much lower than that of ASEAN countries (16.1%). In 2017, the total agricultural trade volume of South Asian countries was US$203.8 billion, of which US$101 billion in import and US$102.8 billion in exports. According to 2017 trade data, China mainly imported fish, vegetable oil, and cotton from India and Pakistan and mainly exported vegetables and fruits with their closest trade partners India, Pakistan, and Bangladesh.

3. Technology Cooperation and Assistance

China established agro-technical cooperation with Sri Lanka in 2013, planning to set up a China-Sri Lanka Agricultural Demonstration Park in tea, vegetable and flowers. According to a newsletter published by the Yunnan government, Yunnan would use its technological advantages in the cultivation of tea, rice, vegetables, and flowers to cooperate with Sri Lanka that lies close to the equator, and has a suitable environment for crop growth. However, the level of intensive farming in Sri Lanka was relatively low. According to this newsletter, a training center on agriculture technology would be established. However, further information cannot be traced on the progress and performance of this technology cooperation.

In recent years, China's assistance to South Asia has focused largely on infrastructure, such as building roads, railroads, ports, oil, and gas pipelines, with the clear aim to advance the economic cooperation between China and South Asia. Unlike Africa and Latin America, South Asia is not a region with rich natural wealth. As China's imports from South Asia mostly are agricultural products and raw materials, China's assistance to South Asia is more related to balancing the power among the South Asian countries rather than resource or market seeking.

VI. Deepening Agricultural Cooperation

From the previous discussion, although data on both investment and development assistance is often incomplete, there is no doubt that China is an important investor, trading partner, and donor to developing countries in Southeast, South, and Central Asia. Several policy actions could be taken by Chinese governments, regulators, and companies to deepen agricultural cooperation.

First, establish a comprehensive agricultural strategy and strengthen overall coordination. At present, diverse mechanisms, strategies, and visions govern China's agricultural cooperation with Southeast, Central, and South Asia. However, without the guidance of a comprehensive strategic plan, questions such as what kind of strategic partnership China wants to build with these regions and the modes of engagement are hard to answer. The *Vision and Actions on Jointly Promoting Agricultural Cooperation on The Belt and Road* that came out of The Belt and Road Forum for International Cooperation in 2017 shows important progress but a specific strategy and action plan have not yet been formulated.

Second, China's lack of a strategic plan for overseas agricultural cooperation leads to inefficient coordination among different government departments. China has signed more than 120 bilateral and multilateral agreements on food and agriculture cooperation with over 60 countries and international organizations and more than 60 inspection and quarantine protocols for food imports and exports. It has established exchanges in agricultural science and economic cooperation with over 140 countries and regions and formed bilateral working groups on agricultural cooperation with more than 50 countries and regions. The Ministry of Agriculture and Rural Affairs, Ministry of Commerce, Ministry of Science and Technology all have agricultural cooperation projects with foreign countries, and the overlapping and duplicated objectives between different departments may result in wasted resources. Additionally, because China's agricultural cooperation has been primarily based on bilateral or multilateral mechanisms governments, other stakeholders such as enterprises and non-governmental organizations have limited participation. As such, there is a need to establish dialogue mechanisms with other countries on planning, reinforce the leading role of these plans for cooperation, and establish communication and coordination mechanisms. Domestic food and nutrition strategies should also be integrated into this framework as the country begins to look outward to improve food security. Only through actively integrating resources on all sides could China promote more sustainable agricultural development cooperation with other countries.

Third, given regional differences, development levels, and agricultural potential, China should consider a more coherent plan that prioritizes key products and industries. In doing so, China should make full use of cooperative methods like aid, investment, and technology transfer in order to establish a long-term cooperation mechanism and partnership.

References

AidData. (2017, October). *AidData's global Chinese official finance dataset 2000–2014 (Version 1.0.).* https://www.aiddata.org/data/chinese-global-official-finance-dataset

Amanor, K.S., & Chichava, S. (2016). South–South Cooperation, agribusiness, and African agricultural development: Brazil and China in Ghana and Mozambique. *World Dev.* 2016, *81*, 13–23.

Asian Development Bank. (2017). *A region at risk: The human dimensions of climate change in Asia and the Pacific.* https://www.adb.org/sites/default/files/publication/325251/region-risk-climate-change.pdf

Asian Development Bank. (2019). *Agriculture development in the Central Asia regional economic cooperation program member countries: Review of trends, challenges and opportunities.* https://www.adb.org//sites/default/files/publication/549916/agriculture-development-carec-countries.pdf

Bossuyt, F. (2016). The EU's and China's development assistance towards Central Asia: Low versus contested impact. *Eurasian Geography and Economics, 59*(5–6), 606–631. https://doi.org/10.1080/15387216.2019.1581635

Charles, W., Wang, X., & Warner, E. (2013). *China's foreign aid and government-sponsored investment activities: Scale, content, destinations, and implications.* RAND Corporation. https://www.rand.org/pubs/research_reports/RR118.html

Chen, C., & Duncan, R. (2008). Achieving food security in China: Implications of WTO accession. In C. CHEN & R. DUNCAN (Eds.), *Agriculture and food eecurity in China: What eEffect WTO accession and regional trade arrangements?* (pp. 1–26). ANU Press. http://www.jstor.org/stable/j.ctt24hd73.9

Cheng, G. (2013). *China's implementation of the general idea of global agricultural strategy.* Development Research Center of the State Council. https://www.drc.gov.cn/DocView.aspx?chnid=386&leafid=1339&docid=2875543

China Embassy. (2011). *Ambassador to Cambodia, Pan Guangxue attended the handover ceremony as Sichuan Provincial Government donated materials to the Cambodian National Assembly.* http://kh.china-embassy.org/chn/dssghd/t826405.htm

China Ministry of Agriculture. (1982–2017). *China agricultural yearbooks.* https://web02.cnki.net/KNavi/yearbook/Detail/GOVY/YZGNV

China Power. (2017). *How is China feeding its population of 1.4 billion?* China Power Project. https://chinapower.csis.org/china-food-security/

COFCO. (2015). COFCO group analyzes Party General Xi Jinping's important speech and *No. 1 Central Document.* http://www.cofco.com/cn/News/Allnews/Latest/2015/0414/40414.html

Consortium for Development Policy Research. (2018). *Agriculture sector opportunities in the context of China-Pakistan Economic Corridor.* https://www.theigc.org/wp-content/uploads/2018/01/

CDPR-2018-final-report.pdf

Dreher, A, Fuchs A, & Parks, B. (2018). Apples and dragon fruits: The determinants of aid and other forms of state financing from China to Africa. *International Studies Quarterly, 62*(1), 182–194.

Ernst and Young. (2015). *Riding the silk road: China sees outbound investment boom: Outlook for China's outward foreign direct investment.* EY Knowledge https://imaa-institute.org/docs/statistics/ey_china_outbound-investment-report-2015.pdf

FAO. (1999). *Implications of economic policy for food security: a training manual.* https://www.fao.org/3/x3936e/x3936e03.htm

FAO. (2018a). *FAO and China set a new milestone for global South–South Cooperation in agriculture.* http://www.fao.org/partnerships/news-archive/news-article/en/c/1171287/

FAO. (2018b). *FAOSTAT database.* http://faostat.fao.org.

FECC. (2017, August 2). China's agricultural assistance and cooperation to developing countries. http://www.fecc.agri.cn/yjzx/yjzx_yjcg/201708/t20170802_293015.html

Fu, L. (2016, April 21). *What China's food safety challenges mean for consumers, regulators, and the global economy.* Brookings. https://www.brookings.edu/blog/order-from-chaos/2016/04/21/what-chinas-food-safety-challenges-mean-for-consumers-regulators-and-the-global-economy/

Grant, J. (2019, December 18). *China looks to Central Asia as an economic alternative.* The Diplomat. https://thediplomat.com/2019/12/china-looks-to-central-asia-as-an-economic-alternative/

Hamidov, A., Helming, K. & Balla, D. (2016). Impact of agricultural land use in Central Asia: A review. *Agronomy for sustainable development, 36*(6),1–23. https://doi.org/10.1007/s13593-015-0337-7

Han, J. (2012). *China: Food security and agricultural going out strategy research.* China Development Press.

IFPRI. (2019). *Overview of the agricultural modernization in Southeast Asia.* http://ebrary.ifpri.org/utils/getfile/collection/p15738coll2/id/133195/filename/133405.pdf

Jusoh, S. (2018). *China's Belt and Road Initiative (BRI) and Southeast Asia.* http://www.lse.ac.uk/ideas/Assets/Documents/reports/LSE-IDEAS-China-SEA-BRI.pdf

Luo, P.M., Donaldson, J.A., & Zhang, Q. F. (2011). The transformation of China's agriculture system and its impact on Southeast Asia. *International Journal of China Studies, 2*(2), 289–310. https://ink.library.smu.edu.sg/soss_research/1087

MFA. (2018). *China-ASEAN 2030 Vision Strategic Partnership.* https://www.mfa.gov.cn/web/ziliao_674904/1179_674909/201811/t20181115_7947869.shtml

Ministry of Agriculture and Rural Affairs of the People's Republic of China. (2014–2019). *No. 1 Central Document.* http://www.moa.gov.cn/ztzl/jj2019zyyhwj/

Ministry of Agriculture and Rural Affairs of the People's Republic of China. (2019). *Agricultural cooperation on the 70th anniversary of the founding of new China*. http://www.moa.gov.cn/hd/zbft_news/qzzhrmghgcl70zndshc/xgxw_25845/201909/t20190911_6327695.htm

OECD. (2018). *China's belt and road initiative in the global trade, investment and finance landscape*. https://www.oecd.org/finance/Chinas-Belt-and-Road-Initiative-in-the-global-trade-investment-and-finance-landscape.pdf

Oh, Y. A. (2019). Chinese development aid to Asia: Size and motives. *Asian Journal of Comparative Politics, 5*(3), 223–234. https://doi.org/10.1177/2057891119836521

Rastogi, C. & Arvis, J. (2014). *The Eurasian connection: Supply-Chain efficiency along the modern Silk Route through Central Asia*. World Bank. https://doi.org/10.1596/978-0-8213-9912-5

Reinsch, W. A. (2019, December 3). *At last, an RCEP deal*. Center for Strategic & International Studies. https://www.csis.org/analysis/last-rcep-deal

Peyrouse, S., Jos, B., & Marlène, L. (2012). *Security and development in Central Asia. The EU compared to China and Russia*. EUCAM. https://eucentralasia.eu/security-and-development-in-central-asia-the-eu-compared-to-china-and-russia/

Rudyak, M. (2019, September 2). *The ins and outs of China's International Development Agency*. Carnegie. https://carnegieendowment.org/2019/09/02/ins-and-outs-of-china-s-international-development-agency-pub-79739

State Council of China. (2011). *China's foreign aid, 2011* [White paper]. Information Office of the State Council. http://english.www.gov.cn/archive/white_paper/2014/09/09/content_281474986284620.htm

Sun, Y. (2019, April 30). *One year on, the role of the China International Development Cooperation Administration remains cloudy*. Brookings. https://www.brookings.edu/blog/africa-in-focus/2019/04/30/one-year-on-the-role-of-the-china-international-development-cooperation-administration-remains-cloudy

Teng, P., & McConville, A. (2016). *Agriculture and ASEAN economies: Still key for growth*. RSIS Commentary. https://www.rsis.edu.sg/wp-content/uploads/2016/05/CO16127.pdf

The Nation. (2020, February 19). *China, India to join hands to fight worst Locust outbreak in Pakistan*. https://nation.com.pk/19-Feb-2020/china-india-may-join-hands-to-fight-worst-locust-outbreak-in-pakistan

Tostevin, M. (2019, November 5). *Explainer: World's biggest trade pact shapes up without India*. Reuters. https://www.reuters.com/article/us-asean-summit-trade-explainer/explainer-worlds-biggest-trade-pact-shapes-up-without-india-idUSKBN1XF0XY

UN. (2019). *World population prospects: The 2019 revision*. https://www.un.org/development/desa/pd/news/world-population-prospects-2019-0

Westad, O.A. (2012, October 18). *Memo to China: Size isn't everything*. Bloomberg. https://www.bloomberg.com/opinion/articles/2012-10-19/china-must-learn-that-size-only-gets-you-so-far-odd-arne-westad

Wong, E. (2013, December 30). *Pollution rising, Chinese fear for soil and food.* New York Times. https://www.nytimes.com/2013/12/31/world/asia/good-earth-no-more-soil-pollution-plagues-chinese-countryside.html?pagewanted=1&_r=0&adxnnlx=1389729664-xekqWDHv%20ERg16ihq6c9CQ

World Bank. (2016). *South Asia economic focus, spring 2016: Fading tailwinds.* https://openknowledge.worldbank.org/handle/10986/24016

World Bank. (2017). *South Asia exports by country and eegion 2017.* World Integrated Trade Solution. https://wits.worldbank.org/CountryProfile/en/Country/SAS/Year/2017/TradeFlow/Export

World Bank. (2019, March 11). Belt and Road Initiative in Central Asia and the Caucasus. https://www.worldbank.org/en/news/feature/2019/03/11/belt-and-road-initiative-in-central-asia-and-the-caucasus

Xinhua. (2014). Myanmar agree to deepen comprehensive strategic cooperation, Xinhua Net. http://www.xinhuanet.com/politics/2020-01/18/c_1125478225.htm

Xinhua. (2016, December 19). *China's Belt and Road Initiative delivers promising initial results.* China Daily. http://www.chinadaily.com.cn/business/2016-12/19/content_27706426.htm

Xinhua. (2018, February 4). *Opinions of the CPC Central Committee and the State Council on the implementation of the rural revitalization strategy.* The State Council of the People's Republic of China. http://www.gov.cn/zhengce/2018-02/04/content_5263807.htm

Xinhua. (2019a, July 23). *Spotlight: China-ASEAN trade continues to boom amid global growth slowdown, uncertainties.* Xinhua Net. http://www.xinhuanet.com/english/2019-07/23/c_138249953.htm

Xinhua. (2019b, October 9). *China, Pakistan vow to strengthen cooperation.* Xinhua Net. http://www.xinhuanet.com/english/2019-10/09/c_138456747.htm

Ye, X. (2014, January 17). *Correctly grasp four new changes in the national food security strategy.* China Development Observer. http://theory.people.com.cn/n/2014/0117/c83865-24152538-2.html

Yu, S. (2017). Complementarity of trade cooperation between China and five Asian countries under the One Belt and One Road strategy. *Agriculture Economics, 7,* 112–114.

Zhang, H. (2019). Looking south for rice. *Securing the "rice bowl."* Palgrave Macmillan.

Zhang, N. (2018, September 3). *China's agricultural techniques reach out to countries along the Belt and Road.* China Focus. http://www.cnfocus.com/chinas-agricultural-techniques-reach-out-to-countries-along-the-belt-and-road/

Zhang, N. (2019). Analysis on China-Central Asia food trade. *Russian Central Asian & East European Market, 2,* 8–21. http://www.oyjj-oys.org/UploadFile/Issue/41zplgum.pdf

Zhang, Z., Yu, H., & Wang, Z. (2019). Development changes and path optimization of China's agricultural foreign cooperation: 1949–2019. *Macroeconomics, 10,* 18–26.

CHAPTER 3

China's Agricultural Trade With Southeast, Central, and South Asia

Mengying Xing, Rui Mao, and Kevin Chen

I. Introduction

Since China's accession to WTO, its agricultural trade has been increasing rapidly to become the fourth largest exporter of agricultural products, following the EU, the United States, and Brazil, and the second largest importer after the EU in 2017. As a result, China not only continues to be the world's largest agricultural producer but also plays a critical role in global agricultural trade. As reported in the *2019 World Trade Statistical Review*, the share in terms of the value of China's agricultural exports in the world increased from 3.0% in 2000 to 4.5% in 2017, while the share of China's agricultural imports in the world increased from 3.3% in 2000 to 10.5%. Closer integration of China in the global food system reflects the overall development of free trade around the world and, more importantly, is driven by China's enormous progress in economic growth, urbanization rate, aging population, and dietary transformation.

China's development of stronger ties in agricultural markets with Asian countries is particularly striking compared to those with other trade partners. As of February 2020, China has signed bilateral free trade agreements (FTAs) with twelve countries and one regional FTA with the Association of Southeast Asian Nations (ASEAN). In the meantime, discussions on eight bilateral negotiations and two regional ones with the Gulf Cooperation Council (GCC) and Regional Comprehensive Economic Partnership (RCEP) are ongoing. These agreements cover 25 Asian countries out of 48, making China strengthen its trade partnership with almost half of its Asian neighbors. In addition, through the Belt and Road Initiative (BRI) launched in 2013 that serves as a comprehensive cooperation platform, China has established closer ties with another

18 Asian countries.[1] In fact, China and the rest of Asia have now become the largest partner in agricultural trade with each other.

Agricultural trade has been recognized in the literature as a key contributor to food security, economic growth, and structural transformation, especially among developing countries (Balié et al., 2019; Baylis et al., 2019; Gong, 2020). Surprisingly, systematic delineations and assessments of China's agricultural trade with its developing neighbors in Central, South, and Southeast Asia are rather limited. Ma et al. (2017) estimated the BRI's contribution to the growth of Sino-Central Asia agricultural trade. Bird et al. (2019) further denoted that these effects varied across countries and industries, with geographical and economic factors such as labor mobility as key drivers of heterogeneities. Based on disaggregated bilateral trade data and domestic production data, Erokhin et al. (2020) provided dynamic trade patterns of agricultural products between China and Central Asia during 2000–2018. They identified competitive advantages of agricultural exports for countries in Central Asia in horticultural products and grains that are labor intensive. In contrast, these countries were uncompetitive in capital and technology-intensive sectors, such as husbandry and food processing. Zhan et al. (2018) examined patterns of Sino-Southeast Asia agricultural trade at regional and national levels during 1990–2015. They found that the trade pattern transformed from a dependent relationship whereby one country consistently exports or imports a much higher value to or from the other to a complementary relationship whereby the product categories traded with each other are different and more equitable in terms of volumes, suggesting a win-win situation. Sun and Xian-de (2018) noted that since the formal establishment of China-ASEAN free trade area in 2010, both the price and quantity of China's agricultural exports to ASEAN countries have increased, though products have largely remained the same.

This chapter contributes to the literature by examining agricultural trade relationships between China and different regions in the rest of Asia in a coherent framework for comprehensive assessment and comparison. It covers the period from 1998 to 2017, which includes China's accession to WTO and the enaction of a number of crucial regional cooperation frameworks such as the China-ASEAN Free Trade Agreements (CAFTA) and Belt and Road Initiative (BRI). It also offers preliminary impact evaluations for these cooperation frameworks using disaggregated data. China's future economic collaborations in the Asia-Pacific region through an enhanced cooperation framework such as the Regional Comprehensive Economic Partnership (RCEP) are also discussed. The paper finds that China's agricultural trade volumes with Southeast Asia, South, and Central Asia have been increasing

---

1. The detailed information for countries involved can be found in Appendix Table A-1.

since its entry to WTO, along with consistent and enlarging deficits. It also finds that, though Central and South Asia make up a very small share of China's agricultural trade basket, Southeast Asia is always a crucial market for China's agricultural exports. The agricultural trade commodity structure between China and developing Asia is divided based on the comparative advantages of each country. There is still potential for China to deepen agricultural trade ties with the least developed Asian countries using frameworks such as RCEP and BRI given the relatively small scale of agricultural trade presently. Last, stronger regional coordination is needed to address disputes and concerns about the effectiveness and sustainability of CAFTA, RCEP, BRI, and other regional collaboration frameworks.

The rest of this report is organized as follows. Section 2 describes the data used in this report and definitions of key terms. In Secton 3, an overview of China's international agricultural trade and that in Asia is provided. Section 4 and Section 5 are analyses of China's agricultural trade in Central, South, and Southeast Asia, respectively, and examinations of China's agricultural trade with five individual countries of interest. Reviews of China's major regional collaboration schemes in Asia and their impacts are reported and discussed in Section 6. Section 7 concludes the report.

II. Data and Definitions

1. Data

In this report, we mainly use the BACI database developed by CEPII, which provides trade information at the HS 6-digit disaggregation for more than 5,000 products and 200 countries. This database has gradually come into popular use in recent studies (Fałkowski et al., 2019; Gong, 2020; Umana-Dajud, 2019;) and employs original procedures including evaluation of the quality of country declarations of mirror trade flows and the cost, insurance and freight (CIF) rates to reconcile data in the United Nations COMTRADE database and scan for measurement errors or duplicates (Gaulier & Zignago, 2010; Imbs & Mejean, 2017). It thus offers more reliable and consistent bilateral trade statistics at the commodity level. We use the dataset from 1998 to 2017 in the analysis below,[2] which identifies products using the Harmonized System (HS) revised in 1996 measured in thousands of current US dollars. The window covers China's pre-WTO period and a number of milestones in regional agricultural cooperation, such as CAFTA and BRI. For the comparability of inter-temporal analysis, consistent with Costa, Garred, and Pessoa (2016), we convert trade values to 2012 US

---

2. This was the latest dataset under HS system revised in 1996 at the end of 2019.

dollars using the US GDP deflator released by the U.S. Bureau of Economic Analysis (BEA) in January 2020.

2. Definitions

Agricultural products refer to food and raw materials in line with World Trade Statistical Review 2019, which is the most current publication of World Trade Organization (WTO). On the basis of the third revision of the Standard International Trade Classification (SITC), food comprises the commodities in SITC sections 0 (food and live animals), 1 (beverages and tobacco), and 4 (animal, vegetable oils, and fats) and SITC division 22 (oil seeds, oil nuts, and oil kernels), and raw materials comprise SITC Section 2 (crude materials except fuels) excluding divisions 22, 27 (crude fertilizers and minerals excluding coal, petroleum, and precious stones), and 28 (metalliferous ores and scrap).[3] Since the BACI database is defined according to the HS system, we utilize the conversion table provided by UN Comtrade to convert the third revision of SITC of agricultural products into the HS 1996 version to generate the agricultural trade data for this report.

With growing attention paid to the factor endowment and global value chain in recent literature, we group agricultural products into four categories by following two steps (Wang, 1997; Chen & Duan, 2001). First, based on the processing degree, products are grouped into three broad categories, i.e., the least processed products, processed intermediates, and processed consumer ready products.[4] Second, according to factor intensity, the least processed products are further classified into two categories, i.e., bulk commodities which are land-intensive and horticultural products that are more labor-intensive. Specifically, bulk commodities are unpackaged products that are inexpensive to ship, including grain, oilseeds, and plant-based fibers such as cotton, raw rubber, and non-manufactured tobacco. Processed intermediates are goods derived from bulk commodities and need further processing for human consumption, including flour, feed, live animals, animal fats/oil, and animal-based fiber such as wool. Horticultural products are consumer-ready, unprocessed fresh commodities, including fresh fruits, vegetables, and flowers. Consumer-ready products are commodities that have been significantly transformed with high value-added, including preserved vegetables,

---

3. We further exclude some products that are typically considered as industrial goods, including those in divisions 232 (synthetic rubber), 24 (cork and wood), 25 (pulp and waste paper), 266 (synthetic fibres suitable for spinning), 267 (other man-made fibres suitable for spinning), 269 (worn clothing and other worn textile articles).

4. In what follows, we use *consumer ready products* to denote this category briefly.

fish, fruits and nuts, fresh and frozen meats, eggs, dairy products, processed meats, manufactured tobacco, and beverages.[5]

III. China's Agricultural Trade From a Global Perspective

1. Trade Scale

Before WTO accession at the end of 2001, China was a net agricultural exporter thanks to its comparative advantage in labor-intensive products, such as vegetables and aquatic products, together with high import tariffs to ensure self-sufficiency and food security (Carter & Li, 2002; Huang et al., 2002; Yang & Tyers, 1989). It was the fifth largest exporter of agricultural products in 2001, following the United States, EU (28), ASEAN (10), and Canada, with a total value of 22.6 billion dollars. To join WTO, China reformed its foreign sector for trade promotion, replacing a regime that featured centralization and import substitution with a new one based on decentralization, market orientation, and openness (Huang et al., 2002). Since 2004, following the dramatic decrease in import barriers and stronger food demand induced by population growth and economic development, China has become a net agricultural

Figure 3.1
Scale of China's Total Agricultural Trade and Trade Surplus

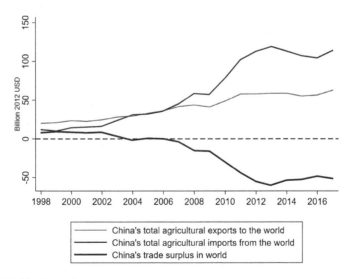

Data. Calculated by the authors.

---

5. The detailed SITC codes under each category can be found in Appendix Table A-2.

importer, as shown in Figure 3.1, and trade deficits have grown over time. In 2017, China's total agricultural imports reached US$114 billion, which is more than seven-fold the amount in 2001 (i.e., US$15.2 billion). Compared with the rapid increase in imports, the scale of China's exports increased steadily to US$62.9 billion in 2017.

2. Commodity Structure

The commodity structure of China's agricultural trade has been generally compatible with its comparative advantage. Due to the relative abundance of labor and scarcity of arable land, China has comparative advantages in labor-intensive products. Figure 3.2 shows that China primarily exports consumer-ready agricultural products such as frozen fish and juice as well as horticultural products, such as vegetables and fruits, which are considered labor-intensive goods. Instead, it mainly imports bulk commodities like soybeans and processed intermediates like wool which are typically land or resource intensive.

Figure 3.2
Commodity Structure of China's Agricultural Trade, 1998–2017

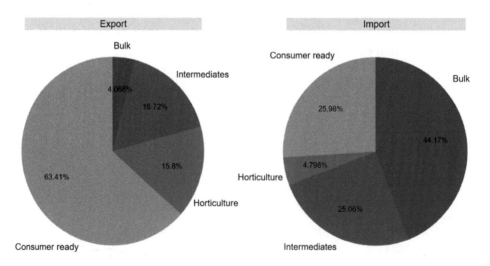

Data. Calculated by the authors.
Note. The commodity structure is measured by trade value.

3. Market Structure

Driven largely by geographical proximity, Asia's export and import markets dominate China's agricultural trade. From 1998 to 2017, Asia accounted for 60.3% of China's total agricultural exports on average. Contrastly, the market distribution of China's agricultural imports is much more diversified. Asia makes up the largest share at 28.9%, followed by North America (25.6%) and Latin America (24.3%) (Figure 3.3).

Figure 3.3
Market Structure of China's Agricultural Trade, 1998–2017

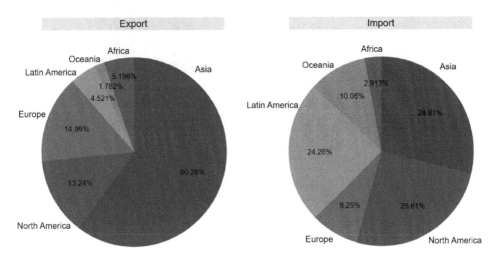

Data. Calculated by the authors.
Note. The market structure is measured by trade value.

4. China's Recent Agricultural Trade in Asia

China kept agricultural trade surpluses with the rest of Asia between 1998 and 2017, although it has shifted from a global exporter to an importer of agricultural products since 2004 (Figure 3.4). The gap between China's agricultural exports to the rest of Asia and its imports narrowed before 2012 and gradually widened afterward. In 2001, China exported agricultural products valued at US$15.7 billion to Asian countries, which accounted for 69.2% of its total agricultural exports. However, since the accession to WTO at the end of 2001, China's agricultural imports from Asia increased from US$5.1 billion in 2001 to US$33.2 billion in 2012. Between 2012 and 2017, however, China's agricultural imports from Asia decreased slightly. In contrast, China's agricultural exports to the rest of Asia grew at a slower pace than imports before 2012, increasing from US$15.7 billion in 2001 to US$33.4 billion in 2012. It remained roughly flat afterward until recently increasing.

Figure 3.4 also shows that Asia has remained an important market for Chinese agricultural imports and exports. However, Chinese agricultural exports to Asia are

Figure 3.4

China's Agricultural Trade in Asia

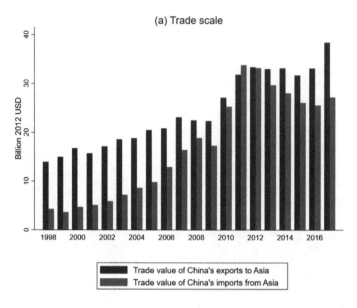

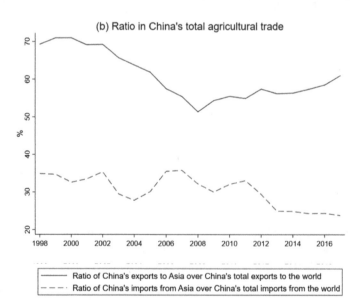

Data. Calculated by the authors.

greater than imports. Imports from Asia are smaller than China's agricultural exports because China primarily imports land-intensive agricultural products such as oil seeds (e.g., soybean) and animal or vegetable oil (e.g., palm oil), which accounted for more than 40%of its total agricultural imports in the period of 1998–2017. China's Asian partners are usually less competitive in these products relative to the US and Brazil (Jha et al., 2010). Meanwhile, Chinese agricultural exports to Asia declined from 69.2% in 1998 to 62.9% in 2017. This is primarily driven by China's increasing exports to the rest of the world, especially the US and EU.

Developed countries in East Asia and developing countries in Southeast Asia are respectively, the most important Chinese trade partners in Asia. China's agricultural exports to Hong Kong, Macau, Taipei of China, Korea, and Japan represent 70% of the total for Asia. Japan, Hong Kong, and Korea ranked as the top three destinations during 1998–2017, to which China exported US$174.4 billion, US$82.2 billion, and US$61.6 billion in agricultural products respectively, accounting for 35.8%, 16.9%, and 12.7% in China's total agricultural exports to Asia. Countries in Southeast Asia dominated China's agricultural import sources in Asia, with a share close to 70% in 2017 (Figure 3.5). China's heavy reliance on agricultural imports from these countries is a result of its rapid economic growth and urbanization, which shifted the general diet of Chinese citizens to products such as fruits, vegetable oil, and meat which SE Asia exports (Radobank, 2016; Salehin & Sirimanne, 2011). Moreover, China's increased agricultural imports from Southeast Asia also benefited from the implementation of CAFTA.

The commodity structure of China's agricultural trade in Asia is largely compatible with comparative advantage. Due to relatively abundant labor and a lack of arable land, China has an advantage in the production of labor-intensive products and a disadvantage in land-intensive products. As is depicted in Figure 3.6 and Figure 3.7, most of China's agricultural exports are consumer-ready and horticultural products, while the majority of its agricultural imports are bulk commodities and processed intermediates.

Figure 3.5
Market Structure of China's Agricultural Trade in Asia

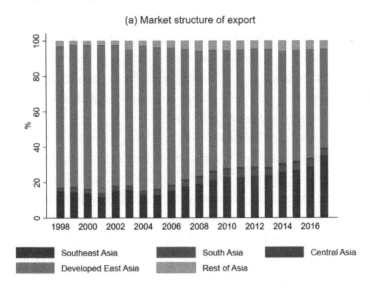

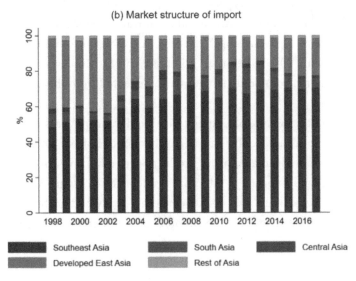

Data. Calculated by the authors.

Note. The market structure is measured by trade value.

Figure 3.6

Commodity Structure of China's Agricultural Exports to Asia

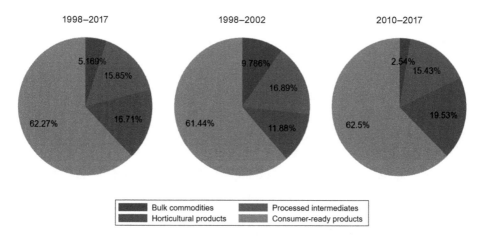

Data. Calculated by the authors.

Note. The commodity structure is measured by trade value.

Figure 3.7

Commodity Structure of China's Agricultural Imports From Asia

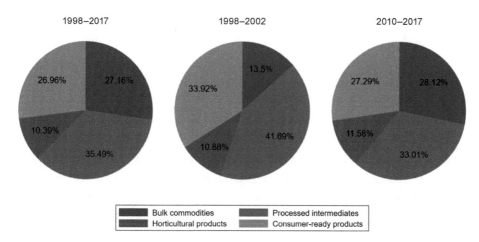

Data. Calculated by the authors.

Note. The commodity structure is measured by trade value.

IV. China's Agricultural Trade With Southeast, South, and Central Asia

1. Expansion of Trade and Widened Trade Deficits

Southeast Asia is an important Chinese market for agricultural imports and exports. The total Chinese agricultural trade volume with Southeast Asia during 1998–2017 was roughly seven times that with South Asia and 28 times that of Central Asia. Figure 3.8 presents the evolution of China's agricultural trade with Southeast, South, and Central Asia.

China's total agricultural exports and imports to Southeast Asia during 1998–2017 were US$105.3 billion and US$230.8 billion respectively, accounting for 12.8% and 19.1% of China's total exports and imports of agricultural products. Between 1998 and 2002, China's agricultural trade with Southeast Asia remained stable, with exports and imports totaling US$11.18 and US$12.22 billion, respectively. After China's accession to WTO, its agricultural trade with Southeast Asia grew rapidly, and the growth rate of imports was significantly higher than that of exports, leading to a widening trade deficit. In 2011, China's agricultural trade deficit with Southeast Asia reached US$16.56 billion. After that, the deficit showed a narrowing trend.

Trade with South Asia is considerably smaller than with Southeast Asia. Between 1998 and 2017, China's total agricultural exports and imports with South Asia were US$16.11 and US$32.37 billion, respectively, accounting for 1.96% and 2.68% of China's total exports and imports of agricultural products. After China's accession to WTO, imports from South Asia grew rapidly. As a result, China has had a deficit in agricultural trade with South Asia since 2004 and peaking in 2012 of US$4.73 billion through narrowing since.

China's agricultural exports and imports with Central Asia are the smallest of the three Asian subregions. From 1998 to 2017, agricultural exports and imports were US$3.8 billion and US$7.98 billion, respectively, accounting for only 0.46% and 0.66% of China's agricultural exports and imports. After China's accession to WTO, agricultural exports to Central Asia rose modestly, though agricultural imports from Central Asia grew more rapidly than exports. Since 2012, however, agricultural imports from Central Asia have shrunk and, as a result, trade deficits have been subsequently narrowed.

Most countries in developing Asia are agricultural economies, which feature abundant natural resources, a high contribution of agriculture to GDP, and a large proportion of population engaged in agriculture, but with inadequate infrastructure and inefficient customs procedures or trade logistics (Jha et al., 2010). On the one hand,

Figure 3.8

China's Agricultural Trade in Southeast, South, and Central Asia

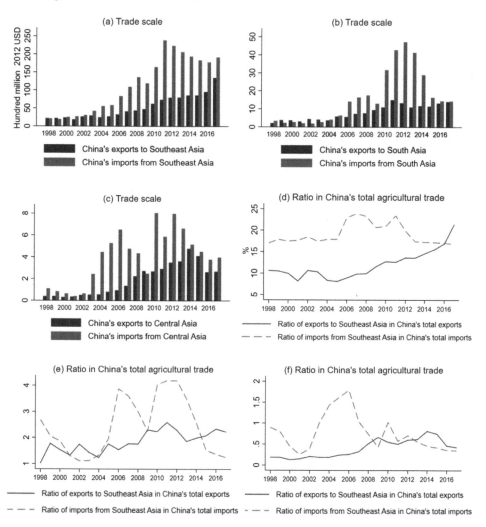

Data. Calculated by the authors.

the relatively rich natural resources and agricultural labor force in these countries could serve as powerful drivers of agricultural exports. On the other hand, the poor infrastructure and poor trade facilitation impairs agricultural exports (Donaldson, 2018).[6] Regardless of the recent increase in their trade volumes and shares, South and

---

6. According to WTO, trade facilitation is defined as "the simplification and harmonisation of international trade procedures," where trade procedures are the "activities, practices and formalities involved in collecting, presenting, communicating and processing data required for the movement of goods in international trade."

Central Asia still account for small shares of China's agricultural exports and imports at less than 5% and 2%, respectively.

However, China is an important export destination of agricultural products for developing Asia (Figure 3.9). From 1998 to 2017, agricultural exports to China accounted for an average of 5.6% and 10.6% of their total for South Asia and Central Asia, respectively. In some years, these shares rose to 10% and 20%. On average, China is the fifth largest agricultural importer for South Asia and second for Central Asia. In contrast, with a great amount of FDI inflows (Shu & Zeng, 2006) and close economic ties based on regional cooperation frameworks such as CAFTA (Qiu et al., 2007), in 2017, ASEAN was China's largest agricultural export market and the second-largest

Figure 3.9
China's Role in Agricultural Trade of Southeast, South, and Central Asia

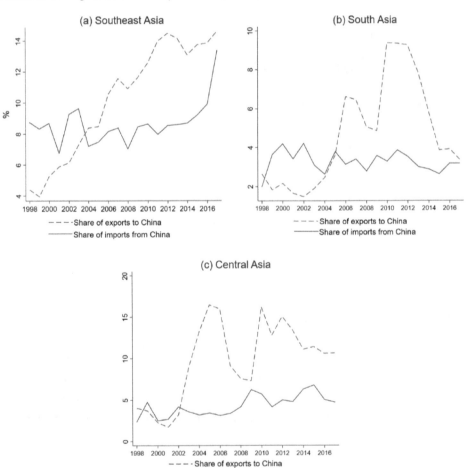

Data. Calculated by the authors.

agricultural import source following Brazil. ASEAN's share of China's agricultural exports and imports in 2017 was 21.3% and 16.8%, respectively. China played an equally important role in terms of agricultural trade for Southeast Asian countries. In 2017, China accounted for 13.4% and 14.6%, respectively, in the total agricultural imports and exports of Southeast Asia.

2. Diversification of Export Commodity Structure and Centralization of Import Commodity Structure

China's exports of bulk commodities remained limited across each of the three Asian regions, which is in line with the fact that China is not a large producer of these resource-intensive goods (Figure 3.10). Over time, the share of processed intermediaries also decreased particularly to South Asia, in which this segment used to make up the primary category. In contrast, the share of horticulture exports to all three regions has substantially increased. In addition, the share of consumer-ready products slightly increased in South and Southeast Asia yet sharply declined in Central Asia.

Table 3.1 lists the top five products in China's agricultural exports to Southeast, South, and Central Asia at the 6-digit HS level.[7] China primarily exported vegetables and fruits to these regions that are typically labor intensive, but also match recent consumption shifts in these regions associated with their economic growth (Kelly,

Figure 3.10
Commodity Structure of China's Agricultural Exports to Southeast, South, and Central Asia

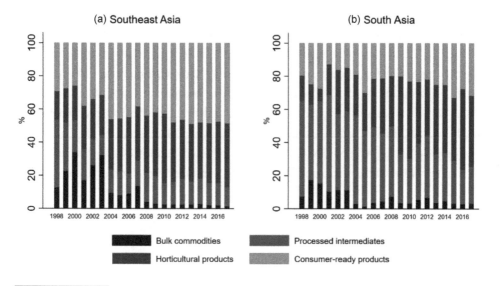

7. These products account for 22% to 63% altogether in China's exports to developing Asian countries.

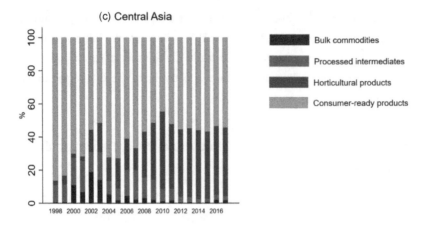

Data. Calculated by the authors.
Note. The commodity structure is measured by trade value.

2016; Reardon et al., 2014). China used to export a lot of cereals, such as maize and rice, to these regions before its accession to WTO, but these were replaced by higher-value products in the later period of 2010–2017. Moreover, China's agricultural export basket shows some diversification supported both by decreasing shares of the top export products and a decreasing Herfindahl-Hirschman Index (HHI).[8]

Figure 3.11 shows China's agricultural import structure from Southeast, South, and Central Asia. Bulk commodities and processed intermediates have dominated China's agricultural imports from these regions for years. In both South and Central Asia, bulk commodities have replaced processed intermediates as the largest imports. While China's imports of processed intermediates from Southeast Asia were still larger than bulk commodities, the gap has notably narrowed. In contrast, China's imports of horticultural and consumer-ready products from these regions have been recently on the rise, especially from Southeast and South Asia. While horticultural and consumer-ready products are typically where China enjoys a comparative advantage, Southeast Asian countries are also competitive globally, and their exports are often complements to those of China (Chen & Duncan, 2008; Nguyen, 2016; Zhan et al., 2018). For example, Southeast Asia possesses advantages in the production of tropical fruits (e.g., bananas), while China performs better in the production of temperate fruits (e.g., apples).

---

8. Herfindahl-Hirschman Index (HHI) is the sum of squared market shares, an indicator of market concentration. Detailed information is available in Appendix Table A-3.

Table 3.1

Top 5 Chinese Agricultural Exports to Southeast, South, and Central Asia

	Rank	1998–2017		1998–2002		2010–2017	
		Products	Share (%)	Products	Share (%)	Products	Share (%)
Southeast Asia	1	alliaceous; garlic	7.05	rice	10.93	alliaceous; garlic	7.92
	2	apples	5.42	maize	10.38	apples	5.50
	3	mandarins	3.94	maize seed	6.26	mandarins	4.28
	4	tobacco	3.08	tobacco	4.14	mushrooms and truffles	3.64
	5	mushrooms and truffles	2.81	apples	3.94	food preparations (n.e.s. in item No. 2106.10)	3.03
South Asia	1	silk	20.94	silk	41.28	apples	15.80
	2	apples	11.98	maize	6.79	silk	13.84
	3	alliaceous; garlic	9.30	sucrose	5.86	alliaceous; garlic	9.57
	4	kidney beans	5.78	alliaceous; garlic	5.08	kidney beans	5.69
	5	ginger	4.66	cotton	4.37	ginger	4.85
Central Asia	1	green tea	15.68	green tea	36.03	green tea	14.38
	2	apples	9.72	yeasts	7.52	apples	9.01
	3	mandarins	7.07	rice (husked)	4.90	mandarins	8.98
	4	tomatoes (vegetable preparations)	4.95	rice	4.48	tomatoes	6.10
	5	swine meat	4.67	pasta (food preparations)	4.02	tomatoes (vegetable preparations)	4.83

Note. Shares are measured by trade value. The top 5 products are defined as those with the highest value shares.

Figure 3.11

Commodity Structure of China's Agricultural Imports From Southeast, South, and Central Asia

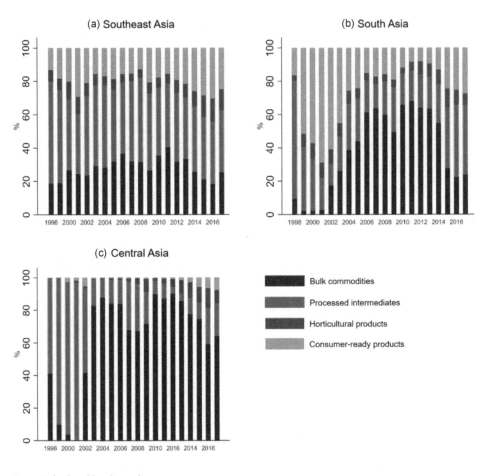

Data. Calculated by the authors.

Note. The commodity structure is measured by trade value.

Table 3.2 lists China's top five agricultural imports from Southeast, South, and Central Asia at the 6-digit HS level.[9] In contrast to China's diversifying agricultural exports to these regions, the results of Table 3.2 suggest that China's import basket is concentrated in only a few categories of products. Export-oriented policies in Malaysia and Indonesia, combined with high yields of palm oil and rubber, make these two countries major sources of Chinese imports (Radobank, 2016). Palm oil and rubber, respectively accounted for 23.8% and 20.3% of China's total agricultural imports from Southeast Asia during 1998–2017. As for South and Central Asia,

___

9. These products account for 53% to 87% altogether in China's imports from developing Asian countries.

Table 3.2

Top 5 China's Agricultural Imports From Southeast, South, and Central Asia

	Rank	1998–2017		1998–2002		2010–2017	
		Products	Share (%)	Products	Share (%)	Products	Share (%)
Southeast Asia	1	palm oil	23.79	palm oil	27.59	rubber	21.25
	2	rubber	20.28	rubber (natural)	8.95	palm oil	20.57
	3	manioc roots and tubers	6.92	rubber	8.00	manioc roots and tubers	7.56
	4	rubber (natural)	4.38	rice	5.05	rice	4.18
	5	rice	3.78	manioc roots and tubers	3.54	fruit (edible)	4.13
South Asia	1	cotton	47.23	fish (frozen)	22.50	cotton	50.13
	2	castor oil	8.86	oil-cake	18.33	castor oil	9.50
	3	fish (frozen)	4.78	shrimps and prawns (frozen)	10.89	rice	3.40
	4	rice	2.51	castor oil	9.25	ramie	3.14
	5	ramie	2.51	molasses	4.30	fish (frozen)	3.10
Central Asia	1	cotton	72.56	hides and skins	23.74	cotton	72.57
	2	cotton linters	4.16	cotton	22.99	meslin and wheat other than durum	5.95
	3	meslin and wheat other than durum	3.42	cotton linters	12.52	cotton linters	3.61
	4	wool tops	2.78	skins; raw, of sheep or lambs	8.68	plants and parts	3.02
	5	hides and skins	2.03	animal products	6.82	sunflower seeds	1.99

Note. Shares are measured by trade value. The top 5 products are defined as those with the highest value shares.

the proportion of cotton is the highest, respectively at 47.2% and 72.6%, among all products during this period.

V. Concentration of Market Shares With Regional Major Partners

1. Southeast Asia

As Table 3.3 shows, China's agricultural exports to Southeast Asia are mainly concentrated in six countries: Malaysia, Indonesia, Thailand, Vietnam, Singapore, and Philippine, accounting for approximately 95% of China's total agricultural exports to Southeast Asia. Among them, Malaysia enjoyed the highest proportion (21.2%) and is followed by Indonesia (19.6%), Thailand (16.9%), Vietnam (15.8%), Singapore (12.6%), and the Philippines (10.2%). Over time, the proportions of Thailand and Vietnam increased from 8.9% and 6.5% over 1998–2002 to 19.1% and 18.2% over 2010–2017, respectively. In contrast, the proportions of the other four countries dropped by a different degree.

China's agricultural imports from Southeast Asia are mainly concentrated in the following four countries: Thailand, Malaysia, Indonesia, and Vietnam, which account for around 90% of China's total agricultural imports from Southeast Asia. Among them, Thailand enjoyed the highest proportion (28.9%), which was followed by Indonesia (24.7%), Malaysia (24.3%), and Vietnam (11.9%).

As indicated by the HHI, the market concentration of China's agricultural trade in Southeast Asia has declined. Nevertheless, it is the diversification among major participants that dominates this trend.[10]

2. South Asia

According to Table 3.4, China's agricultural exports to South Asia are mainly concentrated in three countries: India, Pakistan, and Bangladesh. Between 1998 and 2017, these three countries accounted for 85% of China's total agricultural exports to South Asia. On average, India accounted for the highest proportion (49.4%), followed by Pakistan (18.4%) and Bangladesh (17.6%). The proportion going to Bangladesh increased from 9.4% between 1998 and 2002 to 20.1% during 2010–2017. In contrast, the proportion going to India dropped from 64% to 45.4% between the two periods.

---

10. We first calculated differences of the squared market share between the two period, i.e., and then compared the sum of (SSR) by groups, i.e., the *top group* that includes the major markets and the *others* that includes all markets that are left. For both the export and import basket, SSR of the top group accounted for 99.9% in the total SSR.

Table 3.3

Market Structure of China's Agricultural Trade in Southeast Asia

Countries	Export shares (%)			Import shares (%)		
	1998–2017	1998–2002	2010–2017	1998–2017	1998–2002	2010–2017
Malaysia	21.19	27.56	18.91	24.26	30.67	19.86
Indonesia	19.63	23.29	19.06	24.69	16.99	25.29
Thailand	16.89	8.85	19.14	28.89	30.43	30.08
Vietnam	15.81	6.46	18.23	11.98	12.16	13.66
Singapore	12.58	18.97	10.53	3.91	3.70	3.79
Philippines	10.19	12.20	9.97	2.78	4.71	2.92
Myanmar	2.69	1.95	3.09	2.51	0.86	3.12
Cambodia	0.56	0.44	0.53	0.34	0.39	0.41
Laos	0.24	0.12	0.32	0.64	0.10	0.85
Brunei	0.19	0.15	0.19	0.00	0	0.00
East Timor	0.03	0	0.04	0.00	0	0.00
HHI	0.16	0.19	0.16	0.22	0.23	0.22

Table 3.4

Market Structure of China's Agricultural Trade in South Asia

Countries	Export shares (%)			Import shares (%)		
	1998–2017	1998–2002	2010–2017	1998–2017	1998–2002	2010–2017
India	49.35	64.00	45.37	83.47	83.29	82.16
Pakistan	18.38	15.15	17.89	10.31	8.99	11.65
Bangladesh	17.56	9.37	20.14	3.71	3.26	3.64
Sri Lanka	8.57	6.43	9.78	1.92	1.23	2.08
Nepal	3.96	4.10	4.06	0.34	2.32	0.21
Afghanistan	1.89	0.90	2.39	0.23	0.92	0.23
Maldives	0.26	0.06	0.31	0.02	0.00	0.02
Bhutan	0.04	0.00	0.05	0.00	0	0.00
HHI	0.32	0.45	0.29	0.71	0.70	0.69

Note. Shares are measured by trade value (Table 3.3 and Table 3.4).

China's agricultural imports from South Asia are mainly sourced from India and Pakistan. Between 1998 and 2017, India accounted for 83.5% of China's agricultural imports from South Asia. The proportion of each country changed little over the whole period.

3. Central Asia

As found in Table 3.5, China's agricultural exports to Central Asia are mainly concentrated in Kazakhstan, Kyrgyzstan, and Uzbekistan, which accounted for an average of 90% of the total between 1998 and 2017. Among them, Kazakhstan accounted for the highest proportion (49.96%), followed by Kyrgyzstan (24.52%) and Uzbekistan (17.76%). The share going to Kazakhstan and Kyrgyzstan increased during the period, while the proportion going to Uzbekistan dropped from 39.5% to 16% during 1998–2002 and 2010–2017. As a result, the market concentration increased modestly.

Table 3.5
Market Structure of China's Agricultural Trade in Central Asia

Countries	Export shares (%)			Import shares (%)		
	1998–2017	1998–2002	2010–2017	1998–2017	1998–2002	2010–2017
Kazakhstan	49.96	37.27	52.22	16.67	45.18	16.39
Kyrgyzstan	24.52	11.95	24.15	3.39	20.42	2.32
Uzbekistan	17.76	39.46	16.00	74.19	25.39	75.55
Tajikistan	4.41	1.60	4.47	1.47	5.73	1.18
Turkmenistan	3.35	9.73	3.16	4.28	3.29	4.55
HHI	0.34	0.32	0.36	0.58	0.31	0.60

Note. Shares are measured by trade value.

China's agricultural imports from Central Asia mainly came from Kazakhstan and Uzbekistan between 1998 and 2017, which accounted for 74.19% and 16.67% of China's total agricultural imports from the region respectively. Uzbekistan's share jumped from 25.39% between 1998 and 2002 to 75.55% between 2010 and 2017. On the other hand, Kazakhstan's and Kyrgyzstan's share dropped between the two periods. As a result, the market concentration increased sharply.

4. Summary

Despite disparities, commonalities can be found in the dynamics of China's agricultural trade with Southeast, South, and Central Asia. First, imports generally grew more rapidly than exports, though imports started to decline in recent years. Second, China had agricultural trade deficits with each region shortly after its accession to WTO, although deficits have narrowed since 2012. Third, the Southeast Asian region was a key market for Chinese agricultural trade, while China's agricultural trade with South and Central Asia was relatively small. Finally, China's agricultural trade commodity structure is consistent with its comparative advantages, and this relationship strengthens over time.

VI. China's Agricultural Trade With Targeted Asia Countries

1. Bangladesh

During 1998–2017, the average of China's annual agricultural exports to Bangladesh was US$141 million, accounting for 0.34% of China's total agricultural exports. Meanwhile, China's agricultural imports from Bangladesh averaged US$60 million, accounting for 0.1% of China's total agricultural imports. According to Figure 3.12, China had been running agricultural trade surpluses with Bangladesh since 1999. As the growth rate of China's agricultural exports to Bangladesh was significantly higher than imports, China's agricultural trade surplus with Bangladesh gradually increased. Though Bangladesh was not a crucial market for China in either agricultural exports or imports, its importance has slightly increased over time.

China was relatively more important to Bangladesh's agricultural trade. From 1998 to 2017, China accounted for 6.7% and 3.1% of Bangladesh's agricultural exports and imports respectively. On average, China was the fourth-largest agricultural importer of Bangladesh agricultural goods, following the EU (39.7%), the US (14.3%), and India (10.5%). In addition, China has become an increasingly important destination of Bangladesh's agricultural exports over time. In 2017, the share of Bangladesh's agricultural exports destined for China increased to more than 10%. In contrast, Chinese exports rank ninth largest for Bangladesh.

As Figure 3.13 demonstrates, While China used to export cereals primarily to Bangladesh in 1998–2002, the top category of products has been replaced by fruits and nuts that are typically intensive in labor and thus in line with China's comparative advantages. Shares of other labor-intensive products such as vegetables as well as coffee, tea, mate and spices in China's agricultural exports to Bangladesh have also increased from 2010 to 2017.

As to agricultural imports demonstrated in Figure 3.14, China no longer predominately imported textile fibers and paper yarn from Bangladesh. Instead, aquatic products and crabs, in particular, became the top category of agricultural products in China's import basket.

Figure 3.12
China's Agricultural Trade With Bangladesh

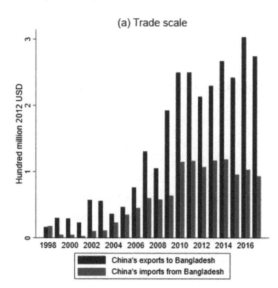

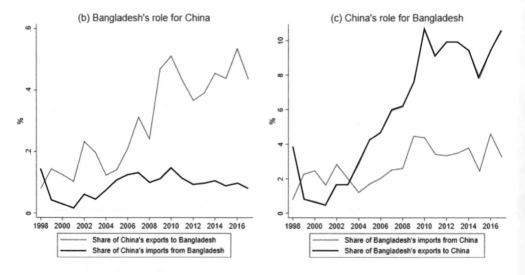

Data. Calculated by the authors.

Figure 3.13

Commodity Structure of China's Agricultural Exports to Bangladesh

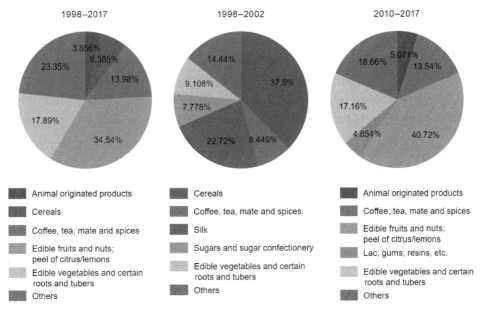

Figure 3.14

Commodity Structure of China's Agricultural Imports From Bangladesh

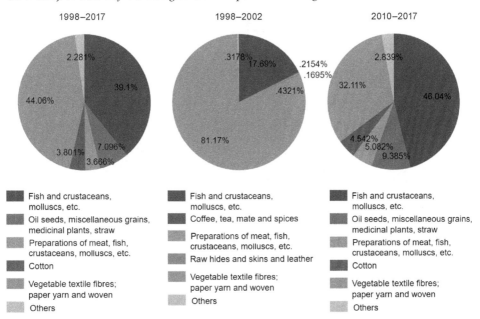

Data. Calculated by the authors (Figure 3.13 and Figure 3.14).

Note. The legends are arranged in a clockwise order from the top. The commodity structure is measured by trade value. The top 5 products are distinguished (Figure 3.13 and Figure 3.14).

2. Cambodia

According to Figure 3.15, Chinese imports of Cambodian agricultural products substantially increased in 2010 when CAFTA was formally established. Over time, China's agricultural exports and imports with Cambodia have increased in importance in China's agricultural trade. From 2010 to 2017, the average annual agricultural exports of China to Cambodia were US$46 million, while imports were US$82 million. They each accounted for 0.08% of China's total agricultural exports or imports.

Figure 3.15
China's Agricultural Trade With Cambodia

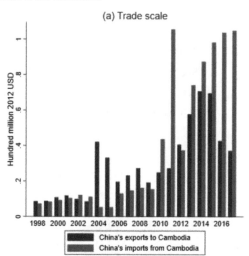

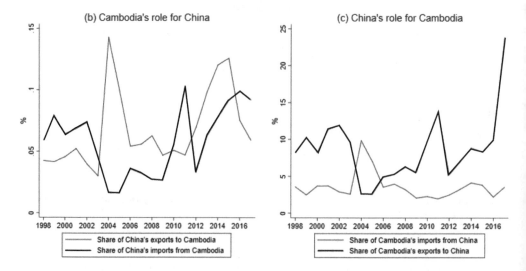

Data. Calculated by the authors.

China remained a more important market for Cambodian agricultural exports and imports. Between 1998 and 2017, agricultural exports to China were 9.0% and imports 3.3% of total Cambodian agricultural exports and imports. China was the third-largest agricultural importer and exporter of Cambodian products, only after ASEAN and the EU.

China's agricultural exports and imports to/from Cambodia have diversified over time. According to Figure 3.16, while China used to predominately export tobacco and manufactured tobacco to Cambodia, this share has decreased substantially from 76.2% of total agricultural exports between 1998–2002 to 19.4% over 2010–2017. Thanks to Cambodia's growing demand for malt and hides, milling products and raw hides, skins, and leather have grown to occupy 16.7% and 10.2% of the total ag exports from China, making them second and third to only tobacco.

In terms of imports shown in Figure 3.17, China used to predominantly import rubber and rubber articles from Cambodia. However, as China shifted imports of these products to Laos, the share of this category declined from 79.6% during 1998–2002 to 36.0% during 2010–2017 in China's total agricultural imports. Cereals, as a result,

Figure 3.16
Commodity Structure of China's Agricultural Exports to Cambodia

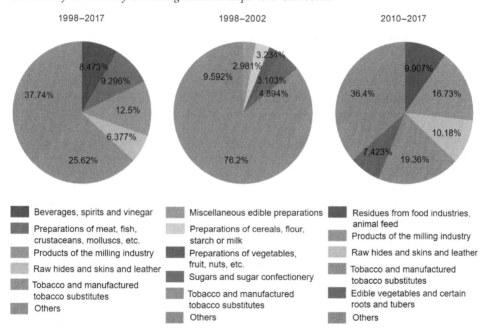

Data. Calculated by the authors.
Note. The legends are arranged in a clockwise order from the top. The commodity structure is measured by trade value. The top 5 products are distinguished.

have now become China's major agricultural imports from Cambodia. The share of this category reached 41.2% of China's total agricultural imports from Cambodia from 2010 to 2017.

Figure 3.17
Commodity Structure of China's Agricultural Imports From Cambodia

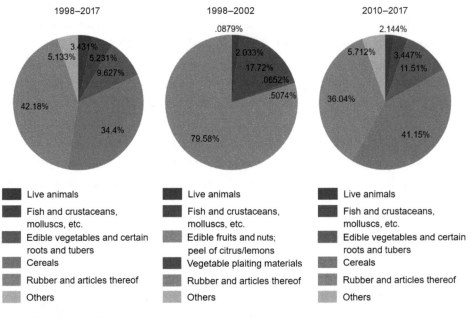

Data. Calculated by the authors.
Note. The legends are arranged in a clockwise order from the top. The commodity structure is measured by trade value. The top 5 products are distinguished.

3. Laos

China's agricultural imports from Laos had rapidly collected since 2006, when it implemented the Early Harvest Program, according to Figure 3.18. This program is generally recognized as the first step of trade liberalization undertaken as part of the CAFTA framework. Under this program, agricultural tariff barriers between China and Laos were gradually reduced, with some sensitive products excluded. The proportion of agricultural imports from Laos in China's total agricultural imports increased from 0.02% between 1998 and 2002 to 0.16% during 2010–2017. In contrast, China's agricultural exports to Laos have remained trivial relatively speaking. As a result, China has always kept a bilateral agricultural trade deficit with Laos, and the scale of deficits has enlarged over time.

Figure 3.18

China's Agricultural Trade With Laos

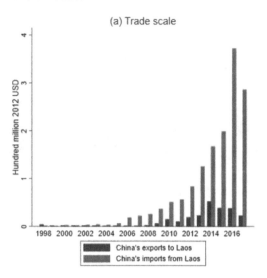

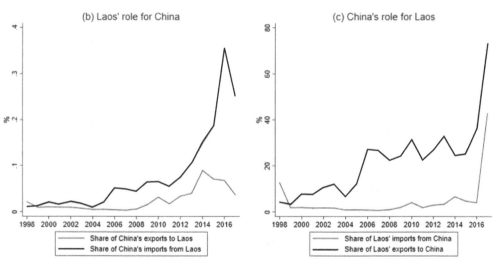

Data. Calculated by the authors.

With a market share of 31.1% from 1998 to 2017, China was the second largest destination for Laos' agricultural exports, and the importance of the Chinese market has increased over time. In 2017, China's share of Laos' agricultural exports was close to 80%. In contrast, China was not a critical source of agricultural imports for Laos, averaging only 3.7% up until 2017, when suddenly agricultural imports skyrocketed in 2017, reaching beyond 40%.

Figure 3.19
Commodity Structure of China's Agricultural Exports to Laos

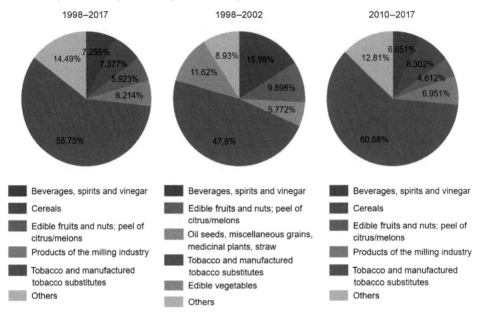

Figure 3.20
Commodity Structure of China's Agricultural Imports From Laos

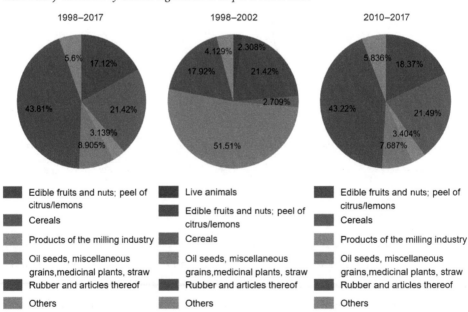

Data. Calculated by the authors (Figure 3.19 and Figure 3.20).
Note. The legends are arranged in a clockwise order from the top. The commodity structure is measured by trade value. The top 5 products are distinguished (Figure 3.19 and Figure 3.20).

As Figure 3.19 demonstrates, tobacco and manufactured tobacco accounted for the largest share of China's agricultural exports to Laos, averaging 58.8% over the period of 1998–2017. Rubber and rubber articles replaced oil seeds as the top category of agricultural products that China imported from Laos, increasing from 17.9% over 1998–2002 to 43.2% over 2010–2017, as manifested by Figure 3.20.

4. Myanmar

Myanmar's importance in China's agricultural imports has notably increased since 2008, according to Figure 3.21. During 1998–2002, its proportion of China's total agricultural imports was 0.15%, but since has increased to 0.58% during 2010–2017. China's growing imports from Myanmar may reflect Myanmar's reexports of sugar from Thailand and India to China (Brough, 2016). These reexports have been substantially expanded in recent years, making China's agricultural imports from Myanmar jump to US$1.52 billion in 2016, more than double that from 2015. China's agricultural exports to Myanmar have grown steadily, consequently making China run bilateral agricultural trade deficits since 2007.

In contrast, between 1998 and 2017, Chinese agricultural exports and imports played a more important role in Myanmar's trade. The proportion of Myanmar's agricultural exports and imports with China, respectively accounted for 10.8% and 19.4% of its total agricultural imports and exports. It should be noted that China has become an increasingly crucial export destination for Myanmar's agricultural products since 2006. In 2016, China's market share in Myanmar's agricultural exports exceeded 40%.

Figure 3.21
China's Agricultural Trade With Myanmar

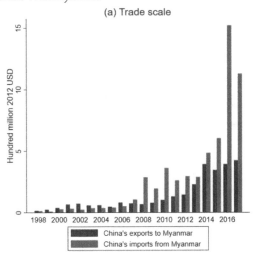

(a) Trade scale

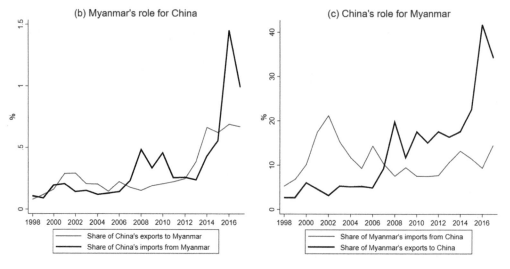

Data. Calculated by the authors.

Figure 3.22

Commodity Structure of China's Agricultural Exports to Myanmar

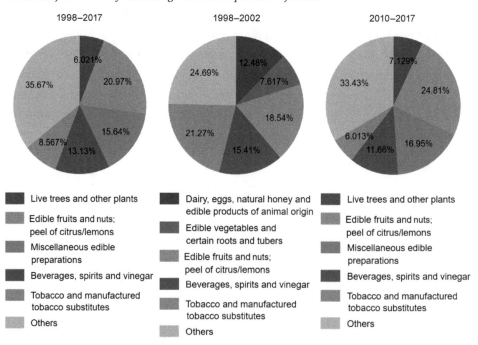

Data. Calculated by the authors.
Note. The legends are arranged in a clockwise order from the top. The commodity structure is measured by trade value. The top 5 products are distinguished.

As demonstrated by Figure 3.22, fruits replaced tobacco as China's top export to Myanmar between 1998 and 2017. Apples accounted for 10.5% of fruit exports, the greatest share, on average. In contrast, sucrose was the single most important agricultural good that China imported from Myanmar, as found in Figure 3.23, with an average market share of 25.5%.

Figure 3.23
Commodity Structure of China's Agricultural Imports From Myanmar

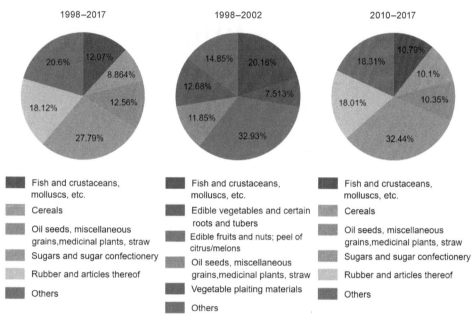

Data. Calculated by the authors.
Note. The legends are arranged in a clockwise order from the top. The commodity structure is measured by trade value. The top 5 products are distinguished.

5. Nepal

Between 1998 and 2017, China's annual agricultural exports to Nepal had an average of US$32 million and accounted for 0.08% of China's total agricultural exports. In the meantime, its annual agricultural imports from Nepal had an average of US$5 million and accounted for 0.01% of China's total agricultural imports. Despite these small shares, Nepal's importance in China's agricultural export markets has increased, as Figure 3.24 finds, with the market share growing from 0.06% during 1998–2002 to 0.09% over 2010–2017. In contrast, Nepal's importance as an import market for China has decreased over time, declining from 0.04% during 1998–2002 to 0.01% during 2010–2017.

Figure 3.24
China's Agricultural Trade With Nepal

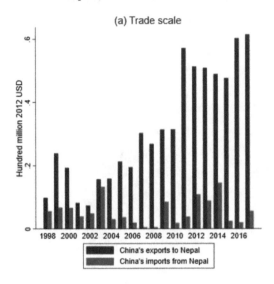

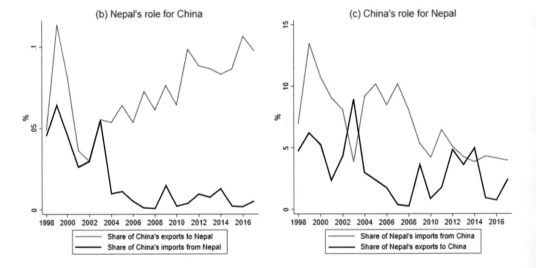

Data. Calculated by the authors.

China was relatively more important to Nepal in terms of both agricultural exports and imports. During 1998–2017, China respectively accounted for 3.0% and 5.3% of Nepal's agricultural exports and imports. In this period, China was Nepal's third-largest agricultural importer, following India (78.8%) and Bangladesh (7.3%). It was Nepal's fourth-largest agricultural export market, following India (54.8%), ASEAN (14.7%), and Argentina (6.8%).

According to Figure 3.25, fruits have replaced raw silk as the top agricultural product that China exported to Nepal, which was driven by economic growth and dietary changes. Fruits, almost exclusively apples, were 58.0% of China's total agricultural exports to Nepal during 2010–2017. As demonstrated by Figure 3.26, in contrast, China's agricultural imports from Nepal used to primarily consist of milling goods, but their combined share has declined from 48.2% to 7.2% over time. Between 2010 and 2017, oilseeds, grains, and plants became the top import item, with a share of 56.7% of China's total agricultural imports from Nepal.

6. Vietnam

Vietnam is one of the largest rice producers and exporters in the world, and the country plays a critical role in China's food security strategy. As Figure 3.27 shows, the establishment of CAFTA in 2010 has driven the rapid growth of Chinese cereal imports from Vietnam. During 2010–2017, China's agricultural exports and imports with Vietnam, respectively averaged US$1.6 and US$2.7 billion, accounting for 2.8% and 2.5% of China's agricultural exports and imports.

Figure 3.25
Commodity Structure of China's Agricultural Exports to Nepal

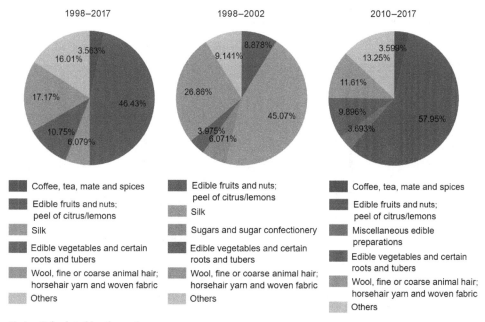

Data. Calculated by the authors.
Note. The legends are arranged in a clockwise order from the top. The commodity structure is measured by trade value. The top 5 products are distinguished.

Figure 3.26

Commodity Structure of China's Agricultural Imports From Nepal

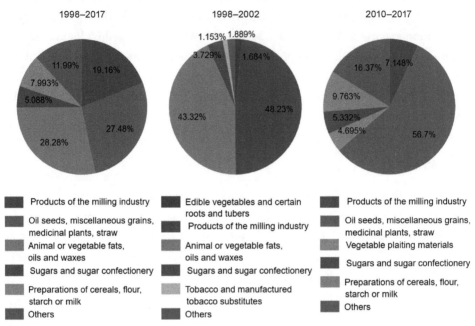

Data. Calculated by the authors.

Note. The legends are arranged in a clockwise order from the top. The commodity structure is measured by trade value. The top 5 products are distinguished.

Figure 3.27

China's Agricultural Trade With Vietnam

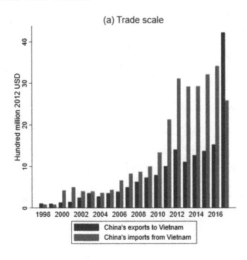

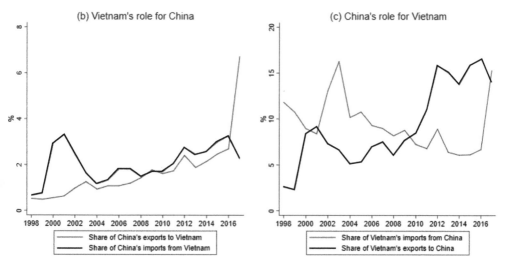

(b) Vietnam's role for China

(c) China's role for Vietnam

Share of China's exports to Vietnam
Share of China's imports from Vietnam

Share of Vietnam's imports from China
Share of Vietnam's exports to China

Data. Calculated by the authors.

China is also a crucial agricultural trade partner for Vietnam. Between 1998 and 2017, China accounted for 11.2% of total Vietnamese agricultural exports and 8.6% of agricultural imports. The importance of Chinese imports to Vietnam's agricultural exports has notably increased since the establishment of CAFTA in 2010.

The agricultural trade commodity structure has changed substantially over time. Vietnam's demand for vegetables, fruits, and animal products has increased rapidly with economic growth. Accordingly, as Figure 3.28 demonstrates, the share of these products in China's agricultural exports to Vietnam rose from 29.4% between 1998 and 2002 to 52.2% from 2010 to 2017.

In contrast, according to Figure 3.29, cereals became the second-largest product category that China imported from Vietnam, following only fruits and nuts. Rice specifically became China's primary agricultural product imported from Vietnam, accounting for nearly one-fifth of China's total agricultural imports from Vietnam.

7. Summary

Myanmar, Laos, and Cambodia make up a small share of China's agricultural trade, generally accounting for less than 1%. In contrast, China plays a relatively important role in agricultural trade for these countries, with notable shares in both their agricultural exports and imports. While China largely runs an agricultural trade deficit with the four Southeast Asian countries, it has kept an agricultural trade surplus with the two South Asian countries, Nepal and Bangladesh.

Figure 3.28

Commodity Structure of China's Agricultural Exports to Vietnam

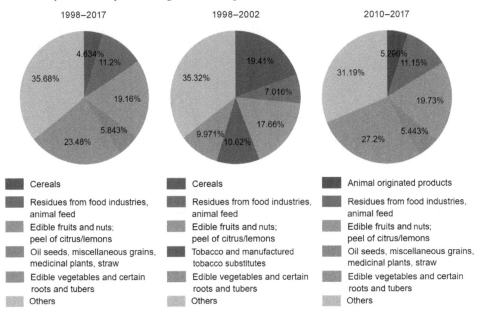

1998–2017

1998–2002

2010–2017

Cereals

Residues from food industries, animal feed

Edible fruits and nuts; peel of citrus/lemons

Oil seeds, miscellaneous grains, medicinal plants, straw

Edible vegetables and certain roots and tubers

Others

Cereals

Residues from food industries, animal feed

Edible fruits and nuts; peel of citrus/lemons

Tobacco and manufactured tobacco substitutes

Edible vegetables and certain roots and tubers

Others

Animal originated products

Residues from food industries, animal feed

Edible fruits and nuts; peel of citrus/lemons

Oil seeds, miscellaneous grains, medicinal plants, straw

Edible vegetables and certain roots and tubers

Others

Figure 3.29

Commodity Structure of China's Agricultural Imports From Vietnam

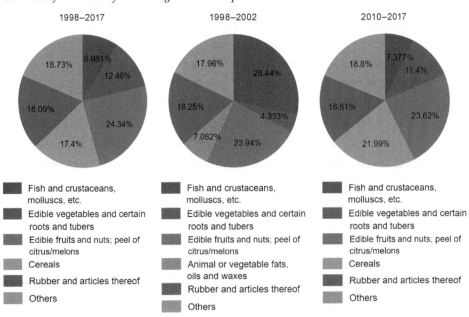

1998–2017

1998–2002

2010–2017

Fish and crustaceans, molluscs, etc.

Edible vegetables and certain roots and tubers

Edible fruits and nuts; peel of citrus/melons

Cereals

Rubber and articles thereof

Others

Fish and crustaceans, molluscs, etc.

Edible vegetables and certain roots and tubers

Edible fruits and nuts; peel of citrus/melons

Animal or vegetable fats, oils and waxes

Rubber and articles thereof

Others

Fish and crustaceans, molluscs, etc.

Edible vegetables and certain roots and tubers

Edible fruits and nuts; peel of citrus/melons

Cereals

Rubber and articles thereof

Others

Data. Calculated by the authors (Figure 3.28 and Figure 3.29).

Note. The legends are arranged in a clockwise order from the top. The commodity structure is measured by trade value. The top 5 products are distinguished (Figure 3.28 and Figure 3.29).

The agricultural trade commodity structure has shifted toward countries' comparative advantages, with China increasingly exporting products that are labor-intensive or relatively processed, such as apples and cigarettes. In contrast, products that are typically land or resource intensive, like rice and rubber, are imported.

VII. Key Regional Agricultural Trade Initiatives

1. China-ASEAN Free Trade Agreement (CAFTA)

Development and Implementation of the Agreement
In November 2001, ASEAN states endorsed China's proposal to establish a CAFTA within ten years, which was expected to boost trade cooperation and increase security confidence between China and Southeast Asia countries. An agreement on the establishment of CAFTA was signed a year later during the ASEAN-China Summit in Phnom Penh. The agreement states that CAFTA would be fully implemented by 2010 for the six original ASEAN members (Brunei, Indonesia, Malaysia, Myanmar, Singapore, and Thailand) and China, and by 2015 for Cambodia, Lao PDR, Vietnam, and the Philippines. January 1, 2010 is usually regarded as the date when CAFTA was formally established. There are three tracks of trade liberalization incorporated in the framework. The first track, the Early Harvest Program (EHP), which came into effect on January 1, 2004, was established to eliminate agricultural tariff barriers by 2006 among China and the six original ASEAN countries, with some sensitive products excluded. The second track, or the Normal Track, was arranged to regulate the liberalization of most traded products other than those included in the EHP and the sensitive list of products and was expected to be fully implemented by 2010. The third track, named the Sensitive Track, includes products that the CAFTA members want to protect, either for development reasons or other ones, was fulfilled in 2015 among all CAFTA members.

Performance of the Agreement and Reflections
China's agricultural trade with ASEAN had expanded rapidly since 2010, when CAFTA was formally established. Between 2010 and 2017, China's total agricultural exports and imports with ASEAN averaged US$8.7 and US$19.8 billion, which are about four and eight times the amount between 1998 and 2002, respectively.

Nevertheless, CAFTA's performance in trade promotion has been hindered by the high usage costs of FTA rules and emerging non-tariff barriers. The utilization rate of the agreement is limited. It was reported that more than 70% of Chinese firms did not make use of the FTA rules when they traded with ASEAN countries in 2018 because of the high costs imposed by rules of origin (CCPIT, 2018; Han et al., 2018). Meanwhile, non-tariff barriers such as SPS are employed by the government of Thailand, Indonesia, and the Philippines to protect domestic industries (Nugroho, 2015). Recent studies suggested that CAFTA could work better in trade promotion if these two problems were alleviated effectively (CCPIT, 2018; Han et al., 2018; Hayakawa et al., 2016).

The establishment of CAFTA also induced a large amount of agriculture-related foreign direct investment from China to Southeast Asian countries, which made notable contributions for them to cope with challenges, including food security, poverty reduction, and agricultural transformation. By the end of 2017, China's total investment in agriculture in ASEAN reached US$4.17 billion, accounting for 24.0% of China's total agricultural-related investment. China also set up 333 agribusiness enterprises, accounting for 39.1% of the total number of China's overseas agricultural enterprises (China Ministry of Agriculture, 2019). Since most ASEAN members are heavily dependent on agriculture and have a high proportion of the population engaged in agriculture, FDI inflows from China could directly contribute to income growth if they positively influence production efficiency (Chandarany et al., 2011). Chinese overseas agribusinesses have created 21,694 jobs in ASEAN countries by the end of 2017 (China Ministry of Agriculture, 2019).

2. Regional Comprehensive Economic Partnership (RCEP)

The RCEP was first introduced during the 19th ASEAN Summit in 2011 with the aim to further boost trade and deepen economic integration in the Asia-Pacific region. Negotiations were formally launched during the 21st ASEAN Summit in 2012 and have been ongoing for several years. Although India pulled out at the last minute for a wide range of reasons, the 15 negotiating parties, including ten-member ASEAN, China, Japan, South Korea, Australia, and New Zealand, plan to sign it in 2020. Once it is put into place, it would be the largest free trade area, accounting for 30% of the world's population and nearly 30% of the world's GDP (Tani, 2020).

Compared with bilateral FTAs signed between negotiating countries, RCEP makes improvements in both the breadth and depth of economic cooperation. Although the details are not yet released, the agreement should progressively lower trade barriers across many countries. According to the framework agreed on in 2017, RCEP will also incorporate more economic considerations into the formulation and implementation of rules. For example, it will allow companies to export the same product within the block but do away with the need to fill out separate paperwork for each country (Tostevin, 2019). RCEP will be committed to improving rule-of-origin and customs procedures, which could improve the rate of participation and potential benefits to businesses that were not seen under previous regional and bilateral FTAs.

However, challenges of the RCEP cannot be neglected. As is mentioned in Section 3, social, political, and economic systems vary across countries, which has the potential to be a threat to cooperation and the stability of the agreement. For instance, many studies predict that industries which are less competitive than others in more industrialized nations may suffer from greater competition (Liu & Zhao, 2017; Xue & Zhang, 2017). Thus, measures to restructure industries or introduce protections should be taken into account in advance to minimize the adverse shock to employment and economic development.

3. Belt and Road Initiative (BRI)

The BRI was announced in 2013 and involved infrastructure development and investments in around 140 countries and 30 international organizations in Asia, Europe, and Africa by the end of January 2020. BRI targets the promotion of economic development and integration through the construction of a unified large market. Though BRI works toward trade promotion and provides trade facilitation such as tariff reductions, it attaches more emphasis on the improvement of connectivity among participants (Li, 2018).

China and other developing Asian countries may benefit from the initiative. Chinese financial resources have been and will continue to be injected into the development of infrastructure to promote the construction of agricultural export production and improved agricultural production efficiency. Constructions of railways, such as Longhai Railway and the Lanxin Railway, will greatly improve the connectivity in developing Asia and contribute to agricultural trade expansion within and outside the region. It is reported that China's total trade with countries involved in the BRI exceeded US$3 trillion and created US$1.1 billion in revenues and 180,000 jobs for the countries involved (Xinhua, 2017; Yu, 2017). Technological exchanges and innovation will also develop new agricultural trade growth points and alleviate food security concerns.

Nevertheless, numerous concerns remain. Domestic debates have centered on whether the initiative will perform as well as hoped since China has provided the bulk of the funding for this initiative. Those countries that have been recipients of investment also worry that China may cut short projects when incomplete because of the heavy fiscal burden (Copper, 2017). Deforestation and losses of habitat for some species are also hot issues given that Chinese-backed hydropower projects along the

Mekong River have caused river flow changes and blocked fish migration while the Pan Borneo Highway caused disastrous landslides and floods (The ASEAN Post Team, 2019).

VIII. Conclusion

This report presents a picture of China's agricultural trade with developing Asia during the period 1998 to 2017 at both the regional and country-level. It sheds light on the trade impacts of China-ASEAN Free Trade Agreement, BRI, and RCEP and their potential implications for food security, poverty reduction, and agricultural transformation.

China's agricultural trade volume has increased since its entry into WTO though imports have increased at a much faster pace resulting in China's consistent and enlarging agricultural trade deficit. Although China has diversified its agricultural trade, Asia has always been China's major trade partner. Most of China's agricultural exports are destined for developed East Asian markets. Though Central and South Asia make up a very small share of China's agricultural trade basket, Southeast Asia has always been an important market for China's agricultural trade. China's agricultural trade commodity structure with each of the Asian subregions has shifted toward each region's comparative advantage. China has begun exporting labor-intensive or consumer-ready products and importing land-intensive or resource-intensive products. Although Chinese trade is relatively concentrated in a few key countries in each sub-region, import and export markets have increasingly diversified in Southeast and South Asia over time. Since agricultural trade among the least developed countries in Asia is highly dependent on intra-regional trade, the share of these countries in China's trade basket remains relatively small, and the commodities are highly concentrated. However, China has gained importance in these countries' agricultural trade baskets. The trade impact of the China-ASEAN Free Trade Agreement is identified while it is limited by the high usage costs of FTA rules and emerging non-tariff barriers. Agricultural-related FDI flows from China under this agreement, and the BRI have contributed to poverty reduction and agricultural transformation in developing Asian countries. Once signed, RCEP should promote economic integration and the establishment of global agricultural supply chains.

A number of implications emerge based on the above findings. First, although China's agricultural trade with the US and EU has substantially expanded since it joined WTO, China and developing Asia still remain important partners to each other. Between 1998 and 2017, developing Asia accounted for 15.2% of China's agricultural exports and 22.5% of agricultural imports. China, in turn, accounted for 10.3% of developing Asia's agricultural exports and 7.1% of agricultural imports. Further consolidation of trade relationships between China and developing Asia holds importance for both parties. Second, because China's agricultural trade was concentrated in only a few countries in each subregion, it will be important for China to develop stronger agricultural trade ties with other countries through enhanced frameworks of regional cooperation to minimize potential region-specific agricultural trade risks. Third, China's growing appetite for land-intensive primary agricultural products may offer opportunities for developing countries to improve their intensity of production and support continued agricultural transformation. Chinese FDI investment and technical cooperation have the potential to support agricultural growth in these countries. Finally, effective implementation of regional cooperation frameworks, including CAFTA, BRI, and RCEP has the potential to improve economic integration between China and developing Asia. These agreements need to offer significant benefits to businesses to improve rule-of-origin and customs procedures and address issues of environmental concerns to reach their full potential.

References

Balié, J., Del Prete, D., Magrini, E., Montalbano, P., & Nenci, S. (2019). Does trade policy impact food and agriculture global value chain participation of Sub-Saharan African countries? *American Journal of Agricultural Economics, 101*(3), 773–789.

Baylis, K., Fan, L., & Nogueira, L. (2019). Agricultural market liberalization and household food security in rural China. *American Journal of Agricultural Economics, 101*(1), 250–269.

Bird, J. H., Lebrand, M. S. M., & Venables, A. J. (2019, April). *The Belt and Road Initiative: Reshaping economic geography in Central Asia?* The World Bank. https://openknowledge.worldbank.org/handle/10986/31536

Brough D. (2016). *Indian, Thai sugar flows to slow to Myanmar for China.* Reuters. https://www.reuters.com/article/india-sugar-china/indian-thai-sugar-flows-to-slow-to-myanmar-for-china-idINKCN0X11O7

Carter, C. A., & Li, X. (2002). Implications of World Trade Organization accession for China's agricultural trade patterns. *Australian Journal of Agricultural and Resource Economics, 46*(2), 193–207.

CCPIT. (2018, November). *Guide for SMEs to use FTA.* http://aaa.ccpit.org/Category7/Asset/2019/Feb/11/onlineeditimages/file71550216560171.pdf

Chandarany, O. U. C. H., Dalis, P., & Chanhang, S. (2011). *Assessing China's impact on poverty reduction in the Greater Mekong Sub-region: The case of Cambodia* (Working Paper No. 52).

Cambodia Development Resource Institute. https://cdri.org.kh/publication/assessing-china-s-impact-on-poverty-reduction-in-the-greater-mekong-subregion-the-case-of-cambodia

Chen, C., & Duncan, R. (2008). Achieving food security in China: Implications of WTO accession. In C. CHEN & R. DUNCAN (Eds.), *Agriculture and food security in China: What effect WTO accession and regional trade arrangements?* (pp. 1–26). ANU Press. http://www.jstor.org/stable/j.ctt24hd73.9

Chen, K. Z., & Duan, Y. (2001). Competitiveness of Canadian agri-food exports against competitors in Asia: 1980–97. *Journal of International Food & Agribusiness Marketing, 11*(4), 1–19.

Chew P. & Soccio M. (2016, February 18). *Asia-Pacific: Agricultural perspectives.* Rabobank. https://economics.rabobank.com/publications/2016/february/asia-pacific-agricultural-perspectives/

China Ministry of Agriculture. (2019). *Report on China's agricultural foreign investment cooperation.* http://www.fecc.agri.cn/xglj/nyzcqxxgx/zyfx_10294/202010/P020201014566497969216.pdf

Donaldson, D. (2018). Railroads of the Raj: Estimating the impact of transportation infrastructure. *American Economic Review, 108*(4-5), 899–934.

Copper, R. N. (2017, July 18). *Opinion: China to confront financial, engineering challenges in "Belt and Road."* Caixin. https://web.archive.org/web/20171002021838/http://www.caixinglobal.com/2017-07-18/101117767.html

Costa, F., Garred, J., & Pessoa, J. P. (2016). Winners and losers from a commodities-for-manufactures trade boom. *Journal of International Economics, 102*, 50–69.

Erokhin, V., Diao, L., & Du, P. (2020). Sustainability-Related implications of competitive advantages in agricultural value chains: Evidence from Central Asia—China trade and investment. *Sustainability, 12*(3), 1117.

Fałkowski, J., Curzi, D., & Olper, A. (2019). Contracting institutions, agro⊠food trade and product quality. *Journal of Agricultural Economics, 70*(3), 749–770.

Gaulier, G., & Zignago, S. (2010). *Baci: International trade database at the product-level (the 1994-2007 version)* (Working Paper No. 2010–23). Center d'Etudes Prospectives et d'Informations Internationales. https://deliverypdf.ssrn.com/delivery.php?ID=4110201260821161230811271250640961180970520730580680051220691191010081121220261241100520500190070450261150840931241171240270670500520350050350041241090730171250940910330031141020891220021151130700701250110250251150990891150100860041071211170650640008EXT=pdf&INDEX=TRUE

Gong, B. (2020). New growth accounting. *American Journal of Agricultural Economics, 102*(2), 641–661.

Han, J., Yue, W., & Liu, S. (2018). Heterogeneous firms, cost of use and FTA utilization rate. *Economic*

Research Journal, 53 (11), 165–181.

Hayakawa, K., Laksanapanyakul, N., & Urata, S. (2016). Measuring the costs of FTA utilization: evidence from transaction-level import data of Thailand. *Review of World Economics, 152*(3), 559–575.

Huang, J. (2002). Trade liberalization and China's food economy in the 21st century. In Bigman D. (Eds.), *Globalization and the developing countries: Emerging strategies for rural development and poverty alleviation* (pp.83–102). CABI Publishing.

Imbs, J., & Mejean, I. (2017). Trade elasticities. *Review of International Economics, 25*(2), 383–402.

Jha, S., Roland-Holst, D., Sriboonchitta, S., & Behnke, D. (2010). Regional trade opportunities for Asian agriculture. In Gilbert J. (Eds.), *New developments in computable general equilibrium analysis for trade policy* (pp. 273–302). Emerald Publishing Limited. 10.1108/S1574-8715(2010)7

Kelly, M. (2016). The nutrition transition in developing Asia: Dietary change, drivers and health impacts. In *Eating, Drinking: Surviving* (pp. 83–90). Springer.

Li Y. (2018, March 24). *"One Belt, One Road" imports of national products increased, how much did Shanghai customs tax last year?* Shanghai Observer. https://www.shobserver.com/news/detail?id=83686

Liu, Y. & Zhao, Y. (2017). Impact of RCEP on Chinese agriculture. *Journal of Agrotechnical Economics, 6*, 118–124.

Ma, J., Balezentis, T., Zhao, Z., & Fang, C. (2017). One Belt One Road (OBOR) Initiative in Central Asia: The study of OBOR on China and Central Asia agricultural trade. *Transformations in Business & Economics, 16*(3), 41–55.

Nguyen, H. (2016). *China's agricultural exports and their effects on other exporters* (Working Paper No. 333-2016-14440). Agricultural and Applied Economics Association. https://ideas.repec.org/p/ags/aaea16/235901.html

Nugroho, G. (2015). *An overview of trade relations between ASEAN States and China.* Organization for Regional and Inter-regional Studies, Waseda University. https://www.waseda.jp/inst/oris/en/

Qiu, H., Yang, J., Huang, J., & Chen, R. (2007). Impact of China–ASEAN free trade area on China's international agricultural trade and its regional development. *China & World Economy, 15*(5), 77–90.

Reardon, T., Tschirley, D., Dolislager, M., Snyder, J., Hu, C., & White, S. (2014). Urbanization, diet change, and transformation of food supply chains in Asia. *Global Center for Food Systems Innovation.*

Salehin, K. M., & Sirimanne, S. (2011). *Facilitating agricultural trade in Asia and the Pacific* (Working Paper No. 74). United Nations Economic and Social Commission for Asia and the Pacific.

Shu, Y., & Zeng, K. (2006). FDI flows between China and ASEAN: Emerging factors and prospect. *China & World Economy, 14*(6), 98–106.

Sun, Z. L., & Xian-de, L. I. (2018). The trade margins of Chinese agricultural exports to ASEAN and their determinants. *Journal of Integrative Agriculture, 17*(10), 2356–2367.

Tani, S. (2020). *India stays away from RCEP talks in Bali.* Nikkei Asia. https://asia.nikkei.com/Economy/Trade/India-stays-away-from-RCEP-talks-in-Bali

The ASEAN Post Team. (2019). *China's BRI egatively impacting the environment.* The ASEAN Post. https://theaseanpost.com/article/chinas-bri-negatively-impacting-environment

Tostevin M. (2019). *Explainer: World's biggest trade pact shapes up without India.* Reuters. https://www.reuters.com/article/us-asean-summit-trade-explainer/explainer-worlds-biggest-trade-pact-shapes-up-without-india-idUSKBN1XF0XY

Umana-Dajud, C. (2019). Do visas hinder international trade in goods? *Journal of Development Economics, 140,* 106–126.

Wang, Z. (1997). *China's agricultural trade in 1996: Commodity structure, geographical distribution, and its role in US and world agricultural trade.* (Report No. WRS–97–3). US Department of Agriculture.

Xinhua. (2017, May 24). *China stresses role of Belt and Road Initiative in UN 2030 Agenda.* Xinhua Net. http://www.xinhuanet.com/english/2017-05/24/c_136311484.htm

Xue, K. & Zhang, J. (2017). Impact of RCEP on China's agricultural trade—From the perspective of tariff reduction. *World Agriculture, 4,* 137–143.

Yang, Y., & Tyers, R. (1989). The economic costs of food self-sufficiency in China. *World Development, 17*(2), 237–253.

Yu, S. (2017). Complementarity of trade cooperation between China and five Asian countries under the One Belt and One Road strategy. *Agriculture Economics, 7.*

Zhan, S., Zhang, H., & He, D. (2018). China's flexible overseas food strategy: Food trade and agricultural investment between Southeast Asia and China in 1990–2015. *Globalizations, 15*(5), 702–721.

AGRICULTURAL DEVELOPMENT IN SELECTED ASIAN COUNTRIES

CHAPTER 4

Agricultural Development in the People's Republic of China

Kevin Chen and Rui Mao

I. Introduction

Since the country's reform in 1978 with a series of liberalization policies, China has made profound improvements in its agricultural and rural development. In particular, the agriculture sector is a crucial component to the development of China's economy. Though agricultural GDP accounted for only 7.9% of total GDP in 2017, the total value of agriculture GDP continued to increase at an annual growth rate of 4.5% on average. Reform and liberalization policies since 1978 have had profound impacts on agricultural and rural development in China (World Bank, 2019). Agricultural productivity and production have been improved with the implementation of agricultural reforms and policies on land use and price support, as well as the goal for rural revitalization. This contributes to continuing annual growth in both GDP and agricultural trade domestically. Further, after the country's accession to WTO, its agricultural trade has made dramatic increases. Although there are still challenging aspects for China to meet considerable and growing agricultural demands with limited land and water resources along with other environmental impacts such as climate change, the gradual economic development has provided the country certain capacity and strength in coping with, if not resolving, these essential challenges in the agricultural development, including production and trade. This chapter reviews Chinese agricultural reform policies and the trends in land use, the natural resource and its constraints, and its regional integration through one of the most recent and ambitious strategies of The Belt and Road Initiative.

II. Agricultural Reforms and Policies

1. Land Reform

Agricultural development in China since 1949 can be described as tortuous, experiencing sustained periods of rapid growth and decline. There are two vital phases of land reforms (Table 4.1) influencing China's agriculture and rural development. First, beginning with land reforms in 1949, rural households were distributed with the land. Farmers have then joined communal farming under centrally-controlled production plans and procurement systems (Lin, 1990). However, agricultural production was still at a very low level during this period, with cotton and oil production decreasing by 11.3% and 16.5%, respectively (Du, 2006). Since 1979, China has initiated the HRS for agricultural development. Agricultural land was then placed under the ownership of rural collectives, while households became eligible to enter fifteen-year contract rights for farmland. Agricultural performance was then improved during this period, with agricultural production increased while the price of rice, wheat, and maize decreased concurrently, supplying cheap, high-quality food products (Zhong et al., 2018). By 1983, almost all arable land was allocated to rural households (World Bank and the Development Research Center of the State Council, P. R. China, 2014).

Table 4.1
Land Reform in China

Period	Program & core	Reforms/policies
Phase I	Equalization of land ownership (1949–1952)	Land was confiscated from landlords and rich farmers and distributed to rural households.
	Collectivization movement (1952–1958)	Private land was replaced by collective ownership (Lin, 1990).
	People's commune (1958–1978)	Collectivization went from voluntary to compulsory participation (Lin, 1990).
Phase II	Household responsibility system (1978–1984)	Households are allowed to contract land, machinery, and other facilities from collective organizations. Quota prices were raised, and the quantities of quotas were reduced.

Source. Bruce & Li (2009); Lin (1990); Zhong et al. (2018).

Rural land reform continued after the introduction of the initial HRS reform. Land-related policies aiming to improve land use efficiency, rationalize land allocation, improve land management, and coordinate urban and rural policies were launched (World Bank and the Development Research Center of the State Council, P. R. China, 2014). More recently, important land reforms have included policies on rural land tenure and land transfer. Land contract rights introduced in the HRS reform largely began in the mid-1980s and ended in 1997. These rights were extended twice for a second and third thirty-year period until 2057. (Zhong, Chen, & Zhu, 2018; The National People's Congress of the People's Republic of China, 2019). Additionally, the government has encouraged the transfer of land use rights to allow enterprises to scale-up production and facilitate higher agricultural productivity and mechanization (Kim, 2018).

2. Agricultural Development Policies

In addition to land reforms, price support measures were also implemented by the government to support agricultural development. China introduced the state monopoly of major agricultural products in 1953, which designated the government as the only legal purchaser of key commodities such as rice, wheat, maize, oilseeds, and cotton (Bruce & Li, 2009). With the introduction of the HRS in 1979, the government initiated the transition to market liberalization in 1985. For example, the uniform grain procurement system was replaced with a dual-track price system, which allowed enterprises to sell surplus production at market prices after fulfilling quotas set by state prices (Zhong et al., 2018). Accession to WTO was a major milestone for China's agricultural development, marking the government's shift to taxes and supports as policy levers. Price support measures included a policy implemented starting in 2014, whereby state-owned grain reserve corporations made intervening purchases if prices fell below a certain level (OECD, 2018; Zhong et al., 2018). While price support measures have encouraged higher production, they also made food products more expensive domestically compared to international prices (OECD, 2018). Agricultural subsidy instruments are used for a variety of functions supporting agriculture as well.

3. Recent National Agricultural Policies

The initial land reforms of 1978 marked the beginning of the current era of China's agricultural development. Though initial concerns were to increase the quantity of agricultural production, objectives have since evolved to include achieving food security and safety, increasing farmers' income, enhancing agricultural competitiveness, and promoting sustainable agricultural development. For example, whereas China had emphasized grain self-sufficiency as a food security strategy during the early stages of reform, a more recent food security strategy introduced in 2014 takes a more expansive view of utilizing both domestic and international resources and markets to secure food supplies (OECD, 2018).

China launched the National Strategy on Rural Revitalization (2018–2022) in 2018, aiming to enhance agricultural and rural development, reduce poverty, and ensure sustained food security. The document pledges support for family and small-holder farms (Ministry of Agriculture and Rural Affairs of the P. R. China, 2018). It also outlines the importance of sustainability, high-quality growth, and environmental concerns in agricultural development (Huang & Rozelle, 2018). Agricultural and rural revitalization are priority issues in the latest annual agricultural policy-setting *No. 1 Central Document* issued in 2019. It also calls for agricultural and rural modernization, poverty reduction, improvement in production quality, stable and sufficient grain production, agriculture industrialization, household income stability, and capacity building for farmers (Ministry of Agriculture and Rural Affairs of the P. R. China, 2019).

III. Trends in Land Use, Agricultural Productivity, and Trade

1. Changes in Land Use and Agricultural Production

China has experienced enormous land use changes, with the HRS introduced in 1979 serving as the foundation of agricultural development. Family-contracted land for 23 million households comprised around 99.4% of total cropland in 2016 (Huang & Rozelle, 2018). Agricultural land increased by 63 million hectares from 1984 to 2016, of which the expansion of permanent meadows and pastures contributed 46 million hectares (FAO, 2019). However, starting in 1990, with rapid economic and industrial growth, arable land area has declined because of widespread construction, environmental degradation, and the Returning Farmland to Forests Program (Wang, 2017; FAO, 2019; Wu, 2011). This program, launched in 1999, converted marginal farmland to forest land (Trac et al., 2013). From Figure 4.1, arable land decreased from 125 million hectares in 1990 to 106 million hectares in 2014 though it rebounded to 119 million hectares in 2016, which was still lower than previous highs. The *No. 1 Central Document* of 2019 addressed that the steady provision of agricultural crops, especially grain, would be a priority of agricultural development. To that end, the document calls for permanent crop planting area to remain steady at 103 million hectares, arable grain production area to be kept above 110 million hectares, and an additional 533,000 hectares of high-quality farmland to be developed by 2020 (Ministry of Agriculture and Rural Affairs of the P. R. China, 2019).

Figure 4.1

Agricultural Land Use in China in Thousands of Hectares, 1961–2016

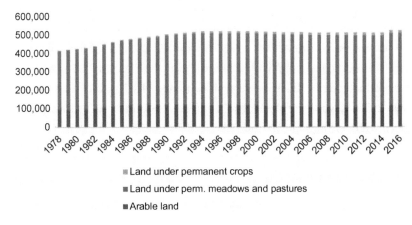

■ Land under permanent crops

■ Land under perm. meadows and pastures

■ Arable land

Source. FAO (2019).

Figure 4.2

Composition of Total Agricultural Production Value in China

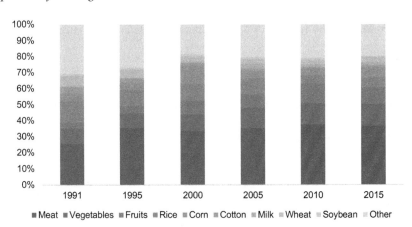

■ Meat ■ Vegetables ■ Fruits ■ Rice ■ Corn ■ Cotton ■ Milk ■ Wheat ■ Soybean ■ Other

Source. FAO (2019).

Owing to policy reforms and improvements in technology, machinery, and inputs, crop and livestock production has expanded since 1978 (Huang & Rozelle, 2018). The production of food crops increased from 567 million tons in 1978 to 1.8 billion tons in 2013 with an annual growth rate of 3.4%. Meanwhile, livestock production increased from 226 million tons to 1.3 billion tons with an annual growth rate of 5.2% over the same period (FAO, 2019). Currently, China is among the world's largest producers of agricultural products such as pork, rice, fruits (e.g., apples, grapes, tangerines, pears, etc.), and vegetables. It is the world's second-largest producer of poultry, wheat, and corn (Chew & Soccio, 2016).

In terms of gross production value, around 69.8% of production came from the crop sector, compared to 30.2% for livestock in 2016 (FAO, 2019). The production share of meat increased from 25.6% to 36.7% from 1991 to 2015, driven by the increase in demand for meat concurrent with economic growth (Figure 4.2). The share of labor-intensive products such as fruit and vegetables increased 2.7 and 1.4 times, respectively, from 1995 to 2019, while the share of land-intensive products such as rice, cotton, and wheat declined over the same period (FAO, 2019).

2. Total Factor Productivity

Figure 4.3 illustrates the growth in total factor productivity (indexed to 2005) since the start of reforms in 1978. Increasing agricultural productivity has been attributed to policy support instruments, farm consolidation, and machinery usage (Liu, 2018). Total factor productivity began its rapid growth during the 1990s, with an annual growth rate of 3.5% between 1990 and 2016 (USDA ERS, 2018). Recent data show rapid increases in partial factor productivity from 2010 to 2015: land productivity increased by 20.3%, and labor productivity increased by 23.0% during this time (Liu, 2018).

Figure 4.3

Total Factor Productivity (Indexed to 2005) and Annual TFP Growth Rate in China, 1978–2015

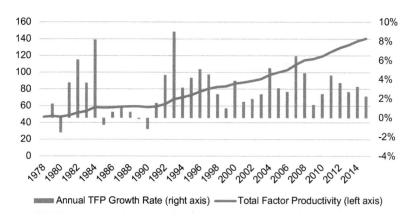

Annual TFP Growth Rate (right axis) ——Total Factor Productivity (left axis)

Source. USDA ERS (2018).

3. Agricultural Trade Trends

Agricultural trade saw dramatic increases after accession to WTO in 2002, in contrast to the relatively slow growth seen after the start of reforms in 1978. The government implemented measures to enhance agricultural trade during this time. Imports outpaced agricultural exports after 2002 (Figure 4.4). Imports reached a high of US$114 billion in 2013 (FAO, 2019).

Figure 4.4

Chinese Agricultural Trade in Millions of US$, 1978–2016

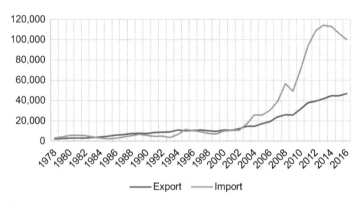

Source. FAO (2019).

Figure 4.5

Major Destinations for Chinese Agricultural Exports

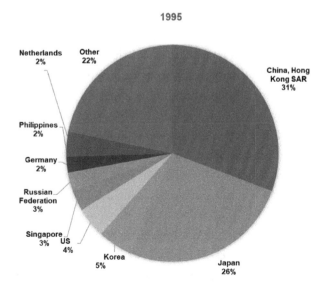

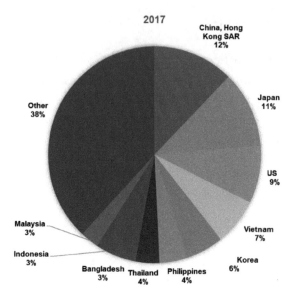

2017

Source. UN Comtrade (2019).

Additionally, the profile of Chinese agricultural trading partners has changed over the years. For example, in 1995, agricultural exports were sent to a limited set of countries and regions, compared to diverse destinations in 2017 (Figure 4.5). Hong Kong was the main export destination and an important transit port in 1995 but it occupies a smaller role in total Chinese exports today (Li & Jiang, 2018).

IV. Perspective by Subsectors

1. Crop Production

The main crops produced in China include maize, rice, vegetables, wheat, sugar cane, and potatoes (FAO, 2019). Total grain production has increased 2.1% annually on average since 1978. Maize, rice, and wheat production from 1978 to 2017 is described in Table 4.2, with the improvement largely driven by the growth of corn production. Research indicates that production growth was mainly due to improvements in land productivity rather than expansion of the sown area (Wang, 2017). Additionally, per capita production of grain increased by 42% during this period, suggesting long-term improvement in the food security situation (National Bureau of Statistics of China, 2019).

China has become a net exporter of vegetables, cotton, coffee, and a net importer of cereal, oilseed, and some processed products in recent years (Figure 4.6). Oilseeds are by far the largest import item category, with a value of US$44.5 billion. Brazil and

Table 4.2

Total Production and Productivity of Cereal, 1978–2017

Year	Production (1000 tons)			Productivity (hg/ha)			Grain per capita output (kg)
	Maize	Rice	Wheat	Maize	Rice	Wheat	
1978	55,950	136,930	53,840	28,030	39,781	18,449	319
1985	63,826	168,569	85,805	36,072	52,563	29,367	365
1990	96,819	189,331	98,229	45,240	57,261	31,941	393
1995	111,986	185,226	102,207	49,169	60,248	35,415	387
2000	106,000	187,908	99,636	45,975	62,716	37,382	366
2005	139,365	182,055	97,445	52,873	62,601	42,753	371
2010	177,425	195,761	115,181	54,592	65,530	47,486	409
2015	264,992	212,142	132,639	58,929	68,913	53,927	453
2017	259,071	212,676	134,334	61,103	69,170	54,812	—

Source. FAO (2019).

Figure 4.6

Net Export Value of Crop and Food Products in Billions of US$ in China, 2008–2017

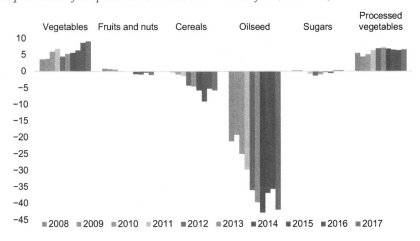

Source. UN Comtrade (2019).

the US are the top two exporters of oilseeds to China, accounting for 47.0% and 32.7% of total oilseed imports, respectively (UN Comtrade, 2019). China's *No. 1 Central Document* in 2019 emphasizes diversifying oilseed imports (Ministry of Agriculture and Rural Affairs of the P. R. China, 2019).

According to the revealed comparative advantage (RCA) index in Table 4.3, agri-food products do not appear to have comparative advantages in the global market. Additionally, RCA indexes appear to have decreased since 2000 for most of the product categories in Table 4.3.

Table 4.3
Revealed Comparative Advantage of Selected Products

RCA	2000	2005	2010	2015	2017
Vegetables	1.9	1.2	1.3	1.0	0.8
Fruits and nuts	0.3	0.3	0.3	0.3	0.3
Coffee, tea, mate, and spices	0.8	0.7	0.4	0.4	0.5
Cereals	1.2	0.4	0.1	0	0.1
Oil seeds	1.1	0.6	0.3	0.2	0.2
Sugars and sugar confectionery	0.3	0.2	0.2	0.3	0.3
Processed cereal	0.6	0.4	0.2	0.2	0.2

Source. UN Comtrade (2019).

2. Livestock

Livestock products have been growing very fast during the past four decades (Table 4.4). Annual meat production rose by an average of 2.6% in the past decade. Dairy production increased at an even more rapid pace, with an average annual increase of 9% during the same period (Huang & Rozelle, 2018). The top-produced livestock products include pork, hen, milk, chicken meat, cattle meat, etc. (FAO, 2019). Animal diseases have periodically caused severe problems for the livestock sector (USDA, 2018). For example, the outbreaks of African swine fever in 2018 decreased the pig population by 16% by March 2019, along with an increase in pork prices.

With the development of China's economy, living standards, and urbanization, the demand for meat has grown, leading to greater production and imports (Gale, 2015). China has become the world's largest importer of animal protein and dairy in recent years. Brazil, US, and Australia are three of the most important meat and offal exporters to China, exporting US$1.8 billion, US$1.6 billion, and US$1.0 billion in 2017, respectively. These three countries together accounted for 42.6% of China's imports in the same year. Meanwhile, New Zealand alone contributed 54.7% of China's dairy imports in 2017 (UN Comtrade, 2019).

Table 4.4

Livestock Production in Thousands of Tons, 1996–2017

Year	Meat	Pork	Beef	Mutton	Milk	Poultry egg
1996	4,584	3,158	356	181	736	1,965
2000	6,014	3,966	513	264	827	2,182
2005	6,939	4,555	568	350	2,753	2,438
2010	7,994	5,138	629	406	3,211	2,777
2015	8,750	5,645	617	440	3,296	3,046
2017	8,654	5,452	635	471	3,149	3,096

Source. National Bureau of Statistics of China (2019).

3. Value Chain Development

The main weaknesses of China's agricultural value chain include transportation, critical infrastructure, and the lack of value-added agricultural production. Transportation and logistics sectors need to be improved in all aspects: ports, rail systems, inland water transport, road infrastructure, vehicular transport, cold chain transportation, and management (Gilmour & Cheng, 2010). China is a major exporter of labor-intensive products such as fruits, vegetables, and pork in the world agricultural market (Huang et al., 2011). Since many of these products are perishable, they rely on cold chain storage, handling, and transportation infrastructure. However, in 2004, the cold storage capacity could only meet 20%–30% of the growing cargo demand. Moreover, 33% of spoilage losses were caused by poor handling procedures (Gilmour & Cheng, 2010).

In addition, only 30% of the nation's food products are processed, whereas this figure typically reaches 70% to 80% in more developed countries. Chinese enterprises should be encouraged to be more market and quality oriented and willing to introduce technologies (Gilmour & Cheng, 2010). Importantly, it would be crucial to support agricultural and agri-food value chains with improved legal, regulatory, and institutional frameworks (Fan, 2017).

V. Natural Resource Constraints, Resilience, and Sustainability

China faces challenges in terms of the availability of natural resources such as water and land. Although the total water supply in the country is approximately 3.5 trillion m³, the per capita water supply is only around 2,200 m³, which is only 30% of the world average (Ministry of Water Resources of the P.R. China, 2016). Per capita arable land is only 0.1 hectares, around 40% of the world average. Additionally, land and water are unevenly distributed throughout the country. The south of the country has sufficient water but lacks land, while the reverse is true for the north (World Bank, 2019; Zhou, 2000).

China is facing problems due to water pollution and water depletion. Agriculture is one of the main sources of water pollution because of the unrestrained usage of fertilizers and pesticides (Li et al., 2015; Qu et al., 2011). The Chinese Ministry of Ecology and Environment has recommended policies to reduce water pollution from agrochemical applications (Yu & Wu, 2018). Besides water pollution, the depletion of agricultural water resources poses a challenge (Jiang, 2009). Regulatory policies, local water management, water infrastructure, and technology must be improved in response (Akiyama et al., 2017).

Climate change may have strong negative impacts on agricultural production in China. A study indicates that cereal yields in 2050 may fall 15% to 25% under 2000 levels because of climate change (Chew & Soccio, 2016). Agriculture may have already had an effect on the climate and environment to some extent. The development of agriculture during the past decades was mainly based on intensive land and water use, as well as the high usage of fertilizers (Ministry of Environmental Protection of the P.R. China, 2014). China's 13th Five-Year Plan (2016–2020) highlights sustainable development by setting targets for expanding environmental protection, increasing energy efficiency, improving access to education and healthcare, and expanding social protection (Yu & Wu, 2018).

VI. The Belt and Road Initiative

1. Regional Integration

The BRI is a development strategy adopted by the Chinese government, laying out the People's Republic of China's aspirations for regional integration. The BRI aims to stimulate economic development through regional economic cooperation. The five main goals of the BRI include: promoting policy coordination, fostering connectivity, facilitating unimpeded trade, integrating finance, and encouraging people-to-people exchanges. Around 153 countries and international organizations in different regions are involved in this initiative.

BRI aims to improve regional- and country-level cooperation in Eurasia. There are abundant agricultural resources along The Belt and Road, which will make agricultural cooperation an important aspect of the project (Li et al., 2018). On agriculture, the BRI framework calls for "deepening cooperation in agriculture, forestry, animal husbandry and fisheries, agricultural machinery manufacturing and farm produce processing." In addition, the AIIB was founded in 2015 to provide financial support for sustainable projects and coordination among BRI-participating countries. Financial support in the agriculture sector included projects focusing on rural infrastructure development, water supply and sanitation, and logistics development (HKTDC Research, 2018).

Chinese Ministry of Agriculture claimed that agricultural cooperation among BRI-participating countries would contribute to sustainable development outlined in the 2030 Agenda by the United Nations (Ministry of Agriculture and Rural Affairs of the P.R. China, 2017). The Second Belt and Road Forum (BRF) held in April 2019 in Beijing reiterated this commitment to environmentally friendly and resource-conserving projects. Participants at the April 2019 BRF also signed 283 agreements related to a host of initiatives supporting BRI activities.

2. Economic Corridors for Development

The BRI involves several economic corridors around which activities and coordination are arranged, including China-Mongolia-Russia, China-Pakistan, and China-Central Asia-West Asia economic corridors. The development of these economic corridors will involve the construction of transportation links and hubs, as well as agriculture-industrial parks that will serve as a base for processing, logistics, and research activities. The following sub-section will look at the major corridors.

The China-Mongolia-Russia Economic Corridor

A tripartite co-operation agreement establishing the China-Mongolia-Russia economic corridor was reached in 2014, aiming to strengthen the construction of transportation infrastructure, enhance connectivity and trade, and promote further cooperation (HKTDC Research, 2018). Cooperation between China and Mongolia was close even prior to BRI. The People's Republic of China has been Mongolia's main trade partner and source of foreign direct investment (FDI). Around 90% of Mongolian products are exported to the People's Republic of China; the value of imports from the People's Republic of China accounts for 30% of Mongolia's total imports (Zhang & Zhang, 2017). Customs authorities from both countries signed agreements on inspection and quarantine cooperation at the Second Belt and Road Forum (Ministry of Foreign Affairs of the People's Republic of China, 2019).

Current priorities for Chinese-Mongolian cooperation, as described by the Chinese Ministry of Agriculture, include: promoting and improving agricultural trade, increasing agricultural investment and employment opportunities throughout the value chain, and enhancing the capacity of farmers (Ministry of Agriculture and Rural Affairs of the P.R. China, 2017). Cooperation on sustainable agriculture is also included, taking into account desertification, water resource usage and protection, renewable energy development, and ecological restoration. Moreover, transportation systems and infrastructure development are key to cooperation. *The Mid- and Long-Term Development Program of Strategic Partnership between China and Mongolia* claims China will invest in highway and railway construction in Mongolia (The State Council of People's Republic of China, 2019). The underlying idea of the program is to improve agricultural cooperation through the upgrading of infrastructure in logistics in Mongolia. Mongolia and China were two of seven countries (including Russia, Kazakhstan, Belarus, Germany, and Poland) to form a joint working group on container train transport at the April 2019 Second Belt and Road Forum (Ministry of Foreign Affairs of the People's Republic of China, 2019).

The China-Pakistan Economic Corridor
China has pledged US$57 billion to support the transport, energy, industry, logistics and agriculture sectors in China-Pakistan Economic Corridor, aiding economic and social development, developing technology, and engineering enterprises, and enhancing Pakistan's industrial capacity. This also includes support for the construction of rail and road links to Northeast Pakistan bordering China's Xinjiang Province and to southwest Pakistan, home to the Gwadar deep-water port. Additionally, a new China-Pakistan-Europe telecommunications network will be built (The Economist, 2016).

In addition, China and Pakistan will cooperate to improve agricultural infrastructure and development, including capacity-building training for farmers and technical exchange in the CPEC. The governments of both countries call for cooperation in a wide range of areas: intensified agro-industrial development, water and irrigation investment, land remediation, disease control, crop research and technical exchange, livestock breeding, and forestry and food growing (P.R. China National Development and Reform Commission; Government of Pakistan Ministry of Planning, Development and Reform, 2016). One example of successful cooperation in research is wheat-breeding technology that was transferred from China to Pakistan, which may have contributed to a 50% increase in hybrid wheat yields in northern Pakistan in 2018 (Zhang, 2018).

Moreover, the topics of disease control and the quality of pesticides are important issues in this corridor. During the Second Belt and Road Forum, the Ministry of Agriculture and Rural Affairs of China, the Ministry of Food Security and Research of Pakistan, and counterpart ministries of Bangladesh, Cambodia, Myanmar, Nepal, the Philippines, Thailand, Sri Lanka, and Vietnam released a joint Statement of Intent for

Cooperation on Promoting Specification-Setting for Pesticide Quality under the BRI (Ministry of Foreign Affairs of the People's Republic of China, 2019).

The China-Central Asia-West Asia Economic Corridor

China-Central Asia-West Asia Economic Corridor mainly covers five countries in Central Asia, including Kazakhstan, the Kyrgyz Republic, Tajikistan, Uzbekistan, and Turkmenistan as well as Iran and Turkey in West Asia (HKTDC Research, 2018). A joint declaration inaugurating the Silk and Road Economic Belt was signed by China and the five Central Asian countries in June 2015 at the third China-Central Asia Co-operation Forum (HKTDC Research, 2018).

In recent years, China and Central Asian countries have increased economic cooperation, which has helped Central Asia improve its global connections. For example, the BRI has helped open trade links between Central Asia and Southeast Asia. Lianyungang's port, as a Belt and Road grain logistic hub, has helped ship wheat from Central Asia to Southeast Asia in recent years. These hubs not only provide transportation services but also provide storage, inspection, and quarantine for traders (FAO, 2019).

However, developing this corridor will have to navigate issues in terms of geography and policies. Improved physical infrastructure and harmonized trading procedures need to be established. It is recommended that China should pay attention to the following tasks: promoting cross-border infrastructure connections, building economic cooperation mechanisms, and maintaining bilateral cooperation in economy, trade, and investment between the People's Republic of China and Central Asian countries (Idan, 2018; Lai & Wu, 2018).

VII. Conclusion

As a country feeding one of the world's largest populations, the development of the agricultural sector serves an important goal for China. Over the years, the share of labor-intensive products composes a large part of Chinese agricultural production due primarily to its large scale of population. Since the country's accession into WTO in 2002, the value of its agricultural imports has surpassed that of the agricultural exports, indicating a greater role of Chinese involvement in the international agricultural trade market. However, challenges are also faced by the country's agricultural value chain, including both a lack of transportation and critical infrastructure support for cold chain transportation and a lack of value addition for basic agricultural goods (Gilmour & Cheng, 2010). In addition, natural resource constraints of water and land continue to rise with the additional effect of climate change.

As an important national strategy, the introduction of The Belt and Road initiative seeks to improve greatly on these challenges through the connections it has illustrated. With an improved condition in the fundamental infrastructures, there could be improved interregional connectivity to foster stronger connections among all countries in the Eurasia continent. In addition, this ambitious policy aims to also foster regional connection and communication, which provides the opportunity for leaders alongside the influencing areas to come together in finding a common path for human prosperity.

Reference

Akiyama, T., Kharrazi A., J. Li, & R. Avtar. (2018). Agricultural water policy reforms in China: A representative look at Zhangye City, Gansu Province, China. *Environmental Monitoring and Assessment, 190* (9), 1–15. doi: 10.1007/s10661-017-6370-z

Bruce, J., & Li, Z. (2009). *Crossing the river while feeling the rocks* (IFPRI Discussion Paper No. 926). International Food Policy Research Institute. https://www.ifpri.org/publication/crossing-river-while-feeling-rocks

Chew, P., & Soccio. M. (2016). *Asia-Pacific: Agricultural perspectives.* Rabobank/RaboResearch. https://economics.rabobank.com/publications/2016/february/asia-pacific-agricultural-perspectives/

Du, R. (2009). The course of China's rural reform. In Governing Rapid Growth in China (1st ed., pp. 51–62). *Routledge.*

FAO. (2019). *FAOSTAT.* https://www.fao.org/faostat.

Fan, S. (2017, September 25). *Reforming China's agrifood sector to face economic and nutrition challenges.* International Food Policy Research Institute. http://www.ifpri.org/blog/reforming-chinas-agrifood-sector-face-economic-and-nutrition-challenges

Gale, F. (2015). China's growing participation in agricultural markets: Conflicting signals. *Choices, 30* (2), 1–6.

Gilmour, B., & G. Cheng. (2010). Enabling China's agri-food sector. *Ideals Institute.*

HKTDC Research. (2018). *The Belt and Road Initiative.* http://china-trade-research.hktdc.com/business-news/article/The-Belt-and-Road-Initiative/The-Belt-and-Road-Initiative/obor/en/1/1X3CGF6L/1X0A36B7.htm

Huang, J., & Rozelle, S. (2018). China's 40 years of agricultural development and reform. *China's 40 Years of Reform and Development* (pp. 487–506). ANU Press.

Idan, A. (2018, May 1). *China's Belt and Road Initiative: Relieving landlocked Central Asia.* The Central Asia-Caucasus Analyst. https://www.cacianalyst.org/publications/analytical-articles/item/13510-chinas-belt-and-road-initiative-relieving-landlocked-central-asia.html

Jiang, Y. (2009). China's water scarcity. *Journal of Environmental Management, 90*(11), 3185–3196.

Kim, G. 2018. *China's annual agricultural policy goals: The 2018 No. 1 Central Document of the CCCPC and the State Council* (GAIN Report No. CH18007). USDA Foreign Agriculture Service.

Lai, Y., & A. Wu. (2018). *China-Central Asia-Western Asia Economic Corridor: Progress, main challenges, and promotion measures* (Report No. 187). Development Research Center of the State Council of the People's Republic of China. http://www.chinadaily.com.cn/m/drc/2019-01/02/content_37421873.htm

Li, F., Liu, Q., Dong, S., & Cheng, H. (2018). Agricultural development status and key cooperation directions between China and countries along "The Belt and Road." In *IOP Conference Series: Earth and Environmental Science, 190* (1), 1–7.

Li, H., Liu, J., Li, G., Shen, J., Bergström, L., & Zhang, F. (2015). Past, present, and future use of phosphorus in Chinese agriculture and its influence on phosphorus losses. *Ambio, 44*, 274–285.

Li, K., & Jiang, W. (2018). China's foreign trade: Reform, performance and contribution to economic growth. China's 40 Years of Reform and Development (pp. 575–593). ANU Press.

Lin, J. Y. (1990). Collectivization and China's agricultural crisis in 1959–1961. *Journal of Political Economy, 98*(6), 1228–1252.

Liu, S. (2018). The structure of and changes to China's land system. *China's 40 Years of Reform and Development* (pp. 427–454). ANU Press.

Ministry of Agriculture and Rural Affairs of the P.R. China. (2017, May). *Vision and action on jointly promoting agricultural cooperation on the Belt and Road.* Belt and Road Portal. https://eng.yidaiyilu.gov.cn/zchj/qwfb/34829.htm

Ministry of Agriculture and Rural Affairs of the P. R. China. (2018). *Joint Statement by MARA, FAO, IFAD and WFP on implementation of China's rural revitalization strategy in support of achieving the 2030 Agenda for Sustainable Development.* Ministry of Agriculture and Rural Affairs of the P. R. China. http://english.agri.gov.cn/governmentaffairs/pi/201811/t20181109_296081.htm

Ministry of Agriculture and Rural Affairs of the P. R. China. (2019, March 21). *No. 1 Central Document.* https://apps.fas.usda.gov/newgainapi/api/Report/DownloadReportByFile Name?fileName=China%27s%202019%20No.1%20Agricultural%20Document%20 Doubles%20Down_Beijing_China%20-%20Peoples%20Republic%20of_3-21-2019

Ministry of Environmental Protection of the P.R. China. (2014). *China's Fifth National Report on the Implementation of the Convention on Biological Diversity.* Ministry of Foreign Affairs of the People's Republic of China.

Ministry of Foreign Affairs of the People's Republic of China. (2019, April 28). *List of deliverables of the Second Belt and Road Forum for International Cooperation.* Ministry of Foreign Affairs of the People's Republic of China. https://www.fmprc.gov.cn/mfa_eng/zxxx_662805/t1658767.shtml

Ministry of Water Resources of the P.R. China. 2016. *Water Resource in China.* Ministry of Water

Resources of the P.R. China

National Bureau of Statistics of China. (2019). *China statistical yearbook.* http://www.stats.gov.cn/sj/ndsj/2019/indexeh.htm

P.R. China National Development and Reform Commission; Government of Pakistan Ministry of Planning, Development and Reform. (2016). *Long term plan for China-Pakistan Economic Corridor (2017–2030).*

Qu, F., A. Kuyvenhoven, X. Shi, & N. Heerink. (2011). Sustainable natural resource use in rural China: Recent trends and policies. *China Economic Review,* 444–460.

The National People's Congress of the People's Republic of China. (2019). *Rural land contracting law of People's Republic of China.* The National People's Congress of the People's Republic of China. http://www.npc.gov.cn/npc/xinwen/2019-01/07/content_2070250.htm

The State Council of People's Republic of China. (2019). *The Belt and Road Initiative.* http://english.gov.cn/beltAndRoad/

The Economist. (2016). *One Belt, One Road: An economic roadmap.* Economist Intelligence Unit. https://www.iberchina.org/files/2016/obor_economist.pdf

Trac, C., A. Schmidt, S. Harrell, & T. Hinckley. (2013). Is the returning farmland to forest program a success? Three case studies from Sichuan. *Environmental Practice, 9,* 350–366.

UN Comtrade. (2019). https://comtrade.un.org/data/

USDA ERS. (2018). *International agricultural productivity.* https://www.ers.usda.gov/data-products/international-agricultural-productivity

USDA. (2018). *Livestock and poultry: World markets and trade.* United States Department of Agriculture Foreign Agriculture Service. https://www.ers.usda.gov

Wang, J. (2017). *Sustainable agricultural development in China: An assessment of problems, policies and perspectives.* Datawyse / Universitaire Pers Maastricht.

World Bank and the Development Research Center of the State Council, P. R. China. (2014). China's urbanization and land: A framework for reform. *Urban China: Toward efficient, inclusive, and sustainable urbanization* (pp. 263–336). World Bank.

World Bank. (2019a). *Data Bank.* https://databank.worldbank.org

World Bank. (2019b). *World integrated trade solution.* https://wits.worldbank.org/datadownload.aspx?lang=en

Wu, R. C. (2011). The revolution of the household registration system: Based on modern country construction. *Inner Mongolia Social Sciences, 11*(6), 15–20.

Yu, J., & Wu, J. (2018). The sustainability of agricultural development in China: The agriculture-environment nexus. *Sustainability, 10*(6),1–17.

Zhang, N. (2018, September 3). *China's agricultural techniques reach out to countries along the Belt and Road.* China Focus. http://www.cnfocus.com/chinas-agricultural-techniques-reach-out-to-countries-along-the-belt-and-road/

Zhang, X, & S. Zhang. (2017). China-Mongolia-Russia economic corridor and environmental protection cooperation. *R-Economy*, *3*(3), 161–166.

Zhong, F., Chen, K., & Zhu, J. (2018). Agricultural and rural policies in China. In *Handbook of international food and agricultural policies* (Vol. 1 pp.393–413). World Scientific Publishing.

Zhou, Y. (2000). *Report on China's development and investment in land and water.* http://www. fao.org/3/ac623e/ac623e0d.htm

CHAPTER 5

Agricultural Development and Cooperation in Central Asia

Kamiljon Akramov, Kevin Chen, Allen Park, Jarilkasin Ilyasov,
and Sarvarbek Eltazarov

I. Introduction

Agricultural development is important national development strategy incorporated into the national policies of Central Asia countries. The five Central Asia countries, including Kazakhstan, the Kyrgyz Republic, Tajikistan, Turkmenistan, and Uzbekistan, experienced a sustained process of transition and reform in the agricultural sector along with Azerbaijan and Georgia from the Caucasus region. Specifically, there exists reforms in land and farm organization from agricultural specialization under the former Soviet system, which later developed separately into national agricultural strategies in each country. Since the dissolution of the Soviet Union in the 1990s, major agricultural industries in the Central Asia region have become grains, livestock, and dairy, and horticulture. Though the agricultural industries from each country could potentially drive productivity improvement, ensuring regional food security and export earnings in the long run, poor physical infrastructure, and policy had been the obstruction to agricultural trade for years in Central Asia and Caucasus. In addition, with the independence of the five Central Asia countries from the former Soviet Union, a huge transformation was made in agricultural production policies: many former crop plantations and livestock grazing areas that existed previously collapsed, and a series of new strategies had to be adopted to provide enough self-sufficient agricultural products from the new regime to feed their citizens.

To provide a better perspective on the development of the agriculture sector in Central Asia region, this chapter will review the agricultural development in primarily five Central Asia countries: Kazakhstan, Kyrgyz Republic, Tajikistan, Turkmenistan, and Uzbekistan. Through a review of the agricultural policies and their reform, the agricultural resources and constraints for agricultural and economic development,and the general trend in agricultural trade within and out of the region, we will provide a full-picture overview of the agricultural sector in the Central Asia region. Along with a review of the conditions in the agricultural sector, we will also conclude with the various policy recommendations for fostering regional cooperation within the region, as well as the potential opportunities brought by several regional integration strategies in enhancing the regional integration within the Central Asia region and around the globe.

II. Agricultural Reforms and Policies

The agricultural sectors we examine in this report for Central Asia include five countries—Kazakhstan, the Kyrgyz Republic, Tajikistan, Turkmenistan, and Uzbekistan. They experienced a sustained process of transition and reform since the early years of their independence. These reforms transformed the fundamental institutional structures of agriculture and produced new patterns in terms of production. This section will briefly discuss the general nature of the transformation that the region underwent, with country-specific examples to illustrate the divergent policy options that governments selected to reform their agricultural sectors.

1. Land and Farm Reorganization

The five countries share a common legacy agricultural system under the former Soviet Union, which was sustained by a heavy reliance on subsidies, specialization, and central planning and marketing networks. However, the dissolution of the Soviet Union severely disrupted all aspects of agriculture in its immediate aftermath, through an absence of strong market institutions to assume essential functions previously undertaken by the state-led agricultural systems provided an obstacle to agricultural production. Moreover, the construction of new national barriers posed an additional challenge for the marketing and supplying of goods and inputs. The cumulative effect of these changes produced a sharp decline in output throughout the region, with widespread socioeconomic ramifications.

It was under these conditions that initial reforms took place. The inefficiencies of existing institutions were exposed and became a focal point for reform-minded policymakers. Among the extensive list of issues that needed to be addressed were land reform, farm reorganization, irrigation and water management, price reform, and the development of market institutions (Rozelle & Swinnen, 2004). Reform efforts in the immediate transition period were largely focused on price liberalization, which every country in the region instituted to varying degrees for most goods. The destabilizing effects of price liberalization included sustained periods of hyperinflation, which all countries in the region experienced during this time. Kazakhstan, for instance, recorded increases in its consumer price index (CPI) of over 1000% from 1992 to 1994.

After price liberalization, land reform was one of the most visible and far-reaching components of agricultural reform in this region (Lerman et al., 2004). Under the Soviet system, all land was owned by the state and all agricultural land fell under the purview of state-run or state-supported collective farms. Small-scale reforms during the Soviet era allowed individuals to use rights for land to grow crops for subsistence on small household plots, but full ownership rights with associated privileges were not granted. Lerman et al. (2004) identify state land control as one of the main reasons for inefficiencies in Soviet agriculture. Individual farmers working state land had little incentive to make long-term investments, while production decisions were made with the primary purpose of satisfying official mandates with only a passing regard to efficiency.

While all governments in the region generally acknowledged the weaknesses of the legacy collective farming system, they offered widely differing responses to land reform, private property, and land redistribution. Privatization occurred most quickly in the Kyrgyz Republic and more slowly in Tajikistan, Turkmenistan, and Uzbekistan. For Kazakhstan, it gradually introduced the concept of private ownership of agricultural land more than a decade after independence (Petrick et al., 2014). Privatization of land differed by country, but the Central Asia countries demonstrated a more conservative approach in general than those in Central and Eastern Europe, which moved quickly to allow full ownership rights, including the right to sell or transfer land. In the Kyrgyz Republic, which had nominally introduced private ownership in 1998, the government initially imposed a moratorium on land transactions to prevent landowners from selling their assets before fully understanding their rights (USAID, 2005). Today, land in Tajikistan and Uzbekistan continues to be state-owned, although agricultural producers can claim use rights.

Along with land reform, farm reorganization was another major pillar of reforms undertaken by the countries in the region during the early transition period. Most policymakers generally acknowledged the weaknesses of collective farming, including inefficiencies due to soft budget constraints, excessively large plots, labor immobility, and centrally-directed production decisions (Lerman et al., 2004). Even during the Soviet period, authorities abided by the subsistence household plots, understanding their relatively high productivity and role in rural welfare. Accordingly, initial reforms throughout the region sought to abolish collective farming. However, the speed and success of de-collectivization varied by country, reflecting the difficulties of adopting replacement institutions.

Farm reorganization in the region resulted in the creation of various types of farm organizations ranging from smallholder family-led farms to large corporate enterprises. Within the first decade of independence, three general forms of farming units emerged throughout the region: agricultural enterprises, individual farming, and household plots. Nomenclature varied depending on the country, but many of the farming organizations that emerged during this period fell under these three categories. Agricultural enterprises—which were variedly known as joint-stock companies, production cooperatives, or corporate farms, depending on the country—largely bore a resemblance to the old collective farms. Individual and private farming were direct beneficiaries of the breakup of collective farms: many farms of this type arose from collective land that was redistributed to individuals. The growth of individual farming drove the transformation of agriculture in Central Asia and was encouraged by regional governments. Household plots continued to exhibit good performance during the transition period and assumed an outsized role in certain sectors, such as livestock and horticultural production, despite their comparatively small land sizes.

The overarching patterns of farm restructuring, characterized by the rise of smallholder farming and the congruent decline of corporate enterprises, were similar throughout the five countries. This held true even for land-abundant Kazakhstan, where large agricultural enterprises still retain a considerable presence. Turkmenistan represents an unusual case in which almost no large agricultural enterprises remain in operation. Large enterprises in Turkmenistan were converted to what were called peasant associations, which consisted of individual leaseholders who are subject to state orders (FAO Investment Center, 2013). Over the years, policymakers have contended with the debate over whether farm sizes have become too small, for example, in the Kyrgyz Republic (Akramov & Omuraliev, 2009). Measures on-farm size optimization and land consolidation such as in Uzbekistan, appear to reflect concerns about land fragmentation.

2. National Agricultural Strategies

Initial reforms generally helped launch agricultural recovery for most of the five countries within a decade of independence. Productivity gains after that period, however, were mixed. The following subsections describe major policies shaping current national agricultural strategies in the five Central Asia countries. With some divergence specific to national conditions, there are a number of common features in national strategies for agricultural development and food security that are noticeable. National agricultural strategies in the region generally aim to modernize their respective agricultural sectors and seek out new opportunities for improved productivity and export earnings.

Kazakhstan

The government of Kazakhstan unveiled its national *Kazakhstan—2050 Strategy* in 2012, which serves as the cornerstone for the long-term multi-sectoral development plan of the country. The strategy prioritized seven key areas, setting a new course for economic and social development policy and a new system of managing natural resources. Former president Nursultan Nazarbayev characterized this as an "all-round economic pragmatism based on the principles of profitability, return on investment and competitiveness of the economy" (Nazarbayev, 2012).

The strategy aims to transform Kazakhstan into a private sector-led, knowledge-based, and diversified economy. The key pillars of the strategy are underlined in an action plan called "100 Concrete Steps," which highlights strengthening institutions, improving physical infrastructure, and raising the quality of human capital. Within this policy paradigm, the program underlines the modernization of the agricultural sector, development of farming, and small and medium enterprises (SME) in agricultural processing and trade as a new course for agricultural development. Specifically, the document sets a national focus on increasing arable land area and agricultural productivity primarily through the introduction of new technologies. Furthermore, Kazakhstan's government envisaged adoption of short and medium-term development plans for agriculture (Nazarbayev, 2012).

In 2013, the government of Kazakhstan approved Agribusiness—2020—its mid-term sectoral program for agricultural development for 2013–2020. With the goal of improving profitability and sustainability, affordability of consumer products, and competitiveness in international markets, the Kazakh government pledged to boost financial and administrative support for the agriculture sector (Government of Kazakhstan, 2013). In the same year, Kazakhstan's Ministry of Agriculture, national holding companies "KazAgro" and "KazAgroInnovation" and regional government administrations agreed upon a memorandum on agricultural diversification and increasing arable land under oil, bean, and forage crops for 2012–2016 (Ministry of Agriculture of the Republic of Kazakhstan, 2013).

In line with Kazakhstan's national strategy and with increased attention to regional development, the Government established a Program for the Development of Regions to 2020 in 2014 with a specific focus on economic development in areas outside of its major cities, Astana and Almaty. The program intends to achieve "level development" through the creation of new industries and infrastructure in different regions. This measure was intended to support local supply chain growth and increase employment opportunities, thus improving livelihoods and sustainable development in both urban and rural areas (Government of Kazakhstan, 2014). Still, the competitiveness of domestic products in international markets has remained one of Kazakhstan's main concerns in achieving the stated goal to become one of the 30 most competitive economies in the world by 2050. The Kazakh government has sought to address this through the State Program for the Development of the Agro-Industrial Complex of the Republic of Kazakhstan for 2017–2021. Specifically, the new multi-sectoral program aims to encourage the involvement of small and medium-sized farms in agricultural cooperation; increase the export potential of domestic products; ensure the effective use of both financial and natural resources in production processes; increase the provision of machinery, and equipment, and fertilizers to producers; develop trade and logistic infrastructure; and support development and implementation of scientific and technological innovations within the agro-industrial complex (Government of Kazakhstan, 2017).

The Kyrgyz Republic

The Kyrgyz Republic adopted its most recent development program for the period 2018–2022 called Unity Trust Creation, which is also part of its long-term vision for sustainable development until 2040. It prioritizes agricultural development through greater state support for the production and the processing of high-value and labor-intensive agricultural products, such as stone fruits, other fruits, berries, certain bean types, and cereals. For the livestock sector, it emphasizes products with high value-added potential, such as honey, wool, organic meat, and dairy products. The government understands that the production of ecologically friendly and organic products can both improve domestic food safety standards and provide additional opportunities to gain a foothold in niche export markets (Government of Kyrgyz Republic, 2018). Moreover, the Kyrgyz government has attempted to link agriculture with nutrition policies that aim to ensure the availability, affordability, quality, and safety of nutritious foods (Government of Kyrgyz Republic, 2015).

The Kyrgyz government continues to seek policies that are compatible with the high prevalence of small-scale agricultural production in the country. It intends to determine several important agricultural products for each region with the goal of introducing regional specialization for certain products. The government intends to create medium and large processing complexes and develop more direct value chains with fewer intermediaries to reduce transaction costs and promote agricultural exports. It plans to develop two large international trade and logistic centers for agricultural products in the southern and northern regions with an additional seven regional logistic centers focused on specific commodities. These trade and logistic centers are expected to be able to collect, store, sort and conduct the primary processing of agricultural products (Government of Kyrgyz Republic, 2018).

Tajikistan

In 2012, Tajikistan adopted its key agricultural reform program for 2012–2020. This program serves as the overarching policy document for agricultural reform and builds upon several other strategies including the National Development Strategy of the Republic of Tajikistan until 2015, Poverty Reduction Strategy for 2010–2012, and Food Security Program until 2015. The program specifies 22 objectives, including the reformation and reorganization of dehkan farms to improve the independent decision-making of farmers in agricultural production and to promote gender empowerment within the farming sector; promoting high-value crops aimed at increasing agricultural exports and expanding area under fruits and horticultural crops; ensuring the sustainable use of natural resources; and improving resilience against climate change and developing agricultural technologies, etc. (Government of Tajikistan, 2012).

In 2016, Tajikistan adopted its latest long-term development strategy until 2030, which lays out a multi-sectoral development program addressing a broad range of social and economic issues such as social protection, access to safe and nutritious food, reduction of gender inequality, and creation of employment opportunities to eradicate poverty. The Tajik government has identified four strategic development goals such as ensuring energy security and the efficient use of electricity; improving external connectivity and moderating international transit; ensuring food security and access to nutritious and high-quality food; and expanding productive employment. In order to achieve these goals, the Tajik government underlines three main principles of the program:

- preventing or minimizing risks to future development;
- industrializing and using national resources efficiently;
- developing through innovation (Government of Tajikistan, 2016).

According to the 2016 strategy, food and nutrition security will be achieved through growth encouraged by reforms in the water and agricultural sectors. The policy document lists specific priority objectives that touch upon all aspects of agriculture, including inputs, technologies, irrigation infrastructure, monitoring systems, agriculture-nutrition linkages, and governance (Government of Tajikistan, 2016).

Turkmenistan

In 2017, Turkmenistan adopted its recent national development program for 2018–2024, which aims to continue its transition into a market-based economy through the promotion of knowledge and innovations, diversification of the economy, and improvement of the living conditions of the general population. According to the document, the agricultural sector fits into these plans by contributing to food security and economic development through food import substitution, supplying the industry sector with raw materials, and providing employment for up to 40% of the population. The Turkmen government's program pledges support to the agricultural sector through technology transfers and modernization (Government of Turkmenistan, 2017).

The Turkmen government has linked agricultural development with its national strategy on climate change, adopted in 2012. The strategy recognizes the threat to water resources and irrigation from global climate change. Therefore, Turkmenistan is paying special attention to agricultural diversification and improving efficiency in water use during the 2018–2024 period. The government also intends to draft and enforce the number of regulations to improve overall efficiency in natural resource use and agricultural production (Government of Turkmenistan, 2017).

Uzbekistan

Changes in Uzbekistan's political leadership following the death of President Islam Karimov in 2016 set forth sweeping reforms in the economy and public administration. They are exemplified by the Strategy of actions on further development of Uzbekistan 2017–2021, which sought to improve public administration, judicial systems, social infrastructure, economic growth, and trade (Government of Uzbekistan, 2017). By the end of 2017, the government had adopted additional 15 laws and issued more than 700 other policy documents as part of its strategy to liberalize social and economic policy. These wholesale reforms also sought to address food and nutrition security and agricultural development in the country (International Food Policy Research Institute, 2018). The 2017–2021 Strategy identified five priority areas for development:

- reformation of public administration;
- reformation of the judiciary system and strengthening the rule of law;
- economic development and liberalization;
- reformation in the area of social development;
- reformation of national security and foreign policy.

As part of its economic development and liberalization agenda, the Uzbek government's strategy specifically addresses the agricultural and food sectors, calling for the modernization and intensive development of agriculture. It intends to deepen structural reforms and develop agricultural production to improve national food security, expand the production of environmentally friendly products, and significantly increase the export potential of the agricultural sector. The new strategy promotes agricultural diversification by reducing crop areas under cotton and cereal crops in favor of vegetables, forage, oilseeds, and perennial fruits. The policy document pays special attention to export promotion and attracting investments for the construction of modern enterprises that can produce high-quality processed foods that would be competitive both in domestic and international markets. It also envisions creating agribusiness clusters as part of an overall goal to direct investment into the country's agricultural storage, transportation, and marketing infrastructure. The Uzbek government's strategy also seeks to improve farmer access to inputs and introduce the latest technology throughout the agricultural value chain (Government of Uzbekistan, 2017).

III. Trends in Land Use and Agricultural Production

The initial reforms in land and farm organization had a transformative effect on the rural landscape and agricultural production in the Central Asia region. Moreover, they were introduced during a time when these countries struggled to transition from agricultural specialization under the Soviet system. This section will focus on the changes in land use and agricultural production.

1. Changes in Land Use

Lerman and Sedik (2009) describe two major periods of agricultural development in Central Asia: a period of sharp decline from the early 1990s and a subsequent recovery phase initiated by reforms in the mid-to-late 1990s (Lerman & Sedik, 2009). With some variation, this pattern generally held true for all Central Asia countries during the first decade of independence. Most countries in the region experienced a windfall in productivity during the late 1990s and early 2000s, which observers attribute to the one-time effect of land reform and farm restructuring.

Over the long term, land reform effectively redistributed agricultural land from large enterprises to smaller farms. For example, in the Kyrgyz Republic, land controlled by collective farms and large agricultural enterprises dropped dramatically from 93% of total cropland in 1990 to 26% in 2000 and less than 5% in the mid-2010s (National Statistics Committee, 2018). Figure 5.1 displays the trend in the distribution of arable land by farm type in the Kyrgyz Republic over nearly three decades. Currently, more

Figure 5.1
Distribution of Arable Land by Farm Type in the Kyrgyz Republic, 1990–2017

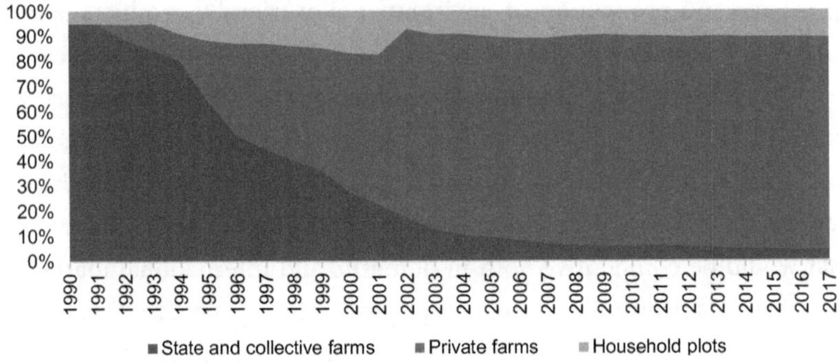

■ State and collective farms   ■ Private farms   ■ Household plots

Source. National Statistics Committee (2018).

than 300,000 individual farms with an average land size of 2.9 hectares control about 82% of the total cropland in the country. The remaining 13% of the total cropland is occupied by more than 900,000 traditional household plots with an average size of 0.11 hectares per holding.[1] Overall cropland in the Kyrgyz Republic saw an increase of more than 40% between 1990 and 2000, though there was a subsequent reduction of more than 104,000 hectares since this early period. In Tajikistan, land reform and farm reorganization accelerated after the end of its civil war that lasted from 1992 to 1997. Currently, large agricultural enterprises occupy only 14% of arable land, compared to 21% under household plots and 65% under private farms (Statistical Agency under the President of the Republic of Tajikistan, 2017).

In contrast to the Kyrgyz Republic and Tajikistan, large agricultural enterprises using leased state land and hired labor are still major actors in agricultural production in Kazakhstan, especially in its northern grain-producing regions (Petrick et al., 2014). Approximately 60% of arable land is cultivated by these enterprises, compared to 39% of arable land for private farms and only 1% for household plots (Statistical Committee under the Ministry of Economy of the Republic of Kazakhstan, 2018).

2. Changes in Agricultural Production

Agricultural production and crop choices in the region have turned in favor of food and high-value commodities since the early reform period. In the past, the Kyrgyz Republic specialized in intensive livestock production, Tajikistan and Uzbekistan on cotton, and Kazakhstan grew mostly wheat. Other essential food products, including

---

1. Partially based on Akramov and Omuraliev (2009) with updated information.

processed foods, were imported from other republics outside of the Central Asia region. However, the instability and collapse in cross-border trade networks following the collapse of the Soviet Union compelled national governments to focus on the availability of food resources and self-sufficiency. This led to an expansion of wheat, potatoes, and vegetable crops in the Kyrgyz Republic, Tajikistan, and Uzbekistan. On the other hand, lands allocated for barley, cotton, and feed crops decreased concurrently. In more recent years, however, regional governments have taken a more expansive approach to food security: prioritizing self-sufficiency and the value in terms of nutrition and earnings. As regional trade links began to regenerate, Kazakhstan has become an important source of cereals for countries in the region, lessening the need to grow wheat in other countries since the early 2000s.

In the Kyrgyz Republic, land allocated for wheat increased from 15% of the total sown area in 1990 to 42% in 2002. Horticulture likewise increased from a combined 8% of total land area to 12% in 2002. Feed crops and barley declined from 48% and 20% of the total sown area in 1990 to 20% and 6% in 2002, respectively.[2] Since that time, wheat in sown areas declined to 24%, as the land was allocated for other crops instead, and wheat availability became less of a concern due to improved international trade, mostly from Kazakhstan. Land allocated for barley and feed crops recovered somewhat during this time, increasing by 27% and 14%, respectively. The share of horticulture continued to expand and reached 16% in 2015 (National Statistics Committee, 2018).

Likewise, in Tajikistan, land allocated for wheat, potatoes, and vegetables increased after initial reforms at the expense of cotton and feed crops. Data show that grains became the dominant crop in Tajikistan by the late 2000s, planted on approximately 51% of arable land in the country, with wheat accounting for 41% of all land alone (Akramov & Shreedhar, 2012). In 2016, grains continued to account for approximately 50% of arable land area. Although reduced in scale, cotton remains a major crop in Tajikistan, representing the second-largest crop type with less than 20% of total land area in 2016. Land allocated for potatoes, melons, and vegetables accounts for a combined 15% of total sown area. These three crops have increased in importance in recent years, representing a growing shift toward horticultural crops. Land area under fruit and vegetable production increased by 16% and 30% by 2011, respectively, compared to 2005 (Development Coordination Council, 2011).[3] With a greater emphasis placed on growing food crops, the share of arable land allocated to feed crops declined significantly and occupied around 12% of arable land in 2016.

---

2. Partially based on Akramov and Omuraliev (2009) with updated information.
3. Partially based on Akramov and Shreedhar (2012) with updated information.

Allocated land for wheat also increased in Uzbekistan at the expense of cotton and feed crops after independence. Between the mid-1990s and mid-2000s, land allocated for wheat and cotton ranged from 70% to 80% of the total sown area. In the past decade, however, the government of Uzbekistan began to prioritize agricultural diversification, specifically by focusing more attention on horticulture. This policy has been supported by international donors such as the World Bank and Asian Development Bank, who have directed financial support to the growth of horticulture in the country. As a result, land allocated for horticultural crops has been steadily increasing and in 2016 reached almost 17%, representing a nearly five percentage point increase from the early 2000s. A notable feature of Uzbek agriculture is the prevalence of double cropping on land allocated for wheat, with vegetables and feed crops often being grown as secondary crops. This has effectively increased the land area and production of vegetable and feed crops.

The government of Kazakhstan has also prioritized crop diversification in recent years. The Kazakh government's strategy has been primarily based on improving wheat production through a technology-driven increase in yield while expanding the area of forage crops and oilseeds. This strategy has encouraged agricultural producers to diversify their crop mix by planting less wheat and directing subsidies to feed and oilseed crops, such as sunflowers, flax, safflowers, rapeseed, and soybeans. The use of direct subsidies has been one of the Kazakh government's most effective tools for implementing crop diversification strategies. The total oilseed area has tripled from 0.7 million hectares in 2006 to more than two million hectares in 2015. Crop diversification has also been driven by a growing livestock industry, which has generated additional demand for forage. Land allocated for feed crops increased from 2.3 million hectares in 2006 to nearly 3.7 million hectares in 2015, with a concurrent 20% reduction in sown area for wheat. Although Kazakhstan is a land-abundant country with large areas of rainfed cropland in the north, agriculture in its southern regions more closely resembles practices found elsewhere in Central Asia.

Although access to reliable production data from Turkmenistan is limited, studies undertaken by international organizations such as FAO suggest that Turkmenistan has also reduced its reliance on cotton. During the Soviet era, Turkmenistan was a cotton monoculture, with over 50% of arable land allocated for cotton (FAO Investment Center, 2013). Like other Central Asian countries during the same period, Turkmenistan prioritized the growth of wheat, rice, and other grain crops while holding cotton production at a relatively steady rate. However, Turkmenistan differs from other Central Asian producers in its use of the state order system to affect policy changes. According to Lerman et al. (2016), 100% of wheat produced in Turkmenistan is governed under the state order system, wherein producers working on leased land receive input supplies at set prices and deliver directly to government producers (Lerman et al., 2016). Horticulture growth in Turkmenistan is limited compared to neighboring countries because of its mostly desert climate and competition with staple crops for arable land (FAO Investment Center, 2013).

Figure 5.2 illustrates long-term changes in crop diversity for Tajikistan, Uzbekistan, and Kazakhstan, demonstrating growing agricultural diversification and the emergence of horticulture. The reduction in land allocated for forage crops during the early stages of agricultural recovery reflected the desire of the governments in the region to respond to food crises that occurred after independence and to ensure self-sufficiency.

Figure 5.2

Crop Diversity, Share of Total Harvested Area in Selected Countries, 1999–2016

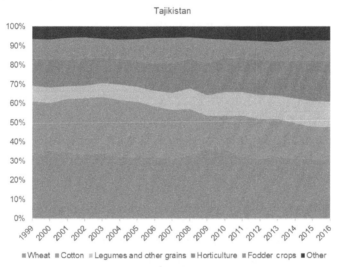

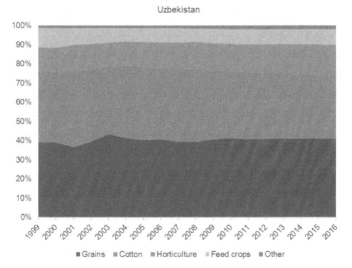

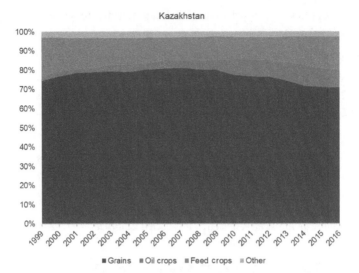

Source. State Committee of the Republic of Uzbekistan on Statistics (2019); Statistical Agency under the President of the Republic of Tajikistan (2017); Statistical Committee under the Ministry of Economy of the Republic of Kazakhstan (2018).

In more recent years, however, higher-value agriculture, such as horticulture in the Kyrgyz Republic and Uzbekistan is seeing an increase in production. In Kazakhstan, oilseeds have become more widely grown since the turn of the century.

3. Changes in Land/Labor Productivity and Agricultural Transformation

Changes in the distribution of arable land and livestock across farm types characterized a fundamental transformation in Central Asian agricultural production. In all countries, the share of private farms (comprised of household plots and individual farms) in total agricultural production increased dramatically. The private sector produced more than 95% of aggregate agricultural output in the Kyrgyz Republic and Uzbekistan, including almost 95% of crops and nearly all livestock by the late 2000s (Akramov & Omuraliev, 2009). While the production of staple crops, primarily cereals, deemed of strategic importance has often been the target of state intervention, horticulture, and livestock have generally been left to the discretion of private and household farmers.

Data have generally demonstrated higher farm productivity in smallholder farms, owing to several possible factors, including lower transaction and administrative costs, better governance, and efficiencies driven by individual crop choices. Unlike small farms, larger farms bear the costly administrative burdens of monitoring operations and enforcing labor discipline, which can offset their advantages from economies of scale (Lerman et al., 2004). The individualization of agriculture may have weakened these problems associated with collective agriculture while simultaneously encouraging private incentives (Akramov & Omuraliev, 2009).

While trends in crop composition, land allocation, and farm organization evidence important changes in agricultural practices, changing labor and land productivity patterns are demonstrative of fundamental transformation within the sector itself (Timmer, 2015). The combination of land and labor productivity captures the pace and extent of agricultural transformation and can be illustrated by a "ruttan-a-gram," which measures the logarithm of productivity per hectare on its vertical axis and productivity per worker on its horizontal axis. This two-dimensional perspective provides the most general representation of the process of agricultural transformation (Hayami & Ruttan, 1971). Figure 5.3 shows the recent historical track of agricultural productivity in Central Asia. Some trends are evident in this graph. The first is a severe reduction in both land and labor productivity after the fall of the Soviet Union. The second is a recovery in both indicators that reverse the initial trend. The slope and length, indicating comparative trends across the two factors, and the rate of change, respectively, of both trend lines, differ significantly by country.

The point of reversal, representing the start of recovery, also differs but is relatively similar. The Kyrgyz Republic and Uzbekistan both experienced relatively early rebounds in land and labor productivity in the mid-1990s. However, the pace of productivity increases has been much faster in Uzbekistan than in the Kyrgyz Republic. Both land and labor productivity rebounded in Kazakhstan, Turkmenistan, and Tajikistan in

Figure 5.3
Land and Labor Productivity in Central Asian Agriculture, 1990–2014

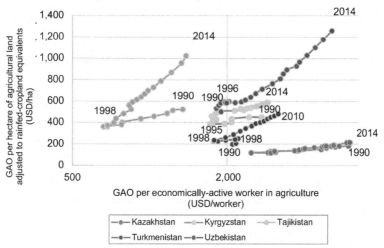

Source. FAO (2019).

the late 1990s. One of the most striking features from Figure 5.3 is the stagnation of growth in land productivity in Kazakhstan. Yields per hectare grew very slowly between 1998 and 2014, and only in recent years has labor productivity recovered to pre-independence levels. The reorganization of farms, which was underway in the mid-to-late 1990s in most countries, strongly influenced the flow of labor to and from the agricultural sector. In some countries, this period was marked by an influx of urban dwellers with little farming experience who entered agriculture after independence. Moreover, some countries experienced high rates of rural migration overseas, which were often not accounted for in official data. This can cloud the picture regarding labor productivity in agriculture.

IV. Perspectives by Subsectors

Grains, livestock, and horticulture make up the major components of agriculture in Central Asia. Wheat, rice, meat, dairy products, and vegetables are also important components of regional diets. Each subsector has the potential for productivity improvement and will play an important role in ensuring regional food security and export earnings in the long run. This section will discuss the specific features of these subsectors and the development of value chains in the region.

1. Grain Production and Trade

The importance of grain as a staple food cannot be overstated in Central Asia. Even as households in the region have improved their economic welfare since independence, they continued to consume grain products as a major source of calorie intake. Although contemporary diets in the region have become more diverse with added wealth, demand for grain has remained constant. Moreover, households have especially relied on grain consumption to sustain their diets during times of economic crisis, such as the food price shocks that occurred in 2007–2008 or downturns caused by falling remittances (Akramov & Shreedhar, 2012).

The share of wheat and animal products, which are two important food groups with somewhat inverse dietary consumption patterns, is illustrated in Figure 5.4. Consumption of wheat products is very high by world standards throughout the five Central Asian countries, with the notable exception of Kazakhstan, where calorie intake via animal products has overtaken intake from grains. The consumption of wheat products reached its peak in the late 1990s in all Central Asian countries and has receded since then. Still, according to FAO data, wheat products comprise around half of the total daily calorie intake in Tajikistan, Turkmenistan, and Uzbekistan (FAO, 2019).

Figure 5.4

Share of Daily Dietary Intake in the Central Asia and Caucasus Region (Kcal/Capita/Day)

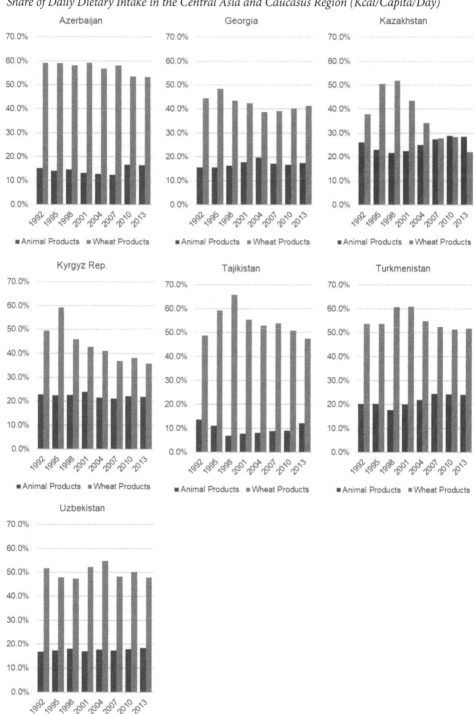

Source. FAO (2019).

The importance of wheat products in household consumption makes wheat the single most crucial crop for regional food availability and explains why the wheat subsector has been the target of heavy intervention by policymakers in their national agricultural production strategies over the years. For example, around 40% to 45% of wheat production in Uzbekistan from 2009 to 2013 was subject to the state order system; this figure was nearly 100% in Turkmenistan in the late 2000s (Lerman et al., 2016). Regardless of their productive capacity, all countries in the region regard domestic wheat production as a key pillar of their national food security, illustrated by the drive by nearly all countries in Central Asia to concentrate on wheat farming amid economic crises following independence. Although some countries, such as Uzbekistan were able to achieve self-sufficiency in grain, this emphasis had a detrimental effect on other capital-intensive agricultural subsectors, such as cotton and livestock (Musaev et al., 2010). Moreover, increased grain production meant more competition for land with higher-value crops such as fruits and vegetables. With most countries in the region treating wheat as a strategic staple crop and a target of intervention to varying degrees, land allocation is a useful indicator of state policy priorities. Figure 5.5 shows the area of land allocated with wheat in addition to productivity yields. The share of land allocated for wheat was highest in Tajikistan at 65.4%, followed by Kazakhstan (59.7%), Uzbekistan (53.9%), the Kyrgyz Republic (32.7%), and Turkmenistan (20.4%) in Central Asia (FAO, 2019).

A shift away from wheat production in more recent years has been aided by the increase in wheat and wheat product imports from Kazakhstan. For Kazakhstan, the only major net exporter of wheat in the region, this subsector takes on added importance as a source of export earnings. In 2016, Kazakhstan was the world's twelfth largest exporter of wheat and was by far the main supplier of wheat and grain to other countries in Central Asia (Simoes & Hidalgo, 2011). Figure 5.6 shows the breakdown of wheat imports to selected Central Asian countries by source. Nearly all of the wheat imported into the rest of Central Asia originates in Kazakhstan. This represents about 43% of Kazakhstan's total wheat exports (United Nations, 2019).

For countries such as the Kyrgyz Republic, Tajikistan, and Uzbekistan, which had not traditionally grown wheat to such a large degree as they did during the late 1990s and early 2000s, imports are an important component of the national wheat balance. Figure 5.7 illustrates the wheat commodity balance of the countries in the region, demonstrating the importance of the wheat trade in augmenting domestic production.

Policy reforms supporting structural changes in the agricultural sector have had positive impacts on wheat production in conjunction with land re-allocation programs. For example, in Tajikistan, land and farm restructuring encouraged productivity growth, as less productive farms were redirected to other crops (Akramov

Figure 5.5

Wheat Area and Productivity (MT/Ha) in Selected Countries, 1992–2014

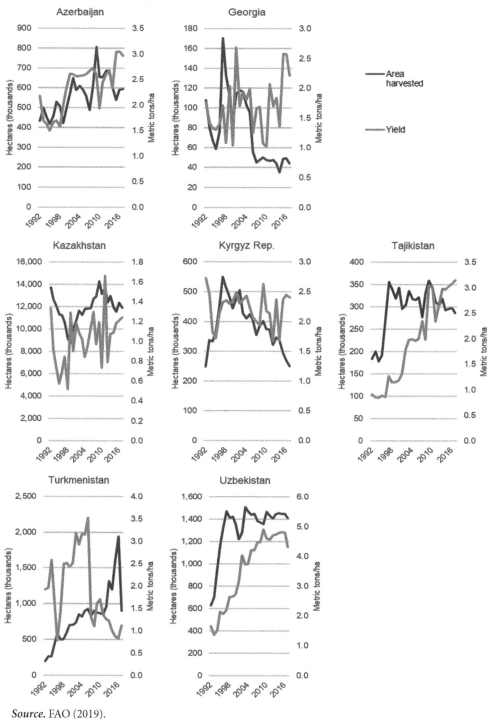

Source. FAO (2019).

Figure 5.6

Share of Wheat Imports From Major Producers, Central Asia, 2006–2013

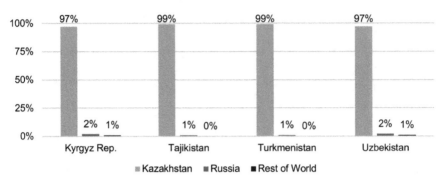

Source. Svanidze et al. (2016).

Figure 5.7

Wheat Commodity Balance in Central Asia and Caucasus, 1992–2012

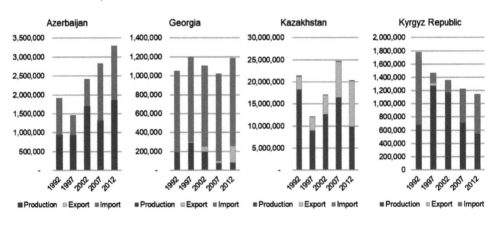

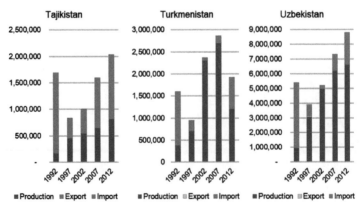

Source. FAO (2019).

& Shreedhar, 2012). Average Central Asian wheat productivity is estimated at 1.6 tons per hectare, which remains less than half of the average world level of 3.3 tons per hectare (FAO, 2019).

Although the longer-term trend has de-emphasized wheat production in favor of a set of more diverse, higher-value crops, the more recent crises that took place in the late 2000s have reignited calls for domestic food availability including wheat. Wheat-importing countries found it difficult to tame rising domestic prices for bread and other wheat products. In 2015, the Kyrgyz Republic called for 95% self-sufficiency in wheat products over a three-year period (Government of Kyrgyz Republic, 2015). In 2010, Tajikistan passed food security legislation that called for domestic production to comprise 80% of wheat consumption (Government of Tajikistan, 2010). However, consumer preferences for higher-quality Kazakh wheat flour (Abassian, 2005), poor bread-making quality of domestic wheat varieties (Pena et al., 2002), and the benefits of agricultural diversification and regional integration have encouraged national governments to focus more attention to value-added activities and trade. For example, Tajikistan has increased its wheat flour milling capacity in recent years while maintaining wheat imports from Kazakhstan.

Transportation of wheat relies on existing railway links connecting Kazakhstan to the rest of the region. Kazakh wheat is directly delivered to Northern Kyrgyz Republic and Uzbekistan. Railroad shipments to Southern Kyrgyz Republic, other Central Asian countries, and Northern Afghanistan pass through Uzbekistan. In the Kyrgyz Republic and Tajikistan, wheat is reloaded onto trucks, whose loading capacity is comparatively limited and is challenged by mountainous terrain. These direct and indirect access routes between Kazakhstan and other Central Asian countries create a substantial range in transportation costs estimated at between US$50 and US$90 per ton (Ilyasov et al., 2016; Svanidze et al., 2016). Kazakhstan's access to international wheat markets is mainly realized through Black Sea ports and shipments across Russian territory, which incur high expenses and competition from Russian wheat during high trade seasons. The government of Kazakhstan has diversified its export routes by building grain terminals on the Caspian Sea and establishing new trade links with China, Iran, and other Middle Eastern and Asian countries. It has also recently focused on higher-value processing and exporting wheat flour to neighboring countries (Petrick et al., 2014).

Kazakhstan will remain a major producer and supplier of wheat in the region. Evidence suggests that Kazakhstan's climatic and land conditions, which in its northern grain-producing regions are similar to those found in North America, can host large productivity increases if farmers receive appropriate price incentives, governance structures, and technology transfers. Coupled with greater trade integration and improved transport infrastructure, the entire region can benefit from improved

Kazakh wheat and grain productivity if other Central Asian countries direct their own production according to their comparative advantages in higher-value activities, such as horticulture and livestock while importing wheat from Kazakhstan (Pomfret, 2016).

2. Livestock and Dairy Production

Livestock production in Central Asia also experienced transformation, experiencing a sharp decline following independence with an eventual recovery in the early 2000s (see Figure 5.8). Trends in livestock production over the years not only witnessed fluctuating output levels but fundamental changes to the nature of production itself. Whereas the Central Asia countries hosted large-scale production on state farms during Soviet times, livestock today is largely the domain of household farms and other smallholders. The transition from a Soviet system supported by generous inputs and intensive management to today's fragmented household holdings was initialized by a collapse in animal stocks following independence, as farmers liquidated much of their herds to eliminate costs. This applied especially to Kazakhstan and the Kyrgyz Republic and less so to Uzbekistan, where meat and milk production remained steady during the early transition period. Livestock operations were less intensive in Uzbekistan prior to independence, and the government remained more conservative in its macroeconomic and agricultural policies at the time (Suleimenov & Oram, 2000).

Throughout the region, household farms became the main setting for livestock production. For many households, livestock represented an important income-

Figure 5.8
Total Meat Production in Tons, 1992–2017

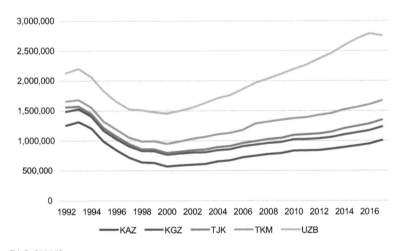

Source. FAO (2019).

generating asset and source of food security. For example, in Uzbekistan, peasant farmers owned 95% of cattle and 83% of all sheep, producing 95% and 96% of meat and milk production, respectively (IFAD, 2015). Likewise, in Tajikistan, livestock inventories increased rapidly after the agricultural recovery period, even as feed production failed to keep pace (Sedik, 2009). More than 90% of cattle in Tajikistan is held by households (Statistical Agency under the President of the Republic of Tajikistan, 2017). In Kazakhstan, however, the growth in the number of animals held by household farms stagnated in the late 2000s, while other types of private farms and agricultural enterprises witnessed somewhat of a recovery (Fileccia et al., 2010).

While livestock plays a crucial role in food security and income for rural households, a reliance on small-scale production can hinder the adoption of improved practices and benefits from economies of scale. Fragmentation of the region's animal stocks has been accompanied by a shortage of crucial support services, which has been detrimental to productivity. This has had broad effects for milk, egg, and meat production. For example, egg production faced a decline in every Central Asia country because of the loss of intensively supported chicken factories (Suleimenov & Oram, 2000). In general, however, evidence suggests that changes in land distribution and household livestock ownership have made positive contributions to the recovery in protein consumption (FAO, 2007).

Recognizing the importance of the livestock sector for rural households, policymakers have been attempting to fill the institutional void in livestock support services, including a renewed focus on marketing and value chains. Policymakers understand that the under-commercialization of livestock production has led to foregone opportunities and have sought to provide opportunities for regional farmers to access new markets and improve household earnings. Projects initiated by foreign donors have been aimed at transitioning from subsistence livestock production in favor of broader commercialization of the sector. These programs seek to direct broad upgrades throughout the meat and dairy production value chain process.

Improvements to livestock production will play an important role in satisfying growing demands for meat and milk products throughout the Central Asia region. Rising incomes in the region stemming from a sustained period of economic growth since the 1990s have led to higher consumer demand for meat and dairy. Moreover, growing demand from elsewhere, including China and the Middle East, could open opportunities for Central Asian exporters. These regional and international consumer trends have placed additional pressure on existing production and marketing infrastructure. The marketing network for livestock varies widely in quality, including in terms of access to processing facilities and investment. Where meat or dairy processing facilities are unavailable, many household producers sell their products at nearby markets or directly to neighbors (UNDP Uzbekistan, 2010). Moreover, the transportation of meat requires cold storage capacity, which is often not available in many parts of the region. High transaction costs due to poor infrastructure and limited information continue to burden small farmers, encouraging the use of informal "middlemen" dealers to fill a void left by a lack of viable producer-to-market value chains in many parts of Central Asia and the Caucasus. Some donor agencies have encouraged the organization of producer associations as one way of strengthening marketing functions (World Bank, 2007).

Dichotomous value chain networks have developed in certain countries: Kazakhstan's livestock sector is an illustrative example. There are distinct livestock value chains in Kazakhstan that cater to distinct consumer profiles ranging from low-income consumers buying meat products directly from local butchers to high-income urban consumers that shop at modern supermarkets. The quality of the products in the latter value chain is relatively high, having been subject to sanitary controls and inspection (Fileccia et al., 2010). Between these two value chain types is what Fileccia et al. (2010) describe as an intermediate option in which consumers buy meat products from a local bazaar. While these meat products must undergo veterinary inspection, regulatory coverage is uncertain, and there remains significant risk that some consumers will purchase uninspected meat. Apart from the consumer market, public sector institutions in some countries, for example, in Uzbekistan, remained an important buyer of meat through the late 2000s (UNDP Uzbekistan, 2010).

Dairy production largely occurs on smallholder farms in the region. For example, household farms comprised approximately 90% of dairy production in Kazakhstan in the late 2000s (Van Engelen, 2011), where per capita dairy consumption is among the highest in the world (FAO, 2019). The production profile is similar in other countries in the region. Productivity of the dairy sector is generally low across the board due to factors including the low quality of pastures and forage, deficiency of feed supplements, poor breeding and management of genetic lines, and weak veterinary services and disease control. Small household farms often do not have access to the complex array of services and inputs required to boost productivity levels.

Milk yields in Central Asia, particularly in the Kyrgyz Republic, Tajikistan, and Uzbekistan, are lower than world averages (FAO, 2019). Milk yields in Tajikistan have still not recovered to pre-independence levels, even as they have increased significantly since the mid-1990s (FAO, 2019). Figure 5.9 demonstrates milk productivity in the five Central Asia countries, along with Azerbaijan and Georgia from the Caucasus region, over a 25-year period starting from independence.

Although Kazakhstan's milk productivity has generally been the highest of the Central Asia countries, it has lagged behind other similarly situated transition

Figure 5.9

Milk Productivity, Central Asia, and Caucasus Hg/An, 1992–2017

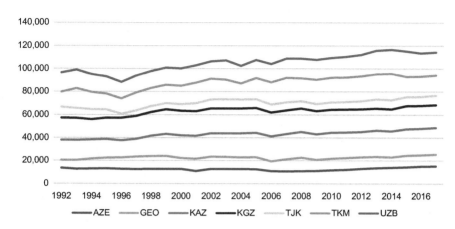

Source. FAO (2019).

Figure 5.10

Milk Productivity, Kazakhstan and Selected Countries in Hectograms per Animal, 1992–2017

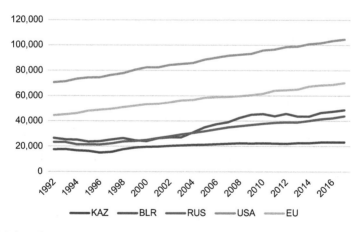

Source. FAO (2019).

countries such as Belarus and Russian Federation (Figure 5.10), which have seen rapid productivity gains since the early 2000s (FAO, 2019). Kazakhstan's national dairy development program is targeting middle and large-scale enterprises with improved value chains and modernized processing facilities. Some of these modern dairy farms used imported cattle and equipment, but overall production volume was low and had to compete with more cheaply produced competitors at the program's inception (Van Engelen, 2011). On the other hand, IFAD (2015) reported that targeted interventions in the region allowed some smallholder dairy farmers to move from subsistence roduction to commercialization. These farmers received improved access to land and finance, training, collection services, linkages to agribusiness enterprises, and financial incentives (IFAD, 2015).

Like other livestock products, dairy value chains also exhibit fragmentation in the region. In Uzbekistan, which according to IFAD (2015) is characteristic throughout Central Asia, household farmers possess the majority of cows in the country, but private and commercial farms are more likely to have access to dairy plants and processors. This latter group has an additional advantage in that processing facilities will also provide technical assistance and services such as refrigeration. Organized collection outside of the largest cities is nonexistent, forcing small dairy farmers to sell their products to local traders or nearby bazaars to sell their goods (IFAD, 2015). Fragmented value chains and a lack of technical capacity negatively affect animal health and public food safety.

Better yields and quality of dairy products can provide export opportunities for regional farmers. For example, the Kyrgyz Republic's entry into the Eurasian Economic Union (EEU) theoretically granted it access to a large common market. However, one of the hurdles for Kyrgyz farmers in being able to fully take advantage of this opportunity was the country's weak reputation for regulatory and veterinary standards. The Kyrgyz Republic faced immediate controls at EEU member state borders despite existing trade agreements (USDA, 2016). With increased regional integration in Central Asia in recent years, national policymakers are focusing attention on improving regulatory standards for livestock products.

Veterinary services were among the support services that fell by the wayside following the fall of the Soviet Union. Bovine tuberculosis, brucellosis, rabies, and anthrax are endemic to Central Asia, making veterinary services an essential component of support to the livestock sector. Veterinary practices as practiced during independence were designed to meet the needs of large-scale livestock farms and became less suitable for private smallholders that emerged in subsequent years. In more recent years, veterinary services have been handled by a mix of government and private sector actors, depending on the country. Privatization of veterinary services has been the general trend in the region. Kazakhstan's law on veterinary services, which was revised in 2009, has sought to decentralize the practice and entrust most fieldwork to the private sector apart from disease outbreak control and inspection (Fileccia et al., 2010). Likewise, Uzbekistan has sought to encourage private veterinary services to supplement government services that had faced shortages in supply and coverage (IFAD, 2015; UNDP Uzbekistan, 2010). As of the early 2010s, veterinary services were almost completely provided by the state in the Kyrgyz Republic, where the government maintained that it needed to control the immunization of livestock in order to ensure the safety of vaccines (USAID, 2013). However, a law on veterinary medicine was passed in 2014 outlining the responsibilities of private providers (USDA, 2016). Barriers to achieving better veterinary practices may involve more than simply access to services. Even a free vaccination program against diseases in 2005 reached only about 50% to 60% of livestock, indicating that logistics and farmers' attitudes may also be obstacles (Swinnen et al., 2011).

Moreover, policymakers have been paying more attention to selective breeding practices in recent years. Distinct genetic lines for livestock, which were rigorously managed under the Soviet system, had become lost after independence because of indiscriminate breeding and poor regulation. This was an especially pertinent problem for livestock grazing on shared pastures, which is a common practice throughout the region. Initiatives such as pedigree breeding systems were undertaken in countries such as the Kyrgyz Republic and Uzbekistan to reintroduce selective breeding, though their reliability was often inconsistent (UNDP Uzbekistan, 2010; World Bank, 2007). Regional governments imported high-productivity animal breeds from Western countries, particularly dairy cows and beef cattle, but their transition to Central Asia was not always successful due to a number of factors, including lack of proper care and health issues.

Artificial insemination services exist throughout the region, but not all farms use them, owing to a lack of resources and familiarity among many farmers about the process. In one study in Uzbekistan, only 2% of household farmers reported using artificial insemination for their cattle, although those that did report satisfactory experiences (UNDP Uzbekistan, 2010). The survey suggested that private and household farmers were more likely to be unaware of these services compared to those working on larger commercial farms. Even among the latter group, only one-eighth of the respondents recalled being familiar with artificial insemination. Kazakhstan, which played an important role in pedigree sheep breeding and farming during Soviet times, has maintained breeding farms that register purebred sheep for meat and wool. There, scientists have bred local sheep with productive foreign breeds (Fileccia et al., 2010).

The availability of animal feed and pasture management is additionally important livestock support mechanisms that have undergone much transformations throughout the past few decades (Figure 5.11). During the early years of independence, many countries overlooked pasture reforms, largely because the sharp decrease in animal stocks made the issue less urgent at the time (USAID, 2011). Because farmers were no longer able to benefit from the Soviet-style system of intensive winter feed and imports of concentrated feed, they sold off or liquidated their herds. The remaining

Figure 5.11

Animal Feed Production in Central Asia, Indexed to 1992 (=100), 1992–2015

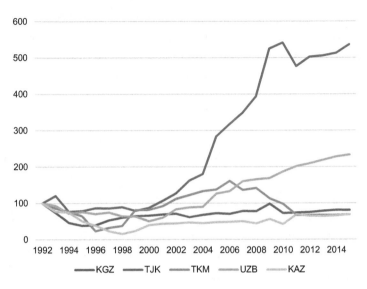

Source. USDA (2018).

animals were left reliant on grazing, placing heavy pressure on shared pastures, which had not received the same attention as cropland during initial reforms. Moreover, animal feed crops were negatively impacted by the shift to food crops during the early stages of agricultural recovery. For example, in Tajikistan, pastureland declined by at least 300,000 hectares in the decade following the end of the civil war (Lerman, 2008). Pastures near populated villages tend to be overgrazed, as many herders prefer that their animals graze on easily accessible fields and do not have the resources or willingness to pursue seasonal migration requiring expensive transportation (Crewett, 2012). Such a case can be seen in mountainous countries like Tajikistan and the Kyrgyz Republic, which contain sufficient amounts of summer pastures that are often left unused while fall-spring pastures are utilized all year long (Sedik, 2009). Sedik (2009) estimated that only 10% of all pasture land in Tajikistan was serving the needs of 43% of all livestock.

Central Asian farmers depend on what is available locally for animal feed, which results in a wide variability by location. In Kazakhstan, medium- and large-scale livestock farms produce their own animal feed, such as grass and Lucerne hay. Some large farms even possess their own feed mills and produce concentrated feed based on a variety of plant materials (Van Engelen, 2011). Even as pastureland degraded during the 1990s and 2000s, cultivated land reserved for fodder crops generally shrank across the region around the same time. Food demands took precedence over animal fodder in countries like the Kyrgyz Republic, where land allocated for forage crops was halved in the decade after independence in favor of staple crops (Dzunusova, 2008). In the mid-to-late 2000s, Sedik (2009) estimated that Tajik livestock obtained only between 53% and 72% of their dietary needs from the carrying capacity of feed resources. As a result, even while many rural Tajik households hold livestock, productivity is very low due to the overreliance on grazing and scarcity of feed crops and concentrates (IFAD, 2015). Similar observations were made in Uzbekistan around the same time, where only 57% of household farms claimed that they were able to supply their livestock with sufficient feeds (UNDP Uzbekistan, 2010).

3. Horticulture

Whereas grain self-sufficiency was the preferred policy for food security for most of the countries in Central Asia and the Caucasus during the period of recovery that took place between the late 1990s and the mid-2000s, regional governments in recent years have begun to emphasize agricultural diversification. Pingali and Rosegrant (1995) describe agricultural diversification as a change in production choices coinciding with commercialization and overall development of the sector. In this definition of agricultural diversification, commercialization is intertwined with economic growth, and staple food self-sufficiency is at odds with this development (Pingali & Rosegrant, 1995). In Central Asia, agricultural diversification is often identified with an increased focus on horticulture, which can be grown under the climatic conditions of most countries in the region. Encouraging horticulture production has been an attractive policy option for national policymakers, who understand the sector's export and income-generating potential. Moreover, the concept of agriculture-nutrition linkages supports the idea that agricultural diversification offers clear pathways toward healthy diets.

Horticulture in Central Asia resembles livestock production in terms of the scale of participation of the private and household sector. Most horticulture is grown in the private sector with little support and direction from the government. Even in Turkmenistan, where state control of agricultural production is by far the most rigid, over 80% of both vegetables and fruits are grown by private farms (FAO Investment Center, 2013). While horticulture continues to grow, there is evidence that farms in the region are producing less than in comparable countries around the world. Many farmers do not have access to information on the latest production technologies, improved seeds and saplings, or modern irrigation and technical equipment to raise yields. Still, countries like Uzbekistan are major producers, even by global standards, for specific horticultural crops such as sweet cherries (FAO, 2019).

A shift from relatively low-value cotton and grain to higher-value horticulture has been observed throughout most of the region in recent years. In the Kyrgyz Republic, for instance, land allocated to horticulture increased from 8% of the total sown area in 1990 to 12% in 2002 and 16% in 2015 (National Statistics Committee, 2018). Land allocated to fruits and vegetables increased by 16% and 30%, respectively, between 2005 and 2011 in Tajikistan (Akramov & Shreedhar, 2012; Development Coordination Council, 2011). After 2010, the government of Uzbekistan began to prioritize horticulture and received loans from the World Bank and the Asian Development Bank to promote the sector's growth. The share of horticultural crops in the total land area reached 17% by 2016.

Most countries in the region benefit from favorable climatic conditions for growing agriculture, especially in the Fergana Valley area that lies among eastern Uzbekistan, Southern Kyrgyzstan, and northern Tajikistan. Natural endowments in Uzbekistan, for example, in terms of weather, water, and soil, are comparable to those found in major horticultural-producing countries such as Chile, Turkey, and the California region of the United States (Larson et al., 2015). In addition, the relatively mild climate in the southern regions of Central Asia allows for multiple vegetable growing seasons in irrigated areas.

A World Bank study in 2015 analyzed relative income outcomes among wheat, cotton, and selected horticultural crops in various regions of Uzbekistan. The results of that analysis validated the idea of horticulture as a productive and profitable sector in the country. While wheat and cotton producers were given extensive supports from the state, they were outperformed in terms of revenue and profit margins by horticultural producers (World Bank, 2015). Horticultural farmers, despite having to arrange their own credit, inputs, and sales, were given greater freedom to make crop decisions. On a per hectare basis, horticulture was also found to employ more workers than either wheat or cotton. Moreover, it was found to be relatively efficient in terms of water usage. In this respect, the growth of horticulture can play a key role in supporting the country's aspirations to modernize its agriculture (World Bank, 2015).

Moreover, these countries can take advantage of great and growing demand from Russia, which has been an important market for regional horticultural goods. Fruits and vegetables from Central Asia were also imported to other parts of the former Soviet Union and many consumers are familiar with horticultural products from the region. Trade between regional countries and Russia deteriorated during the 1990s as logistic and economic barriers were erected on major routes. Lucrative trade networks bringing Kyrgyz onions, Tajik dried fruits, and Uzbek produce to Russia collapsed at this time (Pomfret, 2016). Intraregional trade has also suffered from periodic border closures, such as Tajik vegetables losing access to markets in Uzbekistan.

In addition to logistic barriers, a lack of processing and inspection standards prevents regional produce from accessing certain markets in Russia. For example, while certain Uzbek horticultural exports are sold in higher-end Russian supermarket chains, many other producers are unable to access packaging, processing, refrigeration, and storage requirements to satisfy quality standards. Produce of this variety ended up in wholesale or outdoor markets in Russia and is sold for a lower price (Larson et al., 2015). Accessing more lucrative markets within Russia would require significant investment in horticultural value chains.

Figure 5.12 shows historical fruit production from 1992 to 2017. For countries such as Uzbekistan and Kazakhstan, the growth of fruit has expanded rapidly since the mid-2000s. In general, fruit production has increased steadily in all countries of Central Asia over this timeframe.

Similar patterns can be observed when looking at historical trends in vegetable production for the five countries, displayed in Figure 5.13. Uzbekistan has historically been the largest producer of vegetables in the region and has seen production grow steadily over a sustained period since the agricultural recovery in the late 1990s. Likewise, Kazakhstan is also a large producer of vegetables, with areas in the south of its country as the primary horticultural production zone. Vegetable production has seen gradual increases in most of the region with some variation.

Many countries in the region view horticulture as a potentially lucrative subsector that can become an important source of export earnings and a means to achieve food

Figure 5.12
Fruit Production in Tons, 1992–2017

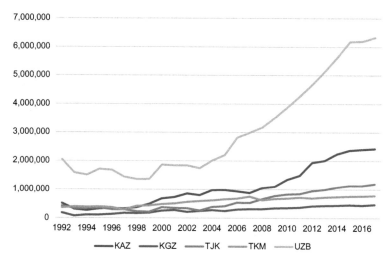

Source. FAO (2019).

Figure 5.13
Vegetable Production in Tons, 1992–2017

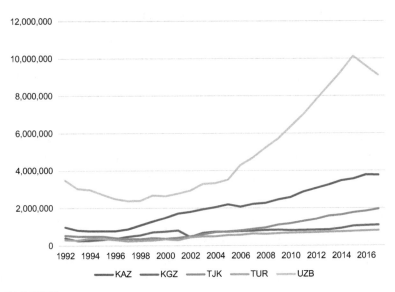

Source. FAO (2019).

and nutrition security. With funding and assistance from international organizations, horticulture has become an important pillar of national agricultural development strategies. Horticulture in the region has supported health policies for dietary diversity and is well-positioned in the current agricultural landscape dominated by smallholder farmers.

V. Trade and Regional Integration Between China and Central Asia

Agricultural trade in the Central Asia region for years had been impeded by poor physical and policy infrastructure to support trade. In its 2016 *Doing Business* survey, the World Bank found that Central Asia lags behind other world regions in terms of the speed and cost of trade. However, in recent years, governments have taken steps to improve regional integration, recognizing the importance of imports in supporting all aspects of the agricultural value chain. Internal and external factors have helped to facilitate trade flows. Some concepts, such as the Chinese BRI and the Russian-led EEU have driven demand for improvements to local infrastructure and trade policies. While long-distance trade originating from Central Asia consists mostly of energy or mineral products, regional trade is more diversified and includes agricultural products as an important component.

Central Asia has been characterized as among the world's least integrated global regions, ranking last among all regions of Asia in various aspects of economic integration (Huh & Park, 2017). Moreover, a 2012 World Bank study on supply chains and trade logistics placed Central Asian countries among the worst in the world with respect to logistics performance, posing a clear impediment to trade. However, the same study demonstrated that the region had improved over a five-year period (Rastogi & Arvis, 2014). Some observers believe that the rise of the EEU and BRI may stimulate regional governments to adopt broad improvements to trade and logistic policies.

1. Eurasian Economic Union

Originally composed of Belarus, Kazakhstan, and Russia, the EEU is a formal trade bloc that succeeded and replaced several minor trade agreements between former republics of the Soviet Union. The EEU formalized the creation of a unified customs and trade bloc, removing customs controls between borders and facilitating trade with non-member states by creating an integrated transit network (Rastogi & Arvis, 2014). Later, the Kyrgyz Republic joined the union in 2015, and other former Soviet republics have also considered joining.

One of the immediate benefits of joining the union is preferential access to the Russian labor market for a member state's citizens. Given the large labor migration that occurs between Central Asia and Russia, joining the EEU has a clear incentive in this respect. Moreover, Russia tightened visa and immigration requirements for foreign guest workers, the requirements for which were often prohibitive in terms of their time and financial costs for many migrants. Following the Russian economic crisis in 2014–2015, the pipeline of remittances between Russia and Central Asia dried up. However, among the three largest labor-sending countries in the region—Uzbekistan, Tajikistan, and the Kyrgyz Republic—the Kyrgyz Republic saw the quickest recovery largely because its citizens were able to take advantage of preferential labor laws, unlike non-EEU citizens. Figure 5.14 illustrates the general trends of labor migration to Russia over an eight-year period and displays the quick recovery in remittances for Kyrgyz citizens compared to those of their Tajik and Uzbek counterparts.

The Kyrgyz Republic's experience in joining the EEU may serve as an important guiding example for other countries that are considering their own bids. A joint study by the International Food Policy Research Institute and the University of Central Asia suggested that the Kyrgyz Republic's accession would provide mixed benefits, though lower-income households participating in labor migration strictly stood to gain provided that regional labor market integration occurred as designed (Mogilevskii et al., 2018). The study found adverse effects for certain sectors including the Kyrgyz

Figure 5.14

Total Remittances From Russia, First Three Quarters, 2010–2017

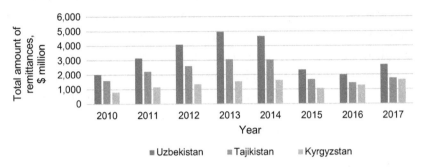

Source. Central Bank of Russian Federation (2018).

Republic's large re-export industry, which imported Chinese goods and re-sold them to other markets in the region.

Moreover, joining the EEU has placed pressure on Kyrgyz authorities to improve the country's regulatory mechanisms and other support structures to meet the rest of the bloc's standards. For example, other EEU countries demanded that the Kyrgyz Republic pass an audit of its food safety standards prior to its accession. Even after sanitary and phytosanitary controls were removed from its border with Kazakhstan after accession, veterinary controls remained to give Kyrgyz authorities a chance to finish implementing the remaining provisions (USDA, 2016). Russia and Kazakhstan have provided financial assistance to the Kyrgyz Republic to help increase its capacity to inspect agricultural goods, including improvements to inspections and laboratory facilities. The Kyrgyz Republic received permission from the bloc to phase out its existing tariff rates by 2020 for a number of selected agricultural products (USDA, 2016). These provisions are not unique to the Kyrgyz Republic, however, as Kazakhstan also received permission to charge different tariff rates for selected products in order to ensure its compliance with its respective responsibilities as a member of the World Trade Organization.

2. Belt and Road Initiative in Central Asia

Previously known as the One Belt One Road Initiative, the BRI in Central Asia provides a conceptual framework for a series of Chinese-led infrastructure and aid projects in the region. The BRI broadly seeks to improve trade connectivity across the Eurasian landmass, linking China with markets in Europe, the Middle East, Africa, and South Asia through heavy investment in infrastructure. Central Asia plays a key role in this concept as it borders both China and the various targeted markets. In turn, Central Asian leaders are seeking to connect their countries to lucrative global markets and improve their poor infrastructure in the process. Two of the proposed belts will cross Central Asian territory: the northern belt will cross Kazakhstan and Russia to Europe, and the central belt will go through several Central Asian countries to the Middle East. Already, major rail infrastructure has been completed to boost trade capacity between China, Kazakhstan, and the Kyrgyz Republic (Rastogi & Arvis, 2014). Moreover, China and Kazakhstan have created a special economic zone on their common border at Khorgos.

The introduction of BRI dovetails with an increasing Chinese economic presence in the Central Asia region. Total trade between China and Central Asia has already surpassed Central Asia's trade with Russia, the region's traditional trade partner. China has signed trade agreements with Kazakhstan, Uzbekistan, and other countries in the region that give access to Chinese markets for Central Asian food products. Chinese companies have also directed investment to the agricultural sector within Central Asia as well. For example, Chinese agribusinesses have invested in underdeveloped sectors of Tajikistan's agriculture, including running individual farms within the country (Hofman, 2016).

3. Regional Reconciliation and Trade

Whereas the first two decades of independence were marked by conflict and disagreements among the countries in Central Asia, regional governments have begun to take a more conciliatory approach in recent years. Namely, the diplomatic opening of Uzbekistan following the death of its preceding leader Islam Karimov has provided a key stimulus to a flourishing of ties that have accompanied greater trade. Uzbekistan is the only country that borders all four other Central Asian countries but has been engaged in a series of running disputes with all of its neighbors.

Among the key diplomatic flashpoints in the region was the issue over Tajikistan's proposed construction of the Rogun Dam. Tajikistan, having suffered from erratic electricity supplies throughout most of its independence, sought to harness its hydroelectric potential by constructing the massive Rogun Dam. Uzbekistan, fearing compromised water supplies for its farmers downstream, opposed the project for decades. The current Uzbek president Shavkat Mirziyoyev dropped his country's categorical opposition to Rogun, which was accompanied by a reopening of borders and trade traffic between the two countries. Uzbek exports to Tajikistan decreased by 39% between 2001 and 2010 (Ganiev & Yusupov, 2012), but the reversal of policies has led to an explosion of cross-border visits and bilateral trade. Tajikistan's exports to Uzbekistan in 2017 totaled US$57 million, over nine times the figure in 2015;

meanwhile, Uzbek exports to Tajikistan increased over tenfold from US$6 million in 2015 to US$69 million in 2017 (Statistical Agency under the President of the Republic of Tajikistan, 2017). Figure 5.15 displays the rapid increase in trade turnover between Tajikistan and Uzbekistan following a warming of ties starting in 2016.

Figure 5.15
Trade Turnover in Millions of US$, Tajikistan-Uzbekistan, 2013–2017

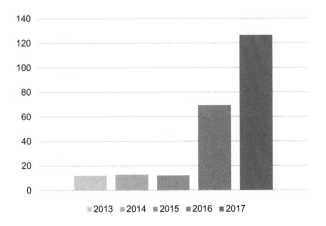

Source. Statistical Agency under the President of the Republic of Tajikistan (2017).

Trade among the Kyrgyz Republic, Kazakhstan, and Uzbekistan also saw increases between 2016 to 2017, although the increase is not as drastic as was the case with Tajikistan. Although Uzbekistan and the Kyrgyz Republic also experienced political friction because of disagreements over land delimitation and water resource sharing, trade during the mid-2010s proceeded steadily. The leaders of the Kyrgyz Republic and Uzbekistan arrived at an accord on a similar hydroelectric project and signed a landmark border demarcation treaty in 2017 that resolved a potential point of conflict. In the same year, representatives of Uzbekistan and Kazakhstan met numerous times after the change in the presidential administration of Uzbekistan, signing agreements for cooperation in a wide range of areas. The leaders of the two countries targeted the total trade turnover of US$5 billion by 2020. Figure 5.16 shows short-term trends in trade turnover between Uzbekistan and its two neighbors, the Kyrgyz Republic, and Kazakhstan. Trade turnover between Uzbekistan and the Kyrgyz Republic totaled US$310 million in 2017; the same figure for Uzbekistan and Kazakhstan in the same year was US$2 billion.

Regional agricultural producers would directly benefit from the improvement of connectivity within the region. Trade among countries in the region is more diversified because the shorter distance to their suppliers makes value-added activities more

Figure 5.16

Trade Turnover With Uzbekistan in Millions of US$, 2015–2017

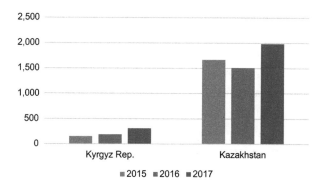

Source. National Statistics Committee (2018); Statistical Committee under the Ministry of Economy of the Republic of Kazakhstan (2018).

Figure 5.17

Food and Agriculture Exports as Percentage of Total Exports, 2017

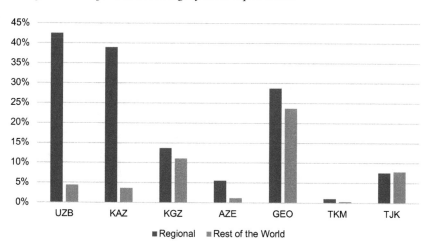

Source. Simoes and Hidalgo (2011).

Note. Figures for UZB, TKM, and TJK do not include bilateral trade between the three countries.

viable (Rastogi & Arvis, 2014). Most countries in the region count China, Russia, and European countries as their main trading partners. However, economic activities and the potential for diversification of those trade routes is constrained by location and the region's low population density (Rastogi & Arvis, 2014).

Figure 5.17 provides a comparison of food and agriculture exports to the region (comprised of the five Central Asia countries, along with Azerbaijan and Georgia) and to the rest of the world. The figure does not include bilateral trade between Tajikistan,

Turkmenistan, and Uzbekistan due to a lack of data. For countries such as Kazakhstan and Uzbekistan, a clear difference is evident in terms of agricultural production sent to the other countries of the region and the rest of the world. These countries are also resource-rich and export a variety of energy products or minerals to markets further abroad. Turkmenistan also falls under this category, but its agricultural exports to other countries in the region were also low, although the lack of data for bilateral trade with Uzbekistan may overstate this tendency. The disparity of agricultural trade within the region and with the rest of the world is narrower for Kyrgyz Republic and Tajikistan. Agricultural and food exports from these countries are often destined for Russia, which is an important market for regional exporters.

Agricultural and food trade between the two Caucasus countries (Azerbaijan and Georgia) and Central Asia is generally low. Kazakhstan imports over two-thirds of all agricultural goods to Central Asia from Azerbaijan and Georgia, totaling over US$44 million in 2017. Turkmenistan is the second-largest Central Asian importer of agriculture from the two countries at US$9 million worth of goods (Simoes & Hidalgo, 2011). These two countries possess seaports on the Caspian Sea, suggesting that the relative lack of trade with the rest of the region is due to transportation and logistics constraints.

VI. Natural Resource Constraints

The quality of land suitable for agricultural production varies widely throughout the Central Asia region. The region contains a great diversity in terms of topography and climate, ranging from arid deserts to mid-latitude steppes and to high mountainous areas. In general, the annual average precipitation is low in lower-lying areas and high in mountain ranges, making agriculture reliant on irrigated land. Apart from Kazakhstan, many of the countries contain limited land resources for agriculture, either because of constrained land area or unfavorable growing conditions. Policymakers and planners, therefore, seek to increase cultivated areas in flat areas and ensure that populations in remote mountainous regions have access to food markets (Akramov & Shreedhar, 2012).

1. Land Resources

Countries in the region are host to many different climate zones, including large areas that are ill-suited for intensive agriculture, such as deserts and mountains. Moreover, soil degradation due to manmade factors, such as from agriculture and industry, is an issue that affects all countries to varying degrees. The proportion of arable land to the

Figure 5.18

Arable Land, Percentage of Total Area, 1992–2016

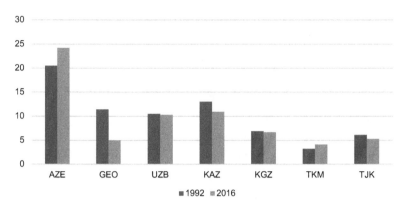

Source. World Bank (2019).

Figure 5.19

Average Arable Land per Person, in Hectares, 1992–2016

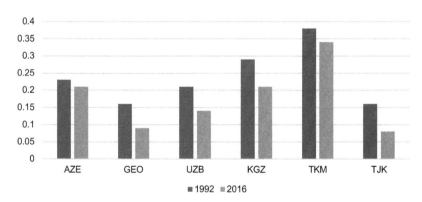

Source. World Bank (2019).

total land area is low in Central Asia, which is pictured in Figure 5.18 Smaller countries of Central Asia and the Caucasus—Azerbaijan, Georgia, the Kyrgyz Republic, and Tajikistan—feature mountainous land, which limits arable land area and increases erosion risk. Arable land as a percentage of the total land in Georgia has sharply decreased between 1992 and 2016, going from 11.4% to 5.0%.

With the exception of Kazakhstan, arable farmland is in short supply throughout the region, measured by the average arable land size per person shown in Figure 5.19. Kazakhstan has been excluded from the figure to highlight the small land sizes of other countries in the region. However, in Kazakhstan, the average arable land area per person has decreased from 2.13 hectares in 1992 to 1.65 hectares in 2016.

2. Climate Change

There is growing evidence on climate change and its ramifications in Central Asia. Climate change poses a risk to the region's agriculture, which accounts for a large share of the population's economic activity. The projected impact of climate change varies by crop and location, adding another layer of uncertainty to the sector. Climate change may have unprecedented effects on the region's water resources (White et al., 2014), agricultural productivity (Sommer et al., 2013), farm incomes (Bobojonov & Aw-Hassan, 2014), economic development, and poverty.

It is generally accepted that climate change could affect the region through increased temperatures, decreased precipitation, changing precipitation patterns over farming areas, and potential political instability. This belief is reflected in a series of studies on Central Asia by the World Bank, as well as Tajikistan's own message to the United Nations Framework Convention on Climate Change. Nevertheless, there is uncertainty about the exact impacts of climate change in Central Asia and the Caucasus, partly due to insufficient data. Some of this uncertainty also stems from the mixed impacts of climate change: whereas overall the region may experience a degradation of growing conditions, there may also be areas that may become more suitable for certain types of agriculture. Short-term and long-term effects may also differ: a joint ADB and IFPRI study in 2009 found that glaciers in Central Asia are already melting at an increased pace because of climate change, which it projected would increase water flows for irrigation (ADB, 2009). In the long term, however, the study's authors projected negative impacts, especially during dry seasons. Furthermore, the study suggested that it was difficult to predict future trends in extreme weather events and anomalies, including the prevalence of pestilence and diseases. Shortcomings in understanding the nature and extent of climate change limit the ability of policymakers to design adaptation and mitigation measures.

In Kazakhstan, climate change is projected to produce a faster increase in mean temperatures of around 4.6 degrees Celsius by 2085. Higher temperatures are projected to accelerate glacier melt, increasing water availability in the medium-term but causing shortages in the longer term (Murisic et al., 2013). In the Kyrgyz Republic, average daily temperatures are expected to increase between 4 and 5 degrees Celsius by 2011. Precipitation there is also expected to decrease in future summers. In the short term, faster-melting glaciers are expected to increase surface water flow by 2025, also increasing the risk of periodic flooding. Like Kazakhstan, the Kyrgyz Republic is also expecting to suffer from longer-term water scarcity (Shah et al., 2013). The projected impact of climate change on crop productivity will vary, for instance, wheat, maize, and sugar beet productivity are expected to fall, while the productivity of tobacco, rice, cotton, and some horticultural crops is expected to increase. Climate change is also projected to have a positive impact on pasture productivity in most regions, subject to stocking rates (Broka et al., 2016).

Around 93% of Tajikistan's territory is covered by mountainous terrain, which is also home to glacial water reserves vital for downstream countries on the Amu Darya River. Temperatures in Tajikistan are expected to increase by around two degrees Celsius by 2030. Precipitation is also expected to become more erratic and intense. One of the principal dangers of climate change for the Central Asian region is the possibility that these glaciers may disappear, which some observers have projected may occur in 30 to 40 years (Shah, 2013). Like other Central Asian countries, Uzbekistan is also expected to witness an increase in temperature of 2 to 3 degrees by the 2050s, along with added volatility in precipitation patterns. These changes are expected to be detrimental to crop and livestock productivity, particularly in the form of damage to harvests caused by extreme weather events that are more likely under this scenario (Sutton et al., 2013).

3. Natural Risks

Natural disasters leading to agricultural crises are projected to increase in the region. Mirroring the region's wide topographic and climatic diversity, Central Asia is also prone to a variety of natural disasters, including earthquakes, floods, avalanches, mudflows, landslides, extreme weather events, wildfires, and epidemics. Seismic threats have been realized throughout much of the region's modern history, and they pose threats to agriculture in addition to public safety.

While many major agricultural zones in Central Asia are heavily irrigated, droughts pose significant risks for areas depending on rainfed agriculture such as northern Kazakhstan, where around four-fifths of the country's grain and oilseed crops are produced. The region's mountainous areas suffer from a myriad of terrain-related disasters and weather risks. For example, floods occur mostly in the southern and eastern parts of Kazakhstan due to heavy rainfall and snowmelt from the area's mountains (Broka et al., 2016). Many of the Kyrgyz Republic and Tajikistan's rural populations reside in areas near mountainous landscapes, making them vulnerable to recurring natural disasters. Natural disasters cause approximately US$30 million in damage annually in the Kyrgyz Republic, though the government's budget allocation for disaster response is many times less (World Bank, 2014).

VII. Conclusion

Agricultural development in Central Asia has largely consisted of managing the transition from the legacy socialist system to a market-oriented one. Although it is constrained by inefficient land organization and limited water resources, efforts need to be made to fully improve agricultural development. Smallholder farming is an important engine of agricultural production and a crucial employer of the large rural population within the Central Asia region. Within this system, a primary and immediate need is to set in place systems that allow farmers access to modern technology, inputs, and knowledge. These are crucial elements that will encourage gains in productivity, especially since per capita arable land resources are limited in most of the region. One negative outcome of post-Soviet land reforms is the over-fragmentation of agricultural land, which has become a serious obstacle to agricultural growth and productivity through its tendency to discourage long-term investment and adoption of mechanization. Hence, providing agricultural support services to small farmers that larger enterprises already have access to may bridge existing gaps in productivity. Besides, due to the unique landscape of the transboundary river basins, five of the Central Asian countries are bounded together by their shared challenges of water resources. These countries must share the limited water resources fairly (see the next chapter for detail), while balancing the needs of upstream hydroelectricity generation and downstream agriculture. In this case, investing in public infrastructure must also focus on improving governance and the institutions that manage irrigation resources, road networks, and border points. The public sector will play a crucial role in attracting investment and generating funds for infrastructure projects and should work in tandem with stakeholders to maximize their benefits. Regional governments could also facilitate cross-border exchange of expertise in developing infrastructure. For instance, China's track record in developing irrigation systems and water saving technologies in its arid western and northern regions can be highly useful for the countries of Central Asia.

Based on the largely developing agriculture, as many of the Central Asian countries' livelihood is dependent on the agricultural sector, the fostering of agricultural cooperation with large importing countries such as China and Russia is hence important. China's introduction of the "BRI could play an important role in stimulating economic development through regional economic cooperation. In particular, both the China-Pakistan Economic Corridor and the China-Central Asia-West Asia Economic Corridor are made to benefit the trade and cooperation between China and Central Asia. Aside from the BRI, regional multilateral cooperation initiatives, such as the CAREC program, could also contribute to a deepened global agricultural integration by the Central Asia region. CAREC has helped establish multimodal transportation networks, increased energy trade and security, facilitated the free movement of people and freight, and laid the groundwork for economic corridor development since its inception in 2001. In 2017, ministers of the program endorsed a new strategic framework of CAREC 2030: Connecting the Region for Shared and Sustainable Development (CAREC 2030), providing a new long-term strategic framework for the program leading to 2030.

References

Abassian, A. (2005). *Tajikistan: Market profile for emergency food security assessments.* World Food Program.

ADB. (2009). *Building climate resilience in the agriculture sector of Asia and the Pacific.* ADB.

Akramov, K., & N. Omuraliev. (2009). *Institutional change, rural services, and agricultural performance in Kyrgyzstan* (Discussion Paper No. 00904). IFPRI. https://www.ifpri.org/publication/institutional-change-rural-services-and-agricultural-performance-kyrgyzstan

Akramov, K., & G. Shreedhar. (2012). *Economic development, external shocks, and food security in Tajikistan* (Discussion Paper No. 1163). IFPRI. https://www.ifpri.org/publication/economic-development-external-shocks-and-food-security-tajikistan

Bobojonov, I., & A. Aw-Hassan. (2014). Impacts of climate change on farm income security in Central Asia: An integrated modeling approach. *Agriculture, Ecosystems and Environment, 188,* 245–255.

Broka, S., A. Giertz, G. Christensen, C. Hanif, & D., Rubaiza, R. Rasmussen. (2016). *Kyrgyz Republic: Agricultural sector risk assessment.* World Bank Group.

Central Bank of Russian Federation. (2018). *Statistical tables.* Central Bank of Russian Federation.

Crewett, W. (2012). Improving the sustainability of pasture use in Kyrgyzstan. *Mountain Research and Development, 32*(3), 267–274.

Development Coordination Council. (2011). *International conference on Agrarian Reform.* Government of the Republic of Tajikistan and Development Coordination Council.

Dzunusova, M. (2008). *Country report on the state of plant genetic resources for food and agriculture in Kyrgyzstan.* Kyrgyz Republic.

FAO. (2007). *Subregional report on animal genetic resources: Central Asia.* FAO.

FAO. (2019). *FAOSTAT.* https://www.fao.org/faostat/en/#home

FAO Investment Center. (2013). *Turkmenistan: Agricultural sector review* (Country Highlights Report No. 7). FAO Investment Center. https://www.fao.org/fileadmin/user_upload/tci/docs/Turkmenistan.pdf

Fileccia, T., A. Jumabayeva, & K. Nazhmidenov. (2010). *Highlights on four livestock sub-sectors in Kazakhstan.* FAO Investment Center.

Ganiev, B., & Y. Yusupov. 2012. *Uzbekistan: Trade regime and recent trade developments* (Working paper No. 4). University of Central Asia.

Government of Kazakhstan. (2013). *Agribusiness—2020: Program for the development of the agro-industrial complex in the Republic of Kazakhstan for 2012–2020* (Resolution No. 151). Government of Kazakhstan.

Government of Kazakhstan. (2014). *Program for the development of the regions 2020* (Resolution No. 728). Governemnt of Kazakhstan.

Government of Kazakhstan. (2017). *State program for the development of the agro-industrial complex of the Republic of Kazakhstan for 2017–2021* (Resolution No. 420). Government of Kazakhstan.

Government of Kyrgyz Republic. (2015). *National food security and nutrition program for 2015–2017* (Government Decree No. 618). Government of Kyrgyz Republic.

Government of Kyrgyz Republic. (2018). *Unity, trust and creation: The development program of the Kyrgyz Republic for the period 2018–2022* (Decree of Jogoru Kenesh of the Kyrgyz Republic No. 2377–VI). Government of Kyrgyz Republic.

Government of Tajikistan. (2010). *On food security* (Law No. 671). Government of Tajikistan.

Government of Tajikistan. (2012). *Program for reforming the agricultural sector for the period of 2012–2020* (Resolution No. 383). Government of Tajikistan.

Government of Tajikistan. (2016). *National development strategy of the Republic of Tajikistan for 2030* (Resolution No. 392). Government of Tajikistan.

Government of Turkmenistan. (2017). *Program of the President of Turkmenistan on socio-economic development of the country in 2018–2024* (Presidential Resolution No. 14530). Government of Turkmenistan.

Government of Uzbekistan. (2017). *Strategy of actions on further development of Uzbekistan for 2017–2021* (Presidential Decree No. 4947). Government of Uzbekistan.

Hayami, Y., & Ruttan, V. W. (1971). *Induced innovation in agricultural development* (Discussion Paper No. 3). https://conservancy.umn.edu/bitstream/handle/11299/54243/1/1971-03.pdf

Hofman, I. (2016). Politics or profits along the "Silk Road": What drives Chinese farms in Tajikistan and helps them thrive? *Eurasian Geography and Economics, 57*(3), 457–481.

Huh, H., & C. Park. (2017). *Asia-Pacific integration index* (Economics Working Paper No. 511). Asian Development Bank.

IFAD. (2015). *Dairy value chains development program: Design completion report* (Report No. 3762–UZ). International Fund for Agricultural Development.

Ilyasov, J., L. Gotz, K. Akramov, & P. Dorosh. (2016). *Market integration and price transmission in Tajikistan's wheat markets: Rising like rockets but falling like feathers?* (IFPRI Discussion Paper No. 1547). International Food Policy Research Institute.

Larson, D., D. Khidirov, & I. Ramniceanu. (2015). *Uzbekistan: Strengthening the horticulture value chain.* World Bank. https://www.academia.edu/48887616/Uzbekistan_Strengthening_

the_horticulture_value_chain

Lerman, Z. (2008). Tajikistan: An overview of land and farm structure reforms.

Sedik, D. (2009). *The feed-livestock mexus in Tajikistan: Livestock development policy in transition* (Policy Studies on Rural Transition No. 2009–2). FAO Regional Office for Europe and Central Asia.

Lerman, Z., Csaki, C., & Feder, G. (2004). *Agriculture in Transition: Land policies and evolving farm structures in post-Soviet countries.* Lexington books.

Lerman, Z., & D. Sedik. (2009). *Agricultural recovery and individual land tenure in Central Asia* (Policy Studies on Rural Transition No. 2009–3). FAO Regional Office for Europe and Central Asia.

Lerman, Z., Sedik, D., Yusupov, Y., Stanchin, I., & Kazakevich, I. (2016). *Wheat production and regional food security in CIS: The case of Belarus, Turkmenistan and Uzbekistan* (Policy Studies on Rural Transition No. 1). FAO Regional Office for Europe and Central Asia.

Ministry of Agriculture of the Republic of Kazakhstan. (2013). *Planted acreage of forage cultures of Kazakhstan to be expanded.* Strategy 2050. https://strategy2050.kz/en/news/343

Mogilevskii, R., Thurlow, J., & Yeh A. (2018). Kyrgyzstan's accession to the Eurasian Economic Union: Measuring economy-wide impacts and uncertainties (working Paper No. 44). Institute of Public Policy and Administration, *University of Central Asia Graduate School of Development.*

Murisic, M., T. Levine, N. Rinnerberger, J. Shah, & J. Srivastava. (2013). *Kazakhstan—Oveview of climate change activities* (Report No. 85559). World Bank.

Musaev, D., Y. Yakhshilikov, & K. Yusupov. (2010). *Food security in Uzbekistan.* UNDP Uzbekistan.

National Statistics Committee. (2018). *Statistical dynamic tables on agriculture.* http://stat.kg/en/statistics/selskoe-hozyajstvo/

Nazarbaev, N. (2012). The message of the President to the People of Kazakhstan "Strategy 'Kazakhstan–2050': New political course of the state." *Kazakhstanskaya Pravda, 15.*

Pena, R., E. Meng, A. Abugalieva, A. Massalimov, & A. Morgounov. (2002). *Milling, baking, and grain factors influencing the quality of tandyr bread (nan) in Central Asia.* CIMMYT.

Petrick, M., D. Oshakbaev, & J. Wandel. (2014). *Kazakhstan's wheat, beef and dairy sectors: An assessment of their development constraints and recent policy responses* (Discussion Paper No. 145). Institute of Agricultural Development in Transition Economies.

Pingali, P., & M. Rosegrant. (1995). Agricultural commercialization and diversification: Processes and policies. *Food Policy, 20*(3), 171–185.

Pomfret, R. (2016). Modernizing agriculture in Central Asia. *Global Journal of Emerging Market Economies, 8*(2), 104–125.

Rastogi, C., & J. Arvis. (2014). *The Eurasian connection: Supply-Chain efficiency along the modern Silk Route through Central Asia.* World Bank.

Rozelle, S., & J. Swinnen. (2004). Success and failure of reform: Insights from the transition of agriculture. *Journal of Economic Literature, 42*(2), 404–456.

Sedik, D. (2009). *The feed-livestock nexus in Tajikistan: Livestock development policy in transition* (Policy Studies on Rural Transition No. 2009–2). FAO Regional Office for Europe and Central Asia.

Shah, J., T. Levine, J. Srivastava, M. Murisic, & N. Rinnerberger. (2013). *Kyrgyz Republic—Overview of climate change activities* (Report No. 85561). World Bank.

Shah, J. (2013). *Tajikistan—Overview of climate change activities* (Report No. 85563). World Bank Group.

Simoes, A., & C. Hidalgo. (2011, January). *The economic complexity observatory: An analytical tool for understanding the dynamics of economic development.* [Conference presentation]. Scalable Integration of Analytics and Visualization, San Francisco, California, USA. https://www.researchgate.net/profile/Cesar-Hidalgo-2/publication/221605462_The_Economic_Complexity_Observatory_An_Analytical_Tool_for_Understanding_the_Dynamics_of_Economic_Development/links/54f472430cf24eb8794e8a6d/The-Economic-Complexity-Observatory-An-Analytical-Tool-for-Understanding-the-Dynamics-of-Economic-Development.pdf

Sommer, R., M. Glazirina, T. Yuldashev, A. Otarov, & M. Ibraeva. (2013). Impact of climate change on wheat productivity in Central Asia. *Agriculture, Ecosystems and Environment, 178*, 78–99.

Statistical Agency under the President of the Republic of Tajikistan. (2017). *Regions of Tajikistan.* https://www.stat.tj/en

Statistical Committee under the Ministry of Economy of the Republic of Kazakhstan. (2018). *Statistical bulletin on sown area of crops in the Republic of Kazakhstan.* https://stat.gov.kz/

State Committee of the Republic of Uzbekistan on Statistics. (2019). *Official statistics/statistical tables.* https://stat.uz/en/

Suleimenov, M., & P. Oram. (2000). Trends in feed, livestock production, and rangelands during the transition period in three Central Asian countries. *Food Policy, 25*(6), 681–700.

Sutton, W., J. Srivastava, J. Neumann, P. Droogers, & B. Boehlert. (2013). *Reducing the vulnerability of Uzbekistan's agricultural systems to climate change: Impact assessment and adaptation options.* World Bank.

Svanidze, M., L. Gotz, I. Djuric, J. Ilyasov, and T. Glauben. (2016, September 28–30). *Spatial integration of wheat markets in the regions of South Caucasus and Central Asia: Evidence from Armenia, Azerbaijan, Georgia, and Kyrgyzstan* [Conference presentation]. 56th Annual Conference, Bonn, Germany. https://ageconsearch.umn.edu/record/244889/

Swinnen, J., K. Van Herck, & A. Sneyers. (2011). *The Kyrgyz Republic: Opportunities and challenges to agricultural growth.* FAO Investment Center.

Timmer, P. (2015). *Managing structural transformation: A political economy approach.* WIDER Annual Lecture 18.

United Nations.(2019) *Comtrade.* https://comtrade.un.org/data/

UNDP Uzbekistan. (2010). *Livestock production in Uzbekistan: Current state, challenges and prospects. Review in The Context of Agricultural Sector Development Trends.*

USAID. (2005). *Land tenure and property rights assessment for Kyrgyzstan. https://www.land-links.org/ wp-content/uploads/2016/09/USAID_Land_Tenure_LTPR_Assessment_for_Kyrgyzstan.pdf*

USAID. (2011). *USAID country profile Kyrgyzstan.* https://www.usaid.gov/kyrgyz-republic

USAID. (2013). *Kyrgyz Republic: An assessment of the agricultural sector.* https://www.usaid.gov/ kyrgyz-republic

USAID. (2013). Kyrgyz Republic: An assessment of the agricultural sector. Unpublished report. United States Agency for International Development.

USDA. (2016). *Eurasian Economic Union: One year on* (Report No. RS1611). Department of Agriculture.   https://apps.fas.usda.gov/newgainapi/api/Report/DownloadReportByFile Name?fileName=Eurasian%20Economic%20Union%20One%20Year%20On_Moscow_ Russian%20Federation_3-11-2016

USDA. (2018). *Livestock and poultry: World markets and trade.* United States Department of Agriculture Foreign Agriculture Service. https://www.fas.usda.gov/data/livestock-and-poultry-world-markets-and-trade

Van Engelen, A. (2011). *Dairy development in Kazakhstan.* FAO. https://www.fao.org/3/al751e/ al751e00.pdf

White, C., T. Tanton, & D. Rycroft. (2014). The impact of climate change on the water resources of the Amu Darya Basin in Central Asia. *Water Resources Management, 28* (15), 5267–5281.

World Bank. (2007). *Kyrgyz Republic livestock sector review: Embracing the new challenges* (Report No. 39026). https://openknowledge.worldbank.org/entities/publication/599385aa-15f5-58be-8078-c52785420573

World Bank. (2014). *Kyrgyz Republic partnership program snapshot.* https://documents.worldbank. org/en/publication/documents-reports/documentdetail/577891486989905356/world-bank-kyrgyz-republic-partnership-program-snapshot

World Bank. (2015). *Project paper on a proposed additional loan in the amount of US$500 Million to the Republic of Uzbekistan for a horticulture development project* (Report No. PAD2583).

CHAPTER 6

Water Resource Management in Central Asia

Kamiljon Akramov, Kevin Chen, Allen Park, Jarilkasin Ilyasov,
and Sarvarbek Eltazarov

I. Introduction

Water is essential to sustaining people's livelihoods and health of ecosystems and to maintaining socio-economic development. Agricultural water use accounts for an estimated 70% of total water withdrawals globally, and in some countries, it is responsible for more than 90% of total withdrawals (Scheierling & Treguer, 2018). Agricultural growth, particularly based on irrigation, in this context presents a clear dilemma for policymakers who must also contend with the looming threat of water scarcity. Central Asia is home to about 73 million people spread across Kazakhstan, the Kyrgyz Republic, Tajikistan, Turkmenistan, and Uzbekistan. With the landlocked geographical landscape, the five countries share common landlocked water resources through the cross-border water basin. This special condition of a shared water resource created disputes on water use management within the region. Particularly, the downstream countries (Kazakhstan, Turkmenistan, and Uzbekistan) need water to supply their irrigated agriculture, while upstream countries (Kyrgyz Republic and Tajikistan) seek to harness their hydroelectric potential through the construction of dams. These countries are thus amid a situation in which their growing populations and economies demand greater use of limited water resources, placing them at risk for conflict. In addition, since the reform in land and farm organization from agricultural specialization under the Soviet system, it is noteworthy that Central Asian countries are facing challenges from shared and limited water resources, undoubtedly increasing pressure on agricultural and economic development. Governments in this region are trying to resolve these challenges. In this chapter, we will review water resources management in five Central Asia countries: Kazakhstan, the Kyrgyz Republic, Tajikistan, Turkmenistan, and Uzbekistan. We will provide an overview on the geographical landscape and water resources, a review on the policies and legislative frameworks abiding the region, and the challenges for water management within the region. We will then conclude with a series of suggestions for future cooperation in water management among the five Central Asia countries.

II. Geographical Conditions for Water in Central Asia

The five main river basins in Central Asia include the Amu Darya, Syr Darya, Balkhash-Alakol, Ob-Irtysh, and Ural (Figure 6.1) river basins. Lake Balkhash is fed by the Balkhash-Alakol basin. The waters of the Ob-Irtysh basin ultimately flow into the Arctic Ocean, whereas those of Ural basin ends in the Caspian Sea. The Amu Darya and Syr Darya rivers previously fed the now largely desiccated Aral Sea.

Figure 6.1
Major River Basins in Central Asia

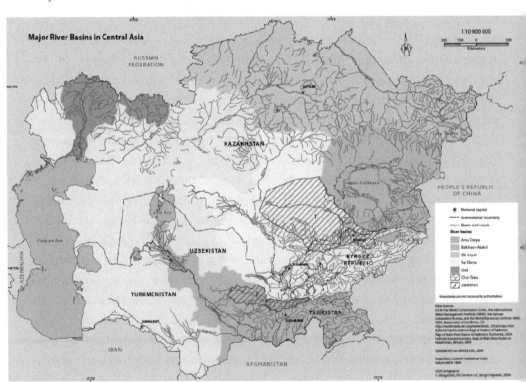

Source. ADB (2010).

The Amu Darya and Syr Darya are the two largest rivers and the main sources of water in Central Asia. When combined, the Amu Darya and Syr Darya rivers contain around 77 m³ of water and 96% of the volume is used for irrigation (Izquierdo et al., 2010). Home to nearly 80% of Central Asia's population, the Amu Darya and Syr Darya river basins provide around 90% of the region's river water and cover about 37% of the land area of Central Asian countries, including most of the Kyrgyz Republic, Tajikistan and Uzbekistan, as well as large parts of Turkmenistan and Kazakhstan (Russell, 2018).

The Amu Darya River is 1,415 km long and possesses the largest capacity in Central Asia. The river originates at the confluence of the Panj and Vakhsh rivers in Tajikistan and flows through Afghanistan, Uzbekistan, and Turkmenistan. Tajikistan contributes 80% of the flow in the Amu Darya River basin, followed by Afghanistan (8%), Uzbekistan (6%), the Kyrgyz Republic (3%), and Turkmenistan and Iran together contribute around 3% (Micklin, 2000). Although it carries less water by volume than the Amu Darya, the Syr Darya is the longest river in the region with a length of 2,212 km. It originates in the Tien Shan mountains and flows through the Kyrgyz Republic, Uzbekistan, Tajikistan, and Kazakhstan before flowing into the Aral Sea. The Kyrgyz Republic contributes 74% of the flow generated in the Syr Darya river basin, followed by Kazakhstan (12%), Uzbekistan (11%) and Tajikistan (3%). Both river basins are served by an extended network of dams, reservoirs and irrigation canals, making up one of the most complex water systems in the world (Allouche, 2007).

Central Asia is landlocked within Eurasia and most of the region contains an arid or semiarid climate. Large daily and seasonal temperature differences, with high solar radiation and relatively low humidity, characterize the area (Bekchanov et al., 2013). There are diversified microclimates due to variances in types of terrain and altitude ranges. Although this region is often subject to humid winds, mountains capture most of the moisture, and little rain falls in the Aral Sea basin. Average annual precipitation is an estimated 273 mm, ranging from 161 mm in Turkmenistan to 691 mm in Tajikistan (Central Asia Water Info, 2011; Frenken, 2013).

The water system in Central Asia is managed by large number of dams, reservoirs, and canals, some of which were constructed during the Soviet period. There are over 1,200 dams across Central Asian countries, and 110 of them are classified as large dams with a height of over 15 m. Many of them have inter-state significance because many of them are located on transboundary rivers like Amu Darya and Syr Darya (UNECE, 2013). The total capacity of dams in Central Asian countries is 176.8 km³. Kazakhstan accounts for 95.5 km³ (54% of the region's total dam capacity), Tajikistan for 29.5 km³ (17%), the Kyrgyz Republic for 23.5 km³ (13%), Uzbekistan for 22.2 km³ (13%), and Turkmenistan for only 6.2 km³ (3%) (Frenken, 2013). Fifteen dams each have a capacity greater than 1 km³, of which six are in Uzbekistan, four in Kazakhstan, two in Turkmenistan, two in Tajikistan, and one in the Kyrgyz Republic. Most of these are multipurpose dams for hydropower production, irrigation, water supply, and flood control. In total, these fifteen large dams account for 130.6 km³, or about 74% of the region's total dam capacity (Frenken, 2013). Bukhtarma dam in Kazakhstan, completed in 1960, has the largest capacity (50 km³). The Toktogul dam in the Kyrgyz Republic, the Kapshagay dam in Kazakhstan and the Nurek dam in Tajikistan follow with capacities of 20 km³, 19 km³ and 11 km³ respectively. The largest dams in Uzbekistan and Turkmenistan are the Tuaymuyun dam (8 km³) and the Zeid dam (2 km³), respectively (Frenken, 2013).

There have been a few studies which have focused on how climate change may impact the availability of water resources and water stress dynamics in Central Asia (Groll et al., 2015; Ibatullin et al., 2009; Immerzeel et al., 2012; Lutz et al., 2012; Nechifor & Winning, 2019). Although there are significant variations in the projections and estimates, all of these studies agree that climate change will affect the four components (rainfall-runoff, snow melt, glacier melt, base flow) that make upstream flow and thus have a negative impact on the availability of water resources in the next several decades. Groll et al. (2015) forecast that available water resources in the region will decline by around 30% due to climate change by 2030 based on analysis of field measurements and meteorological and hydrological data. Ibatullin et al. (2009) employ the water balance equation using air temperature and precipitation data from global and regional climate models, and they forecast that water resources in the Amu Darya basin could decrease by 5% to 8% by 2030 and those in the Syr Darya basin could decrease by 2% to 5% by 2050. Using a spatially distributed glacio-hydrological model based on local and public domain datasets and hydro-meteorological observations, Immerzeel et al. (2012) project that average decreases in water availability for downstream users will be in the ranges of 13% to 17% for 2021–2030 and 22% to 28% for 2041–2050 in the Syr Darya basin and 11% to 15% for 2021–2030 and 26% to 35% for 2041–2050 in the Amu Darya basin.

III. Water Use in Central Asia

Data on water use refers to gross quantity of water withdrawn by different sectors annually for given proposes (FAO, 2018). In Central Asia, there are three main sectors which consume large amounts of water: agriculture, municipalities, and industry. The agriculture sector includes irrigation, aquaculture, and livestock cleaning and watering. The municipalities sector includes water use in houses, villages, towns and cities by the population for domestic proposes. The industry category includes water use for various industrial purposes such as cooling of thermoelectric plants and drying in the leather industry. For most countries, data on water use are obtained from national statistics although there is much uncertainty about the methods used for obtaining data (Frenken, 2013).

Central Asian countries are major producers of water-intensive crops such as cotton and wheat, relying on irrigation due to low annual rainfall (Russell, 2018). Between them, the five countries have a total irrigated area of about 100,000 km², requiring huge amounts of river water and making agriculture by far the biggest water user in Central Asia (Russell, 2018). In all countries, except Kazakhstan, agricultural water use comprises more than 90% of overall use as seen in Figure 6.2 (Frenken, 2013; FAO, 2018). Due to urbanization and industrialization, Kazakhstan's agricultural sector accounts for less than 70% of the country's total water use, with industrial sector making up about 30% of total water use.

Figure 6.2
Water Use by Sector, Percentage of Total Use, Central Asia

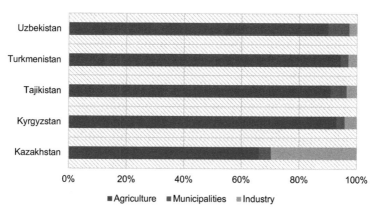

Source. FAO (2018).

Total annual water use for Central Asia is almost 125 km³ (Figure 6.3). Uzbekistan, with 56 km³, has the highest water use, accounting for about 45% of the total in keeping with its large irrigated area. This is around two to four times the irrigated area found in other countries (Frenken, 2013). Turkmenistan accounts for about 22.5% (nearly 28 km³) of the total regional water use. Kazakhstan accounts for another 17% of the total water use in the region with over 21 km³ of water used annually. Tajikistan and the Kyrgyz Republic have the lowest use in the region with 11.5 km³ (9%) and 8 km³ (6.5%), respectively.

Per capita water use in Central Asia is much higher than in other parts of the world. Water use per inhabitant is 2,138 m³/year, but this average does not reflect the

Figure 6.3

Total Water Use, Million m³/Year, Central Asia

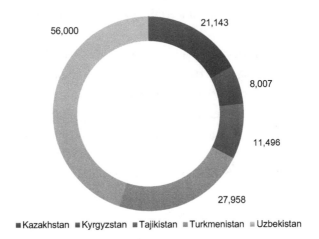

Source. FAO (2018).

Figure 6.4

Total Annual Water Usage per Capita, Central Asia

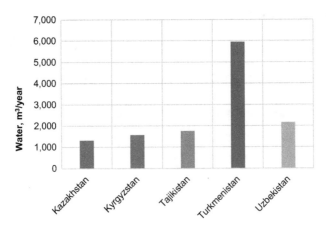

Source. FAO (2018).

wide differences between countries (Frenken, 2013). The figure ranges from 1,319 m³/inhabitant and 1,575 m³/inhabitant in Kazakhstan and the Kyrgyz Republic respectively to 2,158 m³/inhabitant in Uzbekistan and 5,952 m³/inhabitant in Turkmenistan seen in Figure 6.4.

A combination of heavy water use, particularly in agriculture, and limited water resources has put water resources in Central Asia under considerable pressure. Water stress can be measured by total freshwater withdrawal (water use) as a percentage of total renewable water resources. According to the European Environment Agency, a figure of 20% or over indicates water stress (Russell, 2018). By this measure, four of the countries can be classified as under water stress, especially Uzbekistan and Turkmenistan (Figure 6.5).

Figure 6.5
Water Stress, Central Asia

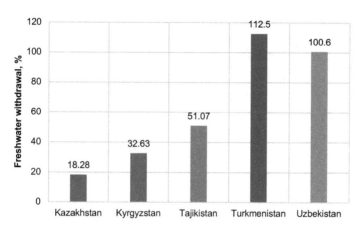

Source. FAO (2018).

It is important to examine the water footprint, which refers to the combined volume of green water (rainfall) and blue water (surface and groundwater) used to produce a given product, of major crops in the region because it could provide information about inefficiencies in water use. As mentioned earlier, the agriculture sector in Central Asia makes up about 90% of the total water use. 75% of the total water use in the agriculture sector consists of water consumption by wheat (39%), cotton (33%) and rice (3%) (Aldaya et al., 2010). Cotton is by far the most important cash crop in the Central Asia, which is one of the major cotton-exporting regions in the world. From 1992 to 2007, the annual average total water footprint for cotton was 15.7 billion m³/year in Uzbekistan, 6.8 billion m³/year in Turkmenistan, 2.8 billion m³/year in Tajikistan, 0.8 billion m³/year in Kazakhstan, and 0.3 billion m³/year in the Kyrgyz Republic. Of the total 26.4 billion m³, almost 94% was blue water. The water footprint of cotton production was 2,423 m³/ton in Kazakhstan, 3,049 m³/ton in the Kyrgyz Republic, 4,426 m³/ton in Uzbekistan, 6,246 m³/ton in Tajikistan, and 7,066 m³/ton in Turkmenistan (FAO, 2018). The variation between the countries was due to differences in evapotranspiration and soil texture (Aldaya et al., 2010).

Shortly after independence, wheat production in Central Asia increased mainly to improve regional food security. From 1992 to 2007, the annual average total water footprint for wheat was 15.8 billion m³/year in Kazakhstan, 7.8 billion m³/year in Uzbekistan, 4.6 billion m³/year in Turkmenistan, 1.7 billion m³/year in the Kyrgyz Republic, and 1.6 billion m³/year in Tajikistan. Of the total 31.5 billion m³, more than 67% was green water. The water footprint of wheat production was 1,440 m³/ton in Kazakhstan, 1,779 m³/ton in the Kyrgyz Republic, 2,068 m³/ton in Uzbekistan, 2,831 m³/ton in Turkmenistan, and 3,931 m³/ton in Tajikistan (FAO, 2018). As can be seen, Kazakhstan is the most efficient in terms of water used for wheat production, and it is completely green water as the crop is cultivated under rainfed conditions in the northern part of the country (Aldaya et al., 2010). The data suggest that countries with more rainfall are better suited for wheat production.

Similarly, to cotton, rice is mainly produced by using blue water resources. From 1992 to 2007, the annual average total water footprint for rice was 1.33 billion m3/year in Uzbekistan, 706 million m³/year in Kazakhstan, 512 million m³/year in Turkmenistan, 172 million m³/year in Tajikistan, and 46 million m³/year in the Kyrgyz Republic. Of the total 2.77 billion m³, more than 94% was blue water. The water footprint of rice production was 2,635 m³/ton in Kazakhstan, 3,498 m³/ton in the Kyrgyz Republic, 4,032 m³/ton in Tajikistan, 4,240 m³/ton in Uzbekistan, and 7,014 m³/ton in Turkmenistan (FAO, 2018).

IV. Legislative and Institutional Frameworks for Water Management

In order to analyze the current issues with regard to the legislative and institutional framework for water management in Central Asia, it is important to understand the region's legislative and institutional history of water management. During the Soviet period, water resources were managed in a unified top-down approach, with the Ministry of Melioration and Water Management in charge of all relevant functions related to their allocation and use. In Central Asia, the main goal was cotton production, and thus, water resources were managed and used in a way to prioritize this goal. This resulted in two significant inter-state management mechanisms. First, there was a water-energy exchange system between the republics. Second, water withdrawal quotas were set for each republic, with the irrigation demands of downstream countries being prioritized to maximize cotton production (Sehring & Diebold, 2012). For all five Central Asian countries, during the Soviet period, the 1970 Law Basics of water legislation of the USSR and Union Republics served as the legal framework for water relations, but this changed after their independence (Frenken, 2013). After the breakup of the Soviet Union, there have been a series of changes and developments in the legislative and institutional framework for water management at the regional and national levels.

At the regional level, different organizations are involved in the management of water resources. The International Fund for Saving the Aral Sea (IFAS), which was established by the presidents of the five Central Asian countries in January 1993, is the leading regional water management organization whose task is to develop and strengthen cooperation among the countries in the Aral Sea basin for socio-economic and ecological improvement, efficient water use, and better environmental protection in the region. The Chairman of IFAS is elected by the heads of the founding countries on a rotation basis (the current chairman is from Turkmenistan for the period of 2017–2019), and the Executive Committee of IFAS serves as a platform for dialogue between the governments of Central Asia and the international community (Dukhovniy & Ziganshina, 2018).

Under IFAS are the Interstate Commission for Water Coordination (ICWC) and the Interstate Commission on Sustainable Development (ICSD) of Central Asia. The ICWC is a regional body of the Central Asian countries tasked with working on issues related to shared water management, efficient use and protection in the Aral Sea basin and implementing jointly elaborated programs based on the collective and mutual interests of the five countries in the region. ICSD is responsible for coordinating and organizing regional cooperation in the areas of environmental protection and sustainable development in Central Asia. Under ICWC are two executive and interdepartmental control bodies, the Amu Darya and Syr Darya River Basin Water Organizations, which are responsible for allocating water resources within mutually established limits in each respective river basin and operating water-intakes, hydropower, reservoirs of common use, and interstate canals under strict adherence to nature protection requirements and implementing measures on the improvement of the ecological situation in the region (Dukhovniy & Ziganshina, 2018).

Water resources management in Kazakhstan is under the responsibility of the Committee for Water Resources of the Ministry of Agriculture. Kazakhstan first adopted a Water Code in 1993, which has since been amended and supplemented several times over the years. The Water Code consists of 32 chapters and 146 articles and aims to establish the key principles governing domestic as well transboundary water resources in Kazakhstan (Janusz-Pawletta, 2015). The territory of Kazakhstan can be divided into eight water management basins: Aralo-Syr Darya, Balkhash-Alakol, Irtysh, Uralo-Caspian, Ishin, Nura-Sarysus, Shu-Talas, and Tobol-Turgai (Ministry of Agriculture of the Republic of Kazakhstan, 2019). The Government of Kazakhstan has developed and implemented National Water Program Ak Bulak 2010–2020 (No. 1176 in November 2010), National Green Economy Concept (No. 577 in May 2013), and the State Program on Water Resources Management (No. 786 of in April 2014) which aims to reduce water consumption per unit of GDP by 33% by 2020 compared to 2012 levels, increase water access in both urban (to 100%) and rural (to 80%) areas, and improve water resource quality (Janusz-Pawletta, 2015; Karatayev et al., 2017).

In the Kyrgyz Republic, the state agency responsible for water resources management is the Department of Water Resources and Land Reclamation of the Ministry of Agriculture, Food Industry, and Land Reclamation. The Department oversees governance, monitoring and regulation of the conditions and use of water resources through irrigation and drainage infrastructure, and fulfills ministerial and legislative functions on the implementation of a unified national water policy. The Kyrgyz Republic adopted a Water Code in 2005 based on integrated water resources management. The Water Code establishes principles for managing water resources, defines the jurisdiction of state bodies concerning water resources and their management, regulates the usage of and payment for surface and underground waters, and sets forth measures protecting water resources from pollution, depletion, and irrigation (Government of Kyrgyz Republic, 2005). It also includes norms related to the establishment and operation of Water Users' Associations (WUAs). Finally, it includes provisions that establish the minimal ecological river flow, requiring government water authorities to define minimal water flow levels for certain rivers and water bodies in order to conserve fish reserves and water ecosystems (The Law Library of Congress, 2013). In 2017, certain improvements were made to legislation related to water and land management. These included amendments to the Water Code and Law on Water to mitigate damage to glaciers, adoption of the State Program for Irrigation Development for 2017–2026 (PP KR No. 440 of 21 July 2017) to construct irrigation infrastructure for the development of newly irrigated land in rural areas, and the reorganization of 26 basin and regional water management organizations into state agencies (PP KR No. 524 of 24 August 2017) (Dukhovniy & Ziganshina, 2018).

In Tajikistan, the state agencies dealing with water management include the Ministry of Energy and Water Resources (MEWR) and the Ministry of Agriculture. Tajikistan signed its Water Code in 1993 and has since made several amendments to it over the past two decades. The Water Code includes provisions on planning and management of water resources for agriculture, water distribution and delivery to the farm inlet, and water quality (Frenken, 2013). The latest developments in the country include the ratification of an agreement on financing of water resources management project in the Pyanj River Basin and the Document on Technical Assistance Agreement Revision between the "Barki Tojik" and European Bank for Reconstruction and Development on rehabilitation of Kairakkum Hydropower Plant (Dukhovniy & Ziganshina, 2018).

In Turkmenistan, the responsibility for water resources management and maintenance of a reliable water supply for agricultural, municipal and the industrial sectors is divided within the Cabinet of Ministers. The Ministry of Water Resources constructs and operates irrigation and drainage systems, the Ministry of Nature Protection is responsible for the control of water pollution and depletion, and State Corporation "Turkmengeologiya" assesses the use of groundwater aquifers and prevents their pollution and depletion (Frenken, 2013). Water resource management is a crucial factor of the economy and environment in the dry climate of Turkmenistan. In January 2017, a new Water Code of Turkmenistan was implemented with the aim of improving water governance relations under sustainable and rational water use, ensuring protection of water from pollution, clogging, and depletion, as well as preventing and mitigating the negative impact of water use, improving conditions of water bodies, and strengthening water infrastructure (Dukhovniy & Ziganshina, 2018).

Until February of 2018, water resources management in Uzbekistan was under the control of the Ministry of Agriculture and Water Resources. However, the Decree of the President of Uzbekistan No. 5330 of February 12, 2018, titled On Measures to Radically Improve the System of Agriculture and Water Sector Governance split the Ministry of Agriculture and Water Resources into the Ministry of Agriculture and Ministry of Water Management (Government of Uzbekistan, 2018). Thus, Ministry of Water Management is now responsible for implementing a unified policy on water resource management, as well as coordinating state bodies, water management organizations, and other relevant agencies in the area of rational use and protection of water resources and prevention of harmful effects of water use. There are 13 Basin Irrigation System Administrations, which are territorial branches responsible for water allocation based on hydrological basins and principles, under the Ministry of Water Management. Uzbekistan introduced water rights through the Water Law in 1993, marking the beginning of a series of measures to address water resources (Frenken, 2013).

WUAs are recognized in most countries in the region as fulfilling essential roles in water management at the farm level. WUAs are membership-based, nongovernmental, and noncommercial organizations designed to manage irrigation systems, distribute water among members, collect payments, and arbitrate disputes (Global Water Partnership, 2014; The Law Library of Congress, 2013). Since Central Asia has a complex and extensive irrigation infrastructure requiring substantial financial and material resources for maintenance, it was thought that transferring responsibility for the management, operation, and maintenance of water systems to water users themselves would lessen the burden on the governments. However, many members of the WUAs lack the knowledge, skills, and experience to manage the organization or the irrigation infrastructure. Additionally, the regulatory framework has not kept pace with ongoing changes and requires modifications and improvements (Executive Committee of the International Fund for Saving the Aral Sea, 2010).

In all of the Central Asian countries, lower administrative or inter-farm water use arrangements are determined through established agreements between provincial, river basin, district and water user associations. In Kazakhstan, which was the first nation in the region to implement water fees in 1994, the price of water varies by province, and is determined by volume, depending on the added value irrigation contributes to agricultural production (Frenken, 2013). Water user fees cover the maintenance of water facilities and hydraulic structures. In the Kyrgyz Republic, payment rates for water delivery are established by Parliament, with about 50% of the operation and maintenance costs covered by the state budget and the other 50% by monthly payments for water delivery from water users (Frenken, 2013). In Tajikistan, water fees have been in effect since 1996, but these fees for irrigation water services cover only 20% to 50% of the operation and maintenance costs of irrigation and drainage systems. In Turkmenistan, the costs of operating and maintaining water infrastructure are covered by the state budget, except for the on-farm irrigation systems which are funded by private parties through a 3% deduction from the total of crops produced by the tenants (Frenken, 2013). In Uzbekistan, water consumer associations (WCAs) are responsible for operating and maintaining on-farm water infrastructure through irrigation service fee (ISF) collection. Still, most WCAs have trouble generating adequate capital for the operation and maintenance of infrastructure, placing a significant financial burden on the state (Frenken, 2013).

V. Major Challenges for Water Management

Central Asian countries are bound together by challenges facing their shared water resources. Their growing economies and populations increase pressure on their limited water resources, making the potential for conflict more acute. Central Asia is not unique in this regard, and governments in the regions are seeking solutions to negotiate this situation. A key dilemma stems from inherent conflicts in interest between downstream countries (Kazakhstan, Uzbekistan, and Turkmenistan) and upstream countries (the Kyrgyz Republic and Tajikistan) over the optimal distribution of water. Downstream countries rely heavily on irrigated agriculture while upstream countries seek to harness their hydroelectricity potential. Upstream countries prefer to store water during the summer for use in the winter, putting them at odds with downstream countries' planting seasons. A Soviet era arrangement whereby upstream countries were supplied with oil and gas was discontinued, setting the stage for the current impasse. In addition, most water infrastructure in Central Asia was built during the

Soviet period in the early 1960s and is now reaching the end of its design life (Bucknall et al., 2003). Aging infrastructure, exacerbated by heavy water consumption patterns in the agriculture sector across the region, is a major contributing factor to excessive water losses, low irrigation efficiency, waterlogging and widespread soil salinization, and declining crop yields. Further, the rise and predominance of smallholder farming present additional challenges for water management. Often, inexperienced individuals have been left in charge of managing land and water resources. Farmers often face an institutional gap that puts them in a poor position to keep up with changes in public policy (Frenken, 2013; Global Water Partnership, 2014).

As indicated by the figures provided in the section on water use, there is an overreliance on irrigation in the agriculture sector and there are some major inefficiencies in the allocation and use of water resources. Aldaya et al. (2010) suggest one example of shifting grain production to higher-rainfall areas to reduce the need for irrigation. There should also be a consideration to move toward less water-intensive crops that can generate more profits with less water footprint. Moreover, such strategies can save scarce surface and ground water resources in the arid and semiarid areas of the region, which can then be used more productively, such as for domestic, industrial, and recreational purposes. There are also efforts by countries in the region to improve water use efficiency by introducing water saving practices and technologies.

In addition, the emergence of climate change (high air temperature and low rainfall) also presents major challenges. Climate change has two consequences: water requirements will grow because of the expected rise in temperature, and water availability will decline in the long run as a result of glacier retreat (Global Water Partnership, 2014). According to global warming prognoses by the Intergovernmental Panel on Climate Change (IPCC), the glaciered river systems in Central Asia will experience unfavorable hydrological changes (Hagg et al., 2006; Siegfried et al., 2012). Projections suggest that by 2050 temperature increase is expected to be between 1.7°C and 4.7°C (Milanova et al., 2018). The increasing trend of the air temperature in Tajikistan has already significantly impacted flow in the Vakhsh and Pyanj rivers, main tributaries of the Amu Darya River (Chevallier et al., 2014). Specific forecasts already suggest that water flow may potentially decrease by 2%–5% in Syr Darya River Basin and by 10%–15% in Amu Darya Basin by 2050 (World Bank, 2013), worsening the water scarcity situation. Moreover, irregular spring temperatures and precipitation have significant effects on agricultural production, with climate change likely to cause yield reductions of 20%–50% by 2050 for nearly all crops under no adaptation option, thus threatening the food security and rural livelihoods in the region (World Bank, 2013).

World Resources Institute (WRI) has developed a methodology which identifies areas with higher exposure to water-related risks. The methodology allows calculation of an overall water risk indicator, which is an aggregated measure of all selected indicators from the Physical Quantity, Quality and Regulatory & Reputational Risk categories (Gassert et al., 2015). Using this methodology, a map was developed specifically for Central Asia. As can be seen in Figure 6.6, large parts of Central Asian countries face high or extremely high-water risk levels.

Figure 6.7 demonstrates the projected change in water stress, which shows how development and/or climate change are expected to affect water stress (the ratio of water use to supply). The "business as usual" scenario (SSP2 RCP8.5) represents a world with stable economic development and steadily rising global carbon emissions (Gassert et al., 2015). Obtained from WRI (2018) and produced specifically for Central Asia region, the map also shows that large parts of the Kyrgyz Republic, Tajikistan, Uzbekistan and Turkmenistan are expected to face high or extremely high-water risk levels, which indicates a need to improve water management and use practices at regional, national and local levels. A major challenge in improving water resources management will be to improve water use efficiency and productivity in irrigated

Figure 6.6
Overall Water Risk Level in Central Asian Countries

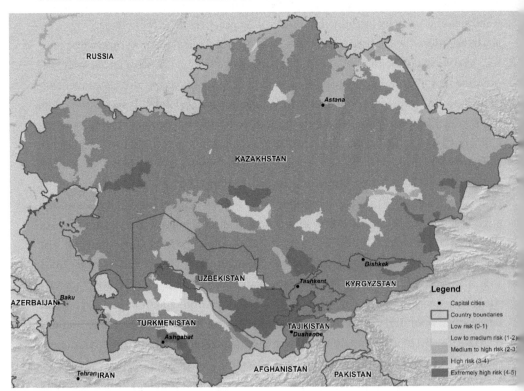

Source. World Resources Institute (2018).

Figure 6.7
Overall Projected Change in Water Stress in 2030

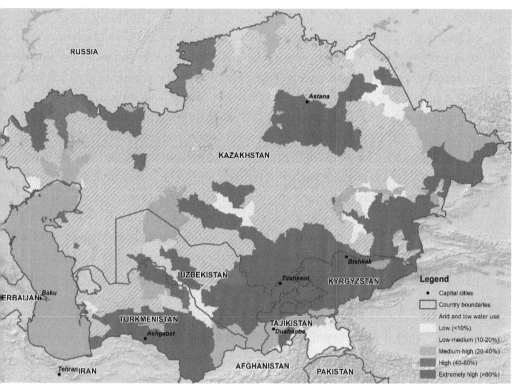

Source. World Resources Institute (2018).

agriculture. Current practices cannot be continued. In this regard, countries such as Uzbekistan and Tajikistan have made efforts to improve water use efficiency through changes in policies and practices, including introducing water saving technologies and considering reducing cultivation of water-intensive crops such as cotton and wheat in irrigated lands.

VI. Opportunities for Regional Integration and Development

In addressing the tensions between upstream and downstream countries, regional cooperation identifying and addressing the needs of both upstream and downstream countries is needed, but recent decades have shown that governments have often resorted to competition and tensions instead. Uzbekistan had long maintained its staunch opposition to upstream countries' interests, but the current administration of president Shavkat Mirziyoyev has adopted a more constructive approach in addressing the region's water problems (Russell, 2018). Therefore, the current geopolitical climate in the region is more conducive to regional cooperation as there are increasing opportunities for carrying out multi-country projects to improve management and use of water resources.

There is also a need for more concerted efforts by the governments and international organizations in the region to rehabilitate and modernize irrigation and drainage infrastructure. In this regard, an important factor will be the development of financial and economic mechanisms to keep crucial institutions and stakeholders such as water management organizations, water user associations, and water users financially feasible. It is vital that the government and water users cover not only day-to-day costs, but also account for longer-term depreciation and its associated costs (Global Water Partnership, 2014). Some approaches to promote the financial sustainability of water management institutions include introducing a volumetric method of payment for water delivery services and water as a resource, charging fees depending on the nature of water use (e.g., for irrigated agriculture, this could be a certain percentage of farm net profit), and implementing financial incentives for water saving by water users and water management organizations and penalties for overuse (Global Water Partnership, 2014).

There is a crucial need to strengthen the capacity of various water organizations, such as national and regional water institutions, educational and academic institutions, and development agencies, and to strengthen extension services (Global Water Partnership, 2014). If more learning opportunities are created, it will allow stakeholders to contribute to more positive outcomes in terms of water management and use in agriculture. Thus, more capacity building work needs to be done to develop and promote a broad range of knowledge and innovation sharing platforms (Global Water Partnership, 2014).

Furthermore, advocacy, regional dialogue, technical assistance, and collective action will also be of paramount importance in addressing the challenges presented under Central Asia's climate change and security context. Climate change presents opportunities for government agencies, international organizations, and civil society to come together and devise strategies for climate mitigation, adaptation, and climate-related security management (Mirimanova et al., 2018). Given that Central Asia is a region with limited data and in need of capacity to develop user-friendly tools to inform decision-making, there are opportunities in the water and agriculture sector to carry out research and capacity building projects which could involve the establishment of user-friendly databases (regional, national, basin, and local), knowledge bases (curricula, guidelines, and other practical and informational materials), analytical tools, and models (Global Water Partnership, 2014). Water and land management organizations could benefit from more advanced use of modern tools such as GIS, remote sensing, and analytical models, the use of which is especially lacking at the local levels (Global Water Partnership, 2014). In Central Asia, increased access to independent data could foster effective early warning and response systems. A comprehensive information and data system would allow regular monitoring and assessment of land and water resources in Central Asian countries with the possibility to evaluate the effectiveness of their use and to make forecasts. An advancement in capacity for independent scientific investigation, and integration into the global climate change monitoring networks could help reduce misinformation and political campaigns which intensify domestic and regional tensions, as well as help foster productive cooperation and management of shared risks.

References

ADB. (2010). *Central Asia atlas of natural resources.* https://www.adb.org/publications/central-asia-atlas-natural-resources

Aldaya, M., G. Munoz, & A. Hoekstra. (2010). *Water footprint of cotton, wheat and rice production in Central Asia* (Value of Water Research Report Series No. 41). UNESCO-IHE, Institute for Water Education.

Allouche, J. (2007). The governance of Central Asian waters: National interestes versus regional cooperation. In *Central Asia at the Crossroads* (pp. 46–55). UN Institute for Disarmament Research. https://unidir.org/sites/default/files/publication/pdfs//central-asia-at-the-crossroads-en-333.pdf

Bekchanov, M., A. Bhaduri, & C. Ringler. (2013). *How market-based water allocation can improve water use efficiency in the Aral Sea basin* (ZEF Discussion Papers on Development Policy No. 177). Leibniz Information Center for Economics.

Bucknall, L., I. Klytchnikova, J. Lampietti, M. Lundell, M. Scatasta, & M. Thurman. (2003). *Irrigation in Central Asia: Social, economic, and environmental considerations.* World Bank. http://web.worldbank.org/archive/website00983A/WEB/OTHER/176B6FDD.HTM?Opendocument

CA Water Info. (2011). *The Aral Sea Basin.* http://www.cawater-info.net/aral/index_e.htm

Chevallier, P., Pouyaud, B., Mojaïsky, M., Bolgov, M., Olsson, O., Bauer, M., & Froebrich, J. (2014). River flow regime and snow cover of the Pamir Alay (Central Asia) in a changing climate. *Hydrological Sciences Journal, 59*(8), 1491–1506.

Dukhovniy, V., & D. Ziganshina. (2018). *2017 water yearbook: Central Asia and around the globe.* Scientific Information Center of Interstate Commission for Water Coordination. http://www.cawater-info.net/yearbook/index_e.htm

Executive Committee of the International Fund for Saving the Aral Sea. (2010). *Serving the people of Central Asia: Aral Sea Basin Program 3.* https://ecifas-tj.org/en/main/

FAO. (2018). *AQUASTAT database.* https://www.fao.org/aquastat/en/databases/

Frenken, K. (2013). *Irrigation in Central Asia in figures: AQUASTAT survey 2012* (Water Reports No. 39). FAO.

Gassert, F., M. Luck, M. Landis, P. Reig, & T. Shiao. (2015, April 6). *Aqueduct global maps 2.1: Constructing decision-relevant global water risk indicators.* World Resources Institute. https://www.wri.org/research/aqueduct-global-maps-21-indicators

Global Water Partnership. (2014). *Integrated water resources management in Central Asia: The challenges of managing large transboundary rivers.* Technical Focus Paper. https://www.gwp.org/en/learn/KNOWLEDGE_RESOURCES/Global_Resources/Technical-Focus-Papers/

Government of Kyrgyz Republic. (2005). *Water code of the Kyrgyz Republic.* FAO. https://faolex.fao.org/docs/pdf/kyr49854E.pdf

Government of Uzbekistan. (2018). *On measures to radically improve the system of agriculture and water sector governance* (Presidential Decree No. 5330). Government of Uzbekistan.

Groll, M., Opp, C., Kulmatov, R., Ikramova, M., & Normatov, I. (2015). Water quality, potential conflicts and solutions—an upstream-downstream analysis of the transnational Zarafshan River (Tajikistan, Uzbekistan). *Environmental Earth Sciences, 73*(2), 743–763.

Hagg, W., Braun, L. N., Weber, M., & Becht, M. (2006). Runoff modeling in glacierized Central Asian catchments for present-day and future climate. Hydrology Research, *37*(2), 93–105.

Ibatullin, S., V. Yasinsky, & A. Mironenkov. (2009). *The impact of climate change on water resources in Central Asia* (Sector Report No. 6). Eurasian Development Bank.

Immerzeel, W., A. Lutz, & P. Droogers. (2012). *Climate change impacts on the upstream water resources of the Amu and Syr Darya River Basins* (FutureWater Report No. 107). Asian Development Bank.

Izquierdo, L., M. Stangerhaugen, D. Castillo, R. Nixon, & G. Jimenez. (2010). *Water crisis in Central Asia: Key challenges and opportunities.* New School University.

Janusz-Pawletta, B. (2015). Current legal challenges to institutional governance of transboundary water resources in Central Asia and Joint Management Arrangements. *Environmental Earth Sciences, 73* (2), 887–893.

Karatayev, M., Rivotti, P., Mourão, Z. S., Konadu, D. D., Shah, N., & Clarke, M. (2017). The water-energy-food nexus in Kazakhstan: Challenges and opportunities. *Energy Procedia, 125,* 63–70.

Lutz, A., P. Droogers, & W. Immerzeel. (2012). *Climate change impact and adaptation on the water resources in the Amu Darya and Syr Darya River Basins* (FutureWater Report No. 110). Asian Development Bank.

Micklin, P. (2000). *Managing water in Central Asia.* Royal Institute of International Affairs.

Milanova, E., A. Nikanorova, A. Kirilenko, & N. Dronin. (2018). Water deficit estimation under climate change and irrigation conditions in the Fergana Valley. In S. Mal, R. Singh & C.

Huggel (Eds.), *Climate Change, Extreme Events and Disaster Risk Reduction*. Springer.

Ministry of Agriculture of the Republic of Kazakhstan. (2019). *Subordinate organizations of the Committee on Water Resources*. https://www.gov.kz/memleket/entities/moa?lang=en

Mirimanova, N., C. Born, P. Nordqvist, & K. Eklow. (2018). *Central Asia: Climate-Related security risk assessment*. Stockholm.

Nechifor, V., & Winning, M. (2019). Global crop output and irrigation water requirements under a changing climate. *Heliyon, 5*(3), 1–27.

Russell, M. (2018). *Water in Central Asia: An increasingly scarce resource*. European Parliamentary Research Service.

Sehring, J., & A. Diebold. (2012). *From the glaciers to the Aral Sea—Water Unites*. Trescher Verlag GmbH.

Scheierling, S., & D. Treguer. (2018). *Beyond crop per drop: Assessing agricultural water productivity and efficiency in a maturing water economy*. World Bank. https://documents.worldbank.org/pt/publication/documents-reports/documentdetail/352321530075399351/beyond-crop-per-drop-assessing-agricultural-water-productivity-and-efficiency-in-a-maturing-water-economy

Siegfried, T., et al. (2012). Will climate change exacerbate water stress in Central Asia? *Climatic Change, 112*, 881–899.

The Law Library of Congress. (2013). *Legislation on use of water in agriculture*. https://blogs.loc.gov/law/2014/04/legislation-on-use-of-water-in-agriculture/

UNECE. (2013). *Dam safety in Central Asia: Capacity building and regional cooperation* (Water Series No. 5). United Nations Economic Commission for Europe. https://unece.org/info/publications/pub/21665

World Bank. (2013). *Uzbekistan: Overview of climate change activities*. https://openknowledge.worldbank.org/entities/publication/c76fae61-9735-5fd8-ad36-c2ef0bfbe3da

World Resources Institute. (2018). *Aqueduct water risk atlas*. https://www.wri.org/applications/map/aqueduct-atlas.

CHAPTER 7

Agricultural Development in Mongolia

Kamiljon Akramov, Kevin Chen, Allen Park, Jarilkasin Ilyasov,
and Sarvarbek Eltazarov

I. Introduction

As a country with a vast area of range land, the agricultural development in Mongolia provides important meat and dairy products to the world. The development of Mongolia, as a current member of the CAREC regional development program, could enhance the promotion of regional agricultural trade integration. In 2001, the Asian Development Bank (ADB) supported an initiative of the CAREC program in the Central Asia region, through a partnership of 11 countries including Afghanistan, Azerbaijan, China, Georgia, Kazakhstan, Kyrgyz Republic, Mongolia, Pakistan, Tajikistan, Turkmenistan, and Uzbekistan. Within this cooperation program, several multilateral financial institutions, including ADB, World Bank, International Monetary Fund, United Nations Development Program, the European Bank for Reconstruction and Development, Islamic Development Bank, and some bilateral assistance organizations in developed countries have also supported projects as partners under the CAREC program. The CAREC region serves an important role in regional cooperation on the Eurasia continent, due to their advanced member countries connecting the Eurasia continent. Mongolia is a country that located to the north central Asia region that occupies a large area of arable or pasture land. Today, its economic growth depends heavily on subsistence herding. However, the country has undergone various agricultural policy reforms that have shifted its agricultural sector since the dissolution of the Soviet Union. In addition, natural conditions are increasingly prominent factors influencing the agricultural development of the country. In this paper, we will explore the agricultural sector in Mongolia, with a particular focus on its specific agricultural conditions focusing primarily on its subsistence herding, its trade and cooperation policies, and the natural resource constraints for its potential in agriculture development under the CAREC framework.

II. Agricultural Reforms and Policies

Mongolia's agricultural GDP accounts for 10.6% of national GDP, while agricultural employment provides 29.8% of the national employment (World Bank, 2019). With an urbanization rate of 68.4% in 2017, most people in the rural areas are engaged in subsistence herding, focused on five animals: sheep, goats, cattle, horses, and camels. Agricultural crops produced include wheat, potato, vegetables, oilseed, and fodder crops (World Bank, 2019). Though Mongolia's agriculture sector experienced depression after the collapse of Soviet Union in 1991, it recovered slowly and smoothly through a series of agricultural reforms.

1. Land Reform

Following the collapse of the Soviet Union in 1991, from which it relied on for trade, Mongolia's economy experienced heavy depression, including in the agriculture sector. In 1992, after the establishment of the new constitution, the government started to introduce reforms. Agricultural land reform was regarded as a priority for its fundamental role in the national economy as well as the government's goal of promoting stable and sustainable economic growth (Hanstad & Duncan, 2001). Before 1991, agricultural land belonged to the state while individuals only had the rights of growing subsistence crops on household plots. No agricultural land was allowed to be sold or transferred by individuals. The new land law adopted in 1994 provided individuals with the expanded land rights including limited ownership, possession (renewable leases between 15–60 years) and usage for foreigners (Myadar, 2009).

The land law launched in 1994 aimed to regulate land possession and usage for individual and business groups in Mongolia. According to the law, agricultural land belonged to the state, but individuals and enterprises were accorded land possession and use rights. Land rights including ownership, possession, use, and limited use rights were further defined in the law. In general, private land holders may lease but not sell use rights, while use rights holders may neither lease nor sell use rights. Additionally, the law gave detailed classifications of different land types including agricultural land, urban and settlement land, public infrastructure land, forest land, water resources land, and reserve lands (Hanstad & Duncan, 2001).

Land transferability and the development of land markets were also important aspects of reform, with the goal of encouraging efficient usage of the land. After reforms, partial transferability of land among farmers and other business entities became permitted. Land was able to be transferred through purchase, sales transactions, rental, or leasing rights. Additionally, it also placed additional controls to regulate the land market (Myers & Hetz, 2004). The agriculture land law was amended in 2002 to further clarify state-owned land possession and land use as well as other related issues. The different forms of land tenure were allowed according to the amended law (Myers & Hetz, 2004).

2. National Agricultural Strategies

There are several important documents outlining Mongolia's national agricultural strategies, including three key documents of the *Millennium Development Goal (MDG)-Based Comprehensive National Development Strategy of Mongolia (2008–2021)*, the *National Program for Food Security (2009–2016)*, and the *"Mongolian Livestock" National Program (2010–2021)*. There are also other plans that are active and effective to the agricultural sector, including the Action Plan of the Government of Mongolia, the State Policy on Food and Agriculture (2003), the State Policy Toward Herders (2009), and the Third Campaign for Reclamation National Program for development of Crop production (2008–2010).

The content and priorities of three key documents are listed in the Table 7.1. In particular, the MDG-based Comprehensive National Development Strategy of Mongolia defines the goals and strategic objectives of food, agriculture, regional and rural development as well as environmental policies. The main strategy document for food and agricultural sector is outlined in the National Program for Food Security (2009–2016), aiming to ensure the sustainable supply of nutritious, secure, and accessible food as well as improve population health and agriculture labor productivity (FAO, 2012). The Mongolian Livestock National Program aims to develop a viable and competitive livestock sector for domestic self-sufficiency and export possibilities.

In addition to these programs, the Mongolian government continued the Third Reclamation Campaign of crop development to promote vegetable and fruit production through supporting crop production in the eastern and western regions. Mongolia also faces many environmental issues including desertification, land degradation, water limitation, water pollution, and air pollution (Lindberg, 2017). To address these issues, the government has introduced a series of policy actions including environmental laws, designation of nature reserve areas, investment in energy-efficient technologies, and pollution reduction programs (FAO, 2012).

Table 7.1
Key Policy Documents on Mongoli's Food, Agriculture and Natural Resources

Agricultural policy documents	Content	Key priorities
The Millennium Development Goal (MDG)-Based Comprehensive National Development Strategy of Mongolia	Defines the goals and strategic objectives of food, agriculture, regional and rural development and environmental policies.	1. Modernize the agricultural and food industrial complex; be self-sufficient of the agricultural products; 2. Implement a regional development policy and reduce the development gap between urban and rural areas; 3. Integrate economic, social and ecological measures to protect the environment.
The Mongolian Livestock National Program (2010–2021)	Develop an economically viable, competitive, and sustainable livestock sector. Be self-sufficient domestically and increase export revenues.	1. Draw attention to the livestock sector as the main traditional economic activity; 2. Improve animal breeding services, increase the productivity and produce high-quality, bio-clean livestock products; 3. Raise the veterinary service standard to international levels and secure livestock health; 4. Develop targeted markets for livestock products; establish proper processing and marketing structures.
National Program for Food Security (2009–2016)	Sustainably supply of nutritious, secure and accessible food. Improve the health and high labor productivity of the population.	1. Create enhanced enabling legal, economic, infrastructure and organizational environment; 2. Stable supply with safe, nutritious, secure and accessible foods; increase the processed and value-added food production; 3. Ensure hygiene and safety of food products and drinking waters through monitoring and information network building; 4. Food safety and nutrition education in the country.

Source. FAO (2012).

III. Trends in Land Use and Agricultural Production

Mongolia's agricultural development experienced a two-phase transition:

- a period of recession in the early 1990s following the collapse of the Soviet Union;
- a recovery and growth phase initiated by agricultural reforms in the early 2000s (Cheng, 2003).

1. Changes in Land Use and Agricultural Production

In general, total agricultural land area in Mongolia is decreasing, going from 140 million hectares in 1961 to 110 million hectares in 2016 (FAO, 2019). As described in Table 7.2, though cropland areas increased from 624,000 hectares in 1960 to 1,369,000 hectares in 1991, it then declined after reforms to 572,200 hectares in 2016. Additionally, in 1961, permanent pastures and meadows in Mongolia covered over 140 million hectares. By 1991, land decreased to 124 million hectares and to 110 million hectares by 2016 (FAO, 2019). The pasture degradation was mainly due to harsh weather, increasing livestock density, and the concentration of the urban population due to urban development (Rasmussen & Prempong, 2015). Additionally, the land composition of cropland changed hands from the collective state to individuals, while the livestock was still held by the latter (Rasmussen & Prempong, 2015).

Table 7.2

Agricultural Land Use in Mongolia in Thousands of Hectares, 1961–2016

Year	Agriculture land	Arable land	Permanent crop	Permanent meadows and pastures
1961	140,683	624	—	140,059
1986	124,531	1,306	1.0	123,224
1991	126,130	1,368	1.0	124,761
1996	118,469	1,321	1.0	117,147
2001	129,704	751	2.0	128,951
2006	114,248	696	2.0	113,550
2011	113,507	611	3.0	112,893
2016	111,062	567	5.0	110,490

Source. FAO (2019).

The economic transition had a negative effect on the agricultural sector until the 2000s. Prior to 1990, Mongolia was self-sufficient in agricultural commodities for domestic consumption and exported products abroad. However, agricultural support systems and production collapsed during the economic transition (Hanstad & Duncan, 2001; Myadar, 2009). As described in Figure 7.1, livestock production alternated between growth and decline from 1991 to 2003, with two big collapses of production in 1991–1994 and 1999–2003. After 2003, livestock production generally increased and reached a peak in 2009. Crop production followed similar trends, collapsing from one million tons in 1989 to 220,000 tons in 2002 and recovering gradually to a peak in 2012 of 840,000 tons. Live animal stocks increased during the agricultural transition period, but collapsed in 2000–2004 and 2009–2010, mainly because of harsh winter weather and pasture land degradation. Additionally, in 2013, production levels of milk (excluding butter), wheat and wheat products, potatoes and potato products, mutton and goat meat, and vegetables reached highs of 510,000, 368,000, 192,000, 157,000, and 93,000 tons, respectively. In general, though agricultural production has recovered since the early 1990s, it remains vulnerable to natural disasters and harsh weather conditions (FAO, 2019).

Figure 7.1
Value of Agricultural Production in Mongolia, Current Millions US$, 1989–2013

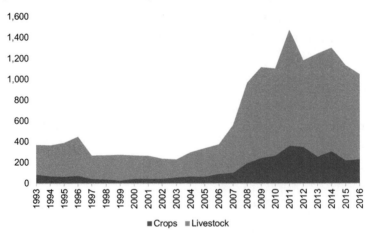

Source. FAO (2019).

2. Total Factor Productivity and Labor Productivity

Mongolia's agricultural productivity has fluctuated greatly since 1990. Total factor productivity (TFP), which is an important factor to evaluate the productivity with the consideration of broad inputs including land, labor, capital, and material resources, went through ups and down through the years, shown in Figure 7.2 (USDA ERS, 2018). Decreasing productivity in 2000–2003 and 2009–2011 is consistent with the production declines during these periods, mainly because of harsh weather and natural disasters. Recent labor productivity has demonstrated a positive trend in recent years.

The year 2002 represented a turning point for labor productivity (Figure 7.3). During the transition period, agricultural labor productivity declined from US$2,534 per worker in 1991 to US$1,248 per worker in 2002. From then, labor productivity increased to US$2,495 per worker in 2012 and thereafter more dramatically to US$4,544 by 2017 (World Bank, 2019).

Figure 7.2

TFP and Annual TFP Growth Rate, Mongolia, Indexed to 2005, 1990–2015

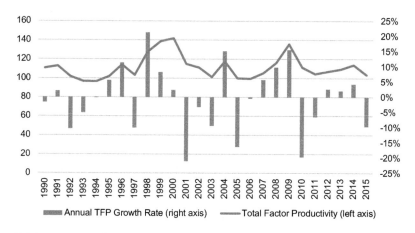

Source. U.S. Department of Agriculture (2018).

Figure 7.3

Agricultural Sector in Mongolia, Value-Added per Worker (2010 US$ Constant)

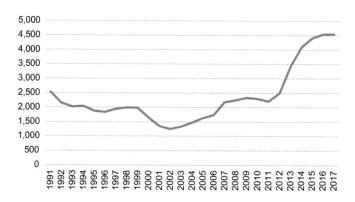

Source. World Bank (2019).

3. Agricultural Trade

Agricultural trade has sharply increased since 2000. Since then, the value of imports has far exceeded the value of exports (Figure 7.4). In 2016, total import values reached US$498 million while total exports were valued at US$325 million (FAO, 2019). Mongolia's agricultural exports include horsemeat, wool, and cashmere, and its major trade partners are China and the Russian Federation. Meanwhile, they also imports large quantities of cereals, vegetables, and processed products.

Figure 7.4
Value of Agricultural Trade in Mongolia in Millions of US$, 1961–2016

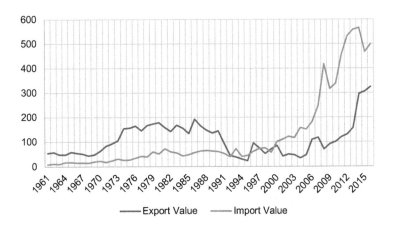

Source. FAO (2019).

IV. Perspective by Subsectors

Livestock production predominates Mongolia's agriculture sector, while arable land covers less than 1% of the total agricultural land area. Value-added agricultural products are limited. Mongolia's agriculture sector is highly susceptible to weather shocks and hazards like droughts and the "dzud," referring to a series of continuous natural disasters, including severe summer droughts, followed by heavy winter snow, winds, and extremely low temperature (FAO & WFP, 2017).

1. Livestock Production and Trade

Extensive Animal Husbandry
Extensive animal husbandry is a dominant sector in Mongolia because of weather and geographic conditions, making up around 80% of overall agricultural production

and 10% of total export value. It is based on traditional extensive grazing, in which livestock are herded on pastures with little supplementary feed. However, this production method leads to not only low productivity but also increasing pressure on pasture resources (Rasmussen & Prempong, 2015). Livestock is also more vulnerable to the harsh winter weather because of increasing density and decreasing pasture land carrying capacity.

The main livestock in Mongolia are sheep, goats, cattle, horses, and camels, also referred to as the "five animals." Generally, livestock holdings have increased in recent decades, apart from the two animal stock collapses in 1999–2002 and 2008–2009 (FAO, 2019). In 1999, livestock counts reached 33 million heads but 9.6 million animals (29%) died over the following three winters because of consecutive severe dzuds that prevented herds from accessing pasture, hay, or fodder. Extremely cold temperatures during the "dzuds" were also fatal for livestock (FAO, 2019; Sayed, 2010). Additionally, in the winter of 2009–2010, around eight million livestock animals died, owing to the cold weather and the condition of the land (IAEA, 2010). Livestock numbers has increased dramatically since 2011 with increased government support. In 2017, the national herd consisted of 30.1 million sheep, 27.3 million goats, 4.4 million cattle, 3.9 million horses, and 0.4 million camels (Figure 7.5) (FAO, 2019).

Figure 7.5
"Five Animal" Stocks in Mongolia, Thousands of Heads, 1991–2017

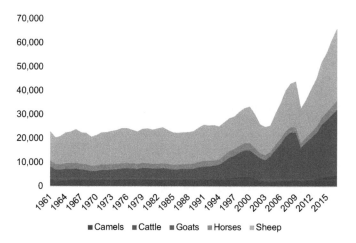

Source. FAO (2019).

Though livestock is a key subsector of Mongolian agriculture, meat export values are relatively minor. Moreover, export products and destinations are limited. As shown in Figure 7.6, horsemeat has overtaken bovine meat in terms of export value since 2005. Before 2007, Russia was Mongolia's main destination for meat exports, though exports to China have increased dramatically in recent years. In 2017, the total meat export value of Mongolia was US$54.9 million, with US$38.4 million exported to China and US$6.9 million to Russia (Figure 7.7). Horse meat comprises 99.5% of China's meat imports from Mongolia. Mongolia also exports cashmere and wool to the global market. The calculated RCA index for meat is 0.41, indicating that Mongolia does not have a comparative advantage in overall meat exports. On the other hand, it shows a strong comparative advantage in exporting horsemeat with an RCA index of 118.3 in 2017. Likewise, Mongolian wool and cashmere RCA index value is 90.6, also indicating a strong comparative advantage in the global market (UN Comtrade, 2019).

Figure 7.6

Composition of Mongolia's Meat Export Value in Millions of US$, 1996–2017

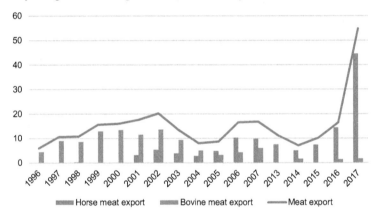

Source. UN Comtrade (2019).

Figure 7.7

Value of Mongolian Meat Export Destinations by Value in Millions US$, 1996–2017

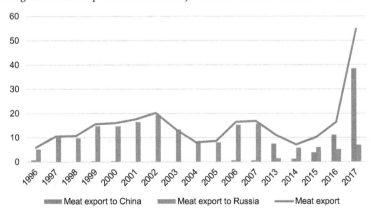

Source. UN Comtrade (2019).

Additionally, though Mongolia is a large producer of milk, it is still a net importer of butter, cheese, and cream. New Zealand is its main trade partner, while others also include Russia, the United States, Germany, and France (UN Comtrade, 2019).

Semi-intensive Livestock

Semi-intensive livestock production in Mongolia includes sheep- and beef-feeding units and dairy farms with supplementary feed, while intensive livestock mainly consists of the production of pork, eggs, and some dairies and feedlots. Semi-intensive and intensive production, especially pork and poultry production, have increased after collapsing in the early 2000s (Rasmussen & Prempong, 2015). Egg, pork, and chicken production generally increased after 2002: on average, 3,957, 500, and 255 tons were produced in 2008–2017, respectively (FAO, 2019). Both intensive and semi-intensive livestock production has increased since 2005. The increasing production of eggs, pork, and chicken is driven by domestic demand, market development, and policy support. Research indicates that the semi-intensive and intensive livestock sector not only brings higher rates of turnover but also facilitates feed and fodder production (Rasmussen & Prempong, 2015).

2. Crop Production

Though only 1% of Mongolia's land area is used to grow crops, approximately 20% of total agricultural production has come from the crop sector on average in the last ten years (FAO, 2019). The crops produced in Mongolia mainly consist of cereals (mainly wheat), potatoes, and different types of vegetables and fruits. Currently, three-fourths of the cropland is sown with grain crops, of which 79% is sown with wheat. Around 238,102 tons of grain were produced in 2017, making up around 52% of total crop production. However, area sown with wheat has recently started declining because of the farmers' preference for growing potatoes and vegetables (FAO, 2019; FAO & WFP, 2017). Potatoes and vegetables are important crops in Mongolia, contributing to 121,808 and 82,102 tons of production, on 4% and 2% of sown area, respectively. Oilseeds, including rapeseed and canola, are becoming more and more important, with the sown area increased to 9% of the total. Other products include fodder crops (4% of sown area) and corn grown for silage (Rasmussen & Prempong, 2015).

Total crop production in Mongolia increased sharply from 2005 to 2012 but has since fluctuated from 2012 to 2017 (FAO, 2019). This is mainly due to severe droughts in 2013 and 2015, reflecting the constraints posed by weather conditions on Mongolia's crop production. A study from Oxford Business Group (2015) indicates that though Mongolia is self-sufficient in wheat, it is hard for the country to be totally self-sufficient in vegetables and other crops given its short cropping season and extreme weather conditions (Oxford Business Group, 2015). Additionally, as seen in Figure 7.8, crop yields are relatively low and vary greatly year by year (FAO, 2019). Poor crop yields are mainly attributed to poor seed quality, lack of irrigation infrastructure, low machinery usage, plant diseases, and severe weather condition (FAO, 2019).

Mongolia is a net importer of several crops and processed products (Table 7.3). The products with the highest net import value in 2017 include processed edible goods, tobacco, sugar and sugar confectionery, cereals and processed cereals, vegetables, and processed vegetables. Of these products, except for processed cereals, net import values have increased. Mongolia has become less reliant on cotton, fruits, and nuts imports, and is beginning to export fruits and nuts, with a net export value of US$41 million in 2017 (UN Comtrade, 2019).

Table 7.3
Net Trade Balance of Selected Products, Mongolia, in Millions of US$

Products	2000	2005	2015	2017
Vegetables	−2.0	−5.3	−15.4	−15.4
Fruits and nuts	−2.0	−4.2	0.9	41.0
Coffee	−1.1	−2.4	−5.3	−5.7
Cereals	−23.6	−21.3	−22.1	−27.4
Processed cereals	−17.4	−21.4	−15.7	−9.4
Oil seed	0.0	−0.4	17.8	4.4
Sugar and sugar confectionery	−8.8	−18.4	−44.1	−54.0
Cocoa products	−2.5	−9.6	−39.7	−43.2
Processed cereals	−3.8	−9.5	−47.3	−53.3
Processed vegetables	−3.8	−7.6	−27.9	−33.5
Miscellaneous edible preparations	−3.8	−10.1	−54.8	−75.7
Beverage	−12.7	−10.1	−32.8	−36.1
Tobacco	−10.3	−11.2	−57.6	−57.5
Cotton	−22.6	−25.4	−2.7	−2.6

Source. UN Comtrade (2019).

Figure 7.8

Mongolian Grain Yields (Kg/Ha), 1961–2017

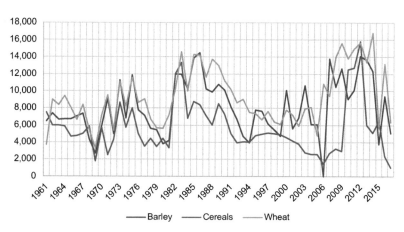

Source. FAO (2019).

V. Trade and Regional Integration

Mongolian meat exports are limited despite the importance of the subsector domestically. Moreover, fragmented value chains, poor logistics, resource constraints, and extreme weather renders meat exports highly seasonal (Enkhbold, 2018). Mongolia has limited cold storage capacity and temperature-controlled warehouse space. This poses a challenge to both the crop and livestock sectors and limits the availability of safe food items by season (Oxford Business Group, 2015; Rasmussen & Prempong, 2015).

Moreover, insufficient sanitary and phytosanitary standards (SPS) are another barrier to Mongolia's meat exports, especially regarding foot-and-mouth diseas. This limits access to markets with stronger SPS controls (FAO, 2019; Rasmussen & Prempong, 2015). Research from the ADB indicates that the shortage of SPS laboratories leaves Mongolia vulnerable to animal and plant diseases. Research from Enkhbold (2018) also indicates that the lack of international accredited laboratories is the main reason why Mongolia cannot meet SPS requirements for cross-border trade (Enkhbold, 2018). Horsemeat exports are more stable because they are not affected by foot-and-mouth disease (Rasmussen & Prempong, 2015).

Additionally, a lack of large processing facilities limits the capacity of production. For example, very little cashmere is processed domestically for this reason. Most raw or semi-processed cashmere products were exported to China, where they were finished (Oxford Business Group, 2015).

ADB has helped Mongolia upgrade laboratories and border inspection facilities and establish SPS inspection systems since 2015 (ADB, 2018). This project included an upgrade of laboratories, inspections, and quarantine facilities; establishing SPS inspection management systems; and aligning SPS control and inspections to meet international standards (ADB, 2018).

VI. Natural Resource Constraints and Sustainability

1. Land and Water Resources

Mongolia's natural resources are limited and have been heavily exploited since the 2000s for agricultural and economic development. Only 567,200 hectares of land is arable, making up around 0.5% of its total agricultural land area (FAO, 2019). Moreover, pasture land has been decreasing due to population growth and land degradation. Water is also a scarce resource in Mongolia; the issue is becoming increasingly acute due to climate change and human activity. According to FAO data, only 14% of the land in Mongolia was irrigated compared to the 518,000 hectares of potentially irrigable land (FAO, 2019). Moreover, Mongolia's rivers and lakes are also facing serious problems. Research shows that 551 out of 6,646 rivers and streams are drying or have already dried while 483 out of 3,613 medium- and small-sized lakes and marshes have dried (Zhang & Zhang, 2017). Around 70% of Mongolia's land faces desertification with the figure likely to increase (Juskalian, 2015; Zhang & Zhang, 2017). In response, water policies and laws have been implemented in Mongolia, including the National Water Program, National Program on Reduction of Natural Disasters, National Action Plan on Climate Change, and the National Action Plan for Combating Desertification (Davaa, 2008). The government has also encouraged the establishment of water protection organizations (FAO, 2012).

2. Climate Change and Sustainable Development

Mongolia is also facing serious environmental issues. Climate change is a contributing factor to increasing desertification, occurrences of extreme weather events, and land degradation. Greenhouse gas emission (GHG) in Mongolia was measured at 7.1 metric tons per capita in 2014, which is 29.6% higher than the world average (World Bank, 2019). High per capita GHG emission is mainly contributed to by land use change and forestry (e.g., forest fires, mining activities, illegal logging, and forest disease), agriculture (mainly livestock production), and energy (e.g., coalfired electricity and heat generation) (USAID, 2016). Though policy standards and measures have been launched for environmental protection and sustainable development, there is still a lack of appropriate environmental governance to monitor the implementation of environmental laws or standards in Mongolia (FAO, 2012).

VII. Conclusion

Mongolia's integration into the global agricultural market plays an important role due to the type of its exports. Particularly, with their extensive animal husbandry activities, the Mongolians have produced a variety of livestock products and byproducts as a result. Their integration into the global agricultural market brings not only food exchanges, but also exchanges in the animal byproducts such as wool and cashmere. Due to the nature of their extensive animal husbandry, the import of grain products such as cereals, vegetables, and processed products from other countries could provide important food intake for the Mongolian citizens. However, the efforts of integration involve first an improvement on the poorly managed domestic value chain and the safety and sanitary controls, and a fixation on the poor logistics behind it.

Over the past decades, there has been a growing demand for the improvement of socio-economic connections between Europe and Eastern Asia. However, the over-fragmentation of agricultural land due to the post-Soviet land reforms has become a serious obstacle for agricultural growth and productivity. It also discourages long-term investment and adoption of mechanization. Given Mongolia's history and obstacles posed by geopolitical realities, the coordination of an aggregated approach is especially crucial in motivating the national policymakers to face shared challenges and derive ideas from a collective expertise. Particularly, the country's involvement in the CAREC program could contribute as a great opportunity.

On the other hand, China has also been Mongolia's main trade partner and source of FDI. Around 90% of Mongolian products are exported to China; the value of imports from China accounts for 30% of Mongolia's total imports (Zhang & Zhang, 2017). Further, a tripartite cooperation agreement establishing the China-Mongolia-Russia economic corridor was reached in 2014, aiming to strengthen the construction of transportation infrastructure, enhance connectivity and trade, and promote further cooperation (HKTDC Research, 2018). Moreover, China and Mongolia were two of seven countries (including Russia, Kazakhstan, Belarus, Germany, and Poland) to form a joint working group on container train transport at the April 2019 Second Belt and Road Forum (Ministry of Foreign Affairs of the People's Republic of China, 2019). The current priorities for Chinese-Mongolian cooperation include: promoting and improving agricultural trade, increasing agricultural investment and employment opportunities throughout the value chain, and enhancing the capacity of farmers

(Ministry of Agriculture and Rural Affairs of the P.R. China, 2017). Due to the importance of China in its agricultural development, cooperation with China should be an important strategy for the country.

Investments in public goods, such as water, energy, and road infrastructure could greatly enhance the production of household farmers and farm businesses. Improvements in agricultural infrastructure should be understood in a broader context, and incorporate the development of support facilities, such as storage and logistics facilities. The creation of not only the physical infrastructure, but also the accompanying institutional and regulatory frameworks will help regional agricultural products gain access to the global markets. Moreover, improving veterinary, sanitary, and phytosanitary inspections and certification services could also enhance trade in meat and animal products, for instance, which is very low compared to the overall volume of livestock production in almost all the CAREC countries. Improving local capacity coupled with better interregional connectivity must come hand in hand.

References

ADB. (2018). *Mongolia: Regional upgrades of sanitary and phytosanitary measures for trade project.* https://www.adb.org/projects/46315-001/main

Cheng, K. (2003). *Growth and recovery in Mongolia during transition.* International Monetary Fund. https://www.imf.org/external/pubs/ft/wp/2003/wp03217.pdf

Davaa, G. (2008). *Water resources pProblems in Mongolia.* Remote Sensing Technology Center of Japan. https://www.restec.or.jp/geoss_ap2/pdf/0415/wg2/sr1/10.pdf

Enkhbold, E. (2018, December 6). The foreseeable future of Mongolia's agriculture. *Asian Development Blog.* https://blogs.adb.org/blog/foreseeable-future-mongolia-s-agriculture

FAO. (2012). *Country programming framework (CPF) 2012–2016.* Government of Mongolia & Food and Agriculture Organization. https://www.fao.org/publications/card/en/c/59f95 2f6-0f6b-4d99-9a37-109a16c68bcc/

FAO. (2019). *Mongolia at a glance.* Food and Agriculture Organization of the United Nations. http://www.fao.org/mongolia/fao-in-mongolia/mongolia-at-a-glance/en/

FAO & WFP. (2017). *FAO/WFP crop and livestock assessment mission to Mongolia.* https://www.fao.org/in-action/kore/news-and-events/news-details/en/c/1085502/

Hanstad, T., & J. Duncan. (2001). *Land reform from Mongolia: Observations and recommendations* (RDI Reports on Foreign Aid and Development No. 109). Rural Development Institute.

HKTDC Research. (2018, May 3). *The Belt and Road Initiative.* HKTDC Research. http://china-trade-research.hktdc.com/business-news/article/The-Belt-and-Road-Initiative/The-Belt-and-Road-Initiative/obor/en/1/1X3CGF6L/1X0A36B7.htm

IAEA. (2010, September). *Improving livestock productivity in Mongolia.* https://www.iaea.org/sites/default/files/documents/tc/mon5016.pdf

Lindberg, M. (2017, June 28). *Five critical issues facing Mongolia's fifth President.* The Asia Foundation. https://asiafoundation.org/2017/06/28/five-critical-issues-facing-mongolias-fifth-president/

Ministry of Agriculture and Rural Affairs of the P.R. China. (2017, May). *Vision and action on jointly promoting agricultural cooperation on the Belt and Road.* Belt and Road Portal. https://eng.yidaiyilu.gov.cn/zchj/qwfb/34829.htm

Ministry of Foreign Affairs of the People's Republic of China. (2019). *List of deliverables of the second Belt and Road Forum for International Cooperation.* Ministry of Foreign Affairs of the People's Republic of China. https://www.fmprc.gov.cn/mfa_eng/zxxx_662805/t1658767.shtml

Myadar, O. (2009). Nomads in a Fenced land: Land reform in post-socialist Mongolia. *Asian-Pacific Law and Policy Journal, 11*, 161–203.

Myers, G., & P. Hetz. (2004, December). *Property rights and land privatization: Issues for success in Mongolia.* USAID. https://www.land-links.org/wp-content/uploads/2016/09/USAID_Land_Tenure_Property_Rights_and_Land_Privatization_Mongolia.pdf

Oxford Business Group. (2015). *The report: Mongolia 2015.* Oxford Business Group. https://oxfordbusinessgroup.com/reports/mongolia/2015-report

Rasmussen, D., & C. Prempong. (2015). *Agricultural productivity and marketing* (Report No. 101087). World Bank.

Sayed, A. (2010, January 31) Dzud: A slow natural disaster kills livestock—and livelihoods—in Mongolia. *World Bank Blogs.* http://blogs.worldbank.org/eastasiapacific/dzud-a-slow-natural-disaster-kills-livestock-and-livelihoods-in-mongolia

UN Comtrade. (2019). https://comtrade.un.org/data/

USAID. (2016, July). *Greenhouse gas emissions in Mongolia.* https://pdf.usaid.gov/pdf_docs/pa00msrr.pdf

USDA ERS. (2018). *International agricultural productivity.* https://www.ers.usda.gov/data-products/international-agricultural-productivity

U.S. Department of Agriculture. (2018). *Agricultural total factory productivity growth indices for individual countries, 1961–2015.* USDA Economic Research Service.

World Bank. (2019). *Data bank.* https://databank.worldbank.org

World Bank. (2019). *World integrated trade solution.* https://wits.worldbank.org

Zhang, X, & S. Zhang. (2017). China-Mongolia-Russia economic corridor and environmental protection cooperation. *R-Economy, 3*(3), 161–166.

CHAPTER 8

Agricultural Development in Selected South Asian Countries

Kamiljon Akramov, Kevin Chen, Allen Park, Jarilkasin Ilyasov,
and Sarvarbek Eltazarov

I. Introduction

Agriculture plays an important role in the livelihoods of households in the South Asian countries, particularly in Afghanistan and Pakistan. The population of Afghanistan and Pakistan combined is much larger than the countries to their north and represents one of the largest economic markets bordering with the Central Asian region. In terms of labor productivity, the agricultural sector of both countries depends heavily on smallholder farming. Specifically, Pakistan is a country whose population of over 200 million is larger than Central Asia and the Caucasus combined. It also ranks among the world's leading producers of various types of agricultural goods, such as grain and livestock production. As Afghanistan has experienced lots of political tensions in the past decades, agricultural production is most often segmented, and opium poppy production is becoming an increasingly competitive crop plantation due to its lucrative market value. Through the analysis of the land use policies and transformations, the development of specific agricultural sectors, and the challenges and opportunities induced by natural resources, this section will look at the patterns and changes in the development of the agricultural sector in both Afghanistan and Pakistan. Through the detailed investigation of the arable conditions in the two countries, we will then conclude with the opportunities for their potential global agricultural integration.

II. Policy Transformations for Agriculture

Agriculture provides approximately one-fifth of value-added GDP in both Afghanistan and Pakistan, according to World Bank data from 2017. In Afghanistan, the share of agriculture in overall economic activity had shrunk from nearly 39% in 2002—when World Bank statistics first became available—to 20% in 2017. Some sources indicate that agriculture accounted for 71% in 1994 (Leao et al., 2018). The same indicator for Pakistan has remained steady, ranging between 20% and 25% over the same period. However, the government of Pakistan estimates that the share of agriculture in the near future will continue to fall, mostly as the services sector increases (Pakistan Bureau of Statistics, 2019). Agriculture, though experiencing moderate gains, has failed to keep pace with the more rapidly growing industrial and services sectors, falling from 43.7% of value-added GDP in 1960 to 23.1% in 1990 (World Bank, 2019). Figure 8.1 illustrates the medium-term structural trends of agriculture in the two countries.

Figure 8.1

Agriculture as a Percentage of Total Value-Added GDP, 2002–2017

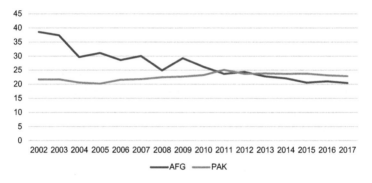

Source. World Bank (2019).

Meanwhile, labor trends in agriculture have mirrored broader trends in the sector. In 2002, over 73% of Afghans were engaged in agricultural production. This figure has since decreased to 60% in 2017, but the importance of agriculture in Afghanistan for its labor force cannot be understated. In 2013, three-fifths of agricultural workers were employed in crop production and the remaining two-fifths were engaged in the livestock sector (Leao et al., 2018). Likewise, in Pakistan, the percentage of the labor force in agriculture has declined over the long term from 38% in 2002 to 33% in 2017. As in Afghanistan, agriculture lags behind other economic sectors in production compared to its role in employment. Figure 8.2 illustrates the long-term decrease in agricultural labor as a percentage of total labor in both countries, with a faster decline observed in Afghanistan.

Afghanistan faces specific challenges stemming from its decades of conflict, which left much agricultural infrastructure underdeveloped or destroyed. Afghanistan had been a major horticultural producer until the 1970s, even leading the world in

Figure 8.2

Percent of Workforce Engaged in Agriculture, 2002–2017

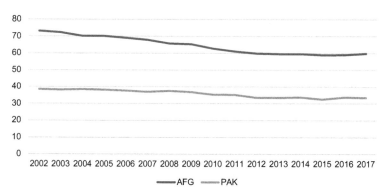

Source. World Bank (2019).

raisin production at that point (Leao et al., 2018). Livestock and horticulture prior to the 1970s were key export commodities for Afghanistan, and the country was self-sufficient in terms of wheat production (World Bank, 2014). Given that history, and the importance of the sector to the rural workforce, agriculture is a priority sector in national development plans.

1. National Agricultural Policies

Afghanistan National Agricultural Development Framework (NADF) outlines the country's short- and long-term agricultural development policies. The stated objective of the NADF is to increase agricultural production and infrastructure to reduce poverty, illicit activity, and national security. Four key areas underpin the NADF concept:

- natural resource management;
- agricultural production and productivity;
- economic regeneration;
- program support and change management (Ministry of Agriculture, Irrigation, and Livestock of the Islamic Republic of Afghanistan, 2009).

In terms of agricultural production and productivity, the government's stated goal is to move closer to self-sufficiency in field crops and expand the growth of cash crops to meet local and export demands. Under the Agriculture Production and Productivity Program (APP), the government seeks to draw attention to several subsectors including cereals and industrial crops, horticulture, livestock, irrigation (both in terms of infrastructure and on-farm support), and nomadic agriculture (named under its Kuchi Support subprogram). Subsequent support strategies and laws have been designed with the NADF framework in mind. The NADF also mentions lucrative export opportunities in large nearby markets such as India as a motivation for improving the quality and production of agriculture (Ministry of Agriculture, Irrigation, and Livestock of the Islamic Republic of Afghanistan, 2009).

Pakistan has adopted a series of national agricultural plans since its founding as a nation in 1947. These policies have focused on aggregate production, land reforms, and governance, which also included the Green Revolution that was envisioned during the 1960s and roughly continued through 1990 (Spielman et al., 2016). Early national agricultural policy plans (known as the Five-Year Plan) were aimed at improving agricultural production and developing governance structures to coordinate the usage of waters in the Indus River basin. Political instability, major droughts, and exogenous shocks (including the global oil crisis of 1973) interrupted the early series of Five-Year Plans even while the Green Revolution was underway. Pakistan's 1980 National Agriculture Policy declared food self-sufficiency as a national priority and outlined the modernization of inputs, irrigation, extension services, and mechanization to support that goal (Spielman et al., 2016).

In recent years, Pakistan has outlined its agricultural development strategies through a series of policy documents including the 11th Five-Year Plan (2013–2018), the Agriculture and Food Security Policy (2013), the National Agriculture and Food Security Action Plan (2015), the National Zero Hunger Action Plan (2012–2017), and the Framework for the Implementation of Climate Change Policy (2014–2030). These various plans fall within Pakistan's Vision 2025 concept, which aims to transform Pakistan into an upper middle-income country by 2025. The 11th Five-Year Plan aims to improve the productivity and profitability of the agricultural sector under sustainable conditions, taking national food security and poverty considerations into account. Linking agricultural production with food security is a common thread among these intersecting plans, and many of the specific interventions outlined aims to support smallholder farming through multiple channels, such as providing disaster relief, increasing market access, implementing social safety nets, promoting dietary diversification, and monitoring food commodity prices (FAO, 2016).

III. Trends in Land Use and Agricultural Production

National land policy has been undermined by an unstable security situation and exists under an uncertain legal environment in Afghanistan. The 2004 Constitution of Afghanistan, the 2007 Land Policy and the 2008 Law on Managing Land Affairs are founding documents that enumerated land rights under the current republic. While the 2007 Land Policy was designed to provide a defined legal framework for land rights, implementation of the policy has faced some hurdles, not the least of which was the simultaneous existence of customary land laws in rural areas. Successive ruling groups since the 1970s have sought to address land issues, starting with the communist government to Taliban rule in the 1990s and 2000s to the current government. De facto land distribution occurred in the 1990s, as wealthy landowners abandoned or redistributed their land. However, land was informally amassed by armed militias during periods of open conflict such as after the fall of the Taliban government (USAID, 2018).

Despite the introduction of legal frameworks for land use during the mid-2000s, Afghanistan has continued to be plagued by serious problems largely due to its experience as a conflict zone. Land grabbing and informal development on land occurred frequently and were committed by a variety of factors including households that returned from abroad, armed groups, and local elites (USAID, 2018). As over five million Afghan refugees have returned to the country in the past fifteen years, additional pressures are created on land distribution. Securing the rights of private owners is a continuing challenge, and policymakers seek to incorporate established procedures to the legal system to improve the robustness of the law. The 2008 Law on Managing Land Affairs outlines land ownership concepts that allow the full rights of private land with arrangements through the Ministry of Agricultural, Irrigation, and Livestock that allow leasing for agricultural purposes for up to 50 years of fertile land and 90 years for previously uncultivated land (Ministry of Justice of the Islamic Republic of Afghanistan, 2008).

Average farm sizes in Afghanistan are very small. According to one survey, 60% are smaller than one hectare and about 90% are smaller than five hectares (World Bank, 2014). Most cultivated land in Afghanistan is used for growing cereal crops, primarily wheat. Cereals accounted for 90% of total cultivated area in 2008–2009 and 2012–2013, though that figure was slightly reduced to 81% in 2016–2017. Wheat alone accounts for a large share of sown land, occupying almost 64% of cultivated land in 2016–2017. In Figure 8.3, other crops include mainly horticultural crops, including fruits, vegetables, and nuts. The area allocated to non-cereal crops has steadily increased since the early 2010s (Central Statistics Organization of Afghanistan, 2018).

Opium production is a significant competitor to crops for resources in Afghanistan and presents an exceptional problem. With other global poppy-growing regions undergoing more stringent enforcement, Afghanistan occupies an increasing role in global opiate production. The total land under poppy cultivation was estimated at 328,000 hectares in 2017, representing a 63% from the previous year despite the

Figure 8.3
Share of Total Cultivated Area by Crop in Afghanistan

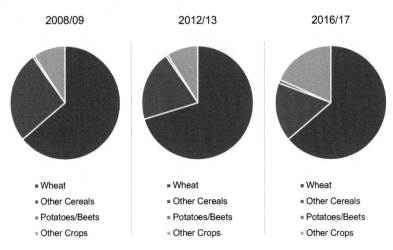

Source. Central Statistics Organization of Afghanistan (2018).

central government's official opposition to the activity (UNODC, 2017). Opium poppy production is an important source of income for poor and itinerant farmers. Compared to wheat and other non-illicit crops, it is a more profitable option for smaller farmers working under leasing or sharecropping arrangements (World Bank, 2014).

Modern land reform in Pakistan was implemented in three major stages in 1959, 1977, and 1992. The purpose of these reforms was to redistribute land from large landowners to smallholders, tenants, and landless farmers. However, land redistribution was largely unsuccessful (Malik et al., 2016). Large landowners claim a wide range of legal mechanisms to protect their holdings, undermining national- and donor-driven efforts to institute privatization and land reforms (Young et al., 2019). Land ownership in Pakistan is out of reach for many small farmers and various forms of tenant farming are common: in 2010, these arrangements constituted over a quarter of total hectares cultivated (Malik et al., 2016).

Farm sizes are generally larger in Pakistan than in Afghanistan. The average farm size, according to the national agricultural census was 2.6 hectares (6.4 acres). Small farms with less than 2 hectares (5 acres) of land comprised 64% of total private farms and only 4% of private farms reported more than 10.1 hectares of land (25 acres) in 2010 (Pakistan Bureau of Statistics, 2010). These large farms accounted for 34% of all farm areas. Some evidence of fragmentation is indicated by the data in terms of the increase in the number of small-sized private farms found in agricultural census data from 2000 and 2010. However, the number of, and area covered by, very large farms owning over 20 hectares has remained relatively constant over the same period, suggesting that land fragmentation is mostly occurring on plots owned by small- and medium-sized landowners while those owned by the wealthy are able to preserve their holdings (Pakistan Bureau of Statistics, 2016). Malik et al. (2016) argue that high transaction costs constrain rural households' ability to buy or sell agricultural land, making fragmentation the most accessible method for new landowners to obtain land. Average farm sizes in the smallest farm category, those under 0.5 hectares, decreased between agricultural census periods of 2000 and 2010, evidencing a tendency toward fragmentation (Prikhodko & Zrilyi, 2013).

Pakistan's agricultural profile has shifted from a focus on crop production to increasing livestock production. Growth rates in the livestock sector has outpaced crop production in the past three decades (Spielman et al. 2016). In 1980, roughly coinciding with the middle of the Green Revolution, the crop subsector represented 60% of total agricultural production, compared to 48% in 2010–2011. Meanwhile, livestock's share increased from 40% to 52% over the same period. Figure 8.4 provides a long-term look at Pakistan's agricultural production statistics, showing large gains in crop production during the approximate period of the Green Revolution.

Figure 8.4

Structural Transformation of Pakistan's Agricultural Sector, Value of Production in US$, 1960–2016

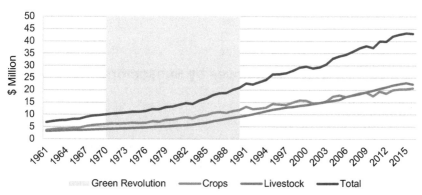

Source. FAO (2019).

The Pakistani statistical agency disaggregates wheat, rice, cotton, and sugar statistics, which reflects the importance of those four crops in national agriculture. These four crops combined for around three-fifths of total value of crop production and share of allocated land (FAO, 2019). Malik et al. (2016) identify several trends in the crop sector. First, production levels have kept pace with population growth, suggesting steady labor productivity. Second, while wheat remains the most important single commodity in Pakistani agriculture, the rate of growth has slowed during the

2010s, even while absolute growth has continued. Third, minor crops (crops besides wheat, rice, cotton, and sugar) have declined in their share of total GDP. Figure 8.5 shows land allocation by major crops in Pakistan in the 21st century, indicating the continued importance of wheat and growth in land allocated for fiber crops, mostly cotton, in the early 2010s. Pakistan is the world's fourth-largest producer of cotton and is home to a major textile processing industry that directly uses domestic output (Valdes, 2013).

Figure 8.5
Land Allocation by Major Crops in Hectares, Pakistan, 2000–2014

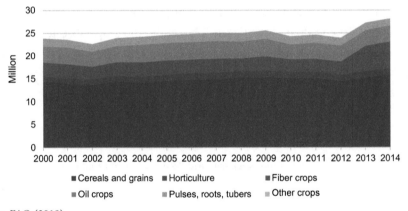

Source. FAO (2019).

IV. Perspectives by Subsectors

1. Grain Production

Wheat is the most commonly consumed cereal in terms of land allocation, production, and consumption in Afghanistan. Afghanistan has one of the world's highest annual per capita wheat consumptions, and wheat flour supplies 57% of daily total calories for the poor population of the country. Afghanistan was previously self-sufficient in wheat production, but a combination of adverse factors including population growth, poor yields, and reduction of irrigated areas has necessitated the import of 1.2 million tons on average per year (World Bank, 2014). Afghanistan also grows a combined average of one million tons of rice, maize, and barley.

Wheat occupies most of the sown land in Afghanistan, accounting for 2.3 million hectares or 64% of total cultivated land area in 2016–2017. Land allocated for wheat reached 70% in 2012–2013, up from 64% in 2008–2009. Although the share of total land is nearly identical in 2016–2017 as it was in 2008–2009, the area allocated for wheat grew in absolute terms because of the growth in cultivated areas. The area sown with wheat expanded from 2.1 million hectares in 2008/09 to 2.3 million in 2016–2017 (Central Statistics Organization of Afghanistan, 2018). The World Bank identified wheat as a promising source of agricultural growth but also noted that Afghanistan's generally arid climate and dependence on irrigation does not lend itself to growing wheat in the longer term. However, in the short term, wheat plays an important role for farmers seeking to ensure their own food security.

Pakistan was the world's eighth-largest producer of wheat, producing 26.7 million tons, and tenth largest producer of rice in 2017 (FAO, 2019). Valdes (2013) notes that rice represented 44% of agricultural export earnings. Wheat and rice also represent the two single most important cereal crops for domestic consumption (FAO, 2012). Wheat yields in Pakistan are comparable to several other major wheat growing nations in terms of productivity, shown in Figure 8.6. Pakistan recorded wheat yields of 3 tons per hectare, which is on par with major wheat exporters such as Russia and the United States. At the same time, FAO estimates that wheat production in Pakistan should be higher given agroclimatic conditions and can reach up to 6 tons per hectare in the eastern Punjab region (the country's major wheat production area) through sustainable crop intensification (Prikhodko & Zrilyi, 2013).

Despite being one of the world's largest producers of wheat, Pakistan exported very little of the product in the mid-2010s (FAO, 2019). Pakistan has alternated between being a net wheat importer or exporter in recent decades, but overall trade volumes are very low and local consumers, and producers are largely disconnected from the global market. Pakistan's government has maintained a policy of strong intervention in

Figure 8.6
Wheat Productivity (Tons per Hectare), Selected Countries, 2013–2017

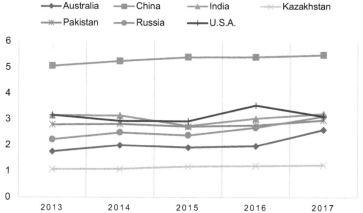

Source. FAO (2019).

restricting both imports and exports of wheat. Official policies have been designed to balance the competing interests of wheat producers, and consumers through income supports for farmers and import substitution policies for the former and subsidies for the latter (Dorosh et al., 2016). Government involvement in the wheat sector reflects the strategic importance of the crop for policymakers. The government actively supports wheat producers through a variety of administrative measures including state procurement mechanisms (Prikhodko & Zrilyi, 2013).

2. Livestock and Dairy Production

Livestock production is another key pillar of Afghan agriculture. The livestock sector accountes for approximately one million out of 2.5 million people employed in agriculture (Leao et al. 2018). However, many of these workers are unpaid family workers. Afghanistan was self-sufficient in meat and milk during the 1970s. Moreover, it exported processed animal products such as wool and higher-value derived products such as carpets and clothing during this time. During the wartime period, livestock herd sizes were significantly reduced, because of a lack of access to important grazing areas and the flight of pastoral herders into Pakistan to escape the conflict. Today, Afghanistan relies on imports to meet domestic demand for meat, eggs, and dairy products from India, Pakistan, Iran, and the UAE (World Bank, 2014).

Livestock faces numerous challenges in Afghanistan, some typical to those in other developing countries and others caused by decades of war. Veterinary and regulatory systems supporting livestock are in poor condition, making poor breeding, diseases, and lack of nutritious feeds an ongoing challenge for livestock farmers. Farmers practicing agriculture in distant rural areas and nomadic herding have especially poor access to livestock support networks. Nomadic livestock production still occurs in Afghanistan, mostly by the Kuchi minority. The nomadic Kuchis are estimated to comprise 5.2% (1.6 million people) of the national population and are mostly engaged in the livestock sector. However, some Kuchis have been forced to adopt sedentary lifestyles or re-settle in urban areas and are more likely to be food insecure than the rest of the population (WFP et al., 2016).

Pakistan's livestock sector on the other hand has demonstrated steady growth in the past two decades, now comprising 56% of value addition in agriculture and employing approximately 30 million people (Rehman et al., 2017). Up until 2012, Pakistan contains the world's third-largest animal herd and is the world's fifth largest producer of milk (FAO, 2012). Livestock production across all categories has generally increased between the mid-2000s and mid-2010s: both milk and beef production has grown by a third since 2006 (Pakistan Bureau of Statistics, 2016). The poultry industry in recent years has enjoyed strong growth, in terms of both meat and egg production, which was largely aided by increased financial investments and adoption of new technologies beginning in the late 1990s (Hussain et al., 2015). Meat and egg production averaged 11% and 6% annual growth, respectively, between 2006 and 2016 (Pakistan Bureau of Statistics, 2016). Despite increased production of poultry products, external trade for poultry products is low and has not shown similar gains: in 2016, total poultry exports were valued at US$2.7 million (FAO, 2019).

A growing population and urbanization of the population are contributing to an increasing demand for livestock products. The recent increase in livestock production is believed to come from increasing animal counts rather than productivity gains. Like other developing countries, the majority of livestock is held by small farmers, and several factors including transport costs and inadequate infrastructure make large-scale livestock production prohibitively expensive (Rehman et al., 2017). Owning livestock creates economic opportunities for small farmers and the landless in Pakistan, who do not often have access to support services that would help sustain high-productivity activity.

3. Horticulture

Afghanistan has a long history of horticultural production aided by its diverse geographic and climate conditions, which was interrupted by the outbreak of conflict at the end of the 1970s. Prior to that period, it was among global leaders in the production of a variety of nuts, dried fruits, and tree fruits including almonds, pomegranates, pistachios, grapes, and apricots (World Bank, 2014). Afghanistan during this time, supplied around 20% of the world's raisins, making it the world's largest raisin producer (Ministry of Agriculture, Irrigation, and Livestock of the Islamic Republic of Afghanistan, 2009). The World Bank has identified horticulture as a subsector in which Afghanistan enjoys a comparative advantage, though the development of value chains, facilities, and markets will require time and investment. However, given the political instability and economic uncertainty of recent decades, many farmers prefer to grow cereal crops over horticulture to guarantee their own food security (World Bank, 2014). Much of Afghanistan's tree-based horticulture occurs in old orchards, which will need significant investment and improvement.

Figure 8.7 indicates that horticulture has been growing in Afghanistan in recent years. Although the land allocated is relatively small compared to grains, horticulture is generally higher-value and accounts for a disproportionately large share in earnings. In 2016–2017, over 550,000 hectares were sown with fruit and vegetable crops. Grapes, grown on over 82,000 hectares, were the most widely planted single fruit crop

Figure 8.7

Land Allocated to Horticulture, Afghanistan, in Hectares, 2009–2017

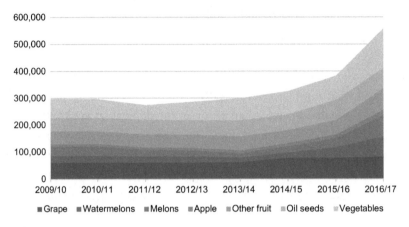

Grape Watermelons Melons Apple Other fruit Oil seeds Vegetables

Source. Central Statistics Organization of Afghanistan (2018).

reported, followed by melons (80,000 hectares), watermelons (75,000 hectares), and apples (19,000 hectares). Although not disaggregated by individual crop type, land sown with vegetable crops rapidly increased from 72,000 hectares in 2009–2010 to 146,000 hectares in 2016–2017. Oil seeds are also being grown at a wider scale, planted on 75,000 hectares in 2016–2017, representing an over 50% increase from 2009–2010 (Central Statistics Organization of Afghanistan, 2018).

Major horticultural crops in Pakistan include citrus fruits, mangoes, apples, dates, and onions. Pakistan is among the world's largest producers of specific horticultural crops and possesses areas that feature a favorable climate for growing subtropical and tropical crops. Up until 2012, it is the world's third-largest producer of dates and fifth largest producer of mangoes (FAO, 2012). In 2016, Pakistan exported US$659 million worth of fruits and vegetables (FAO, 2019). Pakistan is also a large importer of horticulture, importing a total value of US$1.3 billion in the same year. It also produces various spices in large quantities including garlic, chili peppers, coriander, and turmeric. Figure 8.8 displays land allocation statistics of horticultural crops in Pakistan from 2011 to 2016. Total land allocated to fruits and vegetables has remained relatively steady during this period. Potatoes, onions (which have been disaggregated from the spices category below), tomatoes, and carrots are the main vegetable crops grown in Pakistan. (Pakistan Ministry of National Food Security and Research, 2016).

In contrast with other commodities in the agricultural sector, Pakistan's government has largely allowed the private sector to lead the marketing of fruit with little intervention in terms of pricing and restrictions. At the same time, horticultural

Figure 8.8

Horticultural Land Allocation, Pakistan, in Hectares, 2011–2016

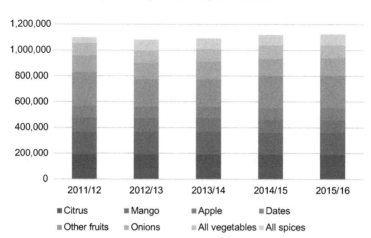

Source. Pakistan Ministry of National Food Security and Research (2016).

value chains are underdeveloped and face constraints in terms of infrastructure, for example, a lack of refrigeration facilities and vehicles, that often limit the reach and marketability of fruit and vegetable products (Khushk et al., 2006).

V. Trade and Regional Integration

Afghanistan's trade is heavily oriented to the two large markets in South Asia, India, and Pakistan. Around 92% of total Afghan exports are directed to India (47%) and Pakistan (45%) in 2017. Agricultural exports made up almost 80% of the total US$879 million exported in 2017. Some of the most commonly exported agricultural crops include grapes, cotton, and a variety of tree crops. India and Pakistan were the destinations for 95% of exported grapes and 100% of cotton exports. Imports from Kazakhstan represent around 11% of total imports, at US$563 million worth of goods in 2017. Of that total, agriculture represented over 75% of all products, with wheat and wheat flour accounting for 66% alone (Simoes & Hidalgo, 2011). However, trade between Afghanistan and Central Asian countries is very low in comparison.

To facilitate trade, the Afghanistan Ministry of Commerce and Industries (MoCI) abolished a dual licensing system for businesses. Previously, domestic businesses had to be issued trade licenses from two domestic agencies (the Afghanistan Investment Support Agency (AISA) and the MoCI) in order to send exports (World Bank, 2017). Moreover, trade has been aided by improvements in connectivity with its largest trading partners. New air routes were established with India and border issues with Pakistan that hindered trade in 2016 were resolved, strengthening Afghanistan's connections with South Asia (World Bank, 2019).

Pakistan's long-term national development plan, known as Vision 2025, aims for the country to become a private sector-led major exporter, with a target of US$150 billion by 2025 (FAO, 2016). However, policies such as the export ban of wheat imposed during the global food price crisis of 2007–2008 and tariffs on imported agricultural products signal lingering opposition to trade liberalization, even after the simplification of tariff systems in the mid-1990s (Valdes, 2013). However, partial and full exemptions were introduced for certain commodities starting in the mid-2000s, and tariff levels for those remained high, hindering Pakistan's greater participation in global value chains. In 2015, the Pakistan government announced a three-year Strategy Trade Policy Framework for 2015 to 2018 that aimed to place exports at the center of economic growth (FAO, 2016). However, from 2015 to 2017 Pakistani exports recorded negative growth each year (World Bank, 2019).

Pakistan has a well-documented history of intervening in foreign trade of certain crops, especially wheat, rice, and sugar. Import controls in addition to tariffs have prevented cheaper international wheat, including competing products from Kazakhstan, Russia, and Ukraine from entering Pakistan (Prikhodko & Zrilyi, 2013). While greater trade with neighboring countries can provide mutual benefits, prospects for greater agricultural trade between Pakistan and India run counter to political sensitivities for domestic producers in both countries having to compete for the market share of similar commodities. India granted Pakistan preferential trade status in the 1990s, shortly after gaining admission into the World Trade Organization. However, trade barriers continued to persist on both sides and India ultimately revoked that status in February 2019, officially citing a skirmish in the Jammu and Kashmir region for the move. Apart from political considerations, price differentials for certain commonly consumed items such as wheat and sugar are fairly small, limiting the demand for the trade of these commodities (Dorosh et al., 2016).

VI. Natural Resource Constraints

1. Land Resources

Arable land only accounts for about 12% of total land in Afghanistan. The country features mountainous terrain with little precipitation, making irrigation an important component of agriculture. There is evidence that the limited arable land in Afghanistan under-irrigated. Prior to the destruction of water infrastructure during the conflict years, almost three million hectares of land were irrigated, compared to two million in the mid-2010s. Afghanistan has the potential to irrigate 4.4 million hectares (World Bank, 2014). Official data suggest that irrigated areas are gradually recovering, as seen in Figure 8.9, adding an average of around 89,000 hectares per year since 2009. Around 16% of households have access to rainfed land (WFP et al., 2016).

Figure 8.9
Irrigated Land in Afghanistan, Thousands of Hectares, 2009–2017

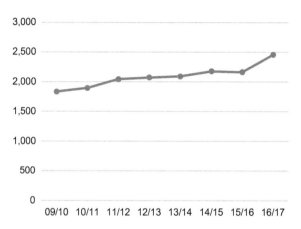

Source. Central Statistics Organization of Afghanistan (2018).

Pakistan features a large diversity in agroclimatic conditions with its major agriculture-producing zones supplied with water from the melting glaciers of several mountain ranges including the Karakoram and Hindu Kush in the north. Pakistan is also home to the world's largest earth-filled dam, providing nearly a quarter of national electricity output (Malik et al., 2016). Eastern areas of the country receive precipitation through the summer monsoon season, which accounts for 60% of the country's annual precipitation. Most of the country can be considered arid or semiarid, though areas bordering the mountain ranges to the north receive substantially more precipitation (Chaudhry, 2017).

Pakistan's major agricultural areas are located in the Indus River basin, which by the 1980s contained around 70% of the country's 31 million hectares of cultivable land (Pinckney, 1989). The Indus River basin also hosts the world's largest gravity-fed irrigation system (Malik et al., 2016), construction for which had begun in the 19th century. Pakistan has invested heavily in expanding irrigated areas in the late 20th century: total irrigated area nearly doubled from 10.4 million to 20.6 million hectares between 1960 and 2010 (Davies et al., 2016).

2. Climate Change and Natural Risks

Afghanistan faces similar risks from climate change as the rest of the Central Asian region, mainly in the form of droughts and floods. Because Afghanistan's agriculture relies mostly on irrigation, but also rainfall, the impacts of climate change will be felt in multiple ways. A joint report by the World Food Program, UN Environment Program, and the National Environment Protection Agency of Afghanistan identifies four climate hazards:

- drought caused by a lack of spring rainfall;
- spring and summer drought caused by reduced snowmelt in upland areas;
- floods caused by localized heavy spring rainfall;
- floods caused by increased snowmelt in highland areas.

These climate hazards are consistent with general projections seen in Central Asia in which higher global temperatures will lead to uncertain weather patterns that will make precipitation more variable than it is today.

Although warmer temperatures over recent decades have lengthened the growing season in most parts of Afghanistan, it is unclear whether this has benefited productivity measures as spring rainfall decreased over the same period. Decreased spring rainfall has been recorded throughout the country's central and northern provinces bordering Central Asia. In addition, reduced snowmelt in nearby mountains threatens irrigation water flows. Between 2000 and 2014, the number of snowfall days has generally decreased throughout the country, but the most severe decreases have been seen in the far eastern Hindu Kush and Pamir Mountain ranges, which is the source of irrigation water for the country's Northeast and parts of Central Asia (WFP et al., 2016). Like droughts, the risk of flooding can be characterized into impacts in terms of rainfall and impacts in terms of snowmelt. Heavy spring rainfall has increased in the country's southern provinces bordering Iran and Pakistan in the past thirty years. Paradoxically, heavy rain events have affected the same northern regions that are experiencing lower overall spring rainfall (WFP et al. 2016).

Afghanistan is vulnerable to some of the same natural risks found in mountainous regions of Central Asia, including earthquakes, floods, landslides, avalanches, and droughts. Many of Afghanistan's populated centers also lie in disaster-prone areas, and Afghanistan is second only to Haiti in terms of the number of fatalities in low-income countries from natural disasters between 1980 and 2015. Economic damage caused by drought is estimated at US$280 million, earthquakes at US$80 million, and food at US$54 million (World Bank, 2017). Droughts are frequent in Afghanistan and are expected to increase in the future due to the impacts of climate change.

Although Pakistan boasts a rich natural endowment for agriculture, water scarcity is a growing problem in arid and semiarid areas of the country. Roughly 80% of the country's total land area can be classified as arid or semiarid and is vulnerable to desertification (UNDP, 2017). Pakistan ranks among the world's most water-stressed countries along with nations mostly in the Middle East and Central Asia, which is defined by a high withdrawal of total renewable resources (Young et al., 2019).

Pakistan has suffered severe weather-related disasters in recent years, including floods and droughts that had serious consequences for agriculture in afflicted areas. Pakistan suffered a series of catastrophic floods in recent years that studies suggest may increase as the impacts of climate change become stronger (FAO, 2012). The country is highly vulnerable to climate change, ranking eighth globally in Germanwatch's Global Climate Risk Index 2018 in terms of nations most affected by climate-related events from 1998 to 2017. According to the authors of that survey, Pakistan has suffered US$3.8 billion worth of damages from climate change during this period (Eckstein et al., 2019).

The annual mean temperature in Pakistan has increased by 0.5 degrees Celsius from 1961 to 2007. Under a moderate scenario, the annual mean temperature is projected to rise by 3 to 5 degrees Celsius by the end of the 21st century, with higher global emissions assumptions producing an even more extreme range of 4 to 6 degrees Celsius (Chaudhry, 2017). Pakistan has already witnessed several extreme heat events in recent years that had significant impacts on agriculture and the wellbeing of rural households. Long-term heat stress may induce migration from afflicted areas in Pakistan, with more lasting implications than other disasters such as flooding (Mueller et al., 2014).

VII. Conclusion

Overall, grain and livestock are two important agricultural subsectors in Afghanistan and Pakistan; though historical factors that shaped the political conditions in Afghanistan has continuously served as a prominent cause for its regional variations. The continuous warfare happening in Afghanistan have resulted in an increasingly inward agricultural development within the country, with most of the smallholder farmers planting crops primarily for their own survival needs. A resolution of the conflicts raised in the region could open an important window for regional and global integration of the agricultural sector in Afghanistan. On the other hand, with the country's abundance land and natural resources, the agricultural sector in Pakistan has the potential of becoming increasingly important to the Asia continent. In particular, the regional integration of its agricultural sector with other Asian countries could contribute Pakistan's Vision 2025 concept that aims to transform Pakistan into an upper middle-income country by 2025. The transformation to a more integrated agriculture market within the Asian region could improve the productivity and profitability of its agricultural sector.

For both Afghanistan and Pakistan, agricultural trade markets are heavily oriented around the South Asian region. Specifically, Afghanistan's exports are highly concentrated in India and Pakistan, with around 90% of its total exports directed to the latter in 2016. Moreover, the improvement in regional connectivity as a result of various regional cooperation initiatives has also enhanced regional connectivity in South Asia. Market interaction, however, between South Asia and Central Asia has been limited due to historical reasons. As perceived by many think tanks, such as the World Bank, there is a huge potential for regional integration between Central and South Asia, increasing regional connectivity within the Asian region is hence an important goal for improved regional economic development. As part of the integration strategy, by 2024, the Khyber Pass Economic Corridor (KPEC) that connects Pakistan and Afghanistan with Central Asia through the Khyber Pass will be officially established as part of Corridors five and six of the CAREC routes. It will provide the shortest trade link between Pakistan, Afghanistan, Tajikistan, Uzbekistan, and the Arabian Sea. Further, other regional integrative policies, such as the Chinese Belt and Road Initiative, could also provide potential development opportunities within the region.

Reference

Central Statistics Organization of Afghanistan. (2018). *Agricultural statistics 2008–2016*. Central Statistics Organization of Afghanistan.

Chaudhry, Q. (2017). *Climate change profile of Pakistan*. Asian Development Bank. https://www.adb.org/publications/climate-change-profile-pakistan

Davies, S., A. Gueneau, D. Mekonnen, C. Ringler, & S. Robinson. (2016). Irrigation and water management in the Indus Basin: Infrastructure and management strategies to improve agricultural productivity. In *Agriculture and the Rural Economy in Pakistan* (pp. 117–170). University of Pennsylvania Press.

Dorosh, D., E. Alonso, S. Malik, & A. Salam. (2016). Agricultural prices and trade policies. *Agriculture and the Rural Economy in Pakistan* (pp. 273–308). University of Pennsylvania Press.

Eckstein, D., M. Hutfils, & M. Winges. (2019). *Global climate risk index 2019*. Germanwatch.

FAO. (2012). *Assessment of the agriculture and rural development sectors in the Eastern Partnership countries*. https://www.eesc.europa.eu/sites/default/files/resources/docs/azerbaijan_assessment.pdf

FAO. (2016). *Pakistan country fact sheet on food and agriculture policy trends.* https://www.fao.org/3/i6054e/i6054e.pdf

FAO. (2019). *FAOSTAT.* https://www.fao.org/faostat/en/#home

Hussain, J., I. Rabbani, S. Aslam, & H. Ahmad. (2015). An overview of poultry industry in Pakistan. *World Poultry Science Journal, 71,* 689–700.

Khushk, A., A. Memon, & M. Lashari. (2006). Marketing system of selected fruits in Pakistan. *Bangladesh Journal of Agricultural Research, 31* (1), 39–68.

Leao, I., M. Ahmed, & A. Kar. (2018). *Jobs from agriculture in Afghanistan.* World Bank Group.

Malik, S., S. Ali, K. Riaz, E. Whitney, M. Malek, & A. Waqas. (2016). Agriculture, land, and productivity in Pakistan. *Agriculture and the Rural Economy in Pakistan* (pp. 41–80). University of Pennsylvania Press.

Ministry of Agriculture, Irrigation, and Livestock of the Islamic Republic of Afghanistan. (2009). *National agricultural development framework.* https://mail.gov.af/en

Ministry of Justice of the Islamic Republic of Afghanistan. (2008). *Law on managing land affairs* (Serial No. 958). Ministry of Justice of the Islamic Republic of Afghanistan.

Mueller, V., C. Gray, & K. Kosec. (2014). Heat stress increases long-term human migration in rural Pakistan. *Nature Climate Change, 4,* 182–185.

Pakistan Bureau of Statistics. (2010). *Agricultural census.* https://www.pbs.gov.pk/publication/agricultural-census-2010-pakistan-report

Pakistan Bureau of Statistics. (2016). *Pakistan statistical yearbook.* https://www.pbs.gov.pk/publication/pakistan-statistical-year-book-2016

Pakistan Bureau of Statistics. (2019). *Agriculture statistics tables.* https://www.pbs.gov.pk/agriculture-statistics-tables

Pakistan Ministry of National Food Security and Research. (2016). *Fruits, vegetables and condiments statistics of Pakistan 2015–16.* https://mnfsr.trancemedia.pk/publications/

Pinckney, T. (1989). *The demand for public storage of wheat in Pakistan* (Research Report No. 77). International Food Policy Research Institute.

Prikhodko, D., & O. Zrilyi. (2013). *Pakistan: Review of the wheat sector and grain storage issues.* World Bank.

Rehman, A., J. Luan, A. Chandio, & I. Hussain. (2017). Livestock production and population census in Pakistan: Determining their relationship with agricultural GDP using econometric analysis. *Information Processing in Agriculture, 4*(2), 168–177.

Simoes, A., & C. Hidalgo. (2011, January). *The economic complexity observatory: An analytical tool for understanding the dynamics of economic development.* [Conference presentation]. Scalable Integration of Analytics and Visualization, San Francisco, California, USA. https://www.researchgate.net/profile/Cesar-Hidalgo-2/publication/221605462_The_Economic_Complexity_Observatory_An_Analytical_Tool_for_Understanding_the_Dynamics_of_Economic_Development/links/54f472430cf24eb8794e8a6d/

The-Economic-Complexity-Observatory-An-Analytical-Tool-for-Understanding-the-Dynamics-of-Economic-Development.pdf

Spielman, D., S. Malik, P. Dorosh, & N. Ahmad. (2016). Food, agriculture, and rural development in Pakistan. *Agriculture and the Rural Economy in Pakistan* (pp. 1–40). University of Pennsylvania Press.

UNDP. (2017, July 24). *Without sustainable land management, Pakistan faces major risks from desertification.* https://www.adaptation-undp.org/without-sustainable-land-management-pakistan-faces-major-risks-desertification

UNODC. (2017). *Afghanistan opium survey 2017.* https://www.unodc.org/documents/crop-monitoring/Afghanistan/Afghan_opium_survey_2017_cult_prod_web.pdf

USAID. (2018). *Property rights and resource governance: Afghanistan.* Landlinks. https://www.land-links.org/country-profile/afghanistan/

Valdes, A. (2013). *Agriculture trade and price policy in Pakistan* (Policy Paper PK 17/12). World Bank. https://openknowledge.worldbank.org/entities/publication/7c1e22da-f8c9-57ca-b958-83f3e27819d2

WFP, UNEP, & NEPA. (2016, November 1). *Climate change in Afghanistan.* https://www.unep.org/resources/report/climate-change-afghanistan-what-does-it-mean-rural-livelihoods-and-food-security

World Bank. (2014, June). *Islamic Republic of Afghanistan agricultural sector review* (Report No. AUS9779). https://documents1.worldbank.org/curated/en/245541467973233146/pdf/AUS9779-REVISED-WP-PUBLIC-Box391431B-Final-Afghanistan-ASR-web-October-31-2014.pdf

World Bank. (2017). *Disaster risk profile: Afghanistan.* https://documents.worldbank.org/en/publication/documents-reports/documentdetail/284301491559464423/disaster-risk-profile-afghanistan

World Bank. (2017). *Doing business in Afghanistan 2017.* https://openknowledge.worldbank.org/entities/publication/a4358f1a-1ed6-534b-9225-480129f17077

World Bank. (2019). *Afghanistan country overview.* https://www.worldbank.org/en/country/afghanistan/overview

Young, W., et al. (2019). *Pakistan: Getting more from water.* World Bank. https://documents.worldbank.org/en/publication/documents-reports/documentdetail/251191548275645649/pakistan-getting-more-from-water

CHAPTER 9

Assessment of Agricultural Trade Comparative Advantage of Myanmar

Huaqi Zhang and Kevin Chen

I. Introduction

Myanmar has been gaining continuous attention from the international community recently. With the gross domestic product (GDP) growth rate of 6.5% in 2016 (World Bank, 2017), Myanmar is one of the world's fastest-growing economies (Kim & Thunt, 2017). Agriculture is the backbone of Myanmar's economy, contributing to 37.8% of the (GDP, 70% of employment, and 27.5% of total export earnings (FAO, 2017). Myanmar's agricultural products are mainly land- and labor-intensive products, such as rice, pulses and beans, maize, sesame, fruits, and vegetables (ADB, 2013; Sri Lanka, EDB, 2014; Embassy of the Republic of the Union of Myanmar, 2017). However, Myanmar's agriculture sector has substantial unexploited potential to underpin its economic development (Raitzer et al., 2015). Agricultural exports were only US$2.02 billion in 2016, compared with neighboring Vietnam's exports of US$19.64 billion in the same year (UN Comtrade, 2017). With vast land in three different agroecological zones (i.e., the delta and coastal zone, the dry zone, and the hill regions), abundant water, low-cost labor resources, as well as a location close to two large markets in India and China, Myanmar's agricultural can become more competitive and has immense potential for growth.

Tight control over agricultural marketing, trading, and pricing during the socialist period (1962–1987) resulted in poor agricultural trade performance (Fujita & Okamoto, 2006). The agricultural trading sector gradually developed after the movement to a more open economy in 1988 (ADB, 2012; Soe, 2004). Furthermore, Myanmar's government has introduced significant political and economic reforms in liberalizing agricultural trading since 2011 (Raitzer et al., 2015), including the opening to global trade, encouraging foreign direct investment, and deepening agricultural policy reforms. In particular, the government is aiming to promote agricultural exports and pursue an export-oriented strategy for agriculture (ADB, 2013) by diversifying markets abroad and improving the quality of exported products (ADB, 2012). Additional significant reforms have also come through the removal or reduction of export taxes, restrictive license requirements, and fixed exchange rates (Tun et al., 2015). Furthermore, in 2016, the Vice Minister of Agriculture, Livestock, and Irrigation called for a change in Myanmar's national strategy in developing and managing its agri-food export sector, aiming to fuel agricultural export as embodied in the 2015 National Export Strategy.

In this chapter, we aim to provide a better understanding of Myanmar's agricultural export performance in relation to its competitors and determine the policy actions for improving Myanmar's export performance. We will use a normalized revealed a comparative advantage (NRCA) index to compare the agricultural competitiveness between Myanmar and its competitors from 2007 to 2016. With the analysis, we found that Myanmar's agricultural export sector enjoys comparative advantage in the global market, but it is not competitive when compared with its major competitors. Particularly, Myanmar's advantage focuses most on large commodity products such as black gram & pigeon peas, natural rubber, sesame seeds, and rice. We argue that diversifying Myanmar's export portfolio, strengthening export promotion and development, and attracting foreign direct investment to upgrade the cross-border value chain are three major important focus of improvement as Myanmar proceed to enhance the export competitiveness.

II. Literature Review

Understanding the competitiveness of Myanmar in agricultural export sectors is essential for developing export policies. Comparative advantage describes the tendency for countries to export commodities for which they are relatively more competitive over the rest of the world and is considered vital to export competitiveness. It is widely used in the international trade to evaluate patterns of trade specialization and export competitiveness in a given sector (Bhattacharyya, 2011; Kilduff & Chi, 2007; Startienė & Remeikienė, 2014).

Export competitiveness can be broadly defined and measured by the RCA index. The RCA index is based on the economic efficiency of industry, revealing a country's weak and strong export sectors and providing implications for trade policy. Additionally, RCA is easily calculated and widely used, and therefore, provides a simple way to evaluate a country's trade policy (Startienė & Remeikienė, 2014). Researchers have utilized the RCA index to analyze the comparative advantage among countries/ regions in various sectors, including agriculture, manufacture, and industry. Table 9.1 summarizes a number of examples of research that utilizes the RCA index to analyze the competitiveness of certain countries or regions in international trade. There are several ways of using the RCA indices in analyzing trade performance, including a) comparing the calculated value with the RCA neutral point, b) comparing given sectors by using the calculated index score, and c) directly comparing the calculated index values (Chandran & Sudarsan, 2012; Ferto & Hubbard, 2002; Kalafsky & Graves, 2016; Sanidas & Shin, 2010; Yu & Qi, 2015).

Despite that utilizing RCA analysis over the past decades, there is little existing literature measuring comparative advantages in the agricultural export sector of Myanmar. Additionally, when analyzing the competitiveness in Myanmar's agricultural export trade, most of the studies choose only limited products (e.g., rice, pulses, fish, etc.) and its neighboring countries (e.g., India, Vietnam) as the competitors for analysis. Estudillo and Fujimura (2015) explored the degrees of comparative advantage of Vietnam and Myanmar in rice production and exporting. They found that although both countries enjoyed a comparative advantage in rice exporting, Vietnam is superior to Myanmar in the degree of comparative advantage. However, Myanmar has the ability to further release its potential in rice export. Aung (2009) calculated the RCAs of Myanmar's major agricultural commodities through 2000–2006, aiming to explore which commodities should be targeted for export to increase economic development. This research indicated that Myanmar was still dependent on exporting natural resources rather than value-added products leading to the recommendation to seek technical assistance from neighboring countries and major trade partners. Kim and Thunt (2017) also utilized the RCA index to explore Myanmar's export competitiveness in different industries. The result revealed that Myanmar had RCAs in most primary commodities, such as the natural resources, agriculture, fishery, and livestock sectors, but the RCAs were in decline from 2010 to 2015.

Moreover, except for the RCA index, there are some other indices for analyzing the comparative advantage in the international trade. For example, trade-cum-production indices containing both trade and production variables, e.g., Lafay index (LI) (Lafay, 1992); export-only indices containing only export variables, e.g., symmetric RCA index (SI) (Dalum et al., 1998), weighted RCA index (WI) (Proudman & Redding, 2000), and additive RCA index (AI) (Hoen & Oosterhaven, 2006); indices using hypothetical situation such as comparative advantage neutral point, e.g., normalized RCA index (NI) (Yu et al., 2009). Each of the indices has pros and cons, thus it is important to well understand the properties of the indices and properly use them. Table 9.2 presented the statistical properties of the six indices with the different perspective, such as the

Table 9.1

Related Literature Utilized Revealed Comparative Advantage Index for Analysis

Country/region	Method	Year	Commodities	Conclusion	Author
Regional and Central and East European	Revealed comparative advantage	1992–1997	Agriculture products	Oceania, South America, the Caribbean, and Africa had a relative revealed a comparative export advantage in agricultural products, while Asia countries showed comparative export disadvantage. The North American Free Trade Agreement countries and Europe had neither a marked relative revealed comparative export advantage nor a disadvantage.	Bojnec (2001)
Hungarian	Balassa revealed comparative advantage; relative trade advantage; revealed competitiveness	1992–1998	Agri-food products	In spite of the significant changes in Hungarian's agriculture during the 1990s, the pattern of revealed comparative advantage has remained fairly stable. Hungary has revealed comparative advantages for eleven of the 22 aggregated product groups.	Ferto & Hubbard (2002)
China	Revealed comparative advantage	2000–2006	Agriculture products	Wood related products showed the highest comparative advantages while vegetables, roots and tubers showed improved export competitiveness between 2000 and 2006.	Aung (2009)
India and Association of Southeast Asian Nations (ASEAN) countries	Revealed comparative advantage and trade intensity index	1990–2007	Fishery sector	Revealed comparative advantage at commodity group level showing that there was trade complementarity between India and ASEAN to be exploited which can enhance bilateral trade.	Chandran & Sudarsan (2012)

(Continued)

Country/region	Method	Year	Commodities	Conclusion	Author
Lithuanian	Revealed comparative advantage index and revealed symmetric comparative advantage index	2007–2011	Industrial products	Food, chemicals, wood, and textile manufactures in Lithuanian took the strongest competitive positions in global markets during the period of 2007–2011.	Startienė & Remeikienė (2014)
China and Central and Eastern European countries	Revealed comparative advantage; Trade complementarity index; Intra-Industry trade index	2013	Agricultural products	There was a big difference in the comparative advantage of agricultural product export of China and five Central and Eastern European (CEE) countries. China and CEE countries should further bring out their comparative advantages and adjust product structure of exports to achieve mutual benefit in the bilateral trade.	Yu & Qi (2015)
Southern states in the United States	Revealed comparative advantage	1995–2013	Manufacturing	Revealed comparative advantage value varied significantly within the southern region between 1995 and 2013. All seven of the states with above-parity revealed comparative advantages in 2013 trended upward in export intensities.	Kalafsky & Graves (2016)

neutral point, symmetry, and comparability cross-sector, country, and over-time, etc. According to the summary, the NI has more favorable features as an RCA index than the others. Especially, its stable means across space and time, comparability across the country and time, and the independence from the selected country can be very helpful in analyzing the trade competitiveness and specialization. However, rarely research utilizes NRCA index assessing Myanmar's comparative advantage of the agricultural export sector and its competitors. The only literature comes from the Myanmar, Ministry of Commerce, Department of Trade Promotion (2018) report, calculating the NRCA score for Myanmar in rice, seeds, fisheries, and crustaceans, and rubber during 2002–2004 and 2009–2011, suggesting a relatively high level of productivity in these prioritized sectors. However, no NRCA score is calculated or analyzed for Myanmar's competitors in the global market. Thus there is also no comparison for the comparative advantage between Myanmar and its competitors for given agricultural commodities for better understanding Myanmar's agricultural export situation across the years, or for developing further recommendations for Myanmar's agricultural sector for enhancing the agricultural competitiveness.

Table 9.2
Statistical Properties of the Six Indices

Index	BI	LI	SI	WI	AI	NI
Comparative advantage neutral point	1	0	0	1	0	0
Independence from reference group of countries	X	X	X	X	X	√
Symmetry	X	√	√	X	√	√
Comparability cross-sector	X	?	X	X	X	√
Comparability cross-country	X	?	X	√	√	√
Comparability over-time	X	√	X	X	?	√

Source. Sanidas and Shin (2010).
Note. BI = Balassa's RCA index; LI = Lafay index; SI = symmetric RCA index; WI = weighted RCA index; AI = additive RCA index; NI = normalized RCA index.

III. Data Source and Agriculture Export Pattern in Myanmar

Agricultural exports in Myanmar are underdeveloped with reliance on exporting primary goods. Myanmar's reformed policy agenda to promote exports went into effect in 2011, and we are interested in comparing the trade value and trends before and after the reforms. To do so, we utilize data collected from 2007 to 2016 in the United Nation Comtrade Harmonized Commodity Description and Coding System (HS) to examine trade values and trends pre and post reform (UN Comtrade, 2017).

The UN Comtrade database provides accurate and disaggregated trade statistics, containing annual imports and exports statistics for more than 160 reporting countries or areas (USITC, 2015). The products can be broken into around 5,000 sub-commodities with detailed descriptions. There are three concerns in the database. First, the exports reported by one country may not exactly coincide with imports reported by its trading partner (UN Comtrade, 2017). Second, in UN Comtrade, Myanmar's export data is not reported, therefore, we use partners' import value as Myanmar's export value. Third, the UN Comtrade database does not include unofficial trade data (Gaulier & Zignago, 2010).

The value of Myanmar's agricultural imports steadily grew from 2009 to 2016, while the export value was comparatively stable throughout the period (Figure 9.1). Moreover, Myanmar shift from a net export to a net import with trade deficit after 2011, and the trade deficit grows larger from 2011 to 2016. The imports products are mainly from consumer-ready and preprocessed intermediate goods which require further processing or value-added technology on the commodities.

Figure 9.1
Myanmar Agricultural Trade Value (US$ Million), 2007–2016

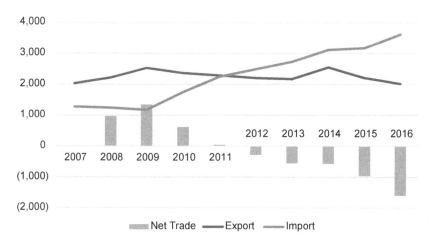

Source. UN Comtrade (2017).

To understand Myanmar's agricultural trade performance, the top export commodities are selected for further analysis. First, we select the top nine exported commodities by 2-digit HS code, and second, under these selected commodities, we choose the top 1 or 2 exported commodities by 4-digit or 6-digit HS code. According to UN Comtrade, Myanmar exports a range of commodities, but these are dominated by dried legumes, natural rubber, crustaceans, rice, and frozen fish (Figure 9.2). Myanmar's agricultural trade partners are mainly concentrated in the Asia Region, especially India, China, Thailand, Japan, and Malaysia (Table 9.3).

Figure 9.2

Myanmar's Agricultural Exports by Commodity (US$ Million)

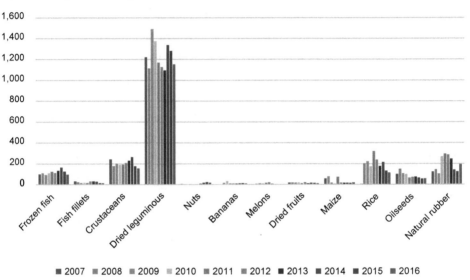

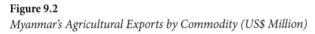

Source. UN Comtrade (2017).

Dried legumes (e.g., black gram, pigeon peas, dried chickpeas, small red beans, kidney beans, cowpeas, etc.) are Myanmar's largest agricultural export by value (Table 9.4). Myanmar is one of the world's largest producers of beans and pulses, accounting for 28% of the total sown area (World Bank, 2017) of the country. Other high-volume producers include Canada, India, Australia, and Tanzania (Myanmar Inside, 2015). However, the export value of dried legumes has fluctuated greatly over the past ten years. There was a tremendous decline in dried leguminous export value from 2009 to 2011, mainly because of the decreasing export volume to India. India is the largest buyer of dried legumes from Myanmar, accounting for 65%–83% of Myanmar's total dried legumes export over the past ten years, partly because of the ease of procurement, short delivery time, and high domestic demand (Myanmar Inside, 2015). Nevertheless, the concentration of dried legume exports to India makes Myanmar's pulses and bean sector vulnerable to India's import and policy changes.

Table 9.3

Export Destinations of Myanmar's Agricultural Products in 2016

HS code	Commodity	Export destinations			
071331 & 071336	Black gram & pigeon peas	India (82.29%)	Malaysia (3.56%)	Indonesia (3.53%)	Sri Lanka (2.53%)
4001	Natural rubber	China (74.41%)	Malaysia (17.92%)	Japan (3.94%)	Korea (3.37%)
0306	Crustaceans	Japan (33.41%)	China, Hong Kong SAR (17.39%)	China (17.08%)	US (11.67%)
1006	Rice	China (31.13%)	Belgium (16.41%)	France (8.65%)	Germany (8.30%)
0303	Frozen fish	UK (33.67%)	Malaysia (15.48%)	US (14.72%)	UAE (11.33%)
120740	Sesame seeds	Japan (53.01%)	other Asia (25.91%)	China (18.6%)	Singapore (1.65%)
0304	Fish fillets	Japan (26.74%)	Malaysia (23.82%)	Korea (17.44%)	UK (14.66%)
0813	Dried fruits	China (80.23%)	Pakistan (10.91%)	Malaysia (8.48%)	UAE (0.27%)
080711	Watermelons	China (92.04%)	Malaysia (4.17%)	China, Hong Kong SAR (3.69%)	Russia (0.10%)
1005	Maize	China (94.4%)	Philippines (3.95%)	Singapore (0.91%)	other Asia (0.74%)
0803	Bananas	China (99.91%)	Korea (0.08%)	Singapore (0.01%)	
0802	Nuts	India (97.46%)	Pakistan (0.98%)	Australia (0.42%)	UK (0.38%)

Source. UN Comtrade (2017).

Note. SAR = Special Administrative Region; UAE = United Arab Emirates; UK = United Kingdom; US = United States.

Table 9.4

Export Value and Commodity Share of Agricultural Products From 2007 to 2016 (US$ Million and Percentage)

HS code	Commodity	2007	2008	2009	2010	2011	2012	2013	2014	2015	2016
0303	Frozen fish	99.03 (1.04%)	109.13 (1.10%)	92.48 (1.02%)	108.93 (1.18%)	124.33 (1.11%)	112.49 (1.00%)	131.82 (0.97%)	165.29 (0.58%)	125.43 (0.87%)	95.05 (0.82%)
0304	Fish fillets	30.88 (0.32%)	23.51 (0.24%)	16.13 (0.18%)	18.47 (0.20%)	15.08 (0.13%)	30.12 (0.27%)	30.81 (0.23%)	27.48 (0.10%)	14.88 (0.10%)	12.71 (0.11%)
0306	Crustaceans	241.88 (2.54%)	179.34 (1.80%)	200.67 (2.21%)	189.72 (2.06%)	192.54 (1.71%)	207.98 (1.85%)	230.72 (1.70%)	264.32 (0.93%)	177.63 (1.23%)	156.14 (1.35%)
0713	Dried legumes	1,220.95 (12.82%)	1,113.87 (11.19%)	1,494.03 (16.45%)	1,375.48 (14.93%)	1,170.96 (10.42%)	1,126.81 (10.05%)	1,095.33 (8.06%)	1,338.38 (4.72%)	1,281.52 (8.90%)	1,151.97 (9.97%)
0802	Nuts	5.43 (0.06%)	1.64 (0.02%)	2.65 (0.03%)	6.63 (0.07%)	4.34 (0.04%)	4.51 (0.04%)	9.14 (0.07%)	16.45 (0.06%)	24.19 (0.17%)	16.87 (0.15%)
0803	Bananas	0.00 (0.00%)	0.83 (0.01%)	15.69 (0.17%)	33.87 (0.37%)	10.67 (0.09%)	10.59 (0.09%)	8.93 (0.07%)	11.56 (0.04%)	12.57 (0.09%)	9.89 (0.09%)
0807	Melons	0.67 (0.01%)	8.00 (0.08%)	10.88 (0.12%)	10.01 (0.11%)	15.83 (0.14%)	20.45 (0.18%)	7.36 (0.05%)	0.86 (0.00%)	0.95 (0.01%)	0.65 (0.01%)
0813	Dried fruits	17.31 (0.18%)	20.40 (0.20%)	18.25 (0.20%)	19.26 (0.21%)	11.70 (0.10%)	20.57 (0.18%)	10.01 (0.07%)	15.34 (0.05%)	13.73 (0.10%)	10.91 (0.09%)
1005	Maize	58.28 (0.61%)	78.00 (0.78%)	17.31 (0.19%)	9.29 (0.10%)	73.51 (0.65%)	16.96 (0.15%)	16.07 (0.12%)	15.10 (0.05%)	14.19 (0.10%)	20.42 (0.18%)

(Continued)

HS code	Commodity	2007	2008	2009	2010	2011	2012	2013	2014	2015	2016
1006	Rice	5.46 (0.06%)	203.08 (2.04%)	223.41 (2.46%)	174.29 (1.89%)	319.14 (2.84%)	237.63 (2.12%)	178.45 (1.31%)	215.42 (0.76%)	132.72 (0.92%)	113.15 (0.98%)
1207	Oilseeds	99.97 (1.05%)	148.78 (1.49%)	104.73 (1.15%)	97.68 (1.06%)	63.64 (0.57%)	70.53 (0.63%)	74.00 (0.54%)	64.16 (0.23%)	53.74 (0.37%)	55.62 (0.48%)
4001	Natural rubber	122.94 (1.29%)	145.47 (1.46%)	102.48 (1.13%)	269.41 (2.92%)	295.21 (2.63%)	285.96 (2.55%)	246.45 (1.81%)	141.41 (0.50%)	125.24 (0.87%)	194.13 (1.68%)

Source. UN Comtrade (2017).

Natural rubber is the second-largest export commodity in Myanmar, accounting for 1.6% of total world rubber exports (Win, 2016). Most of the exports went to China and Malaysia in 2016 (Table 9.3). The export trend of natural rubber export is bell-shaped. The trade value climbed from 2007 to 2011, and then started to decrease till 2015, but bounced back in 2016 with the value of US$194.13 million. This sector helps to utilize underemployed labor resources since it needs intensive labor resource (Aung, 2009). However, the rubber exported by Myanmar is low quality and therefore, the price of Myanmar's rubber is far lower than the world standard rubber price (Win, 2013).

Myanmar has a long coastline with 2,832 km, providing a very good base for the fishery sector (Haggblade et al., 2013). The fishery sector plays an important role in the international export market for foreign exchange earnings (FAO, 2012). Frozen fish, fish fillets and other fish meat, and crustaceans are the major export products in this sector. Crustaceans (e.g., lobster, shrimp, pawn, and crab) account for the highest export share in the fishery sector, with an export value of US$143.99 million in 2016. Japan stands as an important importer of Myanmar's crustaceans, followed by China, Hong Kong (China) Special Administrative Region (SAR), and the United States (US). Frozen fish (e.g., salmon, trout, tilapias, catfish, eels, and plaice) is mainly exported to the United Kingdom (UK), Malaysia, the US, and the United Arab Emirates, with an export value of US$87.51 million in 2016. The export value of frozen fish was the highest in 2014 and then decreased in 2015 and 2016. Fish fillets are mainly exported to Japan, Malaysia, Korea, and the UK, with the highest export value of US$30.88 million in 2007. However, one limitation of export potential of the fishery sector may be the lack of a capital market, insufficient facilities such as ice plants, cold storage, canning factories, and fish-meal plants (Aung, 2009).

Rice is the most important agricultural commodity of Myanmar and is the primary staple food. Myanmar was the largest rice exporter in the 1950s (before General Ne Win seized power in 1962) (Raslan, 2017) though in recent years Myanmar has faced challenges of low productivity (with the average paddy yields of only 2.5 tons per hectare). Although Myanmar faces strong competition from Thailand, Vietnam, and Cambodia, rice is also one of the major sectors prioritized by the Myanmar National Export Strategy (2015), aiming to fuel the country's sustainable development through export promotion (World Bank, 2017). In addition, the demand for the higher-quality rice has put pressure on Myanmar's rice sector, which has been focused on low-quality export markets. This necessitates that Myanmar focuses on improving quality (e.g., developing the high-quality rice like "Paw San" variety) for new market opportunities (World Bank, 2017). The export value of rice has decreased since 2011 from US$319.14 million to US$113.15 million in 2016. The sharp export drop in 2015 was mainly because of the widespread flood that decreased rice production in Myanmar (FAO, 2015; Win & Aung, 2015). The top four export destinations for Myanmar's rice include China, Belgium, France, and Germany. China imports mainly semi-/wholly milled rice and broken rice; France and Germany import mainly husked (brown) rice and semi-/wholly milled rice; and Belgium mainly imports husked (brown) rice and broken rice. The World Bank predicted there are good market prospects to accommodate higher rice exports from Myanmar over the next 10–15 years. China is becoming a large net importer of Myanmar rice, and the EU has opened its markets for duty-free imports from Myanmar. However, Myanmar's rice price fluctuates more profoundly than its neighboring countries.

China is also Myanmar's biggest buyer of maize. In 2016, Myanmar exported US$20.42 million worth of maize to the world, 94.4% of which went to China with other small amounts going to the Philippines and Singapore. However, Chinese officials have recently conducted more rigorous inspections since 2016, pushing Myanmar to pay more attention to the quality of maize exports and encouraging the country to diversify trade partners (USDA, 2016). Myanmar's maize export value was comparatively stable and low after 2011. The Myanmar government may want to provide technical assistance, as well as providing subsidies to farmers to develop this sector (USDA, 2016).

Myanmar is a significant producer of oilseeds. Oilseeds cover around 20% of total crop area and are important crops with higher margins than rice (Wijnands et al., 2014). However, oilseed's export value decreased from US$99.97 million in 2012 to US$55.62 million in 2016. The top export destinations include Japan, China, Thailand, and India. According to the FAO (2014) data, the oilseed sector of Myanmar is heavily regulated on all levels of the chain, resulting in severe distortions (Wijnands et al., 2014). In addition, among all the oilseed crops, sesame oilseed is the most important one, occupying 47% of the oilseed sown area, and the export value accounts for 80% of total oilseed exportation.

Edible fruit and nuts are also vital sectors of agricultural trade in Myanmar. Approximately 97% of nuts (e.g., almonds, walnuts, hazelnuts, chestnuts, pistachios, macadamia, etc.) are exported to India. Other export destinations include Pakistan, Australia, and the UK. China is Myanmar's biggest buyer of bananas, melons and papaws, and dried fruit. In addition, these edible fruit and nuts products are also exported to other Asia counties like Singapore, Malaysia, Pakistan, etc. For example, bananas are also exported to Korea and Singapore; melons and papaws are exported to Singapore; Malaysia; and China, Hong Kong SAR; dried fruit is exported to Pakistan, Malaysia, and the United Arab Emirates. The nuts' export value went steadily up from 2012 to 2016. Export value of melons increased from US$0.67 million in 2007 to US\$20.45 in 2012. However, the trade value declined to US\$0.65 million in 2016. Dried fruit exports fluctuate but have generally decreased, while the export value of bananas was stable after 2011.

In summary, the top exported products are concentrated on primary agricultural products, while there is a lack of value-added products. In addition, the foreign trade is highly dependent on certain Asian countries such as China and India. This makes Myanmar's exports vulnerable to partner's trade policies or external shocks. Appropriate measures should be taken to diversify export commodities and destinations.

IV. Method

Although the Balassa Revealed Comparative Advantage (BRCA) index is useful in assessing whether or not a country has a comparative advantage in a certain commodity (Balassa, 1965), its magnitude has neither the ordinal property nor the cardinal property (Hillman, 1980; Yeats, 1985; Yu et al., 2009). Additionally, the BRCA index has asymmetric properties. This index has a lower bound of zero with 1 being the comparative advantage neutral point, while its upper bound in general is from 1 to $+\infty$, implying the same BRCA score might suggest different levels of comparative advantage for different countries or commodities. Yu et al. (2009) demonstrated that the NRCA index is capable of revealing the extent of comparative advantage more precisely and consistently than BRCA. NRCA not only successfully solves the asymmetric issues but also can be compared across the commodity, country, and time. Furthermore, the NRCA index has a stable mean across space, and time, and the independent aggregation level can be helpful in analyzing trade specialization (Sanidas & Shin 2010; Yu et al., 2009).

The NRCA method generated by Yu et al. (2009) is utilized to compare the competitiveness between Myanmar and its competitors in agricultural export industries. The key to the derivation of the NRCA index is the comparative advantage neutral point. Under the situation of comparative advantage neutral, country j's export of commodity i would be equal to $E^j E_i / E^W$. Country j's actual export of commodity j in the real world would be E_i^j, and the difference would be stated as

$$\Delta E_i^j = E_i^j - E^j E_i / E^W$$

Normalizing ΔE_i by the world export market, E, the NRCA index is obtained as follows:

$$NRCA_{ij} = (E_i^j / E^W) - (E^j E_i / E^W E^W)$$

Where E_i^j refers to country j's export of product i; E^j is the total exports of country j; E_i refers to world export of product i; E^W tells of total world export. An NRCA value greater than zero indicates that a country reveals a comparative advantage in a particular product, while a value of less than zero indicates a revealed comparative disadvantage (Yu et al., 2009). An increasing NRCA value is interpreted as a country gaining the advantage in that product, relative to the world market. Additionally, a higher NRCA value indicates a higher comparative advantage. Since the NRCA index is normalized by the size of world total exports and typically is a huge number compared with a country's trade sector, the numeric value is usually very small. Yu et al. (2009) recommended to scale them by 10,000. Additionally, all trade values are deflated to 2016 prices with the CPI from the World Bank.[1]

To identify Myanmar's agricultural exporting competitors, the following procedures are applied. First, we select the top exported commodities by 4- or 6-digit HS code. Second, for each of the exported products, we find the top four export destinations of Myanmar. Third, for each of these export destinations, we find other leading exporters of the same commodity to the four selected countries and then choose competitors from these countries. There are several rules in choosing the competitors:

- we choose Asian countries as the priority;
- if the non-Asian countries are one of the top exporters to Myanmar's biggest export destinations, or if the non-Asian countries are one of the top four exporters for more than one target destination, we will also take it as the competitor.

The selected commodity, export destinations, and competitors of Myanmar are shown in Table 9.5.

---

1. The CPI index at the world level is the average of the CPI indexes of all the countries.

Table 9.5

Selected Commodity, Export Destinations, and Competitors of Myanmar

HS code	Commodity	Export destinations	Competitors for each export destination	Competitors
071331 & 071360	black gram & pigeon peas	India (82.29%), Malaysia (3.56%), Indonesia (3.53%), Sri Lanka (2.53%)	To India: Myanmar, United Rep. of Tanzania, Mozambique, Sudan To Malaysia: Myanmar, Australia, Thailand, China To Indonesia: Myanmar, Ethiopia, Australia, Thailand To Sri Lanka: Myanmar, Australia, India, Thailand	Australia, China, India, Thailand, United Rep. of Tanzania
0303	fish; frozen	UK (33.67%), Malaysia (15.48%), US (14.72%), United Arab Emirates (11.33%)	To UK: Norway, Myanmar, France, Netherlands To Malaysia: China, Vietnam, Indonesia, Japan To US: China, Canada, Korea, other Asia To United Arab Emirates: other Asia, Myanmar, India, Indonesia	China, India, Indonesia, Japan, Norway, Vietnam
0304	fish fillets and other fish meat (whether or not minced); fresh, chilled, or frozen	Japan (26.74%), Malaysia (23.82%), Korea (17.44%), UK (14.66%)	To Japan: Norway, US, Chile, China To Malaysia: Vietnam, Indonesia, China, US To Korea: Vietnam, US, Russian Federation, China To UK: Iceland, China, Germany, Russian Federation	China, Indonesia, Norway, Russian Federation, US, Vietnam
0306	crustaceans	Japan (33.41%), China, Hong Kong SAR (17.39%), China (17.08%), US (11.67%)	To Japan: Russian Federation, Vietnam, India, Indonesia To China: Canada, US, New Zealand, Argentina To China, Hong Kong SAR: China, Vietnam, Australia, US To US: India, Canada, Indonesia, Ecuador	Canada, China, India, Indonesia, Russian Federation, US, Vietnam
1005	maize (Corn)	China (94.40%), Philippines (3.95%), Singapore (0.91%), Other Asia, nes (0.74)	To China: Ukraine, US, Lao People's Dem. Rep., Myanmar To Philippines: Thailand, Argentina, Brazil, US To Singapore: Malaysia, Pakistan, US, Indonesia	Indonesia, Lao People's Dem. Rep., Malaysia, Thailand, Ukraine, US

(Continued)

HS code	Commodity	Export destinations	Competitors for each export destination	Competitors
1006	rice	China (31.13%), Belgium (16.41%), France (8.65%), Germany (8.30%)	To China: Vietnam, Thailand, Pakistan, Cambodia To Belgium: Spain, Italy, Netherlands, Pakistan To France: Italy, Thailand, Cambodia, Spain To Germany: Italy, Belgium, Netherlands, Cambodia	Cambodia, Italy, Pakistan, Spain, Thailand, Vietnam
120740	sesame seeds	Japan (53.01%), Other Asia, nes (25.91%), China (18.6%), Singapore (1.65%), Korea (0.59%)	To Japan: Nigeria, Paraguay, United Rep. of Tanzania, Myanmar To other Asia: India, Myanmar, Thailand, Sri Lanka To China: Ethiopia, Nigeria, Sudan, United Rep. of Tanzania To Singapore: India, Mexico, Nigeria, Myanmar	India, Nigeria, Sri Lanka, Thailand, United Rep. of Tanzania
0802	nuts (excluding coconuts, Brazils and cashew nuts)	India (97.46%), Pakistan (0.98%), Australia (0.42%), UK (0.38%)	To India: US, Iran, Australia, Sri Lanka To Pakistan: Indonesia, US, Iran, Afghanistan To Australia: US, Turkey, Areas, nes, China To UK: US, Germany, Spain, Italy	China, Indonesia, Iran, Sri Lanka, US
0803	bananas, including plantains	China (99.91%), Korea (0.08%), Singapore (0.01%)	To China: Philippines, Ecuador, Thailand, Vietnam To Korea: Philippines, Ecuador, Guatemala, Peru To Singapore: Philippines, Malaysia, Ecuador, Mexico	Ecuador, Malaysia, Philippines, Thailand
080711	watermelons	China (92.04%), Malaysia (4.17%), China, Hong Kong SAR (3.69%), Russian Federation (0.10%)	To China: Vietnam, Myanmar, Malaysia To Malaysia: Thailand, Korea, Australia, China To China, Hong Kong SAR: Malaysia, China, Japan, Philippines To Russian Federation: Iran, Brazil, Turkey, China	China, Japan, Malaysia, Philippines, Korea, Thailand, Vietnam
0813	fruit, dried; mixtures of nuts or dried fruits of this chapter	China (80.23%), Pakistan (10.91%), Malaysia (8.48%), United Arab Emirates (0.27%)	To China: Thailand, Myanmar, US, Chile To Pakistan: India, Indonesia, Afghanistan, Myanmar To Malaysia: Indonesia, Thailand, China, India To United Arab Emirates: Thailand, India, Turkey, US	China, India, Indonesia, Thailand, US

(Continued)

HS code	Commodity	Export destinations	Competitors for each export destination	Competitors
4001	natural rubber, balata, gutta-percha, guayule, chicle and similar gums	China (74.41%), Malaysia (17.92%), Japan (3.94%), Korea (3.37%)	To China: Thailand, Malaysia, Indonesia, Vietnam To Malaysia: Thailand, Cote d'Ivoire, Vietnam, Philippines To Japan: Indonesia, Thailand, Vet Nam, Malaysia To Korea: Indonesia, Thailand, Vet Nam, Malaysia	Indonesia, Malaysia, Philippines, Thailand, Vietnam

Source. UN Comtrade (2017).
Note. China, Hong Kong SAR = Special Administrative Region; UK = United Kingdom, US = United States, nes = abbr. not elsewhere specified in UN Comtrade database.

V. Result

1. Comparison of NRCA Between Myanmar and Its Main Competitors

The NRCA scores for the agricultural sector and the selected commodities of Myanmar and its competitors are calculated and shown below in Figures 9.3 to 9.16. The NRCA scores of Myanmar were higher than zero from 2007 to 2016, indicating Myanmar enjoyed a comparative advantage in agricultural exports in the global market (Figure 9.3). The NRCA scores are comparatively stable across the ten years for Myanmar, except for the low NRCA score in 2014. This outlier, which is generated because of Myanmar's extremely high total export value, mainly came from exporting pearls, stones, mineral fuel, and apparel in 2014. Myanmar's agricultural export sector is not very competitive when compared with a number of identified competitors. The US shows the highest NRCA score among the countries, followed by Australia, Thailand, India, Vietnam, Indonesia, and Myanmar. Myanmar's agricultural export sector is more competitive than that of Malaysia, Cambodia, the Philippines, Japan, and China. In addition, each country shows different fluctuating trends in export competitiveness. For example, Vietnam reveals decreasing agricultural competitiveness in the global market, while Australia has shown upward competitiveness during the past ten years. Only Myanmar and Thailand show comparatively stable competitiveness.

Figure 9.3
NRCA Scores of Aggregate Agricultural Exports of Myanmar and Its Competitors

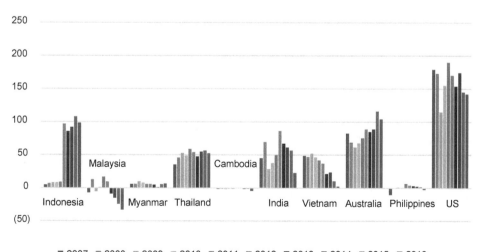

Source. Calculated by the authors.
Note. NRCA = normalized revealed comparative advantage; US = United States.

Figure 9.4 presents NRCA scores across 12 major commodity groups for ten years to identify Myanmar's export comparative advantage. Black gram & pigeon peas enjoy the highest comparative advantage, followed by rice, natural rubber, frozen fish, and sesame seeds. Moreover, the NRCA scores of bananas, fish fillets, maize, nuts, and watermelon in certain years are less than zero, indicating these particular product groups reveal no comparative advantage. The NRCAs of the 12 agricultural commodities fluctuate from 2007 to 2016.

Figure 9.4
NRCA Scores of Myanmar's Agricultural Exports by 4- or 6-Digit Levels

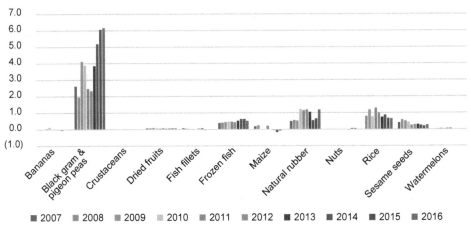

Source. Calculated by the authors.
Note. NRCA = normalized revealed comparative advantage.

The NRCA score is also compared between Myanmar and its competitors by agricultural commodity. Black gram and pigeon peas enjoyed the strongest comparative advantages during the whole period, and although the NRCA scores fluctuated up and down from 2007 to 2012, after 2012, the NRCA trended upward reaching its highest value in 2016 (Figure 9.5). Myanmar's competitors, including Australia, China, India, Thailand, and the United Rep. of Tanzania, have considerably lower NRCA scores than Myanmar, indicating a lower level of competitiveness. Black gram and pigeon peas are land-intensive commodities. Experts in the field suggest the development of value-added beans and pulse products through the development of more processing centers (Myanmar Inside, 2015).

Rice plays a crucial role in the agricultural exporting market in Myanmar. The NRCA value was less than zero in 2007, indicating a comparative disadvantage in rice exporting. After 2007, Myanmar enjoyed positive and stable NRCA scores (Figure 9.6). Among Myanmar's competitors, Thailand shows the highest NRCA score,

Figure 9.5

NRCA Scores of Myanmar and Its Competitors in Black Gram and Pigeon Peas

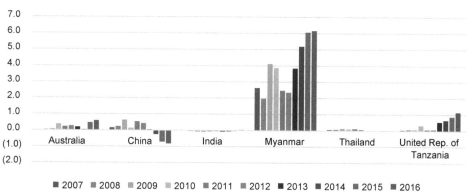

■ 2007 ■ 2008 ■ 2009 ■ 2010 ■ 2011 ■ 2012 ■ 2013 ■ 2014 ■ 2015 ■ 2016

Source. Calculated by the authors.

Note. NRCA = normalized revealed comparative advantage.

Figure 9.6

NRCA Score of Myanmar and Competitors in Rice

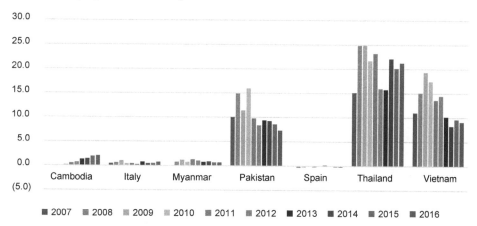

■ 2007 ■ 2008 ■ 2009 ■ 2010 ■ 2011 ■ 2012 ■ 2013 ■ 2014 ■ 2015 ■ 2016

Source. Calculated by the authors.

Note. NRCA = normalized revealed comparative advantage.

followed by Vietnam and Pakistan. Cambodia, Italy, and Myanmar have comparatively low competitiveness in rice exporting, while Spain shows no competitiveness. The potential limitations of rice exporting in Myanmar include low productivity and poor rice quality at the farm level. For example, the average paddy yields of 2.5 tons per hectare are only half of those realized by its competitors in the region. In addition, the milling sector operates with obsolete processing units that cause about 15%–20% losses in quality and quantity during milling (World Bank, 2017). Some policy tactics may be useful for promoting rice production and rice exporting:

- updating the existing seed management system;
- allowing and encouraging direct foreign investment in rice milling, warehousing, and trading;
- reducing transport costs by encouraging the investment in farm-to-market roads (World Bank, 2017).

The NRCA score of natural rubber ranges from 0.49 (Year 2007) to 1.22 (Year 2010) (Figure 9.7). However, Myanmar faces strong competition from Asian countries such as Indonesia, Malaysia, Thailand, and Vietnam. The average NRCA score of the past ten years in Thailand, Indonesia, Malaysia, and Vietnam was around 55.6, 51.1, 18.1, and 8.2 times that of Myanmar, respectively. The shortcomings of Myanmar's rubber exporting include low productivity, high labor cost, and sub-par quality. Myanmar's rubber plantation produces at less than half the international production rate, and a rise in volume must be matched by improvements in product quality (Win, 2016).

Figure 9.7
NRCA Score of Myanmar and Competitors in Natural Rubber

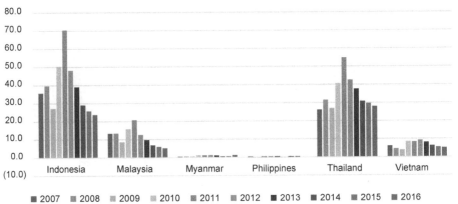

Source. Calculated by the authors.
Note. NRCA = normalized revealed comparative advantage.

The NRCA score of sesame seeds in Myanmar ranged from 0.20 to 0.58 with the highest score in 2008. In addition, the NRCAs were quite stable after 2010 (Figure 9.8). India reveals the highest NRCA value among all the competitors, followed by Nigeria, Tanzania, and Myanmar. Thailand and Sri Lanka reveal no comparative advantage. However, Myanmar's trade value of sesame oilseed is low, considering its strong competitiveness. Improving the quality and efficiency of sesame seed production as well as processing (e.g., proper extraction, roasting and producing snacks) provide potential ways to enhance the trade value and open opportunities to new markets.

Figure 9.8

NRCA Score of Myanmar and Competitors in Sesame Seeds

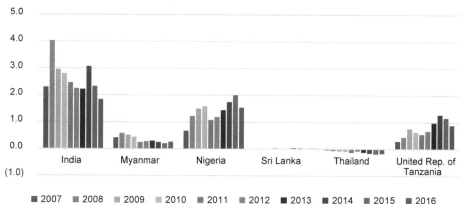

Source. Calculated by the authors.

Note. NRCA = normalized revealed comparative advantage.

Figure 9.9

NRCA Score of Myanmar and Competitors in Frozen Fish

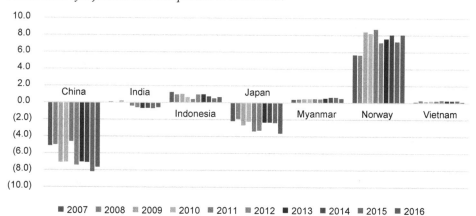

Source. Calculated by the authors.

Note. NRCA = normalized revealed comparative advantage.

Frozen fish and crustaceans reveal a strong competitive advantage, while fish fillets reveal a comparative disadvantage (Figure 9.9 and 9.10). Myanmar's primary competitors in the export of frozen fish include Norway, China, Vietnam, Indonesia, Japan, and India. Myanmar's NRCA score was 0.52 in 2016, higher than most of its competitors except for Norway and Indonesia (Figure 9.10). On average, Norway's NRCA is around 15 times that of Myanmar's. Furthermore, among the other competitors, China, India, and Japan show no competitiveness in exporting frozen fish, while Vietnam and Indonesia do.

Crustacean exports show a considerably lower NRCA score than frozen fish in Myanmar. However, Myanmar has the highest NRCA score among its competitors, followed by Vietnam, Indonesia, India, Canada, the Russian Federation, China, and the US (Figure 9.10). Additionally, the NRCA scores went up and down for all the selected countries, with extremely high values in 2009, 2015, and 2016.

Figure 9.10
NRCA Score of Myanmar and Competitors in Crustaceans

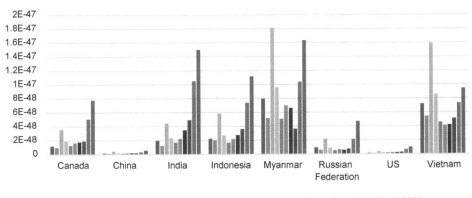

Source. Calculated by the authors.
Note. NRCA = normalized revealed comparative advantage; US = United States.

Fish fillets are mainly exported to Japan, Malaysia, Korea, and the UK. The primary competitors are China, Indonesia, Norway, the Russian Federation, the US, and Vietnam with Norway showing the highest NRCA score. Vietnam, China, and Indonesia also enjoy comparatively higher NRCA scores than Myanmar (Figure 9.11). Myanmar's comparative advantage in fish fillets exports shows some variability with positive values from 2007 to 2013 but no competitiveness from 2014 to 2016.

The Myanmar fishery sub-sector's NRCAs and export values were unstable during the period examined. Fishery production and export needs various special equipment including fishing and transport vessels, ice plants, processing plants, cold storage, fishmeal plants, dehydration plants, etc. However, insufficient facilities in Myanmar maybe restrict the expansion of fishery sector production, exports, or value addition. It is necessary to construct facilities and introduce fishery policies for the development of this sector (Aung, 2009).

Maize's comparative advantage in Myanmar was unstable across the ten years examined. Maize lost its comparative advantage from 2012 to 2015 and gained competitiveness in 2016 (Figure 9.12). The US reveals the highest comparative advantage, followed by Ukraine. Indonesia, Malaysia, and Thailand show no comparative advantage.

Figure 9.11

NRCA Score of Myanmar and Competitors in Fish Fillets

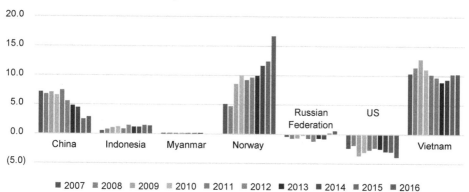

Source. Calculated by the authors.

Note. NRCA = normalized revealed comparative advantage; US = United States.

Figure 9.12

NRCA Score of Myanmar and Competitors in Maize

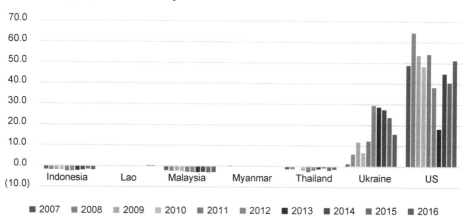

Source. Calculated by the authors.

Note. NRCA = normalized revealed comparative advantage; US = United States.

Nuts (e.g., almonds, walnuts, hazelnuts, and macadamia), bananas, watermelons, and dried fruits show unstable NRCAs across the period (Figure 9.13 to 9.16). The US has the highest NRCA score in nuts exports, followed by Iran and Indonesia. Myanmar only gained a comparative advantage in nuts exports in 2007, 2010, 2015, and 2016 (Figure 9.13).

China is the biggest buyer of bananas, importing 99.91% of Myanmar's bananas. Myanmar's competitors include Ecuador, Malaysia, the Philippines, and Thailand. In the past ten years, Ecuador has had the highest NRCA score, followed by the Philippines

Figure 9.13

NRCA Score of Myanmar and Competitors in Nuts

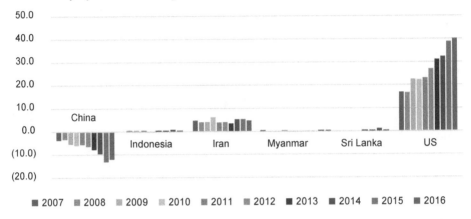

Source. Calculated by the authors.

Note. NRCA = normalized revealed comparative advantage; US = United States.

Figure 9.14

NRCA Score of Myanmar and Competitors in Bananas

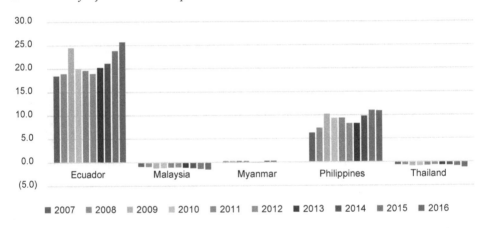

Source. Calculated by the authors.

Note. NRCA = normalized revealed comparative advantage.

and Myanmar. Malaysia and Thailand show no competitiveness in exporting bananas (Figure 9.14). Myanmar lost its competitiveness in 2013 and 2014, and regained competitiveness in 2015 and 2016.

Approximately 92% of Myanmar's watermelons are exported to China though a small amount of exports go to Malaysia; China, Hong Kong SAR; and the Russian Federation. Among Myanmar's competitors in watermelon exporting, only Vietnam enjoys a consistent comparative advantage over the period (Figure 9.15). China, Japan,

Figure 9.15

NRCA Score of Myanmar and Competitors in Watermelons

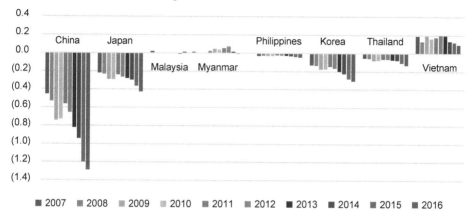

Source. Calculated by the authors.

Note. NRCA = normalized revealed comparative advantage.

Figure 9.16

NRCA Score of Myanmar and Competitors in Dried Fruits

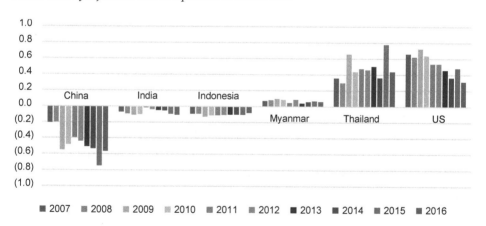

Source. Calculated by the authors.

Note. NRCA = normalized revealed comparative advantage; US = United States.

the Philippines, Korea, and Thailand show no comparative advantage across the years. Myanmar gained and lost comparative advantage over time. Myanmar revealed no comparative advantage in 2007, but gained competitiveness from 2008 to 2013, and again lost competitiveness after 2014. It may be caused by China, which is Myanmar's biggest buyer, banning imports from Myanmar.

Dried fruits have a high NRCA score in Myanmar, though lower than Thailand and the US. Other competitors that include China, India, and Indonesia reveal no comparative advantage (Figure 9.16). However, the trade value of dried fruits has fluctuated in the last ten years. Given the sectors competitiveness globally, policy support and logistic improvement are needed to bolster production and exports.

In summary, Myanmar's black gram and pigeon peas, crustaceans, dried fruits, frozen fish, natural rubber, and sesame seeds reveal comparative advantages in the global market. Myanmar has the strongest NRCA score at the global level in black gram and pigeon peas, followed by rice, natural rubber, frozen fish, and sesame seeds. However, for the other products, such as bananas, maize, fish fillets, nuts, and watermelons, its export competitiveness is unstable; those commodities lost and gained their comparative advantage through the years.

VI. Conclusion

Myanmar is an agrarian county, with the agricultural sector contributing 37.8% to GDP. Agricultural exports make up 27.5% of total export earnings. However, agriculture development and agricultural trade are still far below their potential. This study utilizes UN Comtrade data to compute NRCA scores for a variety of important export commodities based on the methodology used by Yu et al. (2009). Cross-border trade plays a significant role in Myanmar's agricultural trade market, but because of lengthy official licensing requirements and incentives to avoid tariffs, unofficial trade often occurs (Aung, 2009). By relying on the official UN Comtrade data, unofficial trade data is excluded and may be one possible limitation of the study.

The export values and trade patterns from UN Comtrade from 2007 to 2016 demonstrate that Myanmar is dependent on its natural resources rather than value-added products. The major export products include beans and pulses, fishery products, rice, and nuts. In addition, Myanmar's agricultural trade is mainly concentrated with neighboring countries such as China, Thailand, and India and those in the region such as Japan, Singapore, and Malaysia. Agricultural trade with developed countries is still low, and the partners are limited to the United States, the EU, and Japan. Furthermore, for black gram and pigeon peas and nuts, more than 80% of the exports go to India, while for watermelon, natural rubber, and dried fruits, the export market is concentrated in China. As such, the export market of Myanmar is vulnerable to the policies of these major trade partners. Myanmar has thus far shown low product and market diversification in the agricultural export sector.

Myanmar enjoys comparative advantages in the agricultural sector, and these have been relatively stable for the last ten years. Myanmar needs to seize these opportunities. However, thus far, Myanmar's agricultural export sector has not been very competitive when compared with its direct competitors. The US shows the highest NRCA score among the countries, followed by Australia, Thailand, India, Vietnam, and Indonesia. Myanmar's agricultural export sector is only more competitive than Malaysia, Cambodia, the Philippines, Japan, and China. Myanmar enjoys high NRCAs in black gram and pigeon peas, natural rubber, sesame seeds, rice, and frozen fish, while the NRCAs in crustaceans, and dried fruits are low. The competitiveness of bananas, fish fillet, maize, nuts, and watermelon is negative in certain years.

One of the challenges of Myanmar's agricultural export has been greater reliance on a smaller number of exportable commodities, which are mainly land-intensive. Policy action needs to be taken to diversify Myanmar's export portfolio horizontally by adding more commodities to the existing export pattern and vertically including the creation of new commodities lines by means of value-added measures (Oo et al., 2017).

In terms of horizontal diversification, marketing research can determine consumer demand both domestically and abroad for new products. Land development strategies that utilize agriculture research to determine climate and topographic suitability for new crops are needed. Agricultural extension services are necessary to help farmers understand how to grow new crops to encourage their potential adoption and new input markets may be needed to help farmers access seeds and harvesting machinery. Last, basic infrastructure including roads to reduce transaction costs, needs to be developed but also storage and processing facilities. Once developed these same types of facilities can encourage downstream processing of primary commodities to support vertical diversification. Considering the poor storage conditions for perishable commodities (frozen fish, fish fillets, vegetables, etc.), the development of a cold supply chain (including precooling facilities, cold storage, refrigerated carriers, packaging, and traceability systems) is vital to the expansion of these high-value commodities and necessary for international trade where food safety is a primary concern (UN, 2011).

Private and foreign investment is needed to fuel the development of processing facilities as well as input and machinery markets. In India, foreign investment makes up 51% of the total cold value chain. In Australia, public-private partnerships play a significant role in strengthening the cold chain framework (OECD, 2015). Foreign direct investment also provides a good way of fulfilling domestic technology and equipment gaps in Myanmar for high-value products. To ensure the sustained flow of new investments, a favorable investment and business environment needs to be created that removes the barriers to foreign investment.

Several things can be done to support improved market access and facilitate trade with neighboring countries and globally. China, India, Thailand, and Japan are Myanmar's four most important trade partners and entering into more bilateral or multilateral trade agreements can draw the countries closer. The government can support trade promotion through improved branding and trade fairs. Improved trade facilitation can be accomplished through the elimination of complicated and lengthy legal procedures, through tax credits and by making trade policies and procedures stable, transparent, and affordable for small- and medium-sized traders.

Myanmar can learn much from its competitors' trade promotion strategies. For example, Vietnam has operated a national trade promotion program since 2005 that utilized global marketing experts to advise on export development and commodity quality improvement. Additionally, the Vietnam Development Bank (VDB) was established in 2006 to provide financial support to promote trade. The VDB provides export credits, investment credit guarantees, and export project performance security to support exporters needing funding to increase the scale of investment (OECD, 2015). Malaysia is cooperating with Alibaba to launch the Digital Free Trade Zone (e.g., satellite services, eFulfillment Hub, and eServices platform) to encourage international market development and trade. Through the Digital Free Trade Zone, the purchase of commodities via the internet worth up to US$275 will be exempted from taxes (ecommerceIQ, 2017).

Myanmar has prioritized increasing agricultural exports in several recent policy documents and the 2015 National Export Strategy. The purpose of this paper has been to provide a better understanding of Myanmar's agricultural export performance compared to its competitors in different commodities. It has shown that Myanmar has enormous potential to utilize its comparative advantage in several commodities to further expand its exports to achieve more stable export earnings. However, it will take policy reform and investment by both the government and the private sector to achieve these goals, but we are confident that with time Myanmar can achieve them.

References

ADB (Asian Development Bank). (2012, August). *Myanmar in transition: Opportunities and challenges.* https://www.adb.org/publications/myanmar-transition-opportunities-and-challenges

ADB (Asian Development Bank). (2013, December). *Myanmar: Agriculture, natural resources, and environment initial sector assessment, strategy, and road map.* https://www.adb.org/documents/myanmar-agriculture-natural-resources-and-environment-initial-sector-assessment-strategy

Aung, N. M. (2009). *An analysis of the structure of Myanmar's exports and its implications for economic development.* [Unpublished doctoral dissertation]. University of Tokyo.

Aung, W. S. (2009). *The Role of informal cross-border trade in Myanmar.* Institute for Security & Development Policy.

Balassa, B. (1965). Trade liberalization and revealed comparative advantage. *Manchester School of Economic and Social Studies, 33,* 99–123.

Bhattacharyya, R. (2011). Revealed comparative advantage and competitiveness: A case study for India in horticultural products. *Journal of European Economy, 11,* 22–37.

Bojnec, Š. (2001). Trade and revealed comparative advantage measures: Regional and central and East European agricultural trade. *Eastern European Economics, 2,* 72–98.

Chandran, S., & Sudarsan, P. K. (2012). India-ASEAN free trade agreement implications for fisheries. *Economic and Political Weekly, 1,* 65–70.

Dalum, B., Laursen, K., & Villumsen, G. (1998). Structural change in OECD export specialization patterns: De-specialization and "stickiness." *International Review of Applied Economics, 12,* 423–443.

Embassy of the Republic of the Union of Myanmar. (2017). *Trade policy of Myanmar.* http://www.mecairo.org/index.php/en/myanmar/trade-policy-of-myanmar

ecommerceIQ. (2017). *What exactly is the Malaysia digital free trade zone and its impact?* https://e27.co/exactly-malaysia-digital-free-trade-zone-impact-20170512/

Estudillo, J. P., & Fujimura, M. (2015). Comparative advantage in rice production: Vietnam and Myanmar. *The Aoyama Journal of Economics, 68,* 1–24.

FAO (Food and Agriculture Organization of the United Nations). (2012). *Fishery and aquaculture country profiles: The Republic of the Union of Myanmar.* http://www.fao.org/fishery/facp/MMR/en

FAO (Food and Agriculture Organization of the United Nations). (2014). *Country statement of Myanmar Ministry of Agriculture and Irrigation.* http://www.fao.org/fileadmin/user_upload/faoweb/docs/MM3/Statements/Myanmar.pdf

FAO (Food and Agriculture Organization of the United Nations). (2015). *Myanmar floods: Huge impact on agricultural livelihoods, more international support urgently needed.* http://www.fao.org/fileadmin/user_upload/emergencies/docs/Final%20fact%20sheet%201%20-%20web%20version.pdf

FAO (Food and Agriculture Organization of the United Nations). (2017). *Myanmar at a glance.* http://www.fao.org/myanmar/fao-in-myanmar/myanmar/en/

Ferto, I., & Hubbard, L. J. (2002). *Revealed comparative advantage and competitiveness in Hungarian agri-food sectors* (KTK/IE Discussion Papers 2002/8). Institute of Economics, Hungarian Academy of Sciences.

Fujita, K., & Okamoto, I. (2006). *Agricultural policies and development of Myanmar's agricultural sector: An overview* (Discussion Paper No. 63). Institute of Developing Economies, Japan External Trade Organization.

Gaulier, G., & Zignago, S. (2010). *BACI: International trade database at the product-level: The 1994–2007 Version* (WP No. 2010-23). CEPII.

Haggblade, S., Boughton, D., & Denning, G. (2013). *A strategic agricultural sector and food security*

diagnostic for Myanmar (MSU International Development Working Paper). Michigan
State University (MSU) and the Myanmar Development Resource Institute's Center for
Economic and Social Development (MDRI/CESD).

Hillman, A. L. (1980). Observations on the relation between "revealed comparative advantage" and
comparative advantage as indicated by pre-trade relative prices. *Weltwirtschaftliches Arch*,
116, 315–321.

Hoen, A., & Oosterhaven, J. (2006). On the measurement of comparative advantage. *Annals of
Regional Science, 40*, 677–691.

Kalafsky, R. V., & Graves, W. (2016). Reevaluating the position of southern exports on the global
stage. *Southeastern Geographer*, 56, 187–202.

Kilduff, P., & Chi, T. (2007). Analysis of comparative advantage in the textile complex: A study of
Eastern European and former Soviet Union Nations. *Journal of Fashion Marketing and
Management, 11*, 82–106.

Kim, M., & Thunt, H. (2017). An analysis of export competitiveness in Myanmar: Measuring revealed comparative advantage. *Journal of International Trade & Commerce, 13*, 149–172.

Lafay, G. (1992). The measurement of revealed comparative advantages. In M. G. Dagenais and P.-A.
Muet (Eds.), *International trade modeling*. Chapman & Hall.

Myanmar Inside. (2015). *Myanmar's beans and pulses*. http://www.myanmarinsider.com/myanmars-
beans-and-pulses/

Myanmar, Ministry of Commerce, Department of Trade Promotion. (2018.) *Republic of the Union of
Myanmar: National export strategy: Quality management cross-sector strategy, 2015–2019*.
Department of Trade Promotion; International Trade Center.

OECD (Organization for Economic Co-operation and Development). (2015). *Agricultural policies
in Viet Nam*. http://www.oecd-ilibrary.org/agriculture-and-food/agricultural-policies-in-
viet nam 2015/assessment-and-policy-recommendations_9789264235151-4-en

Oo, T. H., Soe, A., & Myat, P. Y. (2017). Agricultural policy and institutional reforms in Myanmar:
Experiences, impacts, and lessons. *Southeast Asian agriculture and development primer
series* (2nd ed.). Southeast Asian Regional Center for Graduate Study and Research in
Agriculture.

Proudman, J., & Redding, S. (2000). Evolving patterns of international trade. *Review of International
Economics, 8*, 373–396.

Raitzer. D., Wong, L., & Samson, J. (2015). *Myanmar's agriculture sector: Unlocking the potential for
inclusive growth* (Economics Working Paper Series. No. 470). Asian Development Bank
(ADB).

Raslan, K. (2017). *Paw San rice: Myanmar's ticket back to the international stage?* http://www.
scmp.com/week-asia/business/article/2077385/paw-san-rice-myanmars-ticket-back-
international-stage

Sanidas, E., & Shin, Y. (2010, June 25–26). *Comparison of revealed comparative advantage indices with application to trade tendencies of East Asian Countries*. 9th Korea and the World Economy Conference, University of Incheon, Incheon, South Korea.

Sri Lanka, EDB (Export Development Board). (2014). *Country report on Myanmar*. EDB. https://www.srilankabusiness.com/pdf/myanmarmarketprofile.pdf

Soe, T. (2004). *Myanmar in economic transition: Constraints and related issues affecting the agriculture sector*. Yangon University of Distance Education.

Startienė, G., & Remeikienė, R. (2014). Evaluation of revealed comparative advantage of Lithuanian industry in global markets. *Journal of Contemporary Issues in Business, Management and Education, 110*, 428–438.

Tun, T., Kennedy, A., & Nischan, U. (2015). *Promoting agricultural growth in Myanmar: A review of policies and an assessment of knowledge gaps* (Working Paper No. 07). International Food Policy Research Institute.

UN (United Nations). (2011). *Facilitating agricultural trade in Asia and the Pacific*. http://www20.iadb.org/intal/catalogo/PE/2012/10040.pdf

UN (United Nations). (2017). *Comtrade*. https://comtrade.un.org/data/

USDA (United States Department of Agriculture). (2016). *Corn production, supply, and demand update 2016*. USDA Foreign Agricultural Service. https://gain.fas.usda.gov/Recent%20GAIN%20Publications/Corn%20Production%20Supply%20and%20Demand%20Update%202016_Rangoon_Burma%20-%20Union%20of_12-2-2016.pdf

USITC (United States International Trade Commission). (2015). Rice: Global competitiveness of the U.S. industry. https://www.usitc.gov/publications/332/pub4530.pdf

Wijnands, J., Biersteker, J., Hagedoorn, L., & Louisse, J. (2014). *Business opportunities and food safety of the Myanmar edible oil sector*. LEI Wageningen UR.

Win, N. (2013). *Experiences of Myanmar agricultural development bank program on value chain finance on agriculture* (Country Report of Myanmar). Regional Training Course on Value Chain Finance in Agriculture.

Win, S. P. (2016). *Low production and quality to blame for rubber sector's export woes*. Myanmar Times. https://www.mmtimes.com/business/22929-low-production-and-quality-to-blame-for-rubber-sector-s-export-woes.html

Win, S., & Aung, H. (2015). *Rice exports suspended as 500,000 acres flood*. Myanmar Times. https://www.mmtimes.com/business/15837-rice-exports-suspended-as-500-000-acres-flood.html

World Bank. (2017). *Myanmar: Capitalizing on rice export opportunities*. The World Bank. http://www.worldbank.org/en/country/myanmar/publication/myanmar-capitalizing-on-rice-export-opportunities

Yeats, A. J. (1985). On the appropriate interpretation of the revealed comparative advantage index: Implications of a methodology based on industry sector analysis. *Weltwirtschaftliches Arch, 121*, 61–73.

Yu, R., Cai, J., & Leung, P. (2009). The normalized revealed comparative advantage index. *Annals of Regional Science, 43,* 267–282.

Yu, C. Y., & Qi, C. J. (2015). Research on the complementarity and comparative advantages of agricultural product trade between China and CEE countries. *Journal of Service Science and Management, 8,* 201–208.

AGRICULTURAL TRADE AMID THE COVID-19 PANDEMIC

CHAPTER 10

Escalated Trade Barriers Amid COVID-19

Kevin Chen and Rui Mao

I. Introduction

The global food system nowadays is more integrated than ever. A risk of shattering ferments, however, as the effects of COVID-19 ripple through the system. From January to February, when the pandemic was mostly confined in mainland China, the country's total export value plunged by 17.2% compared with the same period last year, and the export value of agricultural products plunged by 11.6%.[1] Though worldwide impacts are still invisible in most trade statistics, leading indices such as PMIs suggest severe trade contractions to emerge. WTO predicted the global trade to decline by 13%–32% in 2020, which in the worst case can hit a new low since the global financial crisis.[2] The international agricultural trade will also be likely to stumble. In fact, purchase orders of US farm products have already been reduced by China in the first two months and indefinitely postponed by Morocco in March.[3] The strain of logistics during the pandemic is a key reason of trade contractions, since disrupted transportation has made the delivery of farm products difficult. Yield cuts are likely expected in some regions or certain sectors due to labor shortages and limited input access, which dim the outlook of agricultural trade (Torero, 2020).

---

1. Source: http://www.customs.gov.cn
2. Source: https://www.wto.org/english/news_e/pres20_e/pr855_e.htm
3. Source: https://www.fas.usda.gov/topics/north-africa-march-2020, https://www.tsln.com/news/covid-19-could-alter-agricultural-trade-relationships-change-view-of-globalization-and-interdependency-for-food

II. Escalated Trade Barriers and Institutional Causes

Aside from stresses on the supply side, the erection of tightened border controls in international agricultural trade may further shatter the global food system. WHO and FAO invoke the need for free trade as there is no evidence that suggests the virus spread through food commodities.[4] Historically, however, strict border controls were often observed against agricultural exports from affected regions. For example, Indonesia, Korea, and Russia issued import prohibitions on either wild and live animals or animal-derived products from China in January or February, whereas Egypt forbade imports of garlic, carrots, and green ginger.[5] With rapid spread of the COVID-19 pandemic to other regions, a number of countries, such as Mauritius has restricted imports of animal goods from China, Iran, Korea, Switzerland, and the EU since March.[6] Aside from these import measures that were notified to WTO, countries also adopted unilateral border controls by refusing specific import entries. The US FDA, for instance, has substantially increased import refusals against Chinese agricultural exports this year, with incidents of import refusals and the share in all refusals on agricultural imports rising by 84% and 50%, respectively, in January and by around 30% in February and March from the same period last year.[7] Since FDA enjoys much discretion in making such decisions according to the Federal Food, Drug, and Cosmetic Act,[8] import refusals could be used as an effective tool of trade protection during economic or sectoral downturns (Grundke & Moser, 2019; Jouanjean et al., 2015) and possible means for the prevention of pandemic spread through trade. In fact, heightened refusal and alert incidents against imports from affected regions by FDA and national food safety authorities in EU member states were also observed amid previous epidemics such as Ebola, H1N1, and SARS.[9]

Increased border controls on agricultural trade during epidemics reflect the ineffectiveness of WTO and WHO in regulating trade. One of reasons is a long-existed absence of formal coordination schemes between WHO and WTO on measures to prevent cross-border transmission of epidemics. While both WHO and WTO abide by the principle of minimizing adverse impacts on international traffic and trade in the control of epidemics and acknowledge the justification of trade restrictions only in

---

4. Source: https://www.who.int/news-room/articles-detail/updated-who-recommendations-for-international-traffic-in-relation-to-covid-19-outbreak

5. Source: https://mp.weixin.qq.com/s/rPZt-4m8gpgKzu3ShG0phA

6. Source: https://www.macmap.org/covid19

7. Source: https://datadashboard.fda.gov/ora/cd/imprefusals.htm

8. Source: https://www.fda.gov/industry/import-program-food-and-drug-administration-fda/import-basics

9. For import refusals and alerts of the EU, see: https://ec.europa.eu/food/safety/rasff/portal_en

certain conditions with strong supports by scientific proofs, their judgments of specific measures often differ. For example, Mexico appealed to WTO for trade restrictions imposed by other economies during the H1N1 pandemic using statements of WHO and FAO that such actions have "no justification in the OIE Terrestrial Animal Health Standards Code," but it failed after prolonged debates.[10] A fundamental reason of such disputes is that WHO's epidemic alerts and severity assessments are not directly linked to the use of trade measures within WTO's framework. WTO primarily considers trade-related measures for public health concerns in sanitary and phytosanitary as well as Technical Barriers to Trade agreements. Nevertheless, the declaration of Public Health Emergency of International Concern by WHO does not constitute a specific condition to activate these measures. This typically leads to excessive trade restrictions during epidemics, since judicial obscurity can become obstacles to appeals by affected regions as observed in Mexico's case. Moreover, it is interesting to observe that during reviews of epidemic-related trade policies in WTO committees, public health experts from WHO are hardly involved (Giesecke, 2003).

III. Features and Implications of Additional Trade Barriers

As to the COVID-19 pandemic, however, two additional observations are noted apart from increased border controls. The first is that once established, trade barriers against affected regions might be imposed for a long time even when infections were controlled, as long as the spread is still endured elsewhere. For instance, none of the temporary trade measures against Chinese exports that were notified to WTO during the pandemic have been lifted. Despite that, the country announced on March 12 that the peak of COVID-19 was over in its territory.[11] FDA's import refusals on Chinese agricultural exports still increased by more than 30% in March compared with last year. Second, trade barriers are not only erected by importing countries against exports from coronavirus-affected regions, but also by exporters on vital food products like grain. Between March 12 and April 10, 20 countries established limits or bans on food exports covering rice, wheat, oil, fruit, vegetables, and eggs, mostly for domestic food security concerns, and only half of them have a specified date of end.[12]

Escalated obstacles to both supply and demand of the global food system imply that food surpluses and deficits will likely be observed at the same time across sectors and regions around the world. Such obstacles demonstrate that the trade protectionism

---

10. Source: https://www.wto.org/english/news_e/news09_e/sps_25jun09_e.htm

11. Source: http://www.xinhuanet.com/english/2020-03/12/c_138870547.htm

12. Source: https://www.macmap.org/covid19

emerging during pandemics is of two types, respectively motivated by mitigating shocks on domestic industries and citizens, yet both could result in devastating consequences to usually the most vulnerable stakeholders in the global food system. On the one hand, countries might reinforce trade protections for industries that suffer logistic strains or slacked demand against import competitions. This might threaten the livelihood of related producers in exporting countries, especially small farmers, which has already been felt in China's aquaculture industry since March.[13] On the other hand, trade protections in the form of export restrictions would make access to the global market more difficult, which might become a food security crisis, particularly in the least developed nations where the issue was already acute (Rutten et al., 2013).

IV. Conclusion

To prevent trade barriers established as "fire lines" in the name of controlling the pandemic from becoming "fault lines" that may demolish the global food system, a number of policy options can be considered. First, individual countries should avoid the temptation to enact additional border control measures. In particular, they need to confine discretionary decisions of import refusals and alerts in a collaborative manner, and align these decisions with WTO principles by consolidating requirements about sufficient support of scientific evidence and strengthening information transparency of such evidence to affected exporters. Second, a formal WHO-WTO coordination scheme needs to be established for reviews and assessment of trade measures imposed during the outbreak. This scheme will be of particular importance to the least developed countries with high dependency on food sources overseas. With a stronger voice of public health and food policy experts, the scheme will allow reviews on whether export bans and limitations on vital agricultural products imposed by major food exporters are beyond necessary. Finally, capacity building of quality enhancement by agricultural exporters from the least developed countries is critical, especially in the adoption of food safety regulations that are compatible with mainstream international standards. Import barriers during pandemics often appear outside the WTO framework manifested by import refusals and alerts. Quality upgrading can help exporters from the developing countries to overcome these barriers (Zhou et al., 2019). Higher quality with brand building and product standardization alleviates consumer concerns about pandemic hazards, thus will reduce demand-side vulnerabilities of the food system.

---

13. Source: https://chinadialogueocean.net/13453-coronavirus-hits-sustainable-aquaculture/?lang=zh-hans

References

Giesecke, J. (2003). International health regulations and epidemic control. In R. Smith, R. Beaglehole, D. Woodward, & N. Drager (Eds.), *Global public goods for health: Health economic and public health perspectives* (pp. 196–211). Oxford University Press.

Grundke, R., & Moser, C. (2019). Hidden protectionism? Evidence from non-tariff barriers to trade in the United States. *Journal of International Economics, 117*, 143–157.

Jouanjean, M. A., Maur, J. C., & Shepherd, B. (2015). Reputation matters: Spillover effects for developing countries in the enforcement of US food safety measures. *Food Policy, 55*, 81–91.

Rutten, M., Shutes, L., & Meijerink, G. (2013). Sit down at the ball game: How trade barriers make the world less food secure. *Food Policy, 38*, 1–10.

Torero, M. (2020). *COVID-19 and the risk to food supply chains: How to respond?* FAO. http://www.fao.org/3/ca8388en/CA8388EN.pdf

Zhou, J., Wang, Y., & Mao, R. (2019). Dynamic and spillover effects of USA import refusals on China's agricultural trade: Evidence from monthly data. *Agricultural Economics/Zemedelska Ekonomika, 65*(9), 425–434.

CHAPTER 11

The Impact of COVID-19 on China-ASEAN Agricultural Cooperation

Yanwen Tan, Congxi Li, and Kevin Chen

I. Introduction

China and ASEAN are major economies in the world agricultural trade, capturing large shares of the global agricultural marketplace. From 2010 to 2018, the proportion of total agricultural trade between China and ASEAN in the entire world increased from 13.28% to 15.88% (WTO, 2020). With substantial advantages in agricultural resources, China and ASEAN faced bright prospects for the rapid development of the bilateral agricultural investment. From 2010 to 2018, the flow of China's agricultural investment in ASEAN rose from US$168 million to US$587 million, and the trade volume of agricultural products increased from US$18.166 billion to US$35.405 billion, with an average annual growth rate of 16.93% and 8.70%, respectively. As one of the partners in the international trade of agricultural products, ASEAN found a place as the destination for the movement of China's overseas investment. In 2018, bilateral agricultural trade accounted for 16.36% of China's total agricultural trade, while agricultural investment in ASEAN accounted for 22.93% of China's total overseas agricultural investment. 2020 marked the 17th anniversary of establishing the China-ASEAN strategic partnership and the 10th anniversary of setting up the China-ASEAN Free Trade Area. Therefore, it was of far-reaching and great significance to maintain and develop the bilateral free trade and investment agreements on agriculture.

With the expansion of global and regional economic integration, the risks and challenges, at the same time, significantly increase in the China-ASEAN partnership. Since the outbreak of the COVID-19 pandemic at the end of December 2019, China has cooperated more closely with ASEAN on infection prevention and control regarding their joint battle against the disease. As the pandemic in ASEAN has been spreading rapidly since March 2020, member states in ASEAN have urged to gradually adopt and strengthen the control and trade-restrictive measures in response to the virus pandemic. Trade restrictions during infection prevention and control would inevitably harm China, ASEAN, and even the world. In the short term, it will shock agricultural products' supply and value chain, while in the long term, it may threaten world food security.

II. Main Measures Taken by ASEAN Countries Amid the Pandemic[1]

1. Overview of the Development of the Epidemic

Judging from the timeline of the COVID-19 outbreak in ASEAN countries and according to the information provided by the ASEAN Secretariat, Thailand, as one of the ASEAN members, had confirmed the earliest cases of COVID-19 on January 13, 2020, with continuing growing counts of confirmed cases found in Singapore, Vietnam, and other ASEAN countries. The epidemic spread relatively slowly in ASEAN countries from January to mid-March 2020. However, since mid-to-late March, as the number of COVID-19 confirmed cases in Malaysia, the Philippines, Indonesia, Thailand, and Singapore continued to rise rapidly, the epidemic in ASEAN countries had entered a stage of a concentrated outbreak (Figure 11.1). In just 27 days, from March 15 to April 10, the number of confirmed cases in ASEAN countries increased exponentially from 858 to 16,749, resulting in a dramatic increase of nearly 20 times. During the period, the actual number of confirmed cases in Malaysia, the Philippines, and Indonesia all exceeded 3,000, while Thailand and Singapore exceeded 2,300 and 1,600.

In contrast, Vietnam, Brunei, Cambodia, Myanmar, and Laos reported relatively fewer confirmed cases and slower growth rates. In general, Malaysia, the Philippines, Indonesia, Thailand, and Singapore, which built up economic strength in ASEAN, suffered more severe epidemics. Conversely, the "new four countries" (Vietnam, Cambodia, Laos, and Brunei) in weak economic conditions triggered much milder epidemics.[2] Due to the large gap in the economic situation, medical status, and health conditions among ASEAN member countries, along with the ongoing spread of the global epidemic, ASEAN countries were still confronted with severe hardship in administrative prevention and controls in response to COVID-19.

---

1. The policies and measures involved in this paper are as of April 10, 2020. It is not ruled out that policies and measures will still be introduced in the later period.

2. The milder epidemic situation does not rule out the fact that it is related to poor detection technology or inadequate detection.

Figure 11.1

The Number of COVID-19 Confirmed Cases in ASEAN Countries From March 15 to April 7

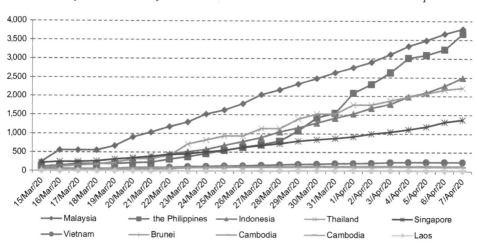

Source. The official website of the World Health Organization (WHO).

2. Main Practices and Measures of ASEAN Countries in Response to the Pandemic

After the outbreak, the ASEAN member states not only took concrete domestic infection prevention and control measures but also called for a stronger collective response to COVID-19 in the whole region of ASEAN "10 + 3," including 10 ASEAN countries, China, South Korea, and Japan.

ASEAN's Overall Response

From January 30, 2020, ASEAN established a regional health management mechanism with China, Japan, and South Korea. From the perspective of the main content of the health mechanism, it was mainly responsible for (a) holding the "ASEAN + 3" senior officials meeting on development and online epidemiological training; (b) Coordinating various health systems among member states through the ASEAN Emergency Operations Center (EOC) network; (c) Building an extensive data network, including a network of health laboratories for sharing information, preparing medical technology, risk communication, and risk assessment of the epidemic (Table 11.1). When WHO declared the COVID-19 outbreak a global pandemic on March 11, 2020, ASEAN countries jointly strengthened control measures. For example, they highlighted the issue of how to respond to COVID-19 in the radio program ASEAN Today. Moreover, they exchanged technical data on COVID-19 and shared the latest information and experience on testing and treatment. On April 9, the foreign ministers of ASEAN countries unanimously agreed to form a foundation. In addition, ASEAN was also actively seeking cooperation with the United States. On April 1, 2020, they held the "ASEAN-US High Level Interagency Video Conference on Public Health Emergencies" to counter COVID-19 (Association of Southease Asian Nations, 2020).

Table 11.1

Content of ASEAN Regional Health System

	Countries	Content
1	Cambodia	ASEAN Senior Officials Meeting on Health Development
2	Malaysia	ASEAN Emergency Operations Center Network
3	Malaysia	ASEAN Plus Three Field Epidemiology Training Network
4	Philippines	ASEAN BioDiaspora Virtual Center
5	Malaysia	ASEAN Biosafety and Biosecurity Network
6	ASEAN countries	Public Health Laboratory Network with ASEAN Health Category II
7	Thailand	Regional Public Health Laboratory Network

Source. Official website from ASEAN Secretariat (https://asean.org/asean-plus-three-senior-health-officials-reaffirm-cooperation-stop-spread-2019-ncov/).

The Main Response Measures of ASEAN Member States

First, strengthen the organizational management of epidemic infection and controls. From January 28 to February 8, 2020, Vietnam established a rapid response team, a national steering committee for epidemic prevention, and four epidemic prevention and control teams responsible for the supervision, treatment, information media, and safeguarding to mobilize and coordinate various departments. The Philippines established the Inter-Agency Task Force on Emerging Infectious Diseases (IATF-EID), with the cabinet minister as the spokesman to guide the work. On April 10, the Cambodian Congress deliberated and approved Cambodia's draft law on the Management of the Nation in a State of Emergency (LMNSE). It is stipulated that when Cambodia suffers from a severe epidemic, a state of emergency will be declared by the king, and the government will be authorized to take emergency martial law and other measures, with the unanimous consent of the prime minister, the president of the National Assembly, and the president of the Senate.

Second, restrict the entry of immigrants and conduct social isolation. With the spread of the epidemic, the restrictions on the entry of foreign personnel in ASEAN countries gradually expanded from China to South Korea, Japan, Europe, the United States, and even all foreigners. At the same time, in order to prevent the pandemic from entering the border areas, ASEAN countries adopted border closures and social distancing measures (Table 11.2). Starting from January 31, 2020, Vietnam has successively closed the Vietnam-China border ports, and it later closed the Vietnam-Cambodia border ports on March 18; Thailand closed the border ports related to Laos, Malaysia, and Cambodia; the Philippines, Malaysia, Thailand, Vietnam, and Singapore successively adopted measures to implement national or regional social isolation measures, close down schools, religious sites, tourism and entertainment venues, traffic control, suspend international flights and suspend domestic passenger services.

Third, strictly control medical supplies and food. To ensure adequate supply and price stability of medical supplies and food during the period of epidemic prevention and control, ASEAN countries (mainly Singapore, the Philippines, and other member states) not only limited the purchase of masks and food but also reduced or remitted exempting tariffs on related items and increase domestic inventory. Moreover, ASEAN countries set the price of medical supplies and severely cracked down on hoarding anti-epidemic supplies and raising prices of medical supplies.

Fourth, implement economic stimulus or assistance programs. To alleviate the sudden economic slowdowns after the outbreak, Singapore, Indonesia, Malaysia, Myanmar, Cambodia, and Vietnam all issued relevant economic stimulus or assistance programs. For example, from February 25 to March 18, 2020, Indonesia unveiled a 181 trillion Rupiah (approximately US$12 billion) stimulus package to alleviate the financial burden. On February 27, Malaysia proposed an economic stimulus plan of 250 billion ringgits (approximately US$57.54 billion). On April 7, the Thailand government launched a loan bill of 1.9 trillion baht (approximately US$58 billion); On April 10, the Vietnamese government officially issued a resolution on an aid plan to assist people affected by COVID-19, with a total of 620,000,100 million VND (approximately US$2.6 billion). The Philippines, Thailand, and the other ASEAN member states also introduced relevant economic stimulus plans. For example, the Philippine government planned to launch a fiscal stimulus of 27.1 billion Philippine pesos (approximately US$527 million).

Table 11.2

Restrictive Measures Taken by ASEAN Countries

Date	Countries	Measures
January 1, 2020	Vietnam	Temporarily closed Vietnam-China border port, and suspended all Vietnam-China round-trip flights from February 1
March 15, 2020	Philippines	Temporarily extended "Enhanced community isolation" measures on Luzon Island to April 30 Declared a state of emergency across the country on March 24
March 16, 2020	Thailand	Ubon Ratchathani closed Thailand-Laos-Cambodia border free trade zone
March 16, 2020	Malaysia	Movement control order temporarily extended to April 28
March 18, 2020	Vietnam	Temporarily closed the Vietnam-Cambodia border port and suspended the issuance of visas for foreigners to enter Vietnam
March 20, 2020	Indonesia	Suspended visa issuance for all countries
March 20, 2020	Laos	Temporarily suspended tourist visa within 30 days
March 20, 2020	Brunei	All immigrants isolated for 14 days
March 20, 2020	Cambodia	Temporarily closed the Cambodia-Vietnam border
March 21, 2020	Burma	Stopped processing visa on arrival and e-visa
March 22, 2020	Philippines	Temporarily prohibited entry of foreigners
March 22, 2020	Thailand	Temporarily closed the third Thailand-Laos friendship bridge, closed Thailand-Malaysia and Thailand-Cambodia border
March 23, 2020	Singapore	Prohibited entry of foreigners
March 26, 2020	Thailand	Implemented emergency laws including closing entry and exit routes, ports, border stations
April 1, 2020	Vietnam	Social isolated for 14 days
April 3, 2020	Thailand	Curfew (10:00 p.m.–04:00 a.m.)
April 7, 2020	Singapore	Temporarily closed most physical stores except for companies that provide food, necessities and import and export trade enterprises in four weeks (until May 4)

Source. Official website of ASEAN countries government.

III. Impact of the Pandemic on Agricultural Production and Trade: Implications for Policies

The pandemic exacerbated a difficult situation of agricultural production and trade in ASEAN countries, leading to an insufficient supply of agricultural products and slow sales of some agricultural products. Ensuring the adequate supply of agricultural products was a major problem for ASEAN countries.

1. The Impact of the Pandemic on Agricultural Production and Trade in ASEAN

Agricultural Production Is Facing a Decline

The significant annual production season is from April to June, with agricultural products such as rice, vegetables, and tropical fruits in ASEAN countries. However, the pandemic has prevented the agricultural production from being effectively carried out. The agricultural production was affected by other disasters. Specifically speaking, Thailand and Vietnam's Mekong Delta suffered from persistent drought. Vietnam's winter and spring rice is in a critical period of growth, and accounts for 60% of Vietnam's rice production. However, since early March 2020, rice blasts have occurred in the Red River Delta, northern and central regions of Vietnam, resulting in reduced rice production in Thailand and Vietnam. According to the Ministry of Agriculture and Rural Development of Vietnam, Vietnam's rice output in 2020 would expect to be 43.4 million tons, 70 thousand tons less than in 2019.[3] In addition, ASEAN member countries, such as Vietnam, the Philippines, and Indonesia, faced African swine fever and highly pathogenic avian flu epidemics (Figure 11.2). The African swine fever and avian flu epidemics have exacerbated the shortage of livestock products in ASEAN. According to FAO data, by March 5, 2020, the number of pigs eliminated by African swine fever in Vietnam, the Philippines, and Indonesia was approximately six million, 73.7 thousand, and 50.2 thousand, respectively. Regarding statistics from the Vietnam Statistics Bureau, as of February 22, 2020, there were 23 bird flu outbreaks in seven provinces in Vietnam, and the total number of dead and slaughtered poultry exceeded 80 thousand.[4] Therefore, due to the occurrence and overlap of the COVID-19 and other disasters, the agricultural production is at risk of reduction in the ASEAN region.

---

3. Data from https://www.mard.gov.vn/Pages/hoi-nghi-truc-tuyen-thuc-day-san-xuat-nong-nghiep-trong-dieu-kien-dich-benh-covid-19-.aspx?item=10

4. Data from https://www.gso.gov.vn/default_en.aspx?tabid=622&ItemID=19526

Figure 11.2
African Swine Fever in Asia

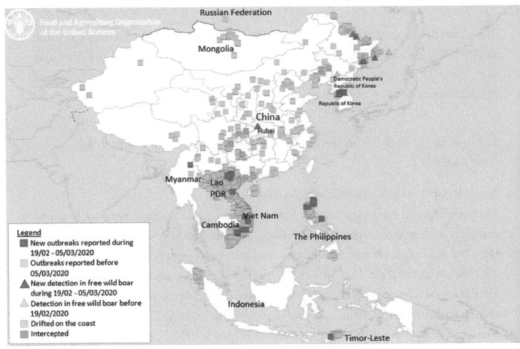

Source. FAO.

The Import and Export Trade of Agricultural Products Is Blocked

China is a leading import and export country for agricultural products from ASEAN countries. However, during the severe epidemic in China from January to February 2020, the import and export trade of ASEAN agricultural products has been severely blocked. The exports of agricultural, forestry, and aquatic products in Vietnam went down to US$5.34 billion, with a decrease of 2.8%, and imports went down to US$4.3 billion, with a decrease of 6.7% (Central Government of Vietnam, 2020a). Thailand's agricultural exports were 181.206 billion baht (approximately US$58.66 billion), and the import value was 85.338 billion baht (approximately US$2.767 billion), with a decrease of 8.22% and 7.12% (Thailand Office of Agricultural Economics, 2020), respectively. In ASEAN countries, the sales season lasts from April to June each year for vegetables, flowers, and tropical fruits such as durian, mangos, mangosteen, rambutan, and longan. However, the temporary suspension of flights to the export markets, especially in South Korea, Japan, and European, resulted in insufficient export capacity and increasing export costs. Also, the slowdown in domestic demand has prevented farmers from selling these products that are not storage-resistant. These influences are therefore leading to a sales stagnation for agricultural products.

2. Agricultural Production and Trade Policies

Large gaps exist in agricultural resource endowments among ASEAN countries. The pandemic has greatly impacted the production and supply of agricultural products in each country. ASEAN countries have mainly adopted the following measures to respond to the pandemic and ensure domestic food security and an effective supply of agricultural products.

Increase the Effective Supply of Agricultural Products

In order to prevent the shortage of agricultural products and the interruption of the supply chain caused by the pandemic, the first measure taken by ASEAN countries is to promote domestic agricultural production. On February 17, 2020, the Vietnamese government urgently implemented a socio-economic development plan, which proposed to promote the production of grain, food, and consumer goods;[5] At the end of March 2020, the Philippines reinforced the promotion of urban agriculture by distributing widespread free vegetable seeds and planting materials (DA Communications Group, 2020a). Second, quarantine measures do not apply to the agricultural production and operation personnel. During the Movement Control Order implementation, Malaysia allowed agricultural product processing and sales of breeding, fishing, and aquaculture. On March 26, 2020, the Department of Agriculture in the Philippines promulgated a policy allowing product transportation, processing, and sales, and healthy people involved in agricultural and fishery production operations to be exempt from home isolation (DA Communications Group, 2020b). Third, it aims to increase imports of essential agricultural products. To increase domestic pork supply and stabilize pork prices, Vietnam has increased its pork imports. From January to March 2020, pork imports in Vietnam amounted to approximately 40,000 tons, a year-on-year increase of nearly three times.[6] The Philippines urgently imported 300 million tons of rice after implementing rice export restrictions in Vietnam to ensure food supply during the epidemic. Last, it is also essential to solve the problem of overstocking agricultural products. With the disruption of agricultural products export and the declining purchasing power of domestic consumers for agricultural products, ASEAN countries have generally adopted several measures to encourage domestic consumption, vigorously develop online marketing and noncash payments, and appropriately lower the prices of agricultural products to promote consumption.

---

5. Central Government of Vietnam, 2022.
6. Data from https://www.mard.gov.vn/Pages/15-doanh-nghiep-chan-nuoi-lon-cam-ket-dua-gia-lon-hoi-xuong-70-000-dong-kg-tu-1-4.aspx

For example, from April 10 to May 2020, Thailand cut milk prices by 25% to lighten the burden of unsalable milk from dairy farmers (Thailand Ministry of Agriculture and Cooperatives, 2020).

Stabilize the Price of Agricultural Products

Strengthening infection control measures in response to COVID-19 has caused ASEAN countries to face supply shortages and rising prices since people rushed to buy food. In order to ensure the supply of agricultural products and stabilize the agricultural product market, related departments of ASEAN countries have tracked agricultural product prices and cracked down on hoarding and price hikes. At the same time, the quota of basic daily necessities has been set. To control the prices of agricultural products, processed agricultural products, and medicines in urban areas, on March 27, 2020, an agreement was reached to restart the Local Price Coordination Committee (LPCC) by the Department of Agriculture in the Philippines, the Department of Trade and Industry, and the Ministry of Health. On April 8, Department of Agriculture monitored basic food supply and price, and strictly implemented the recommended retail price and the "price freeze" policy (DA Communications Group, 2020c). These prevented excessive and unreasonable increases in the prices of agricultural products and their processed products, and medicines.

Restrict the Export of Important Agricultural Products

Due to the rapid growth in rice exports and concerns about domestic food security, Vietnam and Cambodia have successively introduced emergency measures to suspend rice exports. The Myanmar Ministry of Commerce is also considering taking the same actions.[7] From January to March 2020, rice exports in Vietnam and Cambodia increased rapidly. Among them, Vietnam's total rice exports were 1.409 thousand tons, a year-on-year increase of 1.1%, while Cambodia's rice exports were 231 thousand tons, a year-on-year increase of 26.06%, with average monthly growth rates of 17.11% and 36.72%, respectively. On March 25, the Vietnamese government decided to suspend rice exports to assess the situation of its domestic rice supply and export (Central Government of Vietnam, 2020). To ensure food supply during the pandemic, the Cambodian government also suspended the export of rice on April 5.[8] On April 9, the Ministry of Industry and Trade of Vietnam asked the government to resume rice exports, but the total amount of rice exports in April and May will be

---

7. Data from https://www.mmtimes.com/news/myanmar-temporarily-suspends-rice-export-permits.htm
8. Data from https://english.cambodiadaily.com/business/covid-19-cambodia-halts-rice-padi-exports-162259/

limited to 800 thousand tons. At the same time, the Ministry of Agriculture and Social Development of Vietnam requires the 20 largest domestic rice exporters to sign an agreement with at least one supermarket system to ensure circulating grain reserves (Ministry of Agriculture and Rural Development, Vietnam, 2020). In addition, due to the shortage of egg supply, Thailand implemented a seven-day egg export suspension policy starting on March 26.

Enhance Agricultural Financial Support

The economic stimulus plans issued by ASEAN countries include support for agriculture and related enterprises. Due to the food shortage crisis in the Philippines, its agricultural support policies are relatively strong. At the end of March 2020, the Philippines increased its budget for agriculture by 31 billion pesos, including an increase of 8.5 billion pesos for the rice disaster prevention project; On April 3, the Department of Agriculture in the Philippines, through the Agriculture Credit Policy Council (ACPC) has approved initial P1-billion loan assistance to marginal farmers, as well as fishery micro and small enterprises (MSEs) to enable them to cope during this state of national emergency due to the COVID-19 pandemic (DA-AFID, 2020a); The government also implements the subsidy policy for rice farmers on April 6, with a cash subsidy of five thousand pesos per person for 600 thousand rice farmers (DA-AFID, 2020b).

IV. The Impact of Pandemic on China-ASEAN Agricultural Trade and Cooperation

The epidemic has caused a short-term interruption of the agricultural product supply chain between China and ASEAN. The signing of trade agreements and agricultural investment agreements related to agricultural products has been delayed due to the pandemic, which caused significant adverse effects on bilateral agricultural trade and agricultural cooperation.

1. A Short-Term Interruption of the Agricultural Product Supply Chain Impacts Investment and Trade

The epidemic severely impacted the stability of regional and global agricultural product supply chains. Affected by the pandemic, consumers' demand for agricultural products declined, and the transportation of agricultural products was interrupted. It greatly affects the agricultural product value chain network between China and ASEAN. Measures such as the closure of ports and border crossings, ship delays, and grounding of flights have exacerbated the blockage of the agricultural trade network between China and the ASEAN. On January 31, 2020, the Vietnamese government signed relevant instructions requiring the temporary closure of ports and trade with China, discouraging the China-ASEAN trade during the epidemic (Central Government of Vietnam, 2020c). Subsequently, Vietnam also targeted China's excessive prevention and control measures, such as the suspension of all flights and the need to isolate imported cargo ships at designated locations for 14 days, which is not conducive to the normal flow of goods trade, especially for fresh agricultural products with high transportation timeliness requirements. Trade restrictions will increase transportation costs and product corruption risks. Due to the closure of border trade ports, many agricultural products are stranded at China-Vietnam border ports, among which fruits and aquatic products such as watermelon, mango, and dragon fruit exported from Vietnam to China are mainly exported. Until February 7, the Vietnamese government did not allow border cargo clearance (Central Government of Vietnam, 2020d). On February 12, the Prime Minister of Vietnam signed an order on solving the difficulties of import and export activities and cross-border cargo transportation, requiring that fast customs clearance of import and export cargo be implemented at seaports, airports, and highway and railway border ports based on the principle of convenience and promotion. However, due to the excessive backlog of goods in the early stage of customs clearance and the slower flow of goods, the current cargo clearance capacity is only 50%–60% of that before the outbreak.[9] Beginning in late March, as the pandemic spread, ASEAN countries have implemented strict social distancing measures, and the number of border ports closed between member states has also increased. These restrictive measures will have an adverse impact on China's investment in ASEAN agriculture and agricultural trade. The extent of the impact remains to be determined based on the duration of the pandemic and the prevention and control measures of various countries.

Most of the textile raw materials in Vietnam, Myanmar, Cambodia, and other countries are imported from China, while some cassava processing plants in China rely on imports from Vietnam. The pandemic has caused shortages in the supply of raw materials and labor for the agricultural product processing industries on both sides, causing the factories to be forced to stop production. From the perspective of the import and export trade of agricultural products, from January to February 2020, the scale of agricultural product trade between China and ASEAN countries has dropped significantly. Specifically, China's imports of vegetables, fruits, nuts, grains, milling industrial products (mainly tapioca starch), animal and vegetable oils, cotton,

---

9. Vietnam News Agency, March 24, 2020.

and other bulk agricultural products' trade value from ASEAN have all fallen sharply, with a year-on-year decrease of 37.71%, 17.28%, 31.01%, 34.47%, 5.78%, and 8.67%, respectively. China's main agricultural exports to ASEAN, including aquatic products, vegetables, sugar and confectionery, and cotton, also saw a significant decline, with a year-on-year decrease of 16.30%, 8.40%, 6.35%, and 25.12%, respectively (Table 11.3).

Table 11.3

Import and Export Trade of Agricultural Products Between China and ASEAN From January to February 2020 (Unit: Million US$)

Products	Import from ASEAN	Year-on-year increase / decrease	Export to ASEAN	Year-on-year increase / decrease
Chapter 1 live animals	38.12	−76.49%	118.17	11.88%
Chapter 2 meat and edible offal	4,206.91	54.26%	491.92	−3.32%
Chapter 3 fish and other aquatic invertebrates	31,959.41	−0.67%	23,864.18	−16.30%
Chapter 4 milk; eggs; honey; other edible animal products	6,524.34	124.91%	592.49	−1.21%
Chapter 5 other animal products	382.95	−34.47%	5,986.66	−33.42%
Chapter 6 living plants; stems, roots; flower arrangements, clusters of leaves	211.54	−37.48%	1,599.83	20.00%
Chapter 7 edible vegetables, roots and tubers	10,423.43	−37.71%	42,255.39	−8.40%
Chapter 8 edible fruits and nuts; peels of melons and other fruits	57,539.77	−17.29%	57,500.14	20.09%
Chapter 9 coffee, tea, yerba mate and flavoring spices	3,593.08	67.28%	9,210.71	31.08%
Chapter 10 cereals	12,113.13	−31.01%	51.20	−63.16%
Chapter 11 flour mill products; malt; starch	14,228.86	−34.47%	7,419.26	41.70%
Chapter 12 oilseeds; seeds; industrial or medicinal plants; feed	5,149.43	26.72%	6,121.75	−37.91%

(Continued)

Products	Import from ASEAN	Year-on-year increase / decrease	Export to ASEAN	Year-on-year increase / decrease
Chapter 13 shellac; gums, resins and other plant fluids and juices	981.80	−25.64%	1,947.31	−13.68%
Chapter 14 plant fibers; other plant products	467.89	−43.03%	52.51	−40.80%
Chapter 15 animal and vegetable oils, fats, waxes; refined edible fats and oils	79,159.91	−5.78%	3,691.87	219.65%
Chapter 16 products of meat, fish and other aquatic invertebrates	1,358.98	44.78%	12,198.98	−11.75%
Chapter 17 sugar and confectionery	4,374.28	53.26%	10,920.56	−6.35%
Chapter 18 cocoa and cocoa products	2,899.24	−26.53%	883.12	−3.87%
Chapter 19 cereal flour, starch, etc. or milk products; pastries	4,784.89	−26.54%	3,449.85	5.39%
Chapter 20 products of vegetables, fruits, or other parts of plants	6,619.99	31.50%	17,376.52	18.85%
Chapter 21 miscellaneous food	9,868.93	7.51%	16,316.71	17.59%
Chapter 22 drinks, wine and vinegar	1,834.26	51.20%	2,423.73	7.96%
Chapter 23 residues and waste from the food industry; prepared feed	4,264.37	−9.87%	5,899.60	−18.13%
Chapter 24 tobacco	1,860.01	3.73%	2,213.61	−31.11%
Chapter 52 cotton	37,429.36	−8.67%	49,676.02	−25.12%
Total	302,274.89	−9.50%	282,262.08	−4.96%

Source. The General Administration of Customs of the People's Republic of China (GACC).

2. Increasing Measures of Trade Restriction Measures Impacts Regional Food Security

Vietnam and Cambodia's suspension of rice exports may affect the regional food supply situation. In fact, during the global food crisis in 2008, Vietnam and Cambodia introduced policies to restrict rice exports. In late March 2008, Cambodia imposed a two-month export ban on rice, while Vietnam restricted its annual rice export volume to 3.5 million tons. There are huge differences in natural resource endowments among ASEAN countries. Thailand, Vietnam, Myanmar, and Cambodia are the world's major rice exporters. Among the top 10 rice exporters in the world, three ASEAN countries, including Thailand, Vietnam, and Myanmar, ranked second, third, and eighth, respectively. By contrast, the Philippines, Indonesia, and Malaysia are the world's major rice importers, and their rice is in short supply. Vietnamese rice's main export trading partners are the Philippines, Indonesia, Malaysia, and Singapore. In 2018, the proportion of Vietnamese rice imported by these four countries in their total rice imports was 19.10%, 17.02%, 12.76%, and 13.41%, respsectively. Vietnam is the second-largest source of rice imported by these countries (the first largest source of rice is from Thailand). Although the Vietnamese rice imported by the Philippines, Indonesia, and Malaysia accounts for a small proportion of their domestically produced rice, they play an important role in regulating market surpluses and meeting diversified market needs.

There are similarities and differences between the 2008 global food crisis and the ASEAN rice market trade situation during the pandemic. The similarity is that the export prices of rice in the major rice exporting member countries have risen sharply at the beginning of the year. From January to March 2008, Thailand's rice export prices increased by 47.27%, and Vietnam's rice export prices increased by 55.46%. In the same period of 2020, the rice export prices in the two countries increased by 10.70% and 14.50%, respectively (Figure 11.3). The difference was that although rice production in ASEAN countries increased, the supply capacity declined. In particular, rice consumption increased dramatically with the increase in population. The rice export volume in major rice exporting member countries is increasing, but the inventory declined. The rice stocks of major rice-importing member countries have shrunk significantly, and their dependence on imported rice is increasing (Table 11.4). In 2019, the self-sufficiency rates of rice in Indonesia, Malaysia, the Philippines, and Singapore were 96.56%, 65.77%, 83.33%, and 0, respectively.

At present, the number of countries restricting rice export is still growing. India, the world's largest rice exporter, cannot export rice smoothly due to its domestic blockade. The relevant closure measures of ASEAN countries have shown a prolonged

Figure 11.3

Changes in Major International Rice Export Prices From 2008 to March 2020

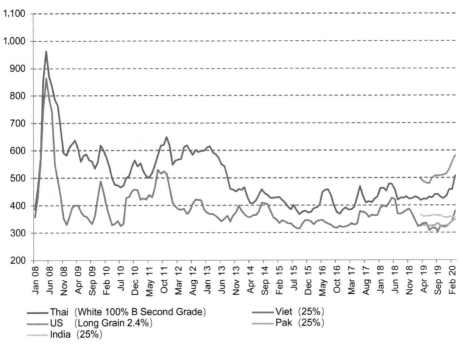

Thai (White 100% B Second Grade)   Viet (25%)
US (Long Grain 2.4%)   Pak (25%)
India (25%)

Source. Data from Food and Agriculture Organization.

trend, which is bound to increase the pressure on Thailand's rice export and force the rice price to go up. From March 25 to April 8, 2020, the prices of various types of rice in Thailand rose sharply. Particularly, the prices of grade B rice with a crushing rate of 100%, rate of 25%, and rate of 5% had increased by 15.09% and 13.02%, and 15.34%, respectively.[10] Therefore, the chain reaction of global rice supply chain capacity transfer, food shortage panic, and rising international food prices that may be triggered by rice trade restrictions deserve further attention.

The rice export restrictions of ASEAN countries do not pose a substantial threat to China's food security. However, as ASEAN is China's largest source of imported rice, the rice export restrictions will not be conducive to satisfying the diversified needs of China's domestic rice market. In addition, an increasing number of countries that restrict rice exports will aggravate the imbalance between supply and demand in the global rice market, which will, in turn, trigger a rise in global rice prices, impacting the stability of China's rice market prices in the short term. Although, in the context of supply-side structural reforms, China's rice imports from ASEAN have dropped

---

10. Data from http://www.thairiceexporters.or.th/price_eng.html

Table 11.4

Rice Market in China and Some ASEAN Countries in 2008 and 2019 (Unit: Million Tons)

Countries	2008					2019				
	Production	Consumption	Year-end inventory	Export amount	Input amount	Production	Consumption	Year-end inventory	Export amount	Input amount
Cambodia	379.1	322	15.7	82	5	568.8	430	49.7	140	1
Indonesia	3,831	3,710	705.7	1	25	3,650	3,780	305.9	0.2	100
Laos	135.2	137	6.6	1.3	4.7	205	200	13.8	5	5
Malaysia	153.6	250	73	0.1	108.6	182.5	277.5	34.4	3	100
Philippines	1,075.5	1,310	467.3	0	260	1,200	1,440	372	0	260
Singapore	0	24.6	0	0	24.6	0	30	0	0	30
Thailand	1,985	950	478.7	857	30	1,850	1,170	378.7	750	25
Vietnam	2,439.3	1,900	196.1	595	50	2,830	2,150	132	700	40
China	13,482.8	13,278.2	3,950	74.7	20.1	14,673	14,293	11,800	320	240

Source. Data from U.S. Department of Agriculture Foreign Agricultural Services.

significantly since 2016. Countries such as Vietnam, Myanmar, and Cambodia are still China's main rice imports. In 2019, China imported 2.5033 million tons of rice. The quantities imported from Myanmar, Thailand, Vietnam, Cambodia, and Laos were 545,700 tons, 526,300 tons, 479,100 tons, 224,900 tons, and 72,500 tons, respectively, accounting for China's rice imports. The proportions of the total amount were 21.80%, 21.02%, 19.14%, 8.98%, and 2.90%, respectively. Guangdong is the Province with the largest permanent population in China, and it is also China's largest rice-consuming and importing Province. In 2019, Guangdong's rice imports amounted to 1,179,500 tons, accounting for 47.12% of China's total rice imports (2.5033 million tons). Specifically speaking, the proportions of rice imports from Thailand, Myanmar, Vietnam, and Cambodia to Guangdong's total rice imports were 29.56%, 17.25%, 14.16%, and 3.03%, respectively. Various types of imported rice can meet the diversified market needs of the Guangdong market. For example, imported Thai long grain polished rice is mainly for the high-end consumer market. The price of rice imported from Vietnam, Myanmar, and other countries is generally lower than that of rice transferred from other provinces in China (Figure 11.4). In particular, there is a large price difference between rice imported from Myanmar and rice transferred from other provinces (Table 11.5), benefiting from reducing the transportation cost of agricultural firms. Taking 2019 as an example, the quantity of long grain rice imported

Figure 11.4

Changes of Rice Price in Guangdong From 2019 to February 2020 (Unit: Yuan/Tons)

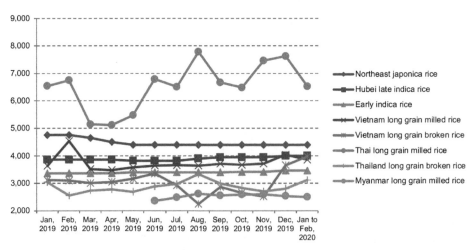

Note. The price of rice in Vietnam and Thailand is the Guangdong port price, and the import price is converted into RMB (average) according to one dollar of the people's Bank of China each month.
Source. Domestic rice prices come from official website of China Agricultural Information. Rice prices in Vietnam and Thailand are based on the data of the General Administration of Customs of China.

Table 11.5

Rice Price Difference Between Vietnam, Myanmar and Provinces Outside Guangdong From 2019 to February 2020 (Unit: Tons)

Dates	Price difference between Vietnam long grain milled rice and Northeast japonica rice	Price difference between Vietnam long grain Milled Rice and Hubei indica rice	Price difference between Myanmar long grain milled rice and Northeast japonica rice	Price difference between Myanmar long grain refined rice and Hubei indica rice
Jan. 2019	−1,129	−229	—	—
Feb. 2019	−223	677	—	—
Mar. 2019	−1,134	−344	—	—
Apr. 2019	−1,023	−383	—	—
May 2019	−825	−245	—	—
Jun. 2019	−760	−180	−2,041	−1,461
Jul. 2019	−748	−168	−1,916	−1,336
Aug. 2019	−761	−261	−1,780	−1,280
Sep. 2019	−688	−238	−1,840	−1,390
Oct. 2019	−730	−280	−1,812	−1,362
Nov. 2019	−685	−235	−1,805	−1,355
Dec. 2019	−358	42	−1,865	−1,465
Jan. to Feb. 2020	−540	−140	−1,898	−1,498

Note. "—" represents no import.
Source. Same to Figure 11.4.

from Vietnam and Myanmar can save US$428 million in the transportation cost of Northeast japonica rice or US$276 million in transportation cost of the Hubei high-quality, late indica rice. However, due to the large amount of imported rice, the rice price in Guangdong is more affected by the global market and is particularly subject to endogenous global market shocks.

The Irrational buying of rice caused by the public panic about the pandemic will also impose a short-term increase in rice prices in China's domestic market. At the end of March 2020, there was a sudden wave of urban residents in Jiangsu, Zhejiang, and Shanghai rushing to buy and hoard rice, and the price of rice in Jiangsu rose by more than 200 yuan per ton within a week. In addition, as far as Chinese companies investing in rice of Cambodia, Myanmar, and other countries are concerned, the rice export ban will block these companies from exporting rice to the country and increase their market development costs and inventory costs. With the upgrading of epidemic prevention and control levels in ASEAN countries, Chinese-funded enterprises face the dilemma of suspension of work and production.

3. ASEAN's Economy Has Declined, and the Risk of Uncertainty in Regional Agricultural Cooperation Has Increased

The pandemic brutally hits ASEAN countries, leading to an economic downturn. Since 2018, the economic growth has been weak or declining in ASEAN countries, especially the major economic entities such as Singapore, Thailand, Malaysia, Indonesia, the Philippines, and Vietnam (Figure 11.5). In the first quarter of 2020, the GDP growth rates of Vietnam and Singapore were 3.82% and −2.2%, respectively, which has reached the lowest points in the past ten years. In order to promote economic development, ASEAN countries have taken measures to stimulate. However, there are few supporting measures for the agricultural sector or poor policy implementation. The current epidemic prevention and control in ASEAN may cause Chinese companies in some ASEAN countries to be buffeted by economic headwinds such as insufficient labor or blocked product sales. China's import and export of agricultural products from ASEAN countries may also be affected by cargo transportation control, which may cause delays in shipping schedules. Therefore, judging from the current situation, the risk of uncertainty in agricultural cooperation between China and ASEAN countries is increasing.

Figure 11.5

Changes in Quarterly GDP Growth Rates of ASEAN Since 2018 (Unit: Tons)

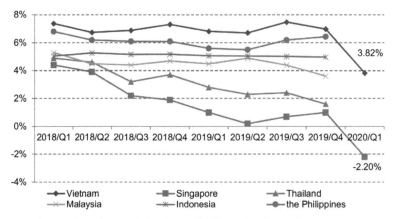

Source. According to the websites of the statistical offices of each member states.

V. Policy Recommendations

1. Strengthen Trade Consultations and Stabilize the Regional Agricultural Product Supply Chain

To jointly fight against the COVID-19 pandemic, a joint ministerial statement was issued by Australia, Brunei Darussalam, Canada, Chile, Myanmar, New Zealand, and Singapore on March 25, 2020, committing to ensure the trade flow unimpeded and maintain an open and connected supply chains.[11] It is currently necessary to prevent the implementation of export controls or tariff and non-tariff barriers, cancel trade restrictions on essential goods, especially medical supplies, and keep key infrastructure such as aviation and seaports open, supporting the feasibility and integrity of the global supply chain. It provides good references for trade negotiations between China and ASEAN.

In response to measures such as border trade closures and trade restrictions during the epidemic, it is recommended to strengthen trade dialogues and consultations with ASEAN countries based on the upgraded version of the China-ASEAN Free Trade Area. The strategic significance of this partnership enabled the two countries to jointly strengthen pandemic monitoring, establish a joint epidemic prevention and control mechanism at border ports, and adopt measures tailored to natural requirements to ensure ports are no longer unilaterally closed. As ports limit the entry and exit of immigrants due to epidemic prevention and control systems, it calls for urgent need to ensure the customs clearance of goods, especially the essential materials, and stabilize the bilateral agricultural product trade supply chain. In addition, concerning the import and export of grain products, trade restrictions should not be imposed unilaterally, and relevant agreements should be signed based on trade negotiations with major trading partners to protect the mutual interests of both parties and maintain regional food supply security.

2. Deepen Cooperation in Epidemic Prevention and Control, Establish Agricultural Product Coordination and Guarantee Mechanism

Although ASEAN has made concerted efforts to respond collectively to the epidemic, almost no coordinated action has been taken among member states.[12] The mutual

---

11. Singapore Government Agency Website: https://www.sgpc.gov.sg/media_releases/mti/press_release/P-20200325-2

12. Straitstimes: https://www.straitstimes.com/opinion/covid-19-challenges-asean-to-act-as-one

adverse effects of the relevant restrictive measures are gradually emerging. From the perspective of cooperation between China and ASEAN countries, up till now, China and ASEAN countries have conducted two high level video conferences on infection prevention and control. However, the meetings are mainly focused on prevention measures and how to provide medical treatment. In response to the current severe situation of the ASEAN and global epidemics, it is suggested to strengthen technical exchanges and cooperation between China and ASEAN in response to the new crown pneumonia, swine fever, and fowl fever. Both should make an overall plan to promote stable agricultural production, appropriately expand the bulk of grain and pork, and release agricultural product stock. Meanwhile, China and ASEAN countries should strengthen agricultural product market governance during the infection prevention and control period, release information on agricultural product supply promptly, enhance the openness and transparency of mutual agricultural investment and trade policies to jointly prevent panic caused by economic downturns, and stabilize prices of agricultural products.

3. Scientifically Study and Judge the Situation of the Epidemic, Establish and Improve an Early Warning Mechanism for Agricultural Cooperation Risks

As the pandemic continues to spread worldwide and numerous countries have successively declared a state of emergency, there is an urgent need to improve guidance for overseas investment and agricultural product trading enterprises. We recommend that enterprises arrange proper plans for importing and exporting agricultural products such as grain, soybeans, oilseeds, pork, cotton, and many more. We should be aware that China's agricultural exports to ASEAN are subject to substantial and continuous growth downgrades reflected in delays of shipping schedules and investment projects being postponed. A further mechanism should be set up for enhancing risk assessment of agricultural investment projects and product trading. Moreover, we recommend establishing an agricultural information platform to expose the risks of investing and trading to promote the development of regional cross-border e-commerce among agricultural products and ensure the adequate supply of regional agricultural products.

References

Association of Southease Asian Nations. (2020). *Co-chairs statement of the ASEAN-United States high level interagency video conference on cooperation to counter COVID-19.* https://asean.org/asean2020/wp-content/uploads/2021/03/30.-Final-Co-Chairs-Statement-for-the-Special-ASEAN-U.S.-Foreign-Ministers-Meeting-on-COVID-19.pdf

Central Government of Vietnam. (2020a, March 12). *Promoting agricultural production in the context of COVID-19 epidemic.* https://www.mard.gov.vn/Pages/hoi-nghi-truc-tuyen-thuc-day-san-xuat-nong-nghiep-trong-dieu-kien-dich-benh-covid-19-.aspx?item=10

Central Government of Vietnam. (2020b, March 25). *Suspend signing rice export contracts.* http://baodientu.chinhphu.vn/Chi-dao-quyet-dinh-cua-Chinh-phu-Thu-tuong-Chinh-phu/Tam-dung-ky-hop-dong-xuat-khau-gao-moi/390910.vgp

Central Government of Vietnam. (2020c, January 31). *The Prime Minister continued to direct the strengthening of measures to prevent and control the COVID-19 epidemic.* http://baodientu.chinhphu.vn/Chi-dao-quyet-dinh-cua-Chinh-phu-Thu-tuong-Chinh-phu/Thu-tuong-tiep-tuc-chi-thi-tang-cuong-cac-bien-phap-phong-chong-dich-benh-nCoV/386247.vgp

Central Government of Vietnam. (2020d, July 2). *The Prime Minister allows the delivery of goods at the border gate, strictly implements the quarantine.* http://baodientu.chinhphu.vn/Chi-dao-quyet-dinh-cua-Chinh-phu-Thu-tuong-Chinh-phu/Thu-tuong-cho-phep-giao-nhan-hang-hoa-tai-cua-khau-thuc-hien-nghiem-viec-kiem-dich/386868.vgp

DA-AFID. (2020a, April 3). *DA-ACPC kays P1-B loan facility for "Plant, Plant, Plant Program."* Department of Agriculture, the Philippine. http://www.da.gov.ph/da-acpc-okays-p1-b-loan-facility-for-plant-plant-plant-program/

DA-AFID. (2020b, April 6). *DA to distribute P5L cash assistance to rice farmers amid COVID-19.* Department of Agriculture, the Philippine. http://www.da.gov.ph/da-to-distribute-p5k-cash-assistance-to-rice-farmers-amid-covid-19/

DA Communications Group. (2020a, March 31). *DA intensifies urban agri through veggie seed distribution amid COVID-19.* Department of Agriculture, the Philippine. http://www.da.gov.ph/da-intensifies-urban-agri-through-veggie-seed-distribution-amid-covid-19/

DA Communications Group. (2020b, March 26). *IATF-EID approves DA's protocol to ease transport of food products to MM, other urban areas nationwide.* Department of Agriculture, the Philippine. http://www.da.gov.ph/iatf-eid-approves-das-protocol-to-ease-transport-of-food-products-to-mm-other-urban-areas-nationwide/

DA Communications Group. (2020c, April 8). *DA reg'l chiefs, LPCCs to enforce SRP, price freeze on major food items.* Department of Agriculture, the Philippine. http://www.da.gov.ph/da-regl-chiefs-lpccs-to-enforce-srp-price-freeze-on-major-food-items/

Ministry of Agriculture and Rural Development, Vietnam. (2020, April 9). *MoIT proposes to resume rice exports.* https://www.mard.gov.vn/en/Pages/moit-proposes-to-resume-rice-exports. aspx

Office of Agricultural Economics (Thailand). (2020). Monthly value of exports and imports of agricultural products. http://impexp.oae.go.th/service/export_import.php?S_YEAR= 2562&E_YEAR=2563&wf_search=&WF_SEARCH=Y

Thailand Ministry of Agriculture and Cooperatives. (2020, April 10). *Deputy Minister Mananya directs DPO to reduce milk prices by 25% to relieve dairy farmers.* https://www.moac.go.th/ news-preview-421191791370

CHAPTER 12

Impacts of Import Refusals on Agricultural Exports During Pandemics

Rui Mao, Ziyi Jia, and Kevin Chen

I. Introduction

During the past two decades, developing countries have experienced four major pandemics: SARS, influenza A (H1N1), Ebola, and COVID-19. All these outbreaks resulted in negative impacts on the economy of epicenter countries due to labor shortages, production stagnation, consumption weakening, and logistic strains. They might also have triggered additional trade barriers to prevent the cross-border transmission of pathogens. For example, in early May 2003, when SARS hit China heavily, Japan issued import bans on China's meat, poultry, and egg products, and extended the time limit for customs clearance on China's vegetable and eel products.[1] During the outbreak of COVID-19, Egypt, Indonesia, South Korea, and Russia established import bans in January and February 2020 on wild or live animals, animal-derived products, and vegetable products such as garlic, carrots, and green ginger from China.[2] Mauritius imposed import restrictions against animal products from Iran, South Korea, Switzerland, and the EU in March 2020.[3] Such measures would increase both trade costs and uncertainty for the export sector of pandemic-hit countries and consequently exacerbate the negative effects on their economy. Specifically, importing countries might increase unilateral border controls such as import refusals against

---

1. News reports about these import restrictions are available from: https://business.sohu.com/11/72/article 210597211.shtml (online; cited May 2020).

2. News reports about these import restrictions are available from: https://mp.weixin.qq.com/s/rPZt-4m8 gpgKzu3ShG0phA (online; cited May 2020).

3. The notification of this import restriction is available from: https://www.macmap.org/covid19 (online; cited May 2020).

exports of pandemic-hit countries; such measures feature relatively greater room for discretion than SPS and Technical Barriers to Trade (TBT) measures regulated by the multilateral framework of the WTO. In this paper, we examine import refusals by the US FDA on agricultural exports from developing countries that were epicenters of these four pandemics, and we evaluate subsequent trade impacts.

There are four reasons for our focus on FDA import refusals instead of other barriers to agricultural trade. First, with the average tariffs on agricultural products being substantially reduced around the world, technical measures on agricultural trade have received increasing research attention (Ghodsi, 2020). A number of empirical studies have revealed that increased technical measures impeded agricultural exports, which was particularly significant for developing countries (Baylis et al., 2010; Grant & Anders, 2011; Tran et al., 2012). Second, while SPS and TBT measures are currently the most prevalent technical barriers to agricultural trade, they are unfortunately de jure regulative actions in that their presence alone could not reflect whether and how strictly they are enforced. Specifically, it is possible that during pandemic outbreaks, importing countries enforced existing yet inactive SPS or TBT measures, instead of imposing new ones. In contrast, FDA import refusals are de facto border control actions that more precisely signal trade costs and uncertainty. Third, WTO's multilateral framework requires that SPS and TBT measures, like other restrictive trade policies, must be based on solid evidence and will not infringe on free trade unnecessarily. The FDA import refusals, however, are unilateral controls by the US in which the food safety inspectors enjoy great discretionary power and can make import refusal decisions based on subjective judgments. According to sections 536 and 801 of the Federal Food, Drug and Cosmetics Act (FD&C), the FDA can refuse agri-food exports to the US that appear (without clear definitions of "appearance") or have been found to be adulterated (e.g., contaminated or incompatible with applicable standards), misbranded, and forbidden or restricted for sale.[4] It means that during pandemic outbreaks, it might be easier for the US to implement unilateral measures, instead of actions that are subject to the multilateral framework, such as SPS and TBT, to restrict agricultural exports of pandemic-hit countries. Finally, the FDA import refusals are also the only available data on unilateral border controls except for data from the EU Rapid Alert System for Food and Feed (RASFF). The crucial difference between the FDA and RASFF is that while FDA features a top-down or vertical organization throughout the US, the RASFF was designed as a flat platform for member states to exchange food safety information and collaborate on potential

---

4. Illustrations of the FDA entry review process are available from: https://www.fda.gov/industry/import program-food-and-drug-administration-fda/import-basics (online; cited May 2020).

threats. It implies that RASFF members could more likely be challenged by taking coordinated border control reactions to exports of pandemic-hit countries due to different consumer food safety concerns across member states.

In this paper, we are primarily concerned with two questions. The first is how the FDA's decisions on import refusals would respond to the agricultural exports of pandemic-hit countries. In particular, we wish to identify whether the outbreak of pandemics, even if not of foodborne diseases, would result in trade barriers to infected countries' exports. If such a reaction exists, how would it differ between China and other developing countries as well as across products and inspection methods? The second question is how FDA import refusals influence agricultural exports of affected countries to the US. While the trade impact of food safety regulations has been assessed in a number of existing studies, we will specifically explore whether the impact was different for pandemic-hit countries during outbreaks. A larger trade impact of pandemic outbreaks suggests that border controls of importing countries could amplify negative shocks of pandemics on the economy of infected countries. This helps to increase our understanding of the economic consequences of pandemics. In this paper we compile monthly data of confirmed cases of pandemic infections, FDA import refusal incidents, and agricultural exports to the US for ten developing countries that were epicenters of the four major pandemics during the past two decades including SARS, H1N1, Ebola, and COVID-19, to answer these questions.

This paper is related both to the literature on determinants of unilateral border controls and to that on the influence of these controls on agricultural trade. Baylis et al. (2009) considered FDA import refusal decisions to depend on three factors, including potential risks, exporter characteristics, and the domestic demand for trade protection. Using country-product level panel data, they confirmed that high-risk products, including those in meat and seafood categories, being perishable, received relatively more EU import refusals in the past and would have more FDA import refusal incidents. They also unveiled that import refusals tended to feature a form of "familiarity breeding contempt" in those refusals were positively associated with cumulative sales to the US and the country being English-speaking. Their findings supported the view that border controls could be motived by trade protectionism as more import refusals arose in industries where the US observed employment reductions, decreased import prices, antidumping cases, and lobby expenditures. With similar data, Jouanjean et al. (2015) identified both the "neighbor reputation effect" and "sector reputation effect." The former indicates that import refusals on a product of neighboring countries could trigger refusals of the same product of a specific country. The latter, in contrast, is defined as refusals on a certain product are dependent on refusals on related products. They found that both effects were quantitatively important factors that determined FDA import refusal decisions. Beestermöller et al. (2018) pointed out that border rejections of the EU on agri-food exports of China were path dependent, targeting producers with a poor history for the limited inspection resources of food safety authorities. Grundke and Moser (2019) also uncovered evidence regarding the protection motive underlying the FDA's import refusal decisions. Specifically, they found that import refusals increased during and after the 2008 global financial crisis when unemployment rates in the US reached historical highs. The pattern was not driven by speculations on stricter product standards or lower product quality in this period. Moreover, they indicated that the increased import refusals were primarily concentrated in non-OECD countries and were likely made as "arbitrary" decisions without being based on sample analysis.

In terms of the influence of unilateral border controls on agricultural trade, Baylis et al. (2010) considered the seafood sector and found reduced agricultural exports with more EU import refusals. Their results implied that, for each refusal, on average, the agricultural exports of the affected country to the EU would decrease by 43.5%. They also identified trade deflections to non-EU markets for countries hit by EU import refusals. Specifically, following an additional EU refusal, agricultural exports of the affected country to other high-income markets would increase by 5.59% on average, and those to low-income markets would increase by 2.3%. Similarly, Grant and Anders (2011) uncovered trade deflections in the fishery and seafood sectors following FDA import refusals. Using a panel structural VAR model, Zhou et al. (2019) noted that the impact of FDA import refusals on China's agricultural exports was mostly confined within a year and substantially differed across products. They also revealed that trade-deflection effects of border controls identified by Baylis et al. (2010) and Grant and Anders (2011) differed across destination markets and import refusal types. Beestermöller et al. (2018) merged EU import refusals with China's firm-level export data to highlight intra-regional and intra-industry spillover effects of border controls on agricultural trade. These effects illustrated the profound impact of border controls arising from the perception of more trade uncertainty by all related exporters. Nonetheless, whether and how to import refusal decisions would be influenced by pandemic outbreaks, and what roles import refusals would play in the economy and especially the export sector of pandemic-hit countries have remained unclear in the current literature.

The rest of this paper is organized as follows. Section II reviews the institutional context of WHO and WTO regarding trade restriction policies for public health concerns and proposes a conceptual framework for the possible strengthening of unilateral border controls during pandemic outbreaks. Section III introduces data and variables. It also characterizes descriptive evidence that FDA increased import refusals against agricultural exports of pandemic-hit developing countries and import refusals would impede agricultural trade. Section IV specifies empirical models and performs the benchmark estimation. Robustness checks for three aspects, including heterogeneities between China and other developing countries, across products, and across inspection methods, are considered in Section V. Section VI concludes the paper and provides some policy implications.

II. Institutional Context and Conceptual Framework

1. Institutional Context of Trade Restrictions During the Period of Pandemics by WHO and WTO

According to the International Health Regulations (IHR), the only binding international agreement on public health events under WHO's framework, countries must "ensure the maximum security against the international spread of disease with a minimum interference with world traffic."[5] On the one hand, WHO recognizes that cross-border transmission of pandemics could result from international personnel and product flows, and therefore border controls are inseparable from strategies to contain the spread. On the other hand, it also agrees that border controls impede free trade; thus, countries need to abide by restrictions when using them.

WHO has the right to review the properness of temporary measures against public health emergencies of international concern (PHEIC), according to amendments to the IHR made in 2005. Measures that WHO considers as proper are those based on scientific principles, no more restrictive to international traffic or trade than reasonable health protection alternatives, and in line with international standards. To ensure that the measures adopted are proper, countries that adopt such controls must provide public health rationales and relevant scientific information to WHO, which will then be shared among WHO member states.

In the meantime, trade-related health measures are also regulated and coordinated under WTO's multilateral framework. WTO considers three types of non-tariff measures that might be adopted for public health concerns, including SPS, TBT, and trade-related intellectual property rights. Trade-related intellectual property rights are mainly used to ensure that consumers can afford pharmaceutical products for public health needs and thus facilitate trade, whereas the first two groups of the non-tariff

---

5. The IHR is available from: https://www.who.int/csr/ihr/ihr1969.pdf (online; cited May 2020). Note that "traffic" in the statement includes "the movement of persons, baggage, cargo, containers, conveyances, goods or postal parcels."

measures are often trade-restrictive. WTO's rationale to justify the use of SPS and TBT measures to control cross-border pandemic spread is that they do not infringe trade unnecessarily.[6] To be specific, SPS measures are used to deal with health risks directly, so they should only be adopted with solid scientific evidence. TBT measures are applied with a broader scope, so they are used when scientific information is fully considered. In rare cases when the situation is urgent yet scientific evidence is lacking, WTO might allow countries to adopt provisional SPS measures.

The principles of WHO and WTO on health-related trade measures are aligned in that countries need to minimize trade impediments. In practice, this "minimal interference" principle is often infringed, unfortunately. During the four pandemics that we studied, many countries insisted on restricting imports from epicenter partners despite the advice of WHO, WTO, and the Food and Agriculture Organization of the United Nations (FAO) against such actions.[7] The negative externality on epicenter partners is a possible reason for these countries to take trade restrictions. In addition, different interpretations of the "minimal interference" principle between WHO and WTO could also impair the enforcement of the principle. In fact, due to the lack of formal coordination schemes between WTO and WHO, the review of specific trade measures imposed for pandemic outbreaks could become prolonged debates between parties due to conflict of interest. For example, Mexico appealed to WTO in 2009 on trade barriers against Mexican products during H1N1 by referring to WHO and FAO's report that such barriers had "no justification in the World Organization for Animal Health (OIE) Terrestrial Animal Health Standards Code."[8] However, its appeal ended in failure because public health experts from WHO were excluded from WTO committee that assessed trade policies (Giesecke, 2003).

2. Conceptual Framework for FDA Import Refusals in Pandemics

Aside from trade measures regulated by the multilateral framework and the "minimal interference" principle of WHO and WTO, countries might also prevent imports from pandemic-hit trade partners by adopting unilateral border controls. The primary

6. This rationale is supported by the joint report by WHO and WTO secretariat: WTO Agreements and Public Health, which is available from: https://www.wto.org/english/res_e/booksp_e/who_wto_e.pdf (online; cited May 2020).

7. The advice against import restrictions for SARS, H1N1, and Ebola, can be found in news reports available from: http://www.fao.org/english/newsroom/news/2003/17263-en.html, http://www.fao.org/news/story/en/item/19349/icode/, and https://www.afro.who.int/media-centre/statements-commentaries/statement-travel-andtransport-relation-ebola-virus-disease, respectively (online; cited May 2020).

8. The news on the Mexican case is available from: https://www.wto.org/english/news_e/news09_e/sps_25jun09_e.htm (online; cited May 2020).

responsibility of the FDA is to protect consumer health and safety with regard to agricultural and medical products.[9] In particular, the FDA oversees the majority of agricultural imports by the US by reviewing electronic documentations submitted for import requests to decide whether examinations or detentions for further information would be required before the shipment can be released into the US market (Baylis et al., 2009; Buzby et al., 2008). Aside from regularly inspecting adulterations, misbranding, and other violations of food safety regulations, the FDA is especially concerned about foodborne bacteria such as Escherichia coli and Salmonella, which can spread through agricultural trade. Because of the limited capacity to conduct inspections, it is typical for the FDA to examine only about 2% of all food-related imports (Buzby et al., 2008; Racino, 2011). The FDA, therefore usually targets countries and products that are perceived to entail the highest food safety risks. It is also common practice for FDA to conduct sensory or "judgment-based" evaluations instead of taking samples or requesting laboratory analyses to make import refusal decisions (Buzby et al., 2008). It reflects the considerable amount of discretionary power of FDA, as specified in FD&C to refuse import entrance simply because of the appearance of violations. Once refused by the FDA, the importer would be notified that further evidence should be submitted within ten business days and that it should request permission to re-label or recondition the shipment as compliant. If the import refusal decision is not withdrawn, the shipment must be re-exported or destroyed within 90 days.

Of course, the four pandemics that we examine in this paper are not foodborne diseases; hence, the outbreak itself should not directly trigger increased FDA import refusals against agricultural exports of infected regions. Nevertheless, the FDA could increase import refusals in response to heightened consumer concerns about possible transmissions through agricultural trade, which would still arise despite statements by WHO and WTO on the low possibility of such transmissions. The likely animal infections and pathogen residuals on either agricultural products or their packages have further fueled consumer concerns and thus might motivate the FDA to strengthen border controls (e.g., Seymour et al., 2020; Shi et al., 2020). As a matter of fact, because of the same logic of making discretionary decisions, the FDA could regulate agricultural imports based on the precautionary principle when there is uncertainty regarding food safety.

For the precautionary principle, the FDA often needs to balance the improved food safety perception against the loss of imports and constraints of inspection capacity. Specifically, although the effect of reducing cross-border transmissions

---

9. Descriptions of the FDA's responsibilities are available from: https://www.fda.gov/about-fda/what-we-do (online; cited May 2020).

might be limited, increased import refusals of products from pandemic-hit countries could signal that the FDA is aware of consumer concerns and is actively preparing for responses, to improve the general public's food safety perception. Increased import refusals, however, would amplify import contractions that might arise during pandemic outbreaks. As US consumers may rely heavily on some imported products from pandemic-hit countries, the FDA might not be able to impose excessive border controls. Furthermore, observed increases in refusal decisions would be restricted by inspection capacity when a high level of import refusals is desired by the FDA. In particular, seeing that the overall ratio of food-related imports with the FDA inspections remained only around 2%, it suggests that when the FDA increased import refusals against products of pandemic-hit countries, border controls on products from elsewhere tended to be relaxed. To allocate inspection resources effectively, the FDA might thus target epicenter countries that have the highest food safety threats during pandemic outbreaks. To sum up, this conceptual framework shows that when the food safety concern of consumers, which is heightened by pandemic outbreaks, outweighs possible import losses following border control measures, the FDA would increase import refusals against agricultural products of countries that are pandemic epicenters.

III. Descriptive Evidence on Pandemic Outbreaks, FDA Import Refusals, and Exports From Pandemic-Hit Developing Countries

1. Data and Variables

To examine the response of the FDA import refusals and associated impacts on agricultural trade during pandemic outbreaks, we considered developing countries that were epicenters of SARS, Ebola, H1N1, and COVID-19. In these countries, the agricultural sector accounted for a large share and non-tariff trade barriers might have wider impacts. China was the epicenter of SARS during 2002–2003. It has the most cumulative confirmed cases of SARS around the world with a share of 66% in July 2003 when WHO declared the pandemic to be over.[10] The pandemic of H1N1 during 2009–2010, by contrast, hit almost all continents heavily. Nevertheless, during the initial stage of the outbreak, three developing countries in America, including Mexico, Argentina, and Chile, were epicenters. The combined cumulative H1N1 cases of these countries accounted for 19% globally and 48% in the world excluding developed

---

10. Data source: https://www.who.int/csr/sars/country/2003_07_11/en/ (online; cited May 2020).

countries by December 2009.[11] The Ebola pandemic broke out in West Africa during 2014–2015, with Sierra Leone, Liberia, Guinea, Nigeria, and Senegal as epicenters. In fact, only less than 20 cases were reported, accounting for less than 1‰ in the world, by January 2016. Like H1N1, COVID-19 was a pandemic that hit many countries heavily. However, the initial outbreak was almost confined to China because, by early March 2020 when the peak of this pandemic was declared to be over in the country, China's cumulative confirmed cases accounted for 68% in the world.[12] For H1N1 and COVID-19, our focus on developing countries with original outbreaks is based on the fact that public attention was particularly heightened in the early development stage of pandemics (Shih et al., 2008).

The first case of SARS was found in Guangdong Province of China in November 2002. The spread was confined in the Province until February 2003. Infections were then reported in other Chinese provinces and outside the country, so WHO issued a global alert on March 12 at the same year. The pandemic was declared to be contained globally on July 5. But in fact, no new cases have been found in China since June 12, 2002. The period from November 2002 to July 2003 is therefore defined as the outbreak window of SARS in China. The first infection of H1N1 that triggered the pandemic was found in Mexico in March 2009. The WHO declared the pandemic to be a PHEIC on April 25; this became the first PHEIC announcement since the IHR revisions in 2005. The pandemic was announced to be globally contained on August 10, 2010. But in Mexico, Argentina, and Chile, almost no additional cases were reported after January 2010. Thus, the period from March 2009 to January 2010 is defined as the outbreak window of H1N1 in these three developing American countries. The Ebola pandemic originated in West Africa. The initial case was reported in December 2013 in Guinea, although the official medical alert was not issued until January 24, 2014. The outbreaks in Sierra Leone, Liberia, Guinea, Nigeria, and Senegal all peaked between August and November 2014, following WHO's announcement of PHEIC on August 8. By the end of 2015, the outbreak of Ebola had been largely contained in these countries. But WHO waited until March 29, 2016 to terminate the PHEIC for the continued sporadic occurrence of the disease globally. We define the outbreak window of Ebola in the five West African countries as the period from December 2013 to January 2016. The first reported case of COVID-19 appeared in Hubei Province of China in December 2019. Rapid transmission to other provinces in China started in January 2020; at

---

11. Data source: https://www.theguardian.com/news/datablog/2009/apr/27/flu-flu-pandemic (online; cited May 2020).

12. Data source: https://voice.baidu.com/act/newpneumonia/newpneumonia#tab0 (online; cited May 2020).

the same time, other countries also reported increasing cases, therefore, on January 30 WHO declared the pandemic to be a PHEIC. The outbreak was mainly confined to China by the end of February 2020, and the cumulative confirmed cases of the country accounted for 91% in the world at that time. On March 12 at that time, China announced that the peak of COVID-19 in the country was over.[13] Afterward, the emergence of new cases in China remained limited. We therefore define the outbreak window of COVID-19 in China as the period from December 2019 to March 2020. Table 12.1 lists the developing countries of study and the associated outbreak period for each pandemic.

Table 12.1
Selected Developing Countries for the Study of Each Pandemic

Pandemic	Selected developing countries	Outbreak window
SARS	China	November 2002–July 2003
H1N1	Mexico, Argentina, and Chile	March 2009–January 2010
Ebola	Sierra Leone, Liberia, Guinea, Nigeria, and Senegal	December 2013–January 2016
COVID-19	China	December 2019–March 2020

Source. Compiled by the authors.

For each selected developing country, we collect monthly data on three variables for empirical analyses. The first variable is the number of newly confirmed cases, which could be used to measure the pandemic outbreaks. We use confirmed cases rather than fatal cases. The former governed the possibility of transmission, which the US as an importing country might be primarily concerned about, whereas the latter would depend heavily on the demographic structure and medical conditions of the developing country.[14] Confirmed cases of SARS since March 17, 2003 have been published by WHO. Earlier cases in China were reported by authorized platforms of the Ministry of Health. Confirmed cases of H1N1 before July 23, 2009 were collected from WHO official reports, and those after this date were collected from the official disease surveillance system of each selected country due to WHO reports ceasing. The official surveillance system was the Pan American Health Organization for Argentina

---

13. The announcement that the peak of COVID-19 was over is available from: http://www.xinhuanet.com/english/2020-03/12/c_138870547.htm (online; cited May 2020).

14. We also re-estimate empirical models using cumulated pandemic cases instead of newly confirmed cases. Results are similar and reported in Appendix B in Table B-1.

and Chile, and the Mexican Institute of Social Security for Mexico. Finally, confirmed cases of Ebola in West Africa and COVID-19 in China were accessible, respectively, from public WHO reports, and the website of the National Health Commission of the People's Republic of China.

The second variable is the incidents of FDA import refusals against agricultural exports of these developing countries to the US. The FDA import refusals were available from the Import Refusal Reports (IRR).[15] Each IRR entry corresponds to an import shipment of the US, with details including the date of refusal, product category, exporting company, charges of import regulation violations, and inspection methods (i.e., sampling, lab analysis and investigator's judgment). The FDA oversees US imports of "the vast majority of food" and medical products (Buzby et al., 2008). Import refusals against medical products are excluded from this paper. We compute all incidents of FDA import refusals by exporting country on a monthly basis. We also break down refusal incidents to the country-product level and conduct robustness checks on inspection methods in our empirical analyses.

The third variable is the value of agricultural exports of these developing countries to the US. Monthly agricultural trade data can be obtained from Trade Map of the International Trade Center.[16] We define agricultural products as those within the first 24 chapters of the HS system (Beestermöller et al., 2018), and compute the total value measured in US dollars of agricultural exports to the US for each developing country.

The FDA import refusals and agricultural exports could feature country-specific seasonality, which typically depends on the country's geographic location and product structure. Thus, we construct a sample period for each pandemic with the outbreak window specified in Table 12.1. We collect monthly data for each pandemic from two years before the outbreak window opens and up to two years after the window closes. Using such a sample period, the behaviors of import refusals and agricultural exports within the outbreak window that were driven by seasonality could be estimated in an average sense. Table 12.2 shows descriptive statistics for our panel dataset.

---

15. The IRR is available from: https://www.accessdata.fda.gov/scripts/importrefusals/ (online; cited May 2020).

16. Data source: https://www.trademap.org/Index.aspx (online; cited May 2020).

Table 12.2

Descriptive Statistics of Key Variables

	Number	Mean	Standard deviation	P10	P90
ln(agri-export value)	688	8.351	3.825	3.526	13.785
ln(new pandemic cases)	688	0.607	1.840	0	2.303
ln(FDA import refusals)	688	1.270	1.691	0	4.357
FDA import refusal dummy (0 = no refusals, 1 = otherwise)	688	0.513	0.500	0	1
Refusals by taking samples/all refusals (%)	688	36.247	34.432	0	1
Refusals with lab analysis/all refusals (%)	688	8.779	15.513	0	1

Note. Since incidents of import refusals and new pandemic cases might take a value of zero, logs of both variables, i.e., ln(FDA import refusals) and ln(new pandemic cases) have been monotonically transformed by adding one to the original value following Grundke and Moser (2019). FDA, Food and Drug Administration; P10 and P90 denote the 10th and 90th percentiles.

2. Stylized Facts

To characterize stylized facts regarding the relationships among the three variables introduced in subsection III.1, we use two scatter plots to present them in Figure 12.1. Figure 12.1 (a) demonstrates the bilateral relationship between the number of newly confirmed pandemic cases and incidents of FDA import refusals that the pandemic-hit developing country received, while Figure 12.1 (b) demonstrates the bilateral relationship for the incidence of FDA import refusals in a one-month lag and agricultural export value to the US of the pandemic-hit developing countries. Note that all variables have been regressed on country-specific month dummies to remove seasonality, and on year dummies to control the possible trend, and are then categorized into 20 quantile groups based on regression residuals. According to Figure 12.1 (a), increased FDA import refusals were, in general, associated with more pandemic outbreaks, which implies an escalation of border controls against agricultural products of pandemic-hit developing countries. According to Figure 12.1 (b), smaller agricultural exports to the US were observed when a pandemic-hit developing country received more import refusals, which implies a negative impact of border controls on trade.

Figure 12.1

Pandemic Outbreaks Trigger Import Refusals by the FDA and Impair Agricultural Exports

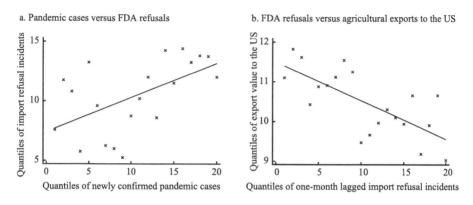

a. Pandemic cases versus FDA refusals

b. FDA refusals versus agricultural exports to the US

Source. Drawn by the authors according to the data introduced in subsection III.1.

In Figure 12.2, we characterize co-movements among the total number of newly confirmed cases displayed in thick solid lines, total incidents of FDA import refusals shown in thin solid lines, and the total value of agricultural exports to the US denoted by thin dashed lines across developing countries for each pandemic. As both import refusals and agricultural exports correspond to the right axes in Figure 12.2, we rescale them using initial values to enable a convenient comparison without changing movement patterns. In the pandemic outbreak windows marked in gray, FDA import refusals increased, and agricultural exports declined significantly. Although the increase in refusal incidents was less notable during COVID-19 than during other pandemics, it should be noticed that, due to the strict lockdowns that China imposed since January 2020, its agricultural exports to the US in the first quarter of this year experienced almost unprecedented declines as shown by the dashed line.

Figure 12.2

Co-Movements Among Cases, Refusals, and Exports During Four Pandemics

a. SARS

b. H1N1

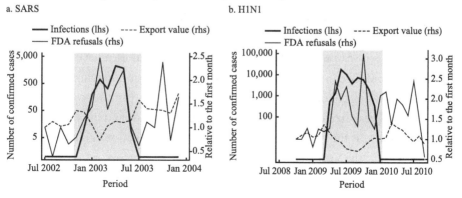

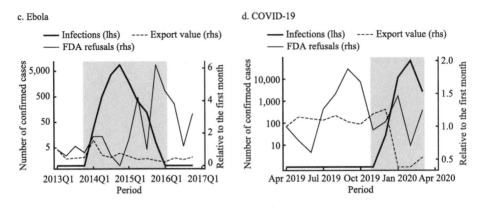

Source. Drawn by the authors according to the data introduced in subsection III.1.

IV. Empirical Analyses of Import Refusals and Trade Impacts in Pandemics

1. Model Specifications

The previous section provided preliminary evidence that, during pandemic outbreaks, the FDA would increase import refusals against agricultural exports of developing countries that were epicenters of infections and these developing countries would experience contractions of agricultural exports to the US. In this subsection, we will empirically identify and estimate the impact of pandemic outbreaks on FDA import refusal decisions and the influence of import refusal incidents on agricultural exports of developing countries, using the panel dataset that we described in subsection III.1. To reveal the response of FDA import refusals to pandemic outbreaks, we consider the following empirical model:

$$\ln REJ_{it} = \alpha_0 + \alpha_1 \ln EXP_{it} + \alpha_2 \ln CASE_{it} + f_{im} + f_y + \epsilon_{it}, \qquad (1)$$

where the dependent variable $\ln REJ_{it}$ is the log value of FDA import refusal incidents that were received by developing country i in period t. Control variables include the value of agricultural exports of country i to the US measured in logs ($\ln EXP_{it}$) seeing that increased exports might be followed by more FDA import refusal incidents, the log number of newly confirmed infection cases ($\ln CASE_{it}$) as a measure of pandemic outbreaks, and the country–month-fixed effects (f_{im}) to capture country-specific seasonality and year-fixed effect (f_y) to capture possible trends and unobservable year-specific shocks; ϵ_{it} is the error term. The coefficient α_1 in Equation (1) thus reflects the impact   of   the agricultural export scale on FDA import refusals, while the coefficient α_2 represents the impact of pandemic outbreaks. As incidents of import refusals and newly confirmed pandemic cases might take a value of 0, we follow Grundke and Moser (2019) and monotonically transform both variables by adding one to the original value before computing logs.

To investigate how agricultural exports to the US of pandemic-hit developing countries react to pandemic outbreaks and incidents of FDA import refusals, we consider the following empirical model:

$$\ln EXP_{it} = \beta_0 + \beta_1 \ln CASE_{it} + \beta_2 \ln REJ_{it-1} + \beta_3 \ln CASE_{it} \times \ln REJ_{it-1} + f_{im} + f_y + \epsilon'_{it}, \quad (2)$$

where the dependent variable $\ln EXP_{it}$ is the agricultural export value of developing country i to the US in year t measured in logs. Control variables include the log number of newly confirmed infection cases ($\ln CASE_{it}$) as a measure of pandemic outbreaks, the log value of FDA import refusal incidents that country i received in the previous period ($\ln REJ_{it-1}$), and the interaction term between the two variables ($\ln CASE_{it} \times \ln REJ_{it-1}$). The coefficient β_1 in Equation (2) reflects the direct impact of pandemic outbreaks on the pandemic-hit developing country's agricultural exports to the US; the coefficient β_2 reflects the direct lagged impact of import refusal incidents, and the coefficient β_3 reflects the indirect impact of pandemic outbreaks that arose through the channel of import refusal incidents. In particular, if both β_2 and β_3 are negative, then we can conclude that import refusal incidents resulted in an export reduction and this negative impact was amplified due to pandemic outbreaks. That is because pandemic outbreaks could lead to increased import refusal incidents, agricultural exporters in pandemic-hit developing countries might be further deterred from serving the US market.

While estimating Equations (1) and (2), we cluster standard errors at the country-year level seeing that both FDA import refusals and agricultural exports could be correlated within country-year pairs. Considering that many observations in our dataset took a value of zero in terms of FDA import refusal incidents, we will also replace $\ln REJ$ with a dummy variable in both equations as a robustness check, denoted by dumREJ.[17] However, due to the possible issue of incidental parameters, we will follow Beestermöller et al. (2018) in using the linear probability model to estimate Equation (1) when the import refusal dummy serves as a dependent variable.

---

17. We also consider the number of FDA import refusals and confirmed pandemic cases as counts. Results are similar to the benchmark case and are reported in the Appendix in Table A-2.

2. Benchmark Results

Table 12.3 reports the benchmark estimation results from Equations (1) and (2). The second and fourth columns of this table show that a greater outbreak of infections would lead to increased FDA import refusals on agricultural exports of the pandemic-hit developing country, in line with the descriptive evidence in Figure 12.1. In particular, with a 1% growth in the number of newly confirmed pandemic cases, FDA import refusal incidents that the pandemic-hit developing country would receive would increase by 0.034%, while the probability of the developing country receiving import refusal incidents would increase by two percentage points. The development of pandemic infections could be extremely swift. Taking January 2020 when the massive outbreak of COVID-19 took place in China as an example, the number of confirmed cases increased by more than 435 times compared to that in the previous month, according to the data on the website of the National Health Commission of the People's Republic of China. Thus, the magnitude of the impact of pandemic outbreaks on FDA import refusal decisions could be large.

Table 12.3
Benchmark Regression Results

	Equation (1)	Equation (2)	ln*REJ* replaced by dum*REJ* Equation (1)	Equation (2)
ln*EXP*$_{it}$	0.005		0.025*	
	(0.033)		(0.012)	
ln*CASE*$_{it}$	0.034***	0.018	0.020***	0.018
	(0.006)	(0.011)	(0.005)	(0.012)
ln*REJ*$_{it-1}$		−0.086*		−0.141**
		(0.049)		(0.066)
ln*CASE*$_{it}$ × ln*REJ*$_{it-1}$		−0.007**		−0.028*
		(0.003)		(0.013)
Country-month FE and -year FE	Yes	Yes	Yes	Yes
Observations	688	678	688	678
Adjusted R^2	0.881	0.973	0.554	0.975

Notes. ***, **, and * represent significance at the 1%, 5%, and 10% levels, respectively. Robust standard errors clustered at the country-year level are reported in parentheses. See subsection IV.1 for the definition of each variable. FDA, Food and Drug Administration. FE, fixed effect.

The third and the last columns of Table 12.3 show that a greater number of FDA import refusals in the past period would lead to significant reductions in agricultural exports of developing countries to the US. The significantly negative estimated coefficient before the interaction term $\ln CASE_{it} \times \ln REJ_{it-1}$ in Equation (2) also suggests that pandemic outbreaks would amplify the negative export impact of import refusal incidents. In particular, with a 1% growth of FDA import refusal incidents in the previous month, agricultural exports to the US in the current month would decline by 0.0086%. This rate of decline would further increase by 0.7 percentage points for each 1% growth in the number of pandemic cases. When import refusal incidents are considered as dummy variables in the last column, we find that the presence of FDA import refusals in the previous month would result in a 14.1% reduction in agricultural exports to the US for the developing countries, and following each 1% growth in the number of pandemic cases this export reduction would be amplified by an additional 2.8 percentage points. Such evidence highlights that FDA import refusals would deter agricultural exports to the US and the effect would be enlarged by pandemic outbreaks. Nevertheless, pandemics would not influence agricultural exports of epicenter countries to the US aside from the channel of increased FDA import refusals, as indicated by the insignificant coefficient before the number of confirmed cases in both the third and the last columns.[18]

V. Robustness Checks

1. China Versus Other Developing Countries

In the past two decades, China has experienced rapid agricultural export growth to the US and an even faster growth of FDA import refusal incidents compared with the other developing countries that we study in this paper. According to the statistics of the General Administration of Customs of China (GACC), the value of agricultural exports of China to the US grew from US\$1.6 billion in 2002 and to US\$6.3 billion in

---

18. The insignificant coefficient before the number of infection cases $\ln CASE_{it}$ in Equation (2) indicates that pandemic outbreaks would not impair agricultural exports from pandemic-hit developing countries directly as long as the FDA did not enact additional import refusals. It might remain a concern, however, that production suspension or other supply-side constraints during pandemic outbreaks would result in a larger export shock that we found for FDA import refusals, especially when these factors happened at the same time. As it is difficult to measure production constraints, we take these developing countries' agricultural exports to the EU as a proxy variable. Table A-3 in the Appendix reports estimated results, which are similar to the benchmark results in Table 3. (May 2020).

2019.[19] As a result, China has now become the fourth-largest agricultural exporter to the US. Compared with the rapid export growth, the increase in China's FDA import refusal incidents was even more noteworthy. According to the records of the IRR, China merely received 718 FDA import refusals, which accounted for 4% of all import refusal decisions by FDA in 2002. In 2018, however, the FDA imposed 2,640 import refusals on China, which accounted for 17% of all FDA import refusals over the year.[20] It would thus be interesting to inspect possibly differential impacts of pandemic outbreaks on FDA import refusal and agricultural exports when China was the epicenter of SARS and COVID-19, compared with the other two pandemics, which mainly hit other developing countries.

To reveal these heterogeneities, we take developing countries other than China as the benchmark and specify two dummy variables, one for China during SARS (denoted as *SARS*) and the other for China during COVID-19 (denoted as *COVID*). Then in Equation (1), we control $\ln CASE_{it} \times SARS$ and $\ln CASE_{it} \times COVID$ alongside $\ln CASE_{it}$. In Equation (2), we similarly introduce interactions between the two dummies for China (i.e. *SARS* and *COVID*) with $\ln CASE_{it}$ and $\ln CASE_{it} \times \ln REJ_{it-1}$. These interaction terms can therefore reflect the heterogeneities between China and other developing countries as well as between the two pandemics, both in China. Estimation results are reported in Table 12.4.

The second column of Table 12.4 shows that coefficients for both interactions terms $\ln CASE_{it} \times SARS$ and $\ln CASE_{it} \times COVID$ are insignificant. The fourth column indicates that an increased probability of receiving FDA import refusals was only observed in epicenter developing countries other than China. The possible reason is that China was the epicenter to SARS and COVID-19, both for a short time.

The third and the last columns in Table 12.4 provide similar results: FDA import refusals resulted in agricultural export contractions of developing countries to the US. However, seeing that the coefficient before $\ln CASE_{it}$ is negative but insignificant, we find no evidence that pandemics in developing countries other than China would amplify the negative impact of FDA import refusals on agricultural trade. On the other hand, FDA import refusals had resulted in larger agricultural export contractions to the US when China was the epicenter of pandemics, especially during COVID-19, according to coefficients before triple interaction terms $\ln CASE_{it} \times \ln REJ_{it-1} \times COVID$ or $\ln CASE_{it} \times \ln REJ_{it-1} \times SARS$. Such additional export declines were especially larger during COVID-19.

---

19. Data source: http://www.customs.gov.cn/customs/302249/302274/302275/9f806879-2.html (online; cited May 2020).

20. Data source: https://www.accessdata.fda.gov/scripts/importrefusals http://www.customs.gov.cn/customs/302249/302274/302275/9f806879-2.html (online; cited May 2020).

Table 12.4

Comparison Between China and Other Developing Countries for the Impact of Pandemic Outbreaks on Import Refusals and Agricultural Exports

	Equation (1)	Equation (2)	lnREJ replaced by dumREJ	
			Equation (1)	Equation (2)
$\ln EXP_{it}$	0.005		0.026	
	(0.033)		(0.016)	
$\ln CASE_{it}$	0.035***	−0.008	0.024***	−0.008
	(0.007)	(0.014)	(0.005)	(0.014)
$\ln CASE_{it} \times COVID$	−0.022	−0.065	−0.024***	−0.067
	(0.017)	(0.068)	(0.005)	(0.061)
$\ln CASE_{it} \times SARS$	0.008	−0.053	−0.024***	−0.052
	(0.014)	(0.084)	(0.005)	(0.087)
$\ln REJ_{it-1}$		−0.080*		−0.147*
		(0.045)		(0.082)
$\ln CASE_{it} \times \ln REJ_{it-1}$		−0.001		−0.001
		(0.002)		(0.001)
$\ln CASE_{it} \times \ln REJ_{it-1} \times COVID$		−0.013**		−0.012**
		(0.005)		(0.005)
$\ln CASE_{it} \times \ln REJ_{it-1} \times SARS$		−0.007***		−0.009***
		(0.002)		(0.003)
Country-month FE and -year FE	Yes	Yes	Yes	Yes
Observations	688	678	688	678
Adjusted R^2	0.903	0.978	0.555	0.978

Note. ***, **, and * represent significance at the 1%, 5%, and 10% levels, respectively. Robust standard errors clustered at the country-year level are reported in parentheses. See subsections IV.1 and V.1 for the definition of each variable. FE, fixed effect.

China's agricultural exports to the US were mostly labor intensive and might trigger a heavier food safety concern in pandemics. According to the GACC statistics, 60% of China's agricultural exports to the US were animal products (particularly aquacultural) aside from oils and 20% were vegetables, fruits, and their products in 2002. In 2019, the share of animal products except oils declined to 43%. but the share of vegetables, fruits, and their products grew to 42%.[21] However, seeing that

---

21. Data source: http://trade.drcnet.com.cn (online; cited May 2020).

COVID-19 was the second pandemic that broke out in China within two decades, the FDA has focused import regulations much more on Chinese products than during SARS. In fact, according to the IRR records, only 7.6% of all FDA import refusals were imposed on Chinese products during the outbreak window of SARS, although they nearly doubled from a share of 4% before the pandemic in 2002. In contrast, the share skyrocketed to 22% during the outbreak window of COVID-19, more than doubling from the share of 10% in 2019.[22]

2. Inter-product Heterogeneities

The impact of infection cases on FDA import refusal decisions and agricultural exports might also differ across products. To reveal such heterogeneities, we first need to compile monthly import refusal and export value data at the product level. Monthly trade statistics at the Harmonized System (HS)-4 digit product level are available from the Trade Map of the International Trade Center for all developing countries in our study except for the five West African countries that were epicenters of Ebola. We therefore, have to consider the other three pandemics to perform the robustness check with disaggregated products. While FDA import refusals were recorded for each rejected shipment, with product information included, the challenge is that the product coding system adopted by the FDA is completely different from the HS system in trade statistics. We matched all FDA product codes to HS-4 codes in line with Grundke and Moser (2019),[23] so the monthly FDA import refusal incidents for each HS-4 product could be computed. Seeing that many observations in the country panel already took a value of zero in FDA import refusal incidents, the situation would become more prevalent when the data is disaggregated into products. Instead of considering each HS-4 digit code as a single product, we therefore categorize HS-4 digit codes into three product groups, with the first group being "animal products, fats, and oils," which are within sections I and III of the HS system and will be the benchmark group in our analysis on inter-product differences; the second group being "vegetable products" (denoted as *Plant*), which are within section II of the HS system, and the third group being "foodstuffs" (denoted as *Food*), which are within section IV of the HS system. Table 12.5 presents our estimation results using this panel dataset with disaggregated product groups for the three pandemics aside from Ebola. The first two columns repeat estimations in Table 12.3 using Equations (1) and (2) but with the new dataset. To uncover inter-product heterogeneities, the last two columns use "animal products, fats,

---

22. Data source: https://www.accessdata.fda.gov/scripts/importrefusals (online; cited May 2020).
23. We are grateful to Professor Christoph Moser for providing the product mapping rules.

Table 12.5

Inter-product Heterogeneities

	Without considering inter-product heterogeneities		Considering inter-product heterogeneities	
	Equation (1)	Equation (2)	Equation (1)	Equation (2)
lnEXP_{it}	0.474***		0.272***	
	(0.058)		(0.040)	
ln$CASE_{it}$	0.017***	0.009	0.020	−0.020*
	(0.005)	(0.005)	(0.018)	(0.010)
ln$CASE_{it}$ × Plant			−0.018	0.005**
			(0.044)	(0.002)
ln$CASE_{it}$ × Food			0.073***	0.003***
			(0.022)	(0.001)
lnREJ_{it-1}		−0.178***		−0.173***
		(0.018)		(0.015)
ln$CASE_{it}$ × lnREJ_{it-1}		−0.003*		0.004
		(0.002)		(0.005)
ln$CASE_{it}$ × lnREJ_{it-1} × Plant				−0.013
				(0.010)
ln$CASE_{it}$ × lnREJ_{it-1} × Food				−0.004**
				(0.001)
Country-month FE and -year FE				
Observations	849	831	849	831
Adjusted R^2	0.797	0.751	0.772	0.749

Note. ***, **, and * represent significance at the 1%, 5%, and 10% levels, respectively. Robust standard errors clustered at the country-year level are reported in parentheses. See subsections IV.1 and V.2 for the definition of each variable. FE, fixed effect.

and oils" as the benchmark product group and introduce interaction terms between infection cases and product group dummies Plant and Food into Equation (1), and introduce additional triple interaction terms among infection cases, import refusal incidents, and product group dummies Plant and Food into Equation (2).

The second column of Table 12.5 confirms that pandemic outbreaks resulted in increased FDA import refusals against agricultural exports of the pandemic-hit developing countries, as we found in Table 12.3. It also reveals that more FDA import refusals were associated with greater exports, which were in line with our expectations but failed to be supported by significant evidence when the country panel was used. The third column of Table 12.5 confirms that FDA import refusal incidents would reduce agricultural exports and such effects would be amplified by pandemic outbreaks, as manifested in Table 12.3. In the fourth column, we set "animal products, fats, and oils" as the reference product group and introduce interaction terms between infection cases and dummy variables for the other two product groups to investigate the differential response of FDA import refusals to pandemic outbreaks across products. As indicated by the positive coefficient before the interaction term between infection cases and the dummy variable for foodstuffs (*Food*), $\ln CASE \times Food$, we find that increased FDA import refusals in pandemic outbreaks were concentrated on foodstuffs in contrast to the other two product groups. This finding is in line with the fact that all three pandemics were not foodborne such that importers' concerns about cross-border transmission would mainly arise from possible contamination during product processing and preparation. In the last column, we further introduce triple interaction terms among infection cases, import refusal incidents, and product group dummies. Estimation results reveal that both direct impacts of pandemics on agricultural exports and indirect amplification effects through the channel of import refusals are different across products. In particular, we find that although import refusals could reduce agricultural exports, only in the group of foodstuffs were such export reductions amplified during pandemic outbreaks. At the product level, pandemics directly impede agricultural exports. However, the effect was smaller for vegetable products and foodstuffs. The relatively large direct impact of pandemics on the "animal products, fats, and oils" group might be related to the fact that these products typically feature longer and more complicated supply chains, which are more likely to be disrupted by pandemic outbreaks.

3. Evidence-Based Versus Judgment-Based Import Refusals

The FDA adopts different inspection methods when making import refusal decisions. Some decisions are more likely to be "evidence-based," for example, samples might have been taken or the product might have been sent for laboratory analysis. Others could more likely depend on investigator's "judgment," referring to the statement in FD&C that the inspection reveals an appearance of violating import regulations in the shipment. Because of the lack of indications of specific causes to FDA's decisions, "judgment-based" import refusals might signal a greater deterrence to potential exporters. We therefore first replace the dependent variable in Equation (1) with the share of "judgment-based" import refusals in all import refusal incidents to investigate how pandemic outbreaks would change the composition of FDA import refusal decisions, which is specified as in Equation (3):

$$\frac{JUD_{it}}{REJ_{it}} = \alpha_0 + \alpha_1 \ln EXP_{it} + \alpha_2 \ln CASE_{it} + f_{im} + f_y + \epsilon_{it} . \tag{3}$$

Then, to find differential impacts of FDA import refusals on agricultural exports due to inspection methods, we distinguish refusals that were "evidence-based" from those that were "judgment-based" in Equation (4):

$$\ln EXP_{it} = \beta_0 + \beta_1 \ln CASE_{it} + \beta_2' \ln EVI_{it-1} + \beta_2'' \ln JUD_{it-1} + \beta_3' \ln CASE_{it} \times \ln EVI_{it-1} + \beta_3'' \ln CASE_{it} \times \ln JUD_{it-1} + f_{im} + f_y + \epsilon_{it}'' . \tag{4}$$

In Equations (3) and (4), "evidence-based" import refusals (denoted as *EVI*) would be alternatively defined as those issued after taking samples and sending for laboratory analysis. In turn, "judgment-based" import refusals (denoted as *JUD*) could be defined as those not "evidence-based." Table 12.6 shows estimation results using Equations (3) and (4).

The second and the fourth columns of Table 12.6 indicate that pandemic outbreaks would increase the share of "judgment-based" import refusals. Together with the estimation results in Table 12.3, it implies that the FDA would tighten border controls on agricultural exports of the pandemic-hit developing countries mainly by making more "judgment-based" import refusals. Such findings are consistent with the precautionary principle, which could serve as the key motive for the FDA to strengthen inspections during pandemic outbreaks. The third and the last columns of Table 12.6 demonstrate that "judgment-based" import refusals would exhibit larger negative impacts on agricultural trade compared with "evidence-based" import refusals. In both the third and the last columns, we also confirmed that pandemic outbreaks would amplify trade-impeding effects only for "judgment-based" import refusals. As "judgment-based" import refusals typically rely more heavily on the FDA's discretionary power, such results lend support to the view that the deterrence of import refusals on agricultural exporters primarily arose from the channel of increased uncertainty regarding border controls in the destination market (Beestermöller et al., 2018).[24]

---

24. Another concern is that pandemic outbreaks not only resulted in increased FDA import refusals but might also trigger other trade restrictions such as SPS and TBT measures. When the appearance of these restrictions was correlated, the negative export impact of FDA import refusals might have been overstated. To alleviate this concern, we re-estimated empirical models, controlling for the number of SPS and TBT measures newly imposed by the US. Table A4 of the Appendix reports our estimated results, which remain similar to the benchmark case.

Table 12.6

Differences by Inspection Methods of Import Entry Examinations

JUD defined as	Not sampled		Not lab analyzed	
	Equation (3)	Equation (4)	Equation (3)	Equation (4)
$lnEXP_{it}$	0.020		0.008	
	(0.017)		(0.015)	
$lnCASE_{it}$	0.020***	0.028	0.013***	0.016
	(0.005)	(0.024)	(0.004)	(0.026)
$lnEVI_{it-1}$		−0.053**		−0.043
		(0.025)		(0.070)
$lnJUG_{it-1}$		−0.087*		−0.082**
		(0.053)		(0.039)
$lnCASE_{it} \times lnEVI_{it-1}$		0.017		0.013
		(0.012)		(0.012)
$lnCASE_{it} \times lnJUG_{it-1}$		−0.020*		−0.025**
		(0.011)		(0.012)
Country-month FE and -year FE	Yes	Yes	Yes	Yes
Observations	688	678	688	678
Adjusted R^2	0.372	0.966	0.362	0.956

Note. ***, **, and * represent significance at the 1%, 5%, and 10% levels, respectively. Robust standard errors clustered at the country-year level are reported in parentheses. See subsections IV.1 and V.3 for the definition of each variable. FE, fixed effect.

VI. Conclusion and Policy Implications

Pandemic outbreaks not only impair the economy of epicenter countries directly but also might induce importing partners to impose stricter unilateral border controls against their exported products. Even for pandemics that are not foodborne, in which the actual chance of cross-border transmissions through trade is limited, the food safety concerns of consumers in importing countries over products from pandemic-hit countries could still be heightened due to possible animal infections and pathogen residuals on product packages. As a result, food safety authorities of importing countries might use their discretionary power to strengthen unilateral border controls based on the precautionary principle, even if lacking scientific evidence. Such escalation of border controls further impeded pandemic-hit countries to stabilize exports and would amplify pandemic impacts on their economy.

In this paper, we compiled monthly data on epicenter countries during four major pandemic outbreaks in the past two decades and identified the responses of border controls in the importing countries and subsequent trade impacts of these restrictions. Our findings confirm that the US FDA increased import refusals on agricultural exports of pandemic-hit developing countries that were epicenters of SARS, H1N1, Ebola, and COVID-19. When China was the pandemic epicenter (i.e., during SARS and COVID-19), the number of FDA import refusals increased; and for other developing countries during H1N1 and Ebola, the probability of receiving FDA import refusals in a period increased. Import refusal increases were primarily noted among foodstuffs and featured a larger share of decisions made by sensory or subjective evaluations. Our findings further reveal the negative effects of FDA import refusals on the agricultural exports of pandemic-hit developing countries to the US. This trade-impeding impact was stronger if there was an increased number of confirmed infection cases in pandemic-hit countries. This supports the view that this indirect channel of pandemics, influencing the economy of infected countries through escalated border controls, is noteworthy. It is interesting to note that the increase in trade-impending effects of border controls was particularly large when China was the pandemic epicenter. They were also larger among foodstuffs and when refusals were based on sensory or subjective evaluations.

Effective measures to reduce the economic impacts of pandemics without impairing the prevention of global pandemic transmission have been discussed in depth since the outbreak of COVID-19. Our findings in this paper have several policy implications for China. First, although production disruption and trade costs have been the main concerns, the deterioration of the external environment, with stricter border controls, would affect the economy negatively amid pandemics. Chinese agricultural exporters, therefore, have to track the movements of food safety authorities closely in importing partners. In the meantime, efficient information disclosure and sharing can be a valuable tool for exporters to contain their risk exposure to border control escalations. Second, as import partners' rejection of product entries for public health concerns is a unilateral decision currently not monitored by WHO or WTO, our results shed light on the importance of China continuously strengthening communications with these international organizations and the food safety authorities of import partners. On the one hand, China needs to play a greater role in establishing coordinated schemes between WHO and WTO to monitor unilateral trade-restrictive measures imposed in the name of preventing health threats. On the other hand, as the world's largest agricultural importer, China also needs to call for an international effort to design unilateral import regulations by sovereign states to meet with WTO's principles of non-discrimination and the use of an evidence-based approach.

References

Baylis, K., A. Martens & L. Nogueira. (2009). What drives import refusals? *American Journal of Agricultural Economics, 91*(5), 1477–1483.

Baylis, K., L. Nogueira & K. Pace. (2010). Food Import Refusals: Evidence from the European Union. *American Journal of Agricultural Economics, 93*(2), 566–572.

Beestermöller, M., A. C. Disdier & L. Fontagné. (2018). Impact of European food safety border inspections on agri-food exports: Evidence from Chinese firms. *China Economic Review, 48*, 66–82.

Buzby, J. C., L. J. Unnevehr & D. Roberts. (2008). Food safety and imports: An analysis of FDA food-related import refusal reports. *Economic Information Bulletin, 39*, Economic Research Service of the United States Department of Agriculture.

Giesecke, J. (2003). International health regulations and epidemic control. In R. Smith, R. Beaglehole, D. Woodward and N. Drager (Ed.s), *Global Public Goods for Health: Health economic and public health perspectives* (pp. 196–211). Oxford University Press.

Ghodsi, M. (2020). The impact of Chinese technical barriers to trade on its manufacturing imports when exporters are heterogeneous. *Empirical Economics, 59* (4), 1667–1698.

Grant, J. & S. Anders. (2011). Trade deflection arising from US import refusals and detentions in fishery and seafood trade. *American Journal of Agricultural Economics, 93* (2), 573–580.

Grundke, R. & C. Moser (2019). Hidden protectionism? Evidence from non-tariff barriers to trade in the United States. *Journal of International Economics, 117*, 143–157.

Jouanjean, M. A., J. C. Maur & B. Shepherd (2015). Reputation matters: Spillover effects for developing countries in the enforcement of US food safety measures. *Food Policy, 55*, 81–91.

Racino, B. (2011, October 3). *Flood of food imported to U.S., but only 2 percent inspected.* NBC News. https://www.nbcnews.com/health/ health-news/flood-food-imported-u-s-only-2-percent-inspected-flna1C9454548.

Seymour, N., M. Yavelak, C. Christian, B. Chapman & M. Danyluk (2020). *COVID-19 FAQ for food service: Receiving and food packaging.* UF/IFAS. https://journals.flvc.org/edis/article/view/121174

Shi et al. (2020). Susceptibility of ferrets, cats, dogs, and other domesticated animals to SARS-Coronavirus 2. *Science, 368*(6494), 1016–1020.

Shih, T., R. Wijaya & D. Brossard. (2008). Media coverage of public health epidemics: Linking framing and issue attention cycle toward an integrated theory of print news coverage of epidemics. *Mass Communication & Society, 11*(2), 141–160.

Tran, N., N. L. W. Wilson & S. Anders. (2012). Standard harmonization as chasing zero (tolerance limits): The impact of veterinary drug residue standards on crustacean imports in the EU Japan and North America. *American Journal of Agricultural Economics, 94*(2), 496–502.

Zhou, J. H., Y. Wang & R. Mao (2019). Dynamic and spillover effects of USA import refusals on China's agricultural trade: Evidence from monthly data. *Agricultural Economics–Czech*, 65(9), 425–434.

Appendix A

Table A-1

China's Economic Partners Involved in FTAs and BRI

Key issues	Countries involved (China +)	Region
FTA (signed)	South Korea	Asia
	Maldives	South Asia
	Pakistan	South Asia
	ASEAN countries (Philippines, Cambodia, Laos, Malaysia, Myanmar, Thailand, Brunei, Singapore, Indonesia, Vietnam)	Southeast Asia
	Singapore	Southeast Asia
	Australia, Chile, Costa Rica, Georgia, Iceland, Mauritius New Zealand, Peru, and Switzerland	Non-Asia
FTA (under negotiation)	GCC countries (United Arab Emirates, Oman, Bahrain, Qatar, Kuwait and Saudi Arabia, Yemen)	Asia
	Israel	Asia
	Japan, South Korea	Asia
	Palestine	Asia
	Sri Lanka	South Asia
	Cambodia	Southeast Asia
	Moldova	Non-Asia
	Norway	Non-Asia
	Panama	Non-Asia
	RCEP countries: India, Japan, South Korea, ASEAN countries, Australia, New Zealand	Non-Asia, (South/ Southeast/ Central) Asia

(Continued)

Key issues	Countries involved (China +)	Region
BRI	Jordan, Palestinian, Qatar, Georgia, Turkey, Japan, Saudi Arabia, Syria, Iran, Lebanon, Russia, Iraq, Mongolia, Kuwait, Azerbaijan, Israel, Bahrain, Yemen, Armenia, Oman, South Korea	Asia
	Kyrgyzstan, Kazakhstan, Tajikistan, Turkmenistan, Uzbekistan	Central Asia
	Bhutan, India, Maldives, Nepal, Sri Lanka, Pakistan	South Asia
	Singapore, Vietnam, Laos, Cambodia, Indonesia, Thailand, Malaysia, Philippines, East Timor, Myanmar, Brunei	Southeast Asia
	Slovenia, Hungary, Estonia, Egypt, Germany, Albania, United Arab Emirates, Lithuania, Poland, Montenegro, Kenya, Belarus, Netherlands, Slovakia, Serbia, French, Ukraine, Czech Republic, Romania, Greek, Macedonia, Italy, Bosnia and Herzegovina, Nigeria, Bulgaria, Croatia, Latvia, Belgium, Moldova	Non-Asia

Table A-2

SITC Codes Under Each of the Four Categories

Categories	SITC code (revision 3)
Bulk commodities	0411, 0412, 0421, 0422, 0430, 0441, 0449, 0451, 0452, 0453, 0459, 1211, 2222, 2223, 2224, 2225, 2226, 2227, 2231, 2232, 2234, 2235, 2237, 2239, 2311, 2312, 2313, 2631, 2641, 2649, 2651, 2658
Processed intermediates	0011, 0012, 0013, 0014, 0015, 0019, 03411, 0423, 0461, 0462, 0471, 0472, 04813, 0482, 0711, 0712, 07132, 0721, 0722, 0723, 0724, 0725, 0811, 0812, 0813, 0814, 0815, 0819, 0910, 1212, 1213, 2111, 2112, 2114, 2116, 2117, 2119, 2121, 2122, 2123, 2613, 2614, 2632, 2633, 2634, 2652, 2654, 2655, 2657, 2681, 2682, 2683, 2685, 2686, 2687, 2911, 2919, 2922, 2923, 4111, 4112, 4113, 4211, 4212, 4213, 4214, 4215, 4216, 4217, 4218, 4221, 4222, 4223, 4224, 4225, 4229, 4311, 4312, 4313, 4314
Horticultural products	0542, 0544, 0545, 0571, 0572, 0573, 0574, 0575, 0576, 0579, 0616, 2221, 2924, 2925, 2926, 2929
Consumer-ready products	0111, 0112, 0121, 0122, 0123, 0124, 0125, 0129, 0161, 0168, 0171, 0172, 0173, 0174, 0175, 0176, 0179, 0221, 0222, 0223, 0224, 0230, 0241, 0242, 0243, 0249, 0251, 0252, 0253, 03412, 0342, 0344, 0345, 0351, 0352, 0353, 0354, 0355, 0361, 0362, 0363, 0371, 0372, 04812, 0483, 0484, 0485, 0541, 0546, 0547, 0548, 0561, 0564, 0566, 0567, 0577, 0581, 0582, 0583, 0589, 0591, 0592, 0593, 0599, 0611, 0612, 0615, 0619, 0621, 0622, 07131, 0731, 0732, 0733, 0739, 0741, 0743, 0751, 0752, 0981, 0984, 0985, 0986, 0989, 1110, 1121, 1122, 1123, 1124, 1221, 1222, 1223, 2927

Table A-3

HHI for China's Product Distribution in Southeast, South, and Central Asia

Region	Export			Import		
	1998–2017	1998–2002	2010–2017	1998–2017	1998–2002	2010–2017
Southeast Asia	0.018	0.038	0.021	0.1103	0.1005	0.1013
South Asia	0.076	0.190	0.064	0.238	0.111	0.266
Central Asia	0.052	0.149	0.052	0.532	0.141	0.534

Note. HHI is the sum of squared market share, an indicator of market concentration.

Table A-4

SPS and TBT Measures Controlled

	Equation (1)	Equation (2)	lnREJ and lnSPSTBT replaced by dumREJ and dumSPSTBT respectively	
			Equation (1)	Equation (2)
$\ln EXP_{it}$	0.006		0.028**	
	(0.033)		(0.013)	
$\ln CASE_{it}$	0.040***	0.017	0.022***	0.017
	(0.008)	(0.011)	(0.005)	(0.012)
$\ln REJ_{it-1}$		−0.090*		0.140**
		(0.049)		(0.066)
$\ln CASE_{it} \times \ln REJ_{it-1}$		−0.008**		−0.032*
		(0.004)		(0.018)
$\ln SPSTBT_{it-1}$	−0.005	−0.047	0.039	−0.163
	(0.036)	(0.056)	(0.048)	(0.129)
$\ln CASE_{it} \times \ln SPSTBT_{it-1}$	−0.016	0.007	−0.007	0.015
	(0.012)	(0.008)	(0.012)	(0.015)
Country-month FE and -year FE	Yes	Yes	Yes	Yes
Observations	678	678	678	678
Adjusted R^2	0.878	0.973	0.549	0.976

Note. ***, **, and * represent significance at the 1%, 5%, and 10% levels, respectively. Robust standard errors clustered at the country-year level are reported in parentheses. See subsections IV.1 and above for the definition of each variable. FE, fixed effect.

Appendix B
Further Robustness Checks for Chapter 12

In the benchmark regression, the severity of pandemic outbreaks was measured by newly confirmed cases, which implicitly assumes that the pandemic impacts on the FDA import refusal decisions and agricultural exports are instantaneous. It is possible, however, that both impacts do not only result from new infections but are also related to cases previously confirmed due to a lagged response. When this is the case, it may be more reasonable to replace new infections in our empirical specifications with cumulated cases. Table 12.1 reports estimated results for this robustness check. Compared with the benchmark results in Table 12.3, we find that, although estimated relationships for variables of interest have remained the same, the impacts of pandemic outbreaks on import refusals and agricultural exports are both attenuated. Thus, previous infections have a smaller effect on increasing FDA import refusals and amplifying subsequent export losses than infections that are currently confirmed, which is as expected.

Table B-1

Pandemic Outbreaks Measured by Cumulated Confirmed Cases

			ln*REJ* replaced by dum*REJ*	
	Equation (1)	Equation (2)	Equation (1)	Equation (2)
lnEXP_{it}	0.005		0.021*	
	(0.030)		(0.010)	
ln$CASE_{it}$	0.015***	0.016	0.018***	0.018
	(0.005)	(0.011)	(0.005)	(0.018)
lnREJ_{it-1}		−0.060		−0.150**
		(0.054)		(0.066)
ln$CASE_{it}$ × lnREJ_{it-1}		−0.002*		−0.014*
		(0.001)		(0.008)
Country-month FE and -year FE	Yes	Yes	Yes	Yes
Observations	688	678	688	678
Adjusted R^2	0.881	0.973	0.557	0.976

Note. ***, **, and * represent significance at the 1%, 5%, and 10% levels, respectively. Robust standard errors clustered at the country-year level are reported in parentheses. See subsections IV.1 for the definition of each variable. FE, fixed effect.

ABOUT THE AUTHORS

Dr. Kevin Chen is Qiushi Chair Professor of the School of Public Affairs at Zhejiang University and International Dean of the China Academy for Rural Development (CARD). He is also the Director of Zhejiang University-International Food Policy Research Institute Center for International Development Studies and the China leader of CGIAR Research Initiative on Mitigate+: Research for Low Carbon Food Systems. He currently serves as editor-in-chief of the *International Food and Agribusiness Management Review* and co-editor of the *China Agricultural Economic Review*. He was an associate professor at the Department of Resource Economics and Sociology at the University of Alberta during 1995–2004. He also served as an editor for the *Canadian Journal of Agricultural Economics* from 2003 to 2004. His interests focus on food systems transformation, agri-food value chain development, public policies on poverty, and agri-food sector modeling.

Dr. Rui Mao is a Professor of the School of Public Affairs at Zhejiang University, Deputy Dean of the China Academy for Rural Development (CARD), Chair of the Department of Agricultural Economics and Management, and Deputy Director of the Zhejiang University-International Food Policy Research Institute Center for International Development Studies. He currently serves as the executive director of the China Rural Development Society, the deputy director of the Youth Work Committee, and the deputy secretary-general of the Urban and Rural Committee of the Chinese Society for Urban Studies. He also serves as the managing editor of the *International Food and Agribusiness Management Review*. His major research area includes agricultural and rural development, industrial structural transformation, and international agri-food trade.